WOMEN AND PHILANTHROPY IN EDUCATION

Philanthropic and Nonprofit Studies

Dwight F. Burlingame and David C. Hammack, editors

WOMEN AND PHILANTHROPY IN EDUCATION

Edited by
Andrea Walton

Indiana University Press
Bloomington and Indianapolis

This book is a publication of

Indiana University Press
601 North Morton Street
Bloomington, IN 47404-3797 USA

http://iupress.indiana.edu

Telephone orders   800-842-6796

Fax orders   812-855-7931

Orders by e-mail   iuporder@indiana.edu

© 2005 by Indiana University Press

The paper used in this publication meets the minimum requirements of American National Standard
for Information Sciences—Permanence of Paper for
Printed Library Materials, ANSI Z39.48-1984.

Manufactured in the United States of America

Library of Congress Cataloging-in-Publication Data

Women and philanthropy in education / edited by
Andrea Walton.
    p. cm.—(Philanthropic and nonprofit studies)
    Includes index.
    ISBN 0-253-34466-2 (cloth : alk. paper)
    1. Women in higher education—United States—
History. 2. Endowments—United States—History. 3.
Women philanthropists—United States—History. I.
Walton, Andrea, date II. Series.

LC1757.W63 2005
378.1'982—dc22
                                        2004010950

1 2 3 4 5 10 09 08 07 06 05

To Claire T. Walton and Frank J. Walton

CONTENTS

CONTENTS

ACKNOWLEDGMENTS

The idea for this book emerged from the synergy between my experiences in teaching the history of education and in developing graduate seminars on the history of philanthropy and education at Indiana University. In designing and teaching these courses I became more keenly aware of philanthropic influences in education and increasingly interested in exploring the role that philanthropy—the actions not only of foundations and the wealthy, as the current narrative of philanthropy suggests, but also of other organizations, communities, and individuals—has played in shaping colleges and universities and, indeed, a much broader array of educational institutions. Arguably, while philanthropy has been one of the most powerful forces shaping education in the U.S. and, in ways this book examines, a salient aspect of women's experience in education, it has also been one of the most understudied influences on education.

Beginning in 2000, I had the opportunity to expand upon my growing interest in the history of educational philanthropy as the director of the Foundation History Network, a project supported with funds from the Lilly Endowment. This three-year project aimed to bring together scholars from various institutions who are interested in the study of philanthropy as a cultural phenomenon and to encourage research and teaching in the history of philanthropy and education. This book was the final product of that project. Each of the scholars whose work appears here—among them, well known scholars of philanthropy and leading historians of women in education, senior and junior scholars—brought her expertise to this volume. I am particularly grateful to the contributors for their insights and wise counsel during our meeting in Bloomington in December of 2001, when we gathered to review and critique the draft chapters. Their generous contributions of time and talent and their encouragement and support throughout the project were invaluable assets to the success of this project.

Because this edited volume has been a collaborative project and in many cases presents research that contributors have been engaged in for a considerable period, a number of individuals and organizations who have supported and facilitated our work (individual and collective) deserve to be thanked here. Generous funding from the Lilly Endowment was crucial to supporting our collaboration and in bringing the idea for this book to fruition. Directing the Foundation History Network and editing this volume has been an intellectually rewarding experience, and I am grateful for having been given this opportunity.

I would like also to extend my personal thanks to the Indiana University Center on Philanthropy for its timely support of my initial research project on women and philanthropy, which paved the way to the ideas I have explored with colleagues in this volume. Special thanks go to Darwin Stapleton, Kenneth Rose, and Thomas Rosenbaum of the Rockefeller Archive Center for assisting a number of the researchers whose work is included in this volume, and to the National Academy of Education, which awarded a grant to support the collaboration of four former Spencer postdoctoral fellows who contributed to this project (Amy Sue Bix, Victoria-María MacDonald, Sarah Henry Lederman, and myself).

My work as director of the Foundation History Network and editor of *Women and Philanthropy in Education* was aided by several colleagues and staff members at Indiana University. Kate Boyle, project assistant for the Foundation History Network, made all arrangements for the seminar meetings and helped in editorial correspondence with contributors. A number of individuals at Indiana University—staff members Sandy Strain, Lisa Brameier, and Jan Ryser and colleagues Barry Bull, Ed McClellan, Mary Ellen Brown, and Myrtle Scott—took an interest in the book project and offered their encouragement. David Smith, former director of the Poynter Center, lent his support by co-hosting two speaker sessions related to the book project at the Poynter Center. A special note of thanks goes to the Indiana University Center on Philanthropy—in particular, to Eugene Tempel, Melissa Brown, and Beverly Ernest, who helped me in various tasks related to administering the grant project.

A number of talented individuals helped with the production of the manuscript. I wish to thank Hamid Tuama Mubarak for reading the draft chapters and critiquing the introduction, and Danille Lindquist and Shoshanna Green for editing the manuscript at various stages. I appreciated the active interest in this book that was shown by series co-editors David Hammack and Dwight Burlingame and the Indiana University Press editors Richard Higgins, Marvin Keenan, Jane Lyle, and Robert Sloan.

As a number of the lives and institutions examined in this volume show, teaching and learning occur in various contexts and forms and have often constituted an important bridge between philanthropy and education. Throughout my studies and career, I have been lucky enough to meet a number of remarkable teachers. I am especially grateful to two women whose knowledge of philanthropy kindled my own interest in the subject. Ellen Condliffe Lagemann, noted historian of the Carnegie philanthropies, introduced me to the history of education and philanthropy during my graduate studies. In addition to respecting her intellectual contributions to the study of educational philanthropy—contributions that a number of the authors represented here draw on—I have valued her support as a mentor and colleague. Working with D. Susan Wisely, former director of evaluation at the Lilly Endowment and project officer on the Foundation History Network project, has been my good fortune. When I first met Susan in 1996 (as I was researching and interviewing for a biography of the Hoosier philanthropist Clementine Miller Tangeman), I saw first-hand her interest in the perspectives that historical scholarship can bring to the study and practice of philanthropy. Susan has supported this book project from its earliest days, attended the December 2001 working session for book contributors, and has given generously of her time, creativity, and counsel. This book would not have been possible without her. I am indebted to these two teachers and colleagues and realize that my exchanges with them over the years inevitably kindled and shaped my ideas about the ties between education and philanthropy and sparked my interest in undertaking a volume on women and philanthropy in education.

While *Women and Philanthropy in Education* is a collaborative work and could not have been possible without the assistance and support of the several individuals and organizations I have mentioned, any editorial errors or oversights are entirely my own.

Finally, I wish to close by recognizing and thanking my family—especially my parents, Claire T. Walton and Frank J. Walton, my "first teachers," for their support and encouragement throughout my schooling and career. This book is dedicated to them.

WOMEN AND PHILANTHROPY
IN EDUCATION

Introduction: Women and Philanthropy in Education— A Problem of Conceptions

Andrea Walton

> Literature has preserved the story. She chronicles the mistakes, warns of pitfalls, and notes what methods have brought blessing. Literature has done more than compilation-service. She has brought Philanthropy out of the chaos of occasional and often misdirected pity into organic structure. . . . It is Nature's inexorable law that undisciplined Charity shall not bless; that unwise Love shall never be beneficent; that Wisdom is born of Experience. Now experience is recorded in Literature; and it is written that Philanthropy cannot be divorced from Education or from Religion. The three are one.
>
> —FRANCES ABIGAIL GOODALE, *The Literature of Philanthropy*, 1893[1]

> I believe it rests largely with us to redeem the word *philanthropy* from the strait and narrow meaning thrust upon it in popular understanding, if not in lexicography. It has come to signify with most of us the giving of money, or of time or effort so considerable as to be the marketable equivalent of money, to relieve sickness, pain, poverty, religious blindness. It should mean far more,—the intelligent exercise of moral and mental power applied directly or indirectly through any and every instrumentality towards the physical, intellectual, spiritual elevation of the race, in the man or in the mass.
>
> —HELEN HISCOCK BACKUS, "The Need and the Opportunity for College-Trained Women in Philanthropic Work," 1887[2]

Since at least the early 1800s, U.S. women have participated in shaping education through philanthropy.[3] They have supported institutions in which education occurs formally, from preschools and kindergartens to colleges and universities, and they have been influential as well in institutions and settings that foster more informal modes of education, sites ranging from the museum and the church to the charity organization. Indeed, by volunteering their time and donating both money and gifts-in-kind, women have fashioned careers as philanthropists and educators, have used education to promote social change, and have been instrumental in establishing and sustaining a wide array of institutions where education occurs. Serving as missionaries, establishing and canvassing for female seminaries, working among the poor as "friendly visitors" for the Charity Organization Society, organizing PTA efforts to support local schools, working through sororities to foster civic pride and race uplift, establishing vocational schools, providing timely funding for women scholars, tapping foundation support in order to implement continuing education programs for women, giving large sums to leverage opportunities for women at male-dominated institutions, and building the country's first museum for female artists—in all these philanthropic activities, women have enhanced the educational experiences of themselves and of others. This volume seeks to document this variety of women's philanthropic experiences in education—both as donors and as recipients—over the last two centuries. In so doing, contributors hope to integrate women's experience more fully into the narratives of both philanthropy and education.

Despite the long list of women's philanthropic engagements, until recent decades women have been virtually absent from dominant accounts of U.S. philanthropy and remain excluded from, or at best marginalized in, the literature on educational philanthropy.[4] As has been the case in many other fields, women were written out of the history of philanthropy by virtue of what "counted" in the minds of those who wrote the conventional histories. However, even a glance at the literature of the past two decades reveals that scholars of women's history have already begun to address this lacuna. For instance, scholars have produced significant works about women's religious philanthropy. Carroll Smith-Rosenberg, Nancy Cott, Jane Hunter, Patricia Ruth Hill, Peggy Pascoe, Susan Yohn, and Amanda Porterfield have explored how the ideals of faith and self-sacrifice have influenced white Protestant women's philanthropy; Evelyn Higginbotham has examined women's leadership within the black church; Shelly Tennenbaum and Susan Chambre have told the story of Jewish women's philanthropy; and Mary Oates and Elizabeth McKeown and Dorothy Brown have considered the role of Catholic nuns who sought to address poverty, child welfare, health, and education long before government involvement in these areas became common.[5] In addition to examining the long-standing traditions of religious philanthropy, scholars interested in women's achievements have also begun to study women's cultural philanthropy. Studies by Helen Horowitz, Karen Blair, Kathleen McCarthy, Bernice Kert, and others have documented women's patronage of artists, museums, and other cultural institutions.[6] During the past two decades, women's efforts to gain power and visibility through voluntary associations and other philanthropic organizations have also drawn scholarly attention. The works of Kathleen McCarthy, Anne Firor Scott, Kathryn Sklar, Nancy Hewitt, Suzanne Lebsock, Lori Ginzberg, Anne Boylan, Darlene Clark Hine, and others have led the way in demonstrating how philanthropy enabled women to exercise considerable power in the public sphere well before the franchise.[7] Indeed, by looking outside the realm of traditional party politics and considering women's political action on its own terms, this literature has contributed new perspectives to both women's history and philanthropic studies.[8]

These efforts notwithstanding, substantial work remains to be done in order to present a fuller portrait of women's experience in philanthropy. In particular, more studies need to shed light on education—an arena in which private donations have figured prominently in shaping opportunities for both sexes and where women's philanthropic contributions have been long-standing, extraordinarily diverse, and significant. Save for the stories of female luminaries like settlement leader and Nobel laureate Jane Addams, of a few women benefactors who had inherited substantial wealth (such as Sophia Smith and Anita McCormick Blaine), and of women like Jane Stanford and Pauline Durant, who gave jointly with their husbands, our knowledge of women's philanthropic action in education remains relatively limited.[9]

It is the premise of this volume that women have been absent from the major literature on educational philanthropy largely because narrow conceptions of both philanthropy and education have dominated scholarship on philanthropic action in education. As I will outline below, and discuss at greater length later in this essay, most works addressing the subject of educational philanthropy have tended to equate philanthropy with large monetary gifts and foundation activity. This frame of reference, reflecting a distinctly twentieth-century mindset, has produced a male-centered "high" history of educational philanthropy—a story of big donor giving focused especially on the influential role of foundations and the largesse of industrialists like Andrew Carnegie and John D. Rockefeller.[10] While studies of wealthy philanthropists are essential to understanding the ways elite private power has shaped education, the emphasis on this type of philanthropy has captured only a narrow range of philanthropic action in education and has restricted our understanding of the history of educational philanthropy. Indeed, disproportionate attention has been paid to settings where foundations have been most active and influential—notably, the male-dominated research university—while the intersection of philanthropy and education in other settings has been relatively ignored. More important, the focus on foundations and big donations has obscured the compelling stories of many who have also left their philanthropic mark on education, including people of color, members of ethnic communities, and—our subject here—women. Therefore, it may be argued that one major reason we have so little insight into the history of women as philanthropic actors in education is that we have underestimated the significance of small but timely gifts—what John Gardner aptly called the "Mississippi River of small gifts"—that even today account for a significant share of giving in the United States.[11]

Simply put, by thinking about educational philanthropy in narrow terms—first by equating philanthropy with large monetary donations and then by conceiving of education only as the formal instructional activities associated with schools and universities—current scholarship has not "seen" women's philanthropic action in education. Indeed, to borrow David Tyack's expression, by focusing attention on one particular "way of seeing," historians (even historians of women in education) have overlooked the expansiveness, complexity, and significance of women's giving to education and have not seen this giving as part of a larger cultural tapestry of women's philanthropy.[12] Accordingly, in seeking to remedy this problem, this volume aims not merely to identify women of great wealth or fame who gave generously to colleges and universities, thereby offering a female image in the mold of the familiar narrative of men's giving to education. Instead, this volume considers women's philanthropy in education on its own terms. To achieve this, the fourteen chapters of this book cast their net widely, adopting very broad definitions of both education and philanthropy. Each chapter provides an in-depth view of a particular figure, group, or institution, and examines the philanthropic impulse within a particular setting or set of circumstances. From these diverse portraits, we reach new understandings of women's philanthropic contributions both to the familiar institutions of formal education—schools, colleges, and universities, where the impact of women's giving has been thought to be insignificant or negligible—and to foundations, where women were thought to be virtually absent.

Beyond helping us to see this familiar terrain in the history of education and the history of philanthropy anew, however, the chapters also help widen our angle of vision on educational philanthropy as a cultural phenomenon. When we consider the variety of organizations and settings where women's education and giving have occurred informally—among them, for instance, the missionary group, the museum, and the voluntary association—the importance of educational philanthropy to the history of women in education and the significance of women's educational philanthropy to the story of philanthropy in the U.S. become more apparent. Collectively, the chapters underscore the variety of means by which women—who often had less access to disposable wealth than men—supported education and adopted education as a means to advance philanthropic ends. In all, though they encountered gender-related barriers in nearly every sphere of life, including education and philanthropy, women were able, through the channels of educational philanthropy, to promote new ideas, to advance their individual and collective goals, and to shape education in the U.S. over the centuries.

WHY STUDY WOMEN'S EXPERIENCE AT THE INTERSECTION OF PHILANTHROPY AND EDUCATION?

Exploring the significance and variety of women's philanthropic action in education is important because both philanthropy and education were among the earliest spaces where women, though still acting within culturally prescribed roles, found opportunities to participate in the public sphere. The founding of the Society for the Relief of Poor Widows with Small Children in 1797 represented one of the earliest examples of women's leadership in a philanthropic organization.[13] The closing decades of the eighteenth century and the early decades of the nineteenth century saw women—often inspired by religious conviction and enabled by a cultural belief in women's morality and nurturing qualities—gain both a modicum of independence and social recognition as teachers in a host of emerging educational institutions: the early summer district schools, parochial and mission schools, and Sunday schools.[14] Also by the early decades of the nineteenth century, the confluence of religious fervor, democratic sentiment, and notions of philanthropy and volunteering had given rise to a wide array of institutions that provided education to women and girls—among them the charity school, the missionary school, the ly-ceum, the academy, and the seminary. For example, rising female lit-eracy and the need for teachers fostered a demand for women's higher schooling as early as the 1820s and, in light of women's exclusion from the established colleges, provided the rationale for creating the female seminary as a new institution founded for women by philanthropic-minded women like Mary Lyon and Catharine Beecher (see chapter 1).[15] These new educational avenues and the collegiate opportunities that soon followed gave social prominence to the moral and intellectual qualities of the educated woman who, as a new counterpart to the leisure-class woman, might contribute to the advancement of society at home and abroad.[16]

Throughout the nineteenth century, the growth of urbanism and the hardships of city life created a special niche for women's entry into the public sphere as volunteers in relief societies and charities that aided widows, unwed mothers, orphans, the sick, and the poor.[17] As settlement leader Jane Addams poignantly described, her generation of educated women often faced the demands of the "family claim," but many felt a special burden to apply their education in broader public arenas in order to give back to society, and in the process they enriched their own lives as well.[18] Throughout the nineteenth century changes in women's education, coupled with changes in women's life cycle and increased economic independence for many women, had opened new horizons for women's philanthropy in the U.S.—and much of this effort was directed to education. For instance, women used philanthropic means and the support of volunteer networks to augment their influence on the affairs of previously all-male institu-tions or male-administered institutions such as the school (see chapter 9 on PTAs). More often, as they faced exclusion from these establish-ments, they sought to create and administer their own institutions. Indeed, by embracing separatism and building what Kathleen Mc-Carthy has described as "parallel power structures," philanthropically minded women were able to sustain their own political culture, par-ticipate in institutional development, and effect social reform.[19] Through a variety of experiences—in all-female or mixed-gender set-tings, in well-established institutions or newly founded ones—women forged identities and opportunities for themselves and contributed to philanthropy and education alike.[20]

PHILANTHROPY BROADLY CONCEIVED: NINETEENTH-CENTURY CHRONICLES OF WOMEN'S PHILANTHROPIC ENGAGEMENTS

Women continued to expand their participation in philanthropic activities throughout the nineteenth century. By the 1890s, when women attempted to chronicle the social significance of their public achievements, they identified philanthropic activity as one of the few arenas where they had made great strides. Frances Abigail Goodale's *The Literature of Philanthropy* (1893) is such an attempt; it sheds light not only on what "counted" as philanthropy in the nineteenth century but also on the connection between philanthropy and education and on women's participation in a variety of philanthropic activities.[21] As one of Oneida County's most prominent clubwomen, Goodale was invited by the Board of Women Managers of New York State to edit a collection of writings on philanthropy by the state's female citizens during the nineteenth century. The board proposed that Goodale's volume on philanthropy would join works on education, such as Anna C. Brackett's *Women and the Higher Education* (1893) and Kate Douglas Wiggin's *The Kindergarten* (1893), as well as compilations of women's writings in other fields. Together, these works were intended to reflect the caliber of women's achievements and be a fitting donation to the Women's Building at the Chicago Exhibition.[22]

As Goodale's volume documents, women were very much at the forefront of the substantive debates and engagements in the major philanthropic enterprises of the nineteenth century—they defined, documented, critiqued, and, in Goodale's case, advocated and promoted the role of philanthropy in a variety of settings. She herself drew attention to activism in the movement for the abolition of slavery, work on prison reform, efforts to improve tenement conditions, and support for the Red Cross, as well as experiments in the education of the blind, settlement life, and manual training institutes. In making clear to the society of her time how important these philanthropic acts were, Goodale argued that these deeds were "variations of one great theme: the invariable, close interdependence and inseparable interests of the different members of the Body Social." In education, Goodale found an especially powerful "agency of reform" and a means for providing for the welfare of the poor—the masses whose condition, if not improved, could become a "desperate menace to the State." Furthermore, she eloquently articulated the connection between inspired philanthropy and education by insisting that "[p]hilanthropy cannot be divorced from Education nor from Religion. The three are one."[23]

Goodale's anthology reflects the tenor of scholarship produced by her generation. It is a work of more limited critical insight and scholarly scope than the philosophical writings of her younger contemporaries (notably Jane Addams and Florence Kelley); nevertheless, the volume remains a significant artifact in the history of women and philanthropy because it sheds light on three important themes. First, the book reveals that women were conscious of the importance of philanthropy to society and of the valuable contributions they made to their communities through this vehicle—a self-awareness evident before the franchise and long before the women's movement that gave rise to women's studies. Until recently, women generally have not been thought of as philanthropists nor identified as commentators and writers on the subject of philanthropy; however, Goodale's volume suggests the contrary—that women were very much engaged in both philanthropic action and in critiquing and documenting philanthropic activity.[24] Second, given the variety of civic activities and humanitarian causes that women engaged in and that Goodale considered philanthropic acts, one begins to understand that the term *philanthropy* in the nineteenth century meant not only the giving of money, but also the giving of time and talent.[25] Third, and hardly least important, Goodale identified education as a vital vehicle for social uplift and an important arena for philanthropic action.[26]

Given Goodale's volume on women and nineteenth-century philanthropy, one is compelled to ask: Why are women often thought of as "new" philanthropists? Why has philanthropy, especially educational philanthropy, become associated most commonly with monetary giving and foundation activity? What are the ramifications of this dominant narrow conception for understanding women's philanthropic experience in education? And what course should scholarship on philanthropy and education take to provide a better understanding of women's philanthropic experience in education? Perhaps a brief review of the major works on philanthropic action in education during the twentieth century may shed light on the historiographical problem at hand.

HISTORIES OF PHILANTHROPIC ACTION IN EDUCATION:
THE PROBLEM OF ABSENT WOMEN

A comprehensive historiography of the literature on philanthropy in the United States lies outside the scope of this short introduction. Moreover, a good overview of the major trends in scholarship on philanthropy may be found in the works of a number of scholars—among them Merle Curti, Robert Bremner, Ellen Condliffe Lagemann, Joseph Kiger, Peter Dobkin Hall, and Lawrence J. Friedman.[27] Rather, our intent here is to review briefly the major works that deal directly with the history of philanthropic action in education in order to help explain how women's experience has been eclipsed. Two interconnected trends, one within the practice of philanthropy and the other within writings about philanthropy, may help us understand why the story of women's philanthropy was relegated to the margins of the larger study of philanthropy and especially of scholarship on educational philanthropy.

The first trend concerns a shift in the common understanding of the term *philanthropy* that may have started well before the beginning of the twentieth century.[28] Philanthropic activity was in the foreground of daily life during the early decades of the twentieth century no less than it was in the nineteenth-century world that Goodale had described in *The Literature of Philanthropy*. Increasingly, however, newspaper accounts of women volunteering in PTAs and charity organizations (for example) became overshadowed by captivating stories of giving at an unprecedented scale; the press focused on the donor who single-handedly funded an academic institution, the millionaire who bequeathed a large sum to the arts, and the activities of great foundations like Carnegie and Rockefeller.[29] Philanthropy, which had been understood as the voluntary giving of time and money on the basis of deeply held religious, benevolent, and humanitarian ideals, became more closely associated with organizational innovations and scientific changes in the closing decades of the nineteenth century and the early decades of the twentieth century: philanthropy became synonymous with monetary donations, professional fundraising, and foundation activity.[30] Since women were not among the few who accumulated vast wealth in the postbellum decades and steered the course of foundation work, women's earlier and continued contributions were eclipsed as histories focused on this crucial but narrow understanding of philanthropy.

Concurrent with late-nineteenth-century accumulations of wealth and shifts in the meaning and scope of philanthropy came a second trend: the rise of universities. This, in turn, led to the emergence of educational philanthropy as a subject of study within the history of education—a field that was striving for legitimacy and direction. In 1919, Jesse Sears's dissertation on "Philanthropy in the History of American Higher Education" became the first work to look at educational philanthropy systematically.[31] Searching for a suitable way to frame his study, Sears turned to economic theory. He chose to regard philanthropy as an economic rather than a cultural phenomenon, charting the gifts-in-kind, bequests, endowments, and gifts that, from his vantage point, were a testament to "social progress" and reflected "growing confidence" in philanthropy's ability to sustain higher education.[32] The story of educational philanthropy as told by Sears began with a recounting of the small gifts that supported the basic survival of fledgling institutions and culminated in explaining how big donors and great foundations not only could meet present needs, but also had the capacity to support expansion and innovation in higher education. It is significant that in Sears's story, women appear only in the early period of educational philanthropy—a period when gifts to colleges were small. As Sears considers the nineteenth century, his focus shifts to major donations and foundation activity, and consideration of "women-as-donors" suddenly disappears from his narrative.

By the appearance of the next major study of educational philanthropy—Ernest Hollis's *Philanthropic Foundations and Higher Education* (1938)—foundations had proliferated in the U.S. Benefiting from well over three decades of insight into foundation activity, Hollis's analysis moved beyond Sears's valuable tabulations to consider the foundation as a social institution that helped "define" the college. Hollis also recognized philanthropy's role in developing a new type of "research" institution; the Brookings and the Carnegie Institutions are examples.[33] As for women, Hollis included just two brief mentions: one reference to studies by Eduard Lindeman, Harold Coffman, and Earl McGrath of the composition of boards of trustees and the other a comment on foundation support for curricular experimentation at Bennington and Sarah Lawrence Colleges.[34] Hollis's focus on foundations placed women as recipients of philanthropy rather than as philanthropists. Reflecting the gender biases and research methods of their times, neither Sears nor Hollis examined women's education in their works on educational philanthropy—and the few paragraphs or pages they included merely celebrated women's increased access to education, with little critical insight into who decided which women would receive which type of education and with scant recognition of women's participation in the broader traditions of philanthropy.

The legacy of women's philanthropic action in education continued to recede from view as the history of education developed into a sub-discipline. Works by Jane Addams, Eleanor Flexner, Mary Beard, and other female authors that captured important aspects of the relationship between women's history and philanthropic action in education were generally discounted as "amateur" writings or minimalized by scholars of education as contributions to the highly feminized field of social work.[35] Works by these women were thought to have little relevance to the study of modern education and, most especially, to the intellectual cornerstone of the history of education as a university study: the history of public schooling. For many historians writing in the early twentieth century, the charitable and voluntary roots of education were to be studied not in their own right but rather as precursors, in a story of progress, to the rise of public schooling.[36] Given these preoccupations, as well as the fact that historians writing about schooling often had different career patterns, institutional affiliations, and audiences than those studying higher education, it is not surprising that interest in educational philanthropy lagged. As Peter Dobkin Hall explains, before the mid-1950s faculty avoided research on philanthropy-related topics "not only because it tended to lead them toward the kinds of essentially political concerns with wealth and power that were unlikely to enhance their career prospects, but also because studying the relation of philanthropy to higher education tended to raise uncomfortable questions about their own power, status, and legitimacy."[37] Such dynamics within the history of education not only made women's contributions to philanthropy and to education far less visible, but they also help explain why, until recently, writing about educational philanthropy was less the work of historians of education than the province of insiders: foundation men.[38]

It would not be until the 1950s, when Merle Curti launched an effort to build philanthropy as an independent field of research, that a major historian would conceptualize and promote the study of philanthropy as a phenomenon that is central rather than tangential to the study of the history of education. Indeed, circumstances in the 1950s presented an opportunity to generate scholarly interest in philanthropy and education. A confluence of factors—among them, government criticism of foundation politics, Cold War interests in expanding higher education and developing area studies (including American studies, where Curti left his mark),[39] and the private funding of new institutions (like the Foundation Center) designed to improve public understanding of foundation activity—created an attractive niche for the study of educational philanthropy within the university.[40] Equally important, the historian who perceived potential in the moment and who tried to galvanize interest in educational philanthropy was also one who viewed education as an agency for cultural transmission and was somewhat conversant with women's history and the histories of other disfranchised groups.[41]

Writing in the 1950s, Curti identified philanthropy as an "agent" and "index" of culture and a "key" to understanding the development of important intellectual and cultural U.S. institutions, including colleges and universities.[42] In addition, Curti was one of the earliest historians to trace the usage of the term *philanthropy* and, especially important here, to underscore that the concept had in fact changed over time—from giving anchored in religious charity and encompassing donations of what are often called "time, talent, and treasure" to giving that is more associated with monetary gifts, and for secular as well as religious reasons.[43] Though Curti's work on philanthropy has received uneven attention from scholars and practitioners over the years, in part because the social sciences have moved away from the concept of "national character," his efforts should be seen as important milestones in philanthropic studies and the study of educational philanthropy. Curti's works pointed to the relationship between philanthropist and recipient, probed issues of donor motivation, examined the ties between philanthropy and innovation, and explored the leverage of philanthropy to promote certain goals.[44] Despite Curti's efforts, which were supported by the Ford and Russell Sage Foundations, the type of sustained interdisciplinary research in the history of philanthropy that he had hoped to kindle at Wisconsin in the 1950s and early 1960s did not gain momentum.[45] Only recently has a history text appeared to replace Bremner's *American Philanthropy* (1960), and Curti's *Philanthropy and the Shaping of American Higher Education* (1965), which he co-authored with his student Roderick Nash, remains the most recent overview of its subject.[46]

Whereas the decades from Sears's pioneering work to Curti's efforts were characterized by intellectual fits and starts, a more sustained interest in the study of philanthropic action in education began to germinate in the 1970s and 1980s. As historians of education debated whether schooling was liberating or an imposition, a number of scholars carried this debate to educational philanthropy, producing a literature that was polarized between advocacy and social control arguments.[47] But despite the divide, scholarship on foundation activity in education broadened as foundations became more self-conscious about their history. Responding to political pressure, they encouraged research by making important resources accessible in such venues as the Rockefeller Archive Center (Sleepy Hollow, New York), the Ruth Lilly Special Collections and Archives (Indiana University–Purdue University Indianapolis), and the Rare Book and Manuscript Collection at Columbia University (New York City).[48] Perhaps reflecting larger debates within U.S. politics, much of the scholarship on philanthropy tended to be preoccupied with the role of private giving in shaping U.S. public policy.[49] Within the field of education, this orientation translated primarily into a focus on foundation involvement in higher education.[50]

Works by Ellen Condliffe Lagemann, Steven Wheatley, Kenneth Ludmerer, Robert Kohler, Donald Fisher, Martin Bulmer, and others offered case studies that explored questions ranging from the functioning of foundations within a democracy to connections between foundations and intellectuals, support for research and the institutionalization of disciplinary knowledge, and standardization and reform within the professions and educational institutions.[51] In addition to such studies, the efflorescence of scholarship on African American education inevitably delved into the motivations and outcomes of foundation action. Studies by John Stanfield, James Anderson, Eric Anderson and Alfred Moss, and, most recently, William Watkins have critiqued the politics of benevolence and, to varying degrees, have depicted the experiences of recipients and their ability to challenge and, in some instances, even to subvert a donor's agenda.[52] Notwithstanding the tremendous value of this recent scholarship in helping to unravel the complex history of educational philanthropy, this literature did not consider the impact of foundations on women's education, nor did it relate the story of foundation activities to women's experience either as recipients of foundation money (see chapter 12) or as program officers and foundation staff (see chapter 5).[53]

Thus, a wide terrain remains open for historians to explore. Fortunately, the works of several scholars writing in the fields of philanthropic studies, women's history, and the history of women in education may help in efforts to retrieve the story of women's philanthropy in education. The work of Kathleen McCarthy, Anne Firor Scott, Suzanne Lebsock, Kathryn Sklar, Anne Boylan, Lori Ginzberg, and others has already pointed the way.[54] Moreover, the discussion of women's philanthropy has been refined as Nancy Hewitt, Darlene Clark Hine, and others have brought the politics of race, ethnicity, and class to the foreground and identified the "fissures" that philanthropy, regardless of the giver's professed intentions, has in some instances opened among women.[55] This volume contributes to this scholarship as the fourteen chapters document various aspects of women's philanthropic experience in education and as the authors reexamine the interconnections of philanthropy and education by reclaiming expansive definitions for both.

CONCEPTUALIZING PHILANTHROPY AND EDUCATION

Robert Payton's conception of philanthropy as all "voluntary action for the public good"[56] is conducive to acknowledging much of the volunteering and financial support that women have given to education during the last two hundred years. The chapters of this book are informed by a similar orientation toward philanthropy; authors regard philanthropy as all voluntary giving of "time, talent, and treasure," by individuals and organizations, for the "public good," regardless of whether the underlying impulse is religious or secular.[57] This broader definition, which embraces financial donations, gifts-in-kind, and voluntary service in associations and organizations (what McCarthy has identified as "an economy of time"), has historical precedent and is particularly useful for considering the variety of women's contributions to education—including the "invisible" careers of female volunteers whose service remains crucial to advancing educational institutions and causes.[58]

Similarly, this volume is informed by a broad definition of education. Definitions of education began to narrow much earlier than did definitions of philanthropy, and the trend continued well into the early years of the twentieth century. As Ellen Lagemann has argued, education became more closely associated with formal schooling (K–12 to university level) at the end of the nineteenth century, to the exclusion of other environments where learning and teaching occur informally.[59] The narrowing conception of education and the politics of writing on the history of education excluded or undervalued many of the experiences and contributions of women.[60] For example, themes related to school administration and the stories of university builders—the likes of Harvard's Charles W. Eliot, Cornell's Andrew D. White, and Johns Hopkins's Daniel Coit Gilman—dominated the literature on education, while "feminized" areas such as teaching and student affairs received scant attention. However, beginning in the 1970s, the dearth of historical research on women in education was challenged as scholars such as Jill Ker Conway, Patricia Albjerg Graham, Anne Firor Scott, Margaret Rossiter, and Geraldine Jonçich Clifford brought the methods of the "new women's history" to the study of education.[61] Such pioneering efforts, attentive to the little-considered connections between the personal and the public, began the initial task of recovering women's achievements in education by drawing upon lively debates in women's history and capitalizing on a wave of cultural revisionism in the history of education, sparked by the writings of Bernard Bailyn and Lawrence Cremin.[62] By considering the dynamics of colonial life on its own terms as well as the institutions that educated individuals long before the rise of public schooling, Bailyn arrived at a very broad conception of education: "The entire process by which a culture transmits itself across the generations." This broad conception of education was refined by Cremin in his trilogy on the history of U.S. education, in which he explored the multiplicity of institutions and settings that figured prominently in shaping the American educational experience over the centuries.[63] Though neither Bailyn nor Cremin was especially concerned with matters related to gender, their latitudinarian approaches together with advances in women's history and gender studies have helped further the challenge of documenting women's achievements as well as the persistent gender barriers women have faced in education.

In the past three decades, scholarship on women has looked outside the institutions that have traditionally dominated the historical literature on education, namely, public schools, colleges, and universities. In so doing, this scholarship identified a myriad of ways and places in which women were educated; it also drew attention to the public spaces, organizations, and institutions that women created, led, and capitalized upon for educational purposes—among them, female academies and seminaries, normal schools, women's clubs, sororities, and social settlements.[64] Ellen Condliffe Lagemann's *A Generation of Women* (1979), for instance, built on Bailyn and Cremin's work and the "new" women's history to provide great insight into the education of women during the Progressive Era.[65] Thus, by employing a broader definition of education, historians have understood women's education on its own terms and have increasingly shifted their focus away from women's exclusion and marginalization and toward an accounting that also acknowledges women's agency. However, in exploring women's forays into male-dominated institutions and alternative pathways to leadership, historians of women in education have not seen women's support of education as part of a larger tapestry of women's philanthropy. Thus, the chapters of this volume, informed by Bailyn and Cremin's broad conception of education, will consider women's contributions to education as philanthropists in a variety of settings—from women's missionary work in the nineteenth century (chapter 7) to feminist grassroots fundraising on behalf of women artists in the twentieth century (chapter 10) and from all-female seminaries (chapter 1) to coeducational research universities (chapter 14).

CHAPTER ORGANIZATION

Though mostly focused on documenting examples of women's agency through philanthropy, the chapters of this volume also depict the types of challenges and limitations women have encountered as both donors and recipients. While any categorization is artificial, and inevitably themes in different chapters will overlap, this volume is organized into three parts and coheres around three broad and interrelated questions. First, how did women's benefaction, their fundraising strategies, and their ability to capitalize on various social and intellectual networks of support contribute to the advancement of education—by helping to found new institutions, by implementing reforms at existing institutions, and by contributing to the organization, creation, and dissemination of knowledge? Second, what has been the role of philanthropists and foundations in shaping the content and mission of women's education, in leveraging (or perhaps limiting) educational and professional opportunities for women, and in defining the needs of the female student, scholar, and professional—thereby becoming a major determinant of women's access to education and to the resources needed for research?[66] And third, how did differences among women—racial, class, ethnic, religious, and regional—play out as women's philanthropic action influenced women's education and as women were influenced by philanthropy generally?

Part I, "Schools, Colleges, Universities, and Foundations," focuses on institutions devoted to providing or supporting formal instruction. More specifically, this group of chapters depicts women's role in the founding and development of educational institutions and in helping to shape the disciplines and the professions. In chapter 1, Frances Huehls's discussion of Catharine Beecher (1800–1878) provides a useful point of departure for this volume by painting a richly textured portrait of Beecher and her recognition of the integral ties among philanthropy, religion, and education. Beecher's biography sheds light on earlier conceptions of philanthropy and provides an early example of women's self-consciousness about the personal and social significance of giving. Huehls notes that Beecher, contrary to the Calvinist tenets of her upbringing, believed good works were a pathway to salvation. As the founder of one of the earliest women's seminaries, Beecher conceptualized the exchange between teacher and student as an expression of good works and, therefore, regarded teaching as a philanthropic activity. Beecher's ability to promote and institutionalize her vision rested on her ability to devote sufficient time to administration, teaching, and fundraising efforts—both at the Hartford Female Seminary and later on the western frontier. In chapter 2, Sarah Henry Lederman also uses biography to explore the life and career of Mary Richmond (1861–1928), who began her career at the Baltimore Charity Organization Society and later headed the Charity Organization Department at the Russell Sage Foundation from 1909 until her death in 1928. Like Beecher, Richmond theorized about the nature of the philanthropic relationship between donor and recipient. But Richmond's most valuable contribution was her attempt to systematize social work long before this feminized field became a university unit. Lederman argues that Richmond was able to codify and promote the tenets of social case work through her publications and teaching institutes but, in an age of growing bureaucracy, was in the end unable to control how case work techniques would be used or to preserve her vision of a caring relationship between social worker and client.

Moving from stories of women like Beecher and Richmond, who worked within female institutions or feminized fields and whose careers were built in the Northeast, in chapter 3 Victoria-María MacDonald and Eleanore Lenington shift the focus to the South by providing a portrait of Martha McChesney Berry (1866–1942). A proud Southerner, born and raised in Floyd County, Georgia, Martha Berry worked tirelessly raising financial support for the industrial schools she founded to educate poor white mountain children. As MacDonald and

Lenington assert, though Berry's efforts have received less attention from historians than the philanthropy of white northern foundations or the work of Booker T. Washington on behalf of black education in the South, she was a well-known figure and champion of vocational schooling in the South. MacDonald and Lenington also show that although Berry's efforts were focused in the South, her fundraising efforts connected her to major national figures in philanthropy and to leaders of the industrial education movement and others who worked to improve southern education, including Booker T. Washington, Robert Ogden, Andrew Carnegie, Olivia Sage, and Berry's most generous benefactor, Henry Ford.

The next three chapters of part I examine facets of how philanthropic action enabled women to shape the enterprise of higher education. In chapter 4, Mary Ann Dzuback focuses on the crucial role of women's patronage for female scholars, who generally lacked access to the foundation resources that promoted the careers of their male counterparts. Capturing women's ability to cultivate and capitalize on "creative financing" in two strikingly different settings—a teaching-oriented private women's liberal arts college and a public land-grant university—Dzuback shows how this small-scale but timely funding was instrumental in enabling women scholars to produce pioneering social science research. As Dzuback points out, much of the research was done on topics that were first deemed relevant only to women's experience, but which later emerged as important areas of social science (e.g., consumer economics).

Providing a rare view of the donor-recipient relationship from the perspective of a female foundation officer, in chapter 5 Amy Wells considers the career and grantmaking philosophy of Sydnor Walker, who joined the Laura Spelman Rockefeller Memorial in 1924 as a "research associate" and eventually became acting director of the Division of Social Sciences at the Rockefeller Foundation. Walker had studied at Vassar and Columbia, and although her career was in some respects limited by her gender, Wells indicates that she successfully used her foundation employment as a platform for promoting her view of research and the social sciences. Displaying an enabling blend of "heart and head" in her grantmaking, Walker exerted a considerable influence through her work in providing foundation support to social scientists in southern universities during the 1920s and 1930s. Chapter 6, by Linda Eisenmann, explores three institutions where university women, seeking to provide a better fit between the structure of higher education and the realities of women's life cycles, capitalized on support from the Carnegie Foundation (and the interest of Carnegie project officer Florence Anderson) to develop pathbreaking continuing education programs for women in the early 1960s. Eisenmann outlines how traditional forms of women's giving to education—"grassroots" alumnae giving and women's local fundraising networks—were dovetailed with support from national foundations; these efforts laid the ground for further foundation involvement in developing women's studies in the 1970s and 1980s.

Whereas part I examines women's giving to institutions where education takes place formally, part II, "Women's Philanthropy as an Agent of Social and Educational Change," explores women's philanthropic activity in informal educational settings. In chapter 7, Roberta Wollons connects Mary Lyon's Mount Holyoke model of women's education to the larger story of evangelical Protestantism by considering the missionary work of Mary and Charlotte Ely (1841–1913; 1839–1915) and Elizabeth Stone (1846–1920), who strove to bring their Christian convictions and Western values to bear on the people of the Ottoman Empire (Turkey). In narrating the journey of these women, Wollons identifies two unexpected outcomes of the philanthropic work to which these women were devoted. First, even as the women students valued their newly acquired literacy, they resisted the particular vision of Christianity the missionaries offered. Second, and more significant, the missionaries, who hoped to save "other" women, were themselves changed—educated, if you will—by them.

Marybeth Gasman provides another view of the relationship between women's education and commitment to philanthropic activity in chapter 8. In this chapter, Gasman gives an overview of the founding and education-related contributions of black sororities, exploring the historical justification for sororities and explaining their conflicted status within the African American community. Further, Gasman shows how the lifetime commitment to service that sorority sisters affirmed translated into a variety of efforts to offset the paucity of resources for African Americans in a segregated and unequal system of education. Among other activities, sorority sisters raised library funds, sponsored teacher development workshops, and administered fellowship programs. As Gasman concludes, the visibility and success sororities achieved in supporting education helped inspire black women to assume leadership in important political causes such as suffrage, desegregation, and, later, the civil rights movement. Much like

Gasman, in chapter 9 Christine Woyshner documents the power of organized womanhood in the service of education. Woyshner's essay focuses on the school-related fundraising of the PTA, a voluntary association founded as the National Congress of Mothers in 1897. As Woyshner notes, the PTA has been understudied—given its long-standing influence on schools—and generally has been seen as a response by communities to the increased bureaucratization of schools. Instead, Woyshner looks at the PTA within the philanthropic framework of the larger women's club movement. She asserts that against the background of a professionalizing school system, gender hierarchies created tensions between white PTA women and male school administrators on the one hand, while on the other, race and class hierarchies defined the subordination of black PTAs to their white counterparts.

In chapter 10, Karen Blair considers women's collective philanthropic action in educating the public about women's art and building and directing museums to provide a space for women's art, thereby challenging traditional canons and establishing alternatives to the museums founded and supported by philanthropic men. Drawing important parallels between women's efforts in the arts during the Progressive Era and the feminist movement of the 1970s, Blair's chapter explores how women activists and artists conceptualized the process of institution-building as an educational process—one that challenged old aesthetics, shaped new cultural sensibilities, and (through both grassroots organizing and large gifts) helped gain public support for the arts.

The third and final section of this book is entitled "The Politics of Philanthropy in Women's Education: Race, Class, and Gender." Chapters in part III provide a closer look at the power of these factors in shaping women's experience as recipients of philanthropy and influencing their effectiveness as donors. Ruth Crocker, in chapter 11, outlines the obstacles that the wealthy heiress Olivia Sage (1828–1918) faced in trying to use her substantial inheritance to advance women's education. Though deeply convinced of the worthiness of this cause by her feminist friends Mary Putnam Jacobi and Elizabeth Cady Stanton, Sage faltered in executing her giving on behalf of women. Crocker argues that a confluence of factors—including class loyalties, the preferences of Sage's lawyers, the ability of institutions to subvert her intentions, and her growing preoccupation with her husband's and her family's legacy—derailed Sage's initial gender consciousness and limited her effectiveness as a donor. In chapter 12, Jayne Beilke explores the impact of philanthropy on women's education from the perspective of the recipient. She focuses on the connection between women's education and race uplift as she considers the stories of African American women from the South who were able to pursue graduate education at northern universities from the early 1930s to the late 1950s under the auspices of the Julius Rosenwald Fellowship program. As Beilke observes, while the fellowship program offered women certain valuable opportunities during the Jim Crow era, racism, limited funding, and the gender biases of the male philanthropists and administrators at the women's home institutions remained great barriers.

Linda Johnson considers the impact of another scholarship program in chapter 13. This chapter traces the career of Tsuda Ume (1864–1929), who attended Bryn Mawr College as the holder of the American Women's Scholarship for Japanese Women. Later she returned to Japan and founded one of her country's earliest colleges for women. Tsuda Ume further championed the cause of Japanese women's education by establishing, with the help of American women, a fellowship program for Japanese women to study at her alma mater, Bryn Mawr College. The collaboration of Japanese and American committees was based on shared beliefs about gender and class, notes Johnson, but certain tensions arose from culturally different imperatives in balancing education and Christianity. And finally, in chapter 14, Amy Bix explores individual and group efforts by women to improve women's status in the engineering profession. Bix focuses on the $1.5 million gift that Katherine Dexter McCormick (class of 1904) gave to MIT in 1960 to build a dormitory for women on MIT's campus. In the latter part of her chapter, Bix turns to the concerted effort of the Society of Women Engineers (founded in 1952) to encourage female high school students to enter engineering programs and to support female engineering students.

In retrospect, there are at least three discernible tendencies that may have facilitated the strong connection between philanthropy and education in U.S. history and that may have played prominent roles in shaping opportunities for women in a variety of settings. The first is a strong tendency to rely on private, local, and voluntary means rather than on centralized governmental agencies to conduct services ranging from municipal works and charity to the vital enterprise of education. The second is the tendency in American social thought to view education (in John Dewey's words) as the "fundamental method of social progress and reform."[67] These two tendencies combined may have given rise to a third trend, in which individuals and foundations have funneled a significant share of the nation's philanthropic dollars and voluntary efforts toward education.[68] The confluence of these three tendencies, reflecting broader currents in U.S. social, cultural, and political history, rendered education a widely contested arena in which social opportunities for individuals and groups were shaped, and where philanthropy—emanating from a host of values, including self-interest—played a salient and complex role. It is with an awareness of this larger context and an eye toward broad conceptions of philanthropy and education that the chapters of this volume have considered women's experience. This approach may also be useful in considering the history of philanthropic action in the lives of other social groups whose stories have yet to be written.

The emphasis on wealth—particularly the largesse of foundations—in the literature on educational philanthropy has related the study of education to important currents in U.S. society (for instance, the role of private power in shaping public policy), but such a focus has also obscured other traditions and persistent themes that have shaped the history of education. One such theme is the story of women's educational philanthropy. The stories of women's giving presented in the chapters that follow challenge the facile assumption, widely touted in the popular media in recent years, that it is only now—when women hold more disposable wealth—that their giving is capable of having a significant impact on education, especially in colleges and universities. While in no way undervaluing the potential impact and leveraging power that women's increased financial resources and independence may bring, this volume argues for greater recognition of the range and effect of women's earlier philanthropic contributions on their own terms. The women whose stories are presented here were not female Carnegies or Rockefellers—only two, Olivia Sage and Nettie Mc-Cormick, had substantial wealth, and only Sage used her wealth to establish a foundation. By comparison to male philanthropists who established foundations and who have become icons in both the history of U.S. philanthropy and the history of education, the impact of the woman-led philanthropic activities discussed in this volume may have been more local, perhaps more relational and institution- or community-specific, than national. But the stories of these women remain equally important to the study of education. Indeed, given the

United States' decentralized approach to education, donations of time and the targeted gift of financial support can have a tangible impact. With relatively limited means and well before government concern with racial or gender equity (before the Brown decision or Title IX, for instance), women used philanthropy to challenge institutional and ideological barriers in education, to fashion roles for themselves as educators who helped to shape new and more equitable modes of social thought, and to pose alternatives to the educational institutions and artistic canon supported by philanthropic men.[69] Simply put, one goal of this volume is to dispel the notion that women are "new givers"; another is to suggest that philanthropy does not emanate only from massive wealth but, as Goodale put it, also from a deep concern for the well-being of the "body social."[70]

Beyond documenting important aspects of the story of women's participation in educational philanthropy, the fourteen chapters of this volume also seek to foster a reconceptualization of the place of women in narratives of both education and philanthropy. Much as scholarship on women's history has looked beyond the narrow framework of the fight for suffrage, historians of women in education have recently begun to look beyond women's access to men's education and to explore the plurality of institutions where the majority of women were educated and where women achieved measurable influence.[71] But scholarship on the history of education has not necessarily viewed many of the female initiatives in education as part of a wider tradition of women's philanthropy, nor has it considered the woman philanthropist as a category for studying women's leadership in education, alongside the faculty member, the student, and the administrator. For example, as mentioned, the PTA has been seen as a reform initiated by women to counter the male-dominated school administrative bureaucracy but not as part of the larger women's club movement (see chapter 9), which is partly a philanthropic enterprise. Thus, this volume may help us not only to document the history of women as philanthropists in education, but also to reconceptualize the place of women in both the history of philanthropy and the history of education. Indeed, by examining the ties between women-as-philanthropists and educational institutions, we may move beyond an approach to writing history that deals with women superficially—or what Geraldine Clifford has described as an "add a woman and stir" approach[72]—to one in which the narratives of both education and philanthropy see women as institution- and discipline-builders.

23

Together, the three parts of this book attempt to capture the variety of both women's philanthropic agency in education and the influence of philanthropy on women's experience; however, it remains beyond the scope of this edited volume to provide a comprehensive discussion of the diversity among women, traditions, and contexts where education and philanthropy have intersected. Difficult choices had to be made about chapter topics, given the necessary constraints on length and the availability of contributors.[73] Because our focus has been on a particular intersection, some interesting—even pivotal—events in the history of philanthropy are not included in this volume. This is the case either because their significance to education per se is less readily apparent, as in the case of the Sanitary Commission during the Civil War, or because they are well documented elsewhere, as in the case of the social settlements.[74] Similarly, notable examples of working women's philanthropy, like women's exchanges or mutual aid societies, are not included here because these were largely entrepreneurial rather than educational ventures.[75]

It is peculiar that today we know relatively little about the complexity of women's philanthropic experience in education—a theme that Frances Goodale so proudly touched upon in *The Literature of Philanthropy* over a hundred years ago. Dealing specifically with an overview of women's philanthropy in education, then, this volume is long overdue. From Mary Richmond's and Sydnor Walker's efforts to enact their ideas through foundation work (a new context for professional women) to the fundraising efforts of the PTAs, we find examples of women theorizing about, documenting, and engaging in philanthropic works that bore directly on educational concerns. Therefore, as we think about the role of women's philanthropy in light of the imminent generational transfer of wealth, and as we witness an increase in the popularity of women's giving circles, women's funds, and university programs designed to attract female donors, these chapters say: here is a history with which to reflect upon women's giving. Indeed, the story of women as philanthropists in education is similar to the larger problem in women's history as articulated by Gerda Lerner, who argued that it is not that women have had no presence in history, but that women have had no consciousness of their history. Here, one might argue that the problem is not that women have no philanthropic legacy in education to reflect upon; rather, the problem lies in the forgetting or erasure of this legacy. Indeed, as is evident in Goodale's 1893 attempt to document women's philanthropy, the story of women's experience in educational philanthropy needs first to be written, so that it may then become a subject of reflection and further refinement.

NOTES

1. Frances Abigail Rockwell Goodale, "The Literature of Philanthropy," in *The Literature of Philanthropy*, ed. Goodale (New York: Harpers, 1893), 1–2.

2. Helen Hiscock Backus (Vassar '73), "The Need and the Opportunity for College-Trained Women in Philanthropic Work," a paper presented to the New York Association of Collegiate Alumnae on 19 March 1887. This is an early example of concern about the narrowing meaning of the term *philanthropy*. The Association of Collegiate Alumnae was the forerunner of the American Association of University Women (AAUW), and its papers are available in the AAUW microfilm papers. The original papers are housed at the AAUW's national headquarters in Washington, D.C.

3. For instance, women helped support the colonial colleges with gifts-in-kind, small donations, and subscriptions. See Jesse Brundage Sears, *Philanthropy in the History of American Higher Education* (1922; reprint, with a new introduction by Roger L. Geiger, New Brunswick, N.J.: Transaction, 1990), 16, 18, 26.

4. Even the second edition of Robert H. Bremner's *American Philanthropy* (Chicago: University of Chicago Press, 1988) contains only scant information regarding women. For a recent critical overview of the history of philanthropy in the United States, see Lawrence J. Friedman and Mark D. McGarvie, eds., *Charity, Philanthropy, and Civility in American History* (Cambridge: Cambridge University Press, 2003).

5. Representative works on Protestant women's philanthropy include Carroll Smith-Rosenberg, *Religion and the Rise of the American City: The New York City Mission Movement, 1812–1870* (Ithaca, N.Y.: Cornell University Press, 1971); Nancy Cott, *The Bonds of Womanhood: "Woman's Sphere" in New England, 1780–1835* (New Haven, Conn.: Yale University Press, 1977); Jane Hunter, *The Gospel of Gentility: American Women Missionaries in Turn-of-the-Century China* (New Haven, Conn.: Yale University Press, 1984); Patricia R. Hill, *The World Their Household: The American Woman's Foreign Mission Movement and Cultural Transformation, 1870–1920* (Ann Arbor: University of Michigan Press, 1985); Peggy Pascoe, *Relations of Rescue: The Search for Female Moral Authority in the American West, 1874–1939* (New York: Oxford University Press, 1990); Susan M. Yohn, *A Contest of Faiths: Missionary Women and Pluralism in the American Southwest* (Ithaca, N.Y.: Cornell University Press, 1995); and Amanda Porterfield, *Mary Lyon and the Mount Holyoke Missionaries* (New York: Oxford University Press, 1997). For African American women's experience, see Evelyn Brooks Higginbotham, *Righteous Discontent: The Women's Movement in the Black Baptist Church, 1880–1920* (Cambridge, Mass.: Harvard University Press, 1993). For Jewish women's philanthropy, see Shelly Tennenbaum, "Gender, Capital, and Immigrant Jewish Enterprises" (working paper 19, Center on Philanthropy and Civil Society, City University of New York, 1993); and Susan M. Chambre, "Parallel Power Structures, Invisible Careers, and the Changing Nature of American Jewish Women's Philanthropy," in *Women, Philanthropy, and Civil Society*, ed. Kathleen D. McCarthy

(Bloomington: Indiana University Press, 2001), 169–89. For Catholic women's philanthropy, see Mary J. Oates, *The Catholic Philanthropic Tradition in America* (Bloomington: Indiana University Press, 1995); and Dorothy M. Brown and Elizabeth
McKeown, *The Poor Belong to Us: Catholic Charities and American Welfare* (Cambridge,
Mass.: Harvard University Press, 1997).

6. See Helen Lefkowitz Horowitz, *Culture and the City: Cultural Philanthropy
in Chicago from the 1880s to 1917* (Lexington: University Press of Kentucky, 1976);
Karen J. Blair, *The Torchbearers: Women and Their Amateur Arts Associations in America,
1890–1930* (Bloomington: Indiana University Press, 1994); Kathleen D. McCarthy,
Noblesse Oblige: Charity and Cultural Philanthropy in Chicago, 1849–1929 (Chicago:
University of Chicago Press, 1982); idem, *Women's Culture: American Philanthropy and
Art, 1830–1930* (Chicago: University of Chicago Press, 1991); and Bernice Kert, *Abby
Aldrich Rockefeller: The Woman in the Family* (New York: Random House, 1993).

7. For representative works of this group, see Kathleen D. McCarthy, ed., *Lady
Bountiful Revisited: Women, Philanthropy, and Power* (New Brunswick, N.J.: Rutgers
University Press, 1990); idem, *Women, Philanthropy, and Civil Society* (Bloomington:
Indiana University Press, 2001); Anne Firor Scott, *Natural Allies: Women's Associations
in American History* (Urbana: University of Illinois Press, 1991); Kathryn Kish Sklar,
Florence Kelley and the Nation's Work (New Haven, Conn.: Yale University Press, 1995);
Nancy Hewitt, *Women's Activism and Social Change: Rochester, New York, 1822–1872*
(Ithaca, N.Y.: Cornell University Press, 1984); idem, *Southern Discomfort: Women's
Activism in Tampa, Florida, 1880s–1920s* (Urbana: University of Illinois Press, 2001);
Suzanne Lebsock, *The Free Women of Petersburg: Status and Culture in a Southern
Town, 1784–1860* (New York: W. W. Norton, 1984); Lori D. Ginzberg, *Women and
the Work of Benevolence: Morality, Politics, and Class in the Nineteenth-Century United
States* (New Haven, Conn.: Yale University Press, 1990); Anne M. Boylan, "Women
in Groups: An Analysis of Women's Benevolent Organizations in New York and
Boston, 1797–1840," *Journal of American History* 71 (December 1984): 497–523; idem,
The Origins of Women's Activism: New York and Boston, 1797–1840 (Chapel Hill: Uni-
versity of North Carolina Press, 2002); Darlene Clark Hine, Wilma King, and Linda
Reed, eds., *"We Specialize in the Wholly Impossible": A Reader in Black Women's History*
(Brooklyn, N.Y.: Carlson, 1995); and Darlene Clark Hine and Kathleen Thompson,
A Shining Thread of Hope: The History of Black Women in America (New York: Broad-
way, 1998).

8. For a discussion of the ways in which feminist literature on women's voluntary
action has contributed to our understanding of civic life, see Kathleen D. McCarthy,
"The History of Women in the Nonprofit Sector," in *Women and Power in the Nonprofit Sector,* ed. Teresa Odendahl and Michael O'Neill (San Francisco: Jossey-Bass,
1994), 17–38; and also idem, *Women, Philanthropy, and Civil Society.* For an overview
of women's role in social welfare history, see Linda Gordon, "The New Feminist
Scholarship on the Welfare State," in *Women, the State, and Welfare,* ed. Linda Gordon
(Madison: University of Wisconsin Press, 1990), 9–35.

9. For an early work that recognized Addams as an educator and philanthropist,
see Ellen Condliffe Lagemann, ed., *Jane Addams on Education* (1985; reprint, Piscataway, N.J.: Transaction, 1994). For a discussion of notable donations to women's
education, see Merle Curti and Roderick Nash, *Philanthropy in the Shaping of American
Higher Education* (Piscataway: Rutgers University Press, 1965), 87–106. For a discus-

sion of Anita McCormick Blaine, see Joyce Antler, "Female Philanthropy and Progressivism in Chicago," *History of Education Quarterly* 21 (winter 1981): 461–69.

10. The idea that the term *philanthropy* has come to mean the giving of money (mostly large sums) seems to have been discussed at least as early as the 1880s, as Backus's commentary suggests in "The Need and the Opportunity." However, the shifting meaning of the term was treated in detail in the 1950s. See Merle Curti, "American Philanthropy and the National Character," *American Quarterly* 10 (winter 1958): 421.

11. John Gardner, "The Independent Sector," in *America's Voluntary Spirit: A Book of Readings,* ed. Brian O'Connell (New York: Foundation Center, 1983), xx. In 2002, individuals were responsible for 76.3 percent of the $240.92 billion total philanthropic contributions in the U.S. (see AAFRC Trust for Philanthropy/Giving USA, 2003, http://www.aafrc.org/bysourceof.html, accessed 1 March 2004). Only recently has scholarship on philanthropy begun to direct attention to pluralism. See Lawrence J. Friedman, "Philanthropy in America: Historicism and Its Discontents," in Friedman and McGarvie, eds., *Charity, Philanthropy, and Civility,* 11–12. Representative of the emergent literature on diverse philanthropic traditions are Emmett Carson, *A Hand Up: Black Philanthropy and Self-Help in America* (Washington, D.C.: Joint Center for Political and Economic Studies Press, 1993); Charles H. Hamilton and Warren F. Ilchman, eds., *Cultures of Giving II: How Heritage, Gender, Wealth, and Values Influence Philanthropy* (San Francisco: Jossey-Bass, 1995); Bradford Smith et al., eds., *Philanthropy in Communities of Color* (Bloomington: Indiana University Press, 1999); Pier C. Roger, "Philanthropy in Communities of Color," ARNOVA Occasional Working Paper Series, 2001; *Cultures of Caring: Philanthropy in Diverse American Communities* (Washington, D.C.: Council on Foundations, 1999); and Laura Tuennerman-Kaplan, *Helping Others, Helping Ourselves: Power, Giving, and Community Identity in Cleveland, Ohio, 1880–1930* (Kent, Ohio: Kent State University Press, 2001).

12. The idea of "ways of seeing" has been used effectively to underscore the interpretive nature of historical inquiry. See David B. Tyack, "Ways of Seeing: An Essay on the History of Compulsory Education," *Harvard Educational Review* 46 (August 1976): 355–89; Elisabeth Hansot and David B. Tyack, "Gender and Public School: Thinking Institutionally," *Signs* 13 (spring 1988): 741–80; and Anne Firor Scott, "On Seeing and Not Seeing: A Case of Historical Invisibility," *Journal of American History* 71 (June 1984): 7–21.

13. Anne Firor Scott, "Women's Voluntary Associations: From Charity to Reform," in *Lady Bountiful,* ed. McCarthy, 37.

14. For a general overview of the history of women's education and a discussion of the ideology of domesticity, see Barbara Miller Solomon, *In the Company of Educated Women: A History of Women and Higher Education in America* (New Haven, Conn.: Yale University Press, 1985). For women's early experience as teachers, see David Tyack and Elisabeth Hansot, *Learning Together: A History of Coeducation in American Schools* (New Haven, Conn.: Yale University Press, 1990), 18–21. For a history of the Sunday school, see Anne M. Boylan, *Sunday School: The Formation of an American Institution, 1790–1880* (New Haven, Conn.: Yale University Press, 1988), 114–32. For a discussion of the volunteerism of teaching nuns, see Oates, *Catholic Philanthropic Tradition,* chapter 7. For relevant overviews of African American women, see Dorothy Sterling, ed., *We Are Your Sisters: Black Women in the Nineteenth*

Century (New York: W. W. Norton, 1984); and Hine and Thompson, *Shining Thread of Hope.*

15. Consider the gains that women in New England made in the period from 1675 to 1790. Within this span, the female literacy rate rose from only 45 percent (compared to 70 percent for men) to 80 percent, approaching the level of male literacy. See Linda Eisenmann, ed., *Historical Dictionary of Women's Education in the United States* (Westport, Conn.: Greenwood, 1998), xii.

16. Mrs. Russell Sage, "Opportunities and Responsibilities of Leisured Women," *North American Review* 181 (November 1905): 712–21.

17. Ginzberg, *Women and the Work of Benevolence;* and Boylan, *Origins of Women's Activism.*

18. Jane Addams, "The College Woman and the Family Claim" (1898) and "The Subjective Necessity for Social Settlements" (1893), both in *Jane Addams,* ed. Lagemann, 64–73 and 49–63. Kathryn Sklar asserts that the relatively high rates of female participation in education in the U.S. may help explain women's prominent contributions to shaping policy. See Kathryn Kish Sklar, "The Historical Foundations of Women's Power in the Creation of the American Welfare State, 1830–1930," in *Mothers of a New World: Maternalist Politics and the Origins of Welfare States,* ed. Seth Koven and Sonya Michel (New York: Routledge, 1993), 43–93.

19. Scholars of women's history were quick to recognize the importance of women's voluntary organizations and all-female associations in expanding women's horizons and fostering a feminist consciousness, but they did not necessarily see these bodies as part of the history of philanthropy and the nonprofit sector. For a classic discussion of separatism in women's history, see Estelle Freedman, "Separatism as Strategy: Female Institution Building and American Feminism, 1870–1930," *Feminist Studies* 5 (fall 1979): 512–29. For a discussion of how women's philanthropic activities constituted "parallel power structures" and promoted institution-building and reform, see Kathleen D. McCarthy, "Women and Philanthropy: Three Strategies in an Historical Perspective" (working paper 22, Center on Philanthropy and Civil Society, City University of New York, winter 1994); and idem, *Women's Culture.* The use of nonprofit organizations as alternative power structures by disfranchised groups is also examined in David C. Hammack, *Making the Nonprofit Sector in the United States: A Reader* (Bloomington: Indiana University Press, 1999), chapter 6.

20. Goodale, ed., *Literature of Philanthropy.*

21. For other works during this period that address women's philanthropy, see Annie Nathan Meyer, *Women's Work in America* (New York: H. Holt, 1891); Backus, "Need and the Opportunity"; Helen L. Bullock, "The Power and Purposes of Women," in *The Congress of Women: Held in the Woman's Building, World's Columbian Exposition,* ed. Mary Kavanaugh Oldham (Chicago: Monarch Book Company, 1894), 143–47; and Helena T. Grossman, *The Christian Woman in Philanthropy: A Study of the Past and Present* (Amherst, Mass.: Carpenter and Morehouse, 1895). This effort at documenting women's achievements continued into the twentieth century; see Scott Nearing and Nellie M. S. Nearing, *Women and Social Progress: A Discussion of the Biologic, Domestic, Industrial, and Social Possibilities of American Women* (New York: Macmillan, 1914), 240–64; and Mary Ritter Beard, *Woman's Work in Municipalities* (New York: D. Appleton, 1915).

22. Anna C. Brackett's *Women and the Higher Education* and Kate Douglas Wig-

gin's *The Kindergarten* were part of the Distaff Series published by Harper and Brothers in 1893. For a general discussion of women's involvement in the Columbian Exposition, see Jeanne Weimann, *The Fair Women* (Chicago: Academy Chicago, 1981).

23. Goodale, "Literature of Philanthropy," 1–5.

24. For a pioneering collection of essays on the history of women's philanthropy, see McCarthy, ed., *Lady Bountiful Revisited.*

25. For early works that dealt with the narrowing conception of philanthropy, see notes 2 and 10. For recent works, informed by historical perspectives, that have called for a broad view of philanthropy, see Robert Payton, *Philanthropy: Voluntary Action for the Public Good* (New York: Macmillan, 1988); Robert Payton et al., *Philanthropy: Four Views* (New Brunswick, N.J.: Transaction, 1988); and Mike W. Martin, *Virtuous Giving: Philanthropy, Voluntary Service, and Caring* (Bloomington: Indiana University Press, 1994). A similar latitudinarian view of giving is adopted in Amy Kass, introduction to *The Perfect Gift: The Philanthropic Imagination in Poetry and Prose*, ed. Kass (Bloomington: Indiana University Press, 2002), 3.

26. Goodale's conception of education as a platform for social change reflected the ethos of late-nineteenth-century progressive thinking that is also found in the writings of contemporary figures like Jane Addams and John Dewey. See for example, Addams, "The Subjective Necessity for Social Settlements"; and John Dewey, "My Pedagogic Creed" (1897), in *Dewey on Education*, ed. Martin S. Dworkin (New York: Teachers College Bureau of Publications, 1959), 19–32.

27. Merle Curti, "The History of American Philanthropy as a Field of Research," *American Historical Review* 62 (January 1957): 352–63; Bremner, *American Philanthropy*, 189–212; Ellen Condliffe Lagemann, *Private Power for the Public Good: A History of the Carnegie Foundation for the Advancement of Teaching* (Middletown, Conn.: Wesleyan University Press, 1983), 194–205; idem, *The Politics of Knowledge: The Carnegie Corporation, Philanthropy, and Public Policy* (Middletown, Conn.: Wesleyan University Press, 1989), 323–34; a bibliography by Susan Kastan in Ellen Condliffe Lagemann, ed., *Philanthropic Foundations: New Scholarship, New Possibilities* (Bloomington: Indiana University Press, 1999), 376–403; Joseph Kiger, *Historiographical Review of Foundation Literature: Motivations and Perceptions* (New York: Foundation Center, 1987); Peter Dobkin Hall, "The Work of Many Hands: A Response to Stanley N. Katz on the Origins of the 'Serious Study' of Philanthropy," *Nonprofit and Voluntary Sector Quarterly* 28 (December 1999): 522–36; and Friedman and McGarvie, eds., *Charity, Philanthropy, and Civility*, 413–39.

28. Backus, "Need and the Opportunity."

29. See Albert Shaw, "Millionaires and Their Public Gifts," *Review of Reviews* 7 (February 1893): 48–60; Sarah Knowles Bolton, *Famous Givers and Their Gifts* (New York: Thomas Y. Crowell, 1896); and Merle Curti and Roderick Nash, "Anatomy of Millionaires," *American Quarterly* 15 (winter 1963): 416–35.

30. Judith Sealander, *Private Wealth and Public Life: Foundation Philanthropy and the Reshaping of American Social Policy from the Progressive Era to the New Deal* (Baltimore, Md.: Johns Hopkins University Press, 1997); and Merle Curti, Judith Green, and Roderick Nash, "Anatomy of Giving: Millionaires in the Late Nineteenth Century," *American Quarterly* 15 (autumn 1963): 416–35. For a discussion of a much earlier shift in the meaning and nature of philanthropy, see Robert Gross, "Giving in

America: From Charity to Organized Philanthropy," in *Charity, Philanthropy, and Civility,* ed. Friedman and McGarvie, 29–48.

31. The importance of private giving in funding schools and colleges had been recognized by earlier works, such as George L. Jackson, *The Development of School Support in Colonial Massachusetts* (1909; reprint, New York: Arno, 1969) and Edwin Slosson, *Great American Universities* (New York: Macmillan, 1910). However, the first historical study to look systematically at the role of philanthropy in U.S. higher education was a dissertation study completed by Jesse B. Sears in 1919 and published three years later by the Government Printing Office. As Roger Geiger notes in his introduction to the 1990 reprint of Sears's *Philanthropy in the History of American Higher Education,* Sears was a pioneer in this area of research and had earlier produced an entry on "educational philanthropy" in the *Cyclopedia of Education* IV (1913), edited by Paul Monroe (Sears's mentor).

32. Sears, *Philanthropy in Higher Education,* 109.

33. Ernest Victor Hollis, *Philanthropic Foundations and Higher Education* (New York: Columbia University Press, 1938), 7.

34. Ibid., 86–87, 153.

35. Addams, "The Subjective Necessity for Social Settlements"; idem, *Democracy and Social Ethics* (New York: Macmillan, 1902); Ellen Condliffe Lagemann, introduction to *Jane Addams,* ed. Lagemann, xii; Beard, *Women's Work;* and Eleanor Flexner, *Century of Struggle: The Women's Rights Movement in the United States* (Cambridge, Mass.: Belknap Press of Harvard University Press, 1959). Similarly, writings by African American scholars on philanthropy and education—a topic that received considerable attention in the *Journal of Negro History,* founded by Carter Woodson—were also marginalized.

36. Bailyn raises the point that, in focusing on the origins of the rationale for public funding, early historians of schooling missed seeing the mix of "public" and "private" funding that had supported education. See Bernard Bailyn, *Education in the Forming of American Society: Needs and Opportunities for Study* (Chapel Hill: University of North Carolina Press for the Institute of Early American History and Culture, 1960), 109. For a similar point, see Geiger, introduction to Sears, *Philanthropy in Higher Education,* ix. For an example of the conventional history of education, see Paul Monroe, *A Text-Book in the History of Education* (New York: Macmillan, 1933); and for a critique of the traditional historiography, see Lawrence A. Cremin, *The Wonderful World of Ellwood Patterson Cubberly: An Essay on the Historiography of American Education* (New York: Teachers College Bureau of Publications, 1965). For a recent provocative qualification of Bailyn's assertion that educational historians focused exclusively on the school and, more centrally, for a critique of Bailyn's argument that educational historians were out of touch with mainstream currents in history, see Milton Gaither, *American Educational History Revisited: A Critique of Progress* (New York: Teachers College Press, 2003).

37. Peter Dobkin Hall, "Teaching and Research on Philanthropy, Voluntarism, and Nonprofit Organizations: A Case Study of Academic Innovations," *Teachers College Record* 93 (spring 1992): 403. An exception was Eduard Lindeman, *Wealth and Culture: A Study of One Hundred Foundations and Community Trusts and Their Operations during the Decade 1921–1930* (New York: Harcourt Brace, 1936).

38. For useful and concise commentary on the philanthropic literature relevant

here, see Ellen Condliffe Lagemann, "Philanthropy, Education, and the Politics of Knowledge," *Teachers College Record* 93 (spring 1992): 362; and idem, "Bibliographic Note," in *Private Power for the Public Good*, 195–205.

39. For a discussion of Curti's career, see John Pettegrew, "The Present-Minded Professor: Merle Curti's Work as an Intellectual Historian," *History Teacher* 32 (November 1998): 67–76; and Frances A. Huehls, "Merle Curti: Remembering a Teaching Life" (Ph.D. diss., Indiana University, 2001).

40. For details about congressional scrutiny of the politics, tax status, and functioning of foundations, see John Lankford, *Congress and the Foundations in the Twentieth Century* (River Falls: Wisconsin State University, 1964); Thomas C. Reeves, ed., *Foundations under Fire* (Ithaca, N.Y.: Cornell University Press, 1970); Hall, "Teaching and Research"; and Eleanor L. Brilliant, *Private Charity and Public Inquiry: A History of the Filer and Peterson Commissions* (Bloomington: Indiana University Press, 2000).

41. Merle Curti, *Social Ideas of American Educators* (New York: Charles Scribner's Sons, 1935), 581. For Curti's early interests in the history of women and African Americans, see chapters 5 and 8. It is also worth noting that Curti and Nash's *Philanthropy in the Shaping of American Higher Education* (1965) included chapters on women and African Americans (see chapters 5 and 8), whereas Bremner's *American Philanthropy*, appearing in 1960, did not. Some work on women's philanthropy came out of the foundation-funded project on the history of philanthropy, which Curti directed at the University of Wisconsin in the 1950s and early 1960s. See, for instance, Kenneth Melder, "Ladies Bountiful: Organized Women's Benevolence in Early Nineteenth Century America," *New York History* 48 (1967): 231–54.

42. Curti, "American Philanthropy and the National Character," 431; and idem, "History of American Philanthropy," 352.

43. Curti argues that the "change in meaning of the term from benevolence and humanitarianism to organized large-scale giving reflects a shift in our society to a greater emphasis on the role of wealth" (Curti, "American Philanthropy and the National Character," 421). See also notes 2 and 10, above.

44. For details of Curti's career, see Pettegrew, "Present-Minded Professor"; and Huehls, "Merle Curti." For a critique of Curti's view of philanthropy in education as roseate, see Walter Metzger's review of Curti and Nash, *Philanthropy and the Shaping of American Higher Education*, in *History of Education Quarterly* 6 (spring 1966): 75–76. Curti is overlooked partly because of the outdated idea of American exceptionalism that is present in his works, but also, I believe, because higher education studies emphasize public funding, and the emerging field of philanthropic studies has been heavily influenced by more contemporary politics and policy concerns. For a view that situates the beginning of philanthropic studies with the 1980 founding of Independent Sector, a coalition of nonprofit and philanthropic organizations (to the exclusion of works like Curti's), see Stanley N. Katz, "Where Did the Serious Study of Philanthropy Come from, Anyway?" *Nonprofit and Voluntary Sector Quarterly* 28 (March 1999): 74–82; and for an alternative view that acknowledges Curti's work, see Peter Dobkin Hall, "Work of Many Hands," 522–36, esp. 524.

45. The recruitment of Robert Bremner to write a general history of philanthropy (Bremner's *American Philanthropy* appeared in Daniel Boorstin's American Civilization Series) was perhaps the most enduring outcome of Curti's efforts to stimulate funded research on philanthropy. The influence of the Wisconsin Project can be traced in

more diffuse ways through the work of Curti's students and research assistants, notably David Allmendinger and Paul Mattingly. For details, see Peter Dobkin Hall, "Work of Many Hands."

46. For the first major study to provide a revisionist alternative to Bremner's classic text, see Friedman and McGarvie, eds., *Charity, Philanthropy, and Civility.*

47. For insight into the debate surrounding the radical revisionist critique of schooling, see Michael B. Katz, *The Irony of Early School Reform: Educational Innovation in Mid-Nineteenth Century Massachusetts* (Cambridge, Mass.: Harvard University Press, 1968); and Diane Ravitch, *The Revisionists Revised: A Critique of the Radical Attack on the Schools* (New York: Basic, 1978). Appearing at this time, David Rothman's *The Discovery of the Asylum: Social Order and Disorder in the New Republic* (Boston: Little, Brown, 1971) provided an early and influential critique of the motives behind benevolence. To some extent, the history of education and the history of social welfare cross-fertilized each other during this period. Katz's own writings have segued into welfare history. See Michael B. Katz, *In the Shadow of the Poorhouse: A Social History of Welfare in America* (New York: Basic, 1986). For a discussion of the ideological currents in the study of foundation philanthropy and patronage, see Gerald Benjamin, ed., *Private Philanthropy and Public Elementary and Secondary Education: Proceedings of the Rockefeller Archive Center Conference Held on June 8, 1979* (North Tarrytown, N.Y.: Rockefeller Archive Center, Rockefeller University, 1980); and Peter Dobkin Hall, "Theories and Institutions," *Nonprofit and Voluntary Sector Quarterly* 24 (spring 1995): 9. See also Donald K. Fisher, "American Philanthropy and the Social Sciences: The Reproduction of Conservative Ideology," in *Philanthropy and Cultural Imperialism: The Foundations at Home and Abroad,* ed. Robert F. Arnove (Boston: G. K. Hall, 1980), 233–68; idem, "The Role of Philanthropic Foundations in the Reproduction and Production of Hegemony: Rockefeller Foundations and the Social Sciences," *Sociology* 17 (June 1983): 206–33; Martin Bulmer, "Philanthropic Foundations and the Development of the Social Sciences in the Early Twentieth Century: A Reply to Donald Fisher," *Sociology* 18 (November 1984): 572–80; and Donald Fisher, "A Response to Martin Bulmer," *Sociology* 18 (November 1984): 580–87. Writing against the background of this debate, Wayne Urban described philanthropy as "one of the more explored pieces of that terrain [history of education] in the last two decades" (Wayne L. Urban, "Philanthropy and the Black Scholar: The Case of Horace Mann Bond," *Journal of Negro Education* 58 [autumn 1989]: 478).

48. Lagemann, "Philanthropy, Education, and the Politics of Knowledge"; and Dobkin Hall, "Teaching and Research."

49. For instance, see Barry D. Karl and Stanley N. Katz, "The American Private Philanthropic Foundation and the Public Sphere, 1890–1930," *Minerva* 19 (summer 1981): 236–70; and idem, "Foundations and Ruling Class Elites," *Daedalus* 116 (winter 1987): 1–40.

50. Even the few works on philanthropy in K–12 schooling tended to focus on foundation activities; see Benjamin, ed., *Private Philanthropy and Public Elementary and Secondary Education;* and Lagemann, *Private Power for the Public Good.* See also the spring 1992 issue of *Teachers College Record,* edited by Lagemann and devoted to an examination of what she refers to as "the politics of knowledge."

51. Representative works include Lagemann, *Private Power for the Public Good;* idem, *Politics of Knowledge;* Steven Wheatley, *The Politics of Philanthropy: Abraham*

Flexner and Medical Education (Madison: University of Wisconsin Press, 1988); Kenneth M. Ludmerer, *Learning to Heal: The Development of American Medical Education* (New York: Basic, 1985); Robert E. Kohler, *Partners in Science: Foundations and Natural Scientists, 1900–1945* (Chicago: University of Chicago Press, 1991); Fisher, "American Philanthropy and the Social Sciences"; and Theresa Richardson and Donald Fisher, eds., *The Development of the Social Sciences in the United States and Canada: The Role of Philanthropy* (Stamford, Conn.: Ablex, 1999). Also see the autumn 1997 issue of *Minerva*, which editor Martin Bulmer devoted to the theme "Philanthropy and Institution-Building in the Twentieth Century." Though not directly concerned with foundations, an example of another important approach to studying voluntary action in higher education would be Hugh Hawkins, *Banding Together: The Rise of National Associations in American Higher Education, 1887–1950* (Baltimore, Md.: Johns Hopkins University Press, 1992).

52. John H. Stanfield, *Philanthropy and Jim Crow in American Social Science* (Westport, Conn.: Greenwood, 1985); James D. Anderson, *The Education of Blacks in the South, 1860–1935* (Chapel Hill: University of North Carolina Press, 1988); William H. Watkins, *The White Architects of Black Education: Ideology and Power in America, 1865–1954* (New York: Teachers College Press, 2001); and Eric Anderson and Alfred A. Moss, Jr., *Dangerous Donations: Northern Philanthropy and Southern Black Education, 1902–1930* (Columbia: University of Missouri Press, 1999).

53. For one of the few studies of a woman whose career was tied to foundation support and employment, see Guy Alchon, "Mary Van Kleeck and Social-Economic Planning," *Journal of Policy History* 3 (winter 1991): 1–23.

54. See note 7.

55. Nancy Hewitt, *Women's Activism;* idem, *Southern Discomfort;* Darlene Clark Hine, " 'We Specialize in the Wholly Impossible': The Philanthropic Work of Black Women," in *Lady Bountiful,* ed. McCarthy, 70–93; Hine, King, and Reed, eds., *"We Specialize in the Wholly Impossible";* and McCarthy, "History of Women in the Nonprofit Sector," 18. I take the term "fissures" from McCarthy.

56. Payton, *Philanthropy: Voluntary Action for the Public Good.*

57. For the reasons why all voluntary action may be considered philanthropy, see Payton, *Philanthropy: Voluntary Action for the Public Good;* and idem, "Philanthropic Values," in *Private Means, Public Ends,* ed. Kenneth W. Thompson (New York: University Press of America, 1987), 21–47, esp. 28. In this definition, the "public good" is not seen as monolithic. For the idea that many publics exist in a democratic and multicultural society and therefore that the "public good" is a contested arena, see Jane Mansbridge, "On the Contested Nature of the Public Good," in *Private Action and the Public Good,* ed. Walter W. Powell and Elisabeth S. Clemens (New Haven, Conn.: Yale University Press, 1998), 3–18. Here, in *Women and Philanthropy in Education,* the definition of philanthropy embraces all giving, including what some might call charity. For the history of the concepts of "charity" and "philanthropy" and the distinction, if any, between these two terms see Payton, "Philanthropic Values"; and Gross, "Giving in America."

58. Kathleen D. McCarthy, "Women, Politics, Philanthropy: Some Historical Origins of the Welfare State," in *The Liberal Persuasion: Arthur Schlesinger, Jr., and the Challenge of the American Past,* ed. John Patrick Diggins (Princeton, N.J.: Princeton University Press, 1997), 143; and Arlene Kaplan Daniels, *Invisible Careers:*

Women Civic Leaders from the Volunteer World (Chicago: University of Chicago Press, 1988).

59. Ellen Condliffe Lagemann raises this point and elaborates on the narrowing of the concepts of education and teaching in her introduction to *Jane Addams*, xiii–xiv, and idem, *An Elusive Science: The Troubling History of Education Research* (Chicago: University of Chicago, 2000), esp. 1. For a relevant discussion of the narrowing views of education and of philanthropy in relation to the social settlements, see Addams, "The Subjective Necessity for Social Settlements" and "A Function of the Social Settlement" (1899), in *Jane Addams*, ed. Lagemann, 49–63 and 74–97, esp. 55 and 84–85.

60. An example of an early woman university scholar who studied women's education is Willystine Goodsell, editor of *Pioneers of Women's Education in the United States: Emma Willard, Catherine Beecher, Mary Lyon* (New York: McGraw-Hill, 1931), who in turn has become a subject of interest. See Robert Engel, "Willystine Goodsell: Feminist and Reconstructionist Educator," *Vitae Scholasticae* 3 (fall 1984): 355–78.

61. For ideas from women's history that influenced the history of women in education, see Gerda Lerner, "Placing Women in History: Definitions and Challenges," *Feminist Studies* 3 (fall 1975): 5–14; idem, *The Majority Finds Its Past: Placing Women in History* (New York: Oxford University Press, 1979); and idem, *Teaching Women's History* (Washington, D.C.: American Historical Association, 1980), esp. 6–13. For early works in the history of women in education, see Jill Ker Conway, "Perspectives on the History of Women's Education in the United States," *History of Education Quarterly* 14 (spring 1974): 1–12; Patricia Albjerg Graham, "So Much to Do: Guides for Historical Research on Women in Higher Education," *Teachers College Record* 76 (February 1975): 421–29; idem, "Expansion and Exclusion: A History of American Women in Higher Education," *Signs* 3 (summer 1978): 759–73; Anne Firor Scott, "What, Then, Is the American: This New Woman?" *Journal of American History* 65 (December 1978): 679–703; idem, "The Ever Widening Circle: The Diffusion of Feminist Values from Troy Female Seminary, 1822–1872," *History of Education Quarterly* 19 (spring 1979): 3–25; Margaret W. Rossiter, *Women Scientists in America: Struggles and Strategies to 1940* (Baltimore, Md.: Johns Hopkins University Press, 1982); and Geraldine Jonçich Clifford, "Shaking Dangerous Questions from the Crease: Gender and American Higher Education," *Feminist Issues* 3 (fall 1983): 3–62. For an overview of studies in the history of women in education, see Sally Schwager, "Educating Women in America," *Signs* 12 (winter 1987): 333–72.

62. Early useful applications of this broader conception of education in relation to women's lives include Ellen Condliffe Lagemann, *A Generation of Women: Education in the Lives of Progressive Reformers* (Cambridge, Mass.: Harvard University Press, 1979); Clifford, "Shaking Dangerous Questions"; and Lois Arnold, *Four Lives in Science: Women's Education in the Nineteenth Century* (New York: Schocken, 1984). For a more recent work influenced by Bailyn and Cremin, see Margaret Smith Crocco and O. L. Davis, Jr., eds., *"Bending the Future to Their Will": Civic Women, Social Education, and Democracy* (New York: Rowman and Littlefield, 1999).

63. Bailyn, *Education in the Forming of American Society*, esp. 14. The general theory of the multiplicity of institutions that educate (forming varied relationships that Cremin described as the "configurations of education") is explained in Lawrence A. Cremin, *Public Education* (New York: Basic, 1976), esp. 29–33. Cremin insisted

that education occurs not only in settings where formal instruction takes place—such as in schools, colleges, and universities—but also in institutions like the family, the church, and the museum.

64. Representatives of this literature are Clifford, "Shaking Dangerous Questions"; Karen J. Blair, *The Clubwoman as Feminist: True Womanhood Redefined, 1868–1914* (New York: Holmes and Meier, 1980); Lagemann, ed., *Jane Addams;* and Crocco and Davis, eds., *"Bending the Future to Their Will."*

65. Lagemann, *Generation of Women.*

66. Though the history of philanthropy in education is understudied, an important discussion of donor intentions in women's education is found in Helen Lefkowitz Horowitz, *Alma Mater: Design and Experience in the Women's Colleges from Their Nineteenth-Century Beginnings to the 1930s* (New York: Knopf, 1984). See also Rossiter, *Women Scientists in America: Struggle and Strategies;* and idem, *Women Scientists in America: Before Affirmative Action, 1940–1972* (Baltimore, Md.: Johns Hopkins University Press, 1995).

67. Dewey, "My Pedagogic Creed," 30.

68. In 2002, education received 13.1 percent of private giving, or $31.64 billion, ranking second to religion, which received 35 percent, or $84.26 billion. See AAFRC Trust for Philanthropy/Giving USA, 2003. But, as Ellen Lagemann noted in a 1992 essay, education's portion in any such reporting becomes considerably larger when one considers that much of the funds that are reported under religious giving are also used to support education-related activities. See Lagemann, "Philanthropy, Education, and the Politics of Knowledge," 1.

69. See, for example, V. P. Franklin's use of Bourdieu's concept of "cultural capital" to explore many of the types of actions in support of African American education that might also be regarded as "philanthropic." See V. P. Franklin, "Introduction: Cultural Capital and African American Education," *Journal of African American History* 87 (spring 2002): 175–81.

70. Goodale, "Literature of Philanthropy," 1–5.

71. For a discussion of the limitations of the concept of "access," see Linda Eisenmann, "Reconsidering a Classic: Assessing the History of Women's Higher Education a Dozen Years after Barbara Solomon," *Harvard Educational Review* 67 (winter 1997): 689–717; and idem, "Creating a Framework for Interpreting U.S. Women's Educational History: Lessons from Historical Lexicography," *History of Education* 30 (fall 2001): 453–70. For a discussion of how the study of philanthropy might help us rethink the meaning of access and illuminate important aspects of the history of women in education, see Andrea Walton, "Rethinking Boundaries: The History of Women, Philanthropy, and Higher Education," *History of Higher Education Annual* 20 (2000): 29–57; Eisenmann, "Creating a Framework"; and idem, "New Frameworks for Women's Educational History: The Importance of Philanthropy," a paper presented at the annual meeting of the History of Education Society, Yale University, New Haven, Conn., 21 October 2001, in the author's possession.

72. Clifford, "Shaking Dangerous Questions," 12.

73. For example, it has not been possible, given these constraints, to include materials addressing the stories of Catholic, Jewish, Muslim, Latina, Asian, Native American, and other minority, religious, and ethnic women's experience in philanthropy.

74. For representative works on the social settlement movement, see Judith Ann Trolander, *Professionalism and Social Change: From the Settlement House Movement to Neighborhood Centers, 1886 to the Present* (New York: Columbia University Press, 1987); Ruth Crocker, *Social Work and Social Order: The Settlement Movement in Two Industrial Cities, 1889–1930* (Urbana: University of Illinois Press, 1992); and Elisabeth Lasch-Quinn, *Black Neighbors: Race and the Limits of Reform in the American Settlement House Movement, 1890–1945* (Chapel Hill: University of North Carolina Press, 1993). For the Sanitary Commission, see Ginzberg, *Women and the Work of Benevolence.*

75. For this aspect of women's philanthropy, see Kathleen Waters Sander, *The Business of Charity: The Women's Exchange Movement, 1832–1900* (Urbana: University of Illinois Press, 1998).

PART I.
SCHOOLS, COLLEGES, UNIVERSITIES, AND FOUNDATIONS

1. Teaching as Philanthropy: Catharine Beecher and the Hartford Female Seminary

Frances Huehls

"I would rather my daughters would go to school and sit down and do nothing, than to study philosophy," wrote a concerned father to the editors of the *Connecticut Courant* in 1829. Notably, education for women was not the object of his criticism. Indeed, by this era in the young republic's history, demand for female literacy together with other social and economic changes had provided a powerful rationale for women's education and, as a result, academies admitting female students dotted New England and the eastern seaboard, and new schools where women might study were being founded in the frontier territories.[1] These institutions offered the most advanced education available to women and in many instances boasted curricula that were substantially similar to course work offered for young men. The question for this worried Connecticut father, then, was not whether women should be educated but rather what type of education women were to receive. He was especially concerned about the wisdom of allowing young women to pursue a course on mental and moral philosophy like the one offered by educator and philanthropist Catharine Beecher at the Hartford Female Seminary. "These branches fill young Misses with vanity to the degree that they are above attending to the more useful parts of an education," he wrote pointedly.[2]

By contrast to the writer to the *Connecticut Courant*, Catharine Esther Beecher did not believe that the study of mental and moral philosophy was an inappropriate pursuit for young women or a certain pathway to female vanity; indeed, such an outcome would have contradicted Beecher's own vision of education and of Hartford Seminary's mission. Nor did Beecher view the introduction of a philosophy course at Hartford solely as an equalizing measure that provided women with the standard fare found in early-nineteenth-century institutions for young men. Rather, to Beecher's mind, the study of philosophy was central to her concept of education and to promoting the values she hoped to institutionalize at Hartford Female Seminary. Indeed, deep intellectual investigation was at the heart of the type of experience Catharine sought to share with her students. She infused this type of inquiry into the curriculum at Hartford to work toward enlarging women's place in society and increasing their contribution to the common good.

From its inception in 1823, Hartford Female Seminary was a laboratory for Catharine's beliefs about education, religion, and the role of women in society. From her vantage point, these were not three separate sets of ideas, but rather ones that could be united under a single framework: philanthropy.[3] God's greatest wish for mankind was happiness, and happiness for oneself could be achieved most effectively through efforts toward making others happy. Education—the sheer exercise of the intellect—and the transmission of cultural values from one generation to the next through teaching were the greatest sources of personal happiness.[4] In opposition to accepted Calvinist doctrine, Catharine taught that good works—including teaching—were a means to eternal salvation. Thus, Catharine conceptualized teaching as a philanthropic activity: proffering the gift of education rewarded both giver and recipient. This chapter will explore Catharine Beecher's philosophy of education during her years at the Hartford Female Seminary (1823–1831), demonstrating how and why she defined teaching as a philanthropic act. In doing so, this chapter will show that women were engaged not only in doing philanthropy but also in articulating teaching—a woman's profession—as a philanthropic activity.

Catharine was born in 1800, the first child of Lyman and Roxana Foote Beecher. Lyman Beecher rose to a position of eminence as an evangelical preacher during the years of the Second Great Awakening in New England. His growing influence was reflected in moves to successively larger and more prestigious churches between 1800 and 1830, including congregations in East Hampton, New York; Litchfield, Connecticut; and Boston. Lyman Beecher's evangelical work stressed active involvement in reform and missionary movements; in order to foster social solidarity in his religious domain, he facilitated the formation of benevolent societies within his congregations. The fruits of a family philosophy that emphasized religion and benevolence are apparent in Lyman Beecher's offspring. In the course of their lives, six of his eleven children—Catharine, Edward, Charles, Henry Ward, Harriet Beecher Stowe, and Isabella Beecher Hooker—would play significant roles in the revision of Calvinist theology and in movements advocating abolition, woman suffrage, and educational reform.[5]

Benevolence was central to more than Beecher family life: during the post-Revolutionary decades, the idea permeated the Protestant tradition. A writer to the *Christian Spectator* in 1822 noted that "the public is forming a habit of benevolent exertion."[6] The attitude of benevolence and its enactment as charity were nested within the universal love and brotherhood understood in the concept *philanthropy*. Further, benevolence was tied to recognition of privilege: those who had been favored with prosperity and good health had an obligation to tend to those who were less fortunate, doing good works and promoting happiness through their efforts. The meaning of *charity* at the end of the colonial era embraced the attitudes of benevolence and Christian love but also included the acts of almsgiving and relief for the poor. The proliferation of benevolent societies in the early decades of the Republic lent a new and institutionally oriented meaning to the term; charity came to include gifts for public goods and the activities of benevolent societies as well as direct aid to the needy. A gift of money or time was deemed uncharitable when it was rooted in self-interest rather than altruism. This, however, did not preclude some level of financial gain. By the 1820s it was not unusual for some workers in benevolent societies—secretaries, nurses, doctors—to be paid for their work.[7]

By 1820, benevolent societies for the relief of children, widows, and orphans, missionary societies, and Sunday schools abounded, particularly in the northeastern states. Women from a range of socioeconomic situations—from members of the working class to the financially affluent—formed the morally elite backbone of social and humanitarian reform movements that aimed to uplift the disadvantaged—including slaves, the physically and mentally handicapped, children, and other women. The church was often the venue through which women entered charitable work, becoming the means of access to an enlarged domestic sphere that included "dependents" beyond the immediate family unit.[8]

As Roberta Wollons points out later in this volume, the religious revivals of the early nineteenth century were linked both to missionary movements, which aimed to spread the gospel, and to reform movements that intended to improve educational opportunities for women.[9] The linkage of religious mission and educational opportunity is evident in the earliest benevolent societies. The Society for the Relief of Poor Widows with Small Children, formed in New York City in 1797, organized schools that enabled widows to support themselves by educating orphans as well as their own children. The goals of female benevolence were religious in nature, whether or not the societies were formed within the confines of the institutional church; the idea was to "save souls as well as bodies."[10] Women, who constituted the majority of church members, were viewed as morally superior to men and the natural purveyors of religious and social values. Moved by the sentiment that only separate education—woman to woman—of future mothers could ensure their ability to rear virtuous citizens, provide Christian guidance for children, and train teachers, women such as Sarah Pierce, Emma Willard, Zilpah Grant, Mary Lyons, Almira Phelps, and Catharine Beecher sought to provide an elite education that would bolster these unique roles of women. Catharine herself was educated in this liberal tradition, having attended Sarah Pierce's Litchfield Academy from 1810 to 1816.[11]

The women educated in the academies did not represent clearly defined socioeconomic classes. Distinctions between "upper-class" and "middle-class" women elude precise economic definition in this era, since virtue, piety, and gentility were mechanisms of social mobility that were available to all but the very poor. Social status was of less concern to educational reformers than the need to arm young women with the moral means to cope with changing social and economic conditions.[12] In 1847, Catharine wrote, "Everything is moving and changing. Persons in poverty are rising to opulence, and persons of wealth are sinking to poverty. There are no distinct classes as in aristocratic lands, whose bounds are protected by distinct and impassable lines, but all are thrown into impassable masses."[13] Despite the egalitarianism of this statement, the economics of running an academy dictated to some extent who attended. Catharine followed the lead of Sarah Pierce, drawing students for her school from Hartford's socially and financially elite families. During these years, Catharine's desire for her own economic independence and the school's financial stability caused her to rely on the financial largesse and approval of Hartford's moral and moneyed elites.[14]

Liberal education for women was justified on a number of grounds, ranging from the need to keep a daughter occupied until marriage to the more enlightened view that a woman's education was a good in its own right and needed no further justification.[15] For women of Catharine's social standing, however, religious conversion constituted a more critical rite of passage to adulthood than did either educational attainment or participation in benevolent work. Although Lyman Beecher's sermons were full of exhortations to perform good works, he did not believe that benevolence was enough to guarantee eternal salvation. Conversion was essential to overcome original sin and guarantee eternal life in God's love; he was determined that Catharine would achieve this moral safeguard before marriage. In 1821, Lyman Beecher began to press Catharine to submit her will to God, renouncing the sin that permeated her life, including her liberal academy education.[16]

In December of 1821, Catharine was officially engaged to Alexander Fisher, a professor of natural theology at Yale. Fisher's death at sea in May of 1822 precipitated a crisis of faith for Catharine: he had died with an unconverted soul and Catharine could not bring herself to believe that God would abandon a man who had led a virtuous life. She wrote to her father, "When I think of Mr. Fisher, and remember his blameless and useful life, his unexampled and persevering efforts to do his duty both to God and man, I believe . . . that God . . . does make the needful distinction between virtue and vice; and that there was more reason to hope for one whose whole life had been an example of excellence than for one who had spent all his days in sin and guilt."[17] Unable to resolve the emotional and intellectual conflicts of submitting her will to God, Catharine remained unconverted.

Beecher's domestic future was also unsettled. Although both Lyman Beecher and Catharine had anticipated that she would marry and move out of the family economic unit, she instead became one of many young women who, by necessity or design, would defer or find an alternative to marriage. With traditional marriage and family at least temporarily out of the picture, she settled on teaching as perhaps the only useful purpose to which she might be allowed to direct her energy and her intellect. In 1824, she made a conscious and irrevocable decision to remain a single and financially independent woman, making the school and its success her primary objective.[18]

EQUAL BUT DIFFERENT: THE MORAL ETHOS OF A SCHOOL

For Catharine, the overall purpose of a woman's education was to prepare her to become a teacher, whether of her own children or those of others. Catharine's ideas about education were first formalized in 1829 as "Suggestions Respecting Improvements in Education Presented to the Trustees of the Hartford Female Seminary and Published at Their Request."[19] Rendering children competent in the "three Rs" was not what she had in mind, however. The role of mothers and teachers was to educate character, to maintain the health of children, and to "form immortal minds" by encouraging intellectual and moral development and by replacing bad habits with proper ones. Women, Catharine felt, had not been trained to fulfill this important, but dishonored, role. If women were educated to improve both themselves and others, they would bring about overall improvements in society.[20]

Catharine asserted her view that these lofty ends could only be accomplished through facilities and a curriculum comparable to those available for young men.[21] In 1826, Catharine mounted a successful fundraising campaign to build what she considered a proper school.[22] From the time the school had opened with seven students in 1823 until the fall term of 1827, when the student body numbered over one hundred, Catharine had lacked equipment, classroom space, and a library. The school had moved from its original rented room above a harness shop to the basement of a church, but it continued to operate in a single room, with a few teachers teaching many subjects to classes of mixed ages and abilities. Furthermore, recitations and lectures occurred simultaneously.[23] One can only imagine the noise created by lecturing, reciting, and coming and going! In 1824, Catharine herself was teaching rhetoric, logic, natural philosophy, chemistry, history, Latin, and algebra.[24] As a result of Catharine's successful campaign efforts, however, the newly incorporated Hartford Female Seminary that opened for the fall term in 1827 included a large hall for general instruction, a library, a lecture room, and recitation rooms. Catharine was able to invest in blackboards and maps, and the division of teaching responsibilities also improved: eight teachers each taught one or two subjects. Promising students were trained to be assistants, further reducing the load on the teaching staff and adding what could be considered in-service training for potential future teachers. The additional classrooms made it possible to have small classes of six to ten students, who were assigned to courses based on ability, as determined by the placement exam administered when students enrolled.[25]

To a great extent, this is where Catharine's push to emulate male academies ended, as the environment she created would not duplicate the competitive spirit prevalent at schools for young men.[26] Properly training the minds of women of the "moral" class required equal facilities and curriculum, but, in Catharine's mind, students needed an environment that was ruled by benevolence, self-discipline, and noncompetition. Not surprisingly, Hartford Female Seminary was also ruled entirely by women. Through three routes—proper preparation, internalized self-discipline, and internalized rewards—Catharine sought to prepare her students for their most important duty: their future roles as teachers. As she wrote in 1835, a woman's most critical responsibility "is the physical, intellectual, and moral education of children. It is the care of health, and the formation of the character, of the future citizens of this great nation."[27]

Although many of Catharine's students came from Hartford's socially and financially elite families, *intellectual* elitism was not fostered. Catharine's philosophy tended to downplay intelligence in favor of common sense and morality. Achievements often ascribed to intelligence could in fact be accomplished through training in "good common sense, persevering energy and high religious principle, and not by remarkable genius, or by the aid of that literary and scientific training sought in our colleges and regarded as a marked privilege of which women have been unjustly deprived."[28] What Catharine referred to as "intellectual defects" could be remedied through individual attention and by presenting the material in a number of ways. Thus, an effective teacher should focus on principles and generalizations, not on the rote memorization of facts. Students needed to see how knowledge was connected instead of merely committing information to memory; they should be able to recognize the common elements of and the relationships between the various disciplines. Students were also encouraged to find alternatives to textbooks for learning, since Catharine believed that being interested in a subject was critical to learning it. She cited her own difficulties in learning mathematics, which had been resolved by applying concepts to real-life situations. In all, then, the Hartford system tended to encourage self-directed learning. Catharine also expected her teachers to socialize with their students and get to know their academic strengths and weaknesses. Teachers and student assistants met regularly to discuss which pupils needed individual attention.[29]

Catharine's goal was the development of conscience and congenial female communities that were also led by women. Because their members had internalized discipline as an ethic of self-examination and self-restraint, these communities would be managed by voluntary submission to the common good. Consequently, disciplinary practices at the school encouraged self-control rather than relying on punishment. Although a governess ultimately enforced the rules of conduct, a system of self-reporting evolved over the years. By 1831, students recorded their infractions in their journals, which were collected and read aloud—anonymously—the following day at the common assembly before being submitted to the governess. "Ratting" on fellow students was discouraged. Perhaps Catharine drew upon her own childhood experience at Miss Pierce's School in Litchfield, an environment that also emphasized moral education and relied upon journals and the self-reporting of rule infractions.[30] The boarding system also operated on principles of example and surveillance. Students and teachers regularly boarded together in the homes of Hartford women of "high position, culture, and religious principle," and the teacher held moral authority over the students in her charge.[31]

Competition between students was diminished through the emphasis on internalized rewards. Although the seminary awarded annual prizes for academic achievement in the early years, Catharine decided to curtail this practice in 1831. She felt the students should excel out of affection for their parents and teachers, out of interest in their own intellectual improvement, and out of duty to God.[32]

Views of Hartford Female Seminary that come from sources other than Catharine's published writing shed light on the atmosphere of the school. Angelina Grimké visited the school in 1831, with the intention of becoming a student there. She found the atmosphere genteel, but purposeful. Catharine encouraged her scholars "to feel that they had no right to spend their time in idleness, fashion and folly, but they as individuals were bound to be useful in Society after they had finished their education, and that as teachers single women could be more useful in this than in any other way."[33]

The emphasis on purposeful piety and gentility should not imply that there were never occasions for high feelings or pranks. Catharine had a reputation for being economical—particularly with food—and sometimes these economies pertained only to the food served to the students. On one occasion, when the girls could not endure what they saw as a double standard, Sara Willis substituted the students' low-grade butter for Catharine's and then graciously returned it to her as soon as the headmistress recognized the disparity in taste. Catharine also experimented with Graham diets, which were essentially vegetarian fare with a strong emphasis on whole-wheat products. The philosophy of Sylvester Graham was dietary temperance—a sound mind in a sound body—leading to a right and moral life. It was an idea that appealed to Catharine. With the aim of remedying physical as well as moral defects, she also introduced a course of calisthenics at the school.[34]

Moral education at Hartford was also overt in the sense that religious practice was a part of daily life as well as a part of the formal curriculum. Catharine read the Bible to students and held daily worship services that all pupils and instructors were required to attend. Private religious counseling for individual students was also available. Even in 1824, when Catharine took responsibility for teaching multiple subjects, she kept afternoons open for worship and prayer with students.[35]

In the spring of 1826, Catharine led a religious revival that included not only her students, but also members of the Hartford community—particularly women. By this time, she had rented her own home and used it for prayer meetings. Conversion in the Calvinist style was her goal, and she adopted the method Lyman Beecher had used in 1823 to direct conversion. She threw herself whole-heartedly into this effort, writing to her brother Edward in August of 1826 that she was so busy molding the character of her students that she had no time to work on her own salvation.[36] The revival produced considerable emotional heat, causing Lyman Beecher to urge Catharine to moderate her conversion activities. He cautioned her that the proper mood was indicated by "a genial warmth of heart, of steady benevolent temperature, compared with the more intense heat and flashings of holy and animal affections and passions, all boiling at once in the heart."[37] Although revivals occurred regularly at the seminary over the years, after 1826 Catharine restricted her conversion activities to the students rather than taking them into the wider Hartford community.[38] Undoubtedly, she was mindful of Lyman's view that the ministry was not a proper role for a woman and that she had clearly been acting in that role.

"ELEMENTS OF MENTAL AND MORAL PHILOSOPHY":
TEACHING AS PHILANTHROPY

The lectures on mental and moral philosophy that were to gain editorial note in the *Connecticut Courant* were a natural outgrowth of Catharine's need to protect and nurture the overall development of her students. The course also provided an academic venue for her ministry, one more acceptable than her efforts at conversion. Catharine had an enduring fear for the unconverted (including herself); at one point she noted, " 'What must we do to be saved' became the agonizing inquiry for myself and all I loved most."[39] She decided to take personal responsibility for this philosophical instruction after she failed to persuade the eminently devout Zilpah Grant to come to Hartford as chaplain and director of religious education.[40] Catharine's lectures on the subject led to the volume *The Elements of Mental and Moral Philosophy Founded upon Experience, Reason, and the Bible.*[41] While the work was never published for public consumption, Catharine did circulate a number of copies for "leaders of thought in both the literary and religious world."[42] Except for the removal of what Catharine said were a few pages that would have been considered heresy by Calvinists of her father's persuasion, the content of *Elements* approximates what the young women heard in class.

On its long and winding path, *Elements* binds together the mental, the physical, and the moral. At the risk of oversimplifying, only the strands that lead most directly to her ultimate thesis will be discussed here. These include happiness for the self and others, the relationship of experience to education, and the roles that both of these elements played in salvation. At the outset of the lectures, Catharine was careful to set out definitions, saying that mental states could be identified and definitions could be applied. In her opinion, philosophy was not an inexact science, but rather one susceptible to logic and reason.

In these lectures, happiness emerges as an emotional state sanctioned by and enabled through the gift of Jesus Christ, who took on the form of man and died for human sins. Catharine enumerated nine forms of pleasurable emotions that result from right and virtuous acts: conscious "being" itself, enjoying intellectual superiority, receiving sympathy, giving and appreciating affection, exercising the intellect, employing physical and moral power (which Catharine defined as the ability to bend the will of another), feeling sympathy for the happiness of others, living a virtuous life ("conscious rectitude"), and enacting benevolence.

Catharine's definition of benevolence, one of the pleasurable emotions and the natural state of the human mind, was "such love for the happiness of other minds, as induces a willingness to make sacrifices of personal enjoyment, to secure a greater amount of good to others." It would, in Catharine's opinion, be difficult to love someone who was not benevolent.[43]

Thus, happiness for the self was important but it was not enough. A higher level of happiness could be gained by adding to the happiness of others. Catharine argued that God created us with minds so that we could be happy and make others happy; the mind continuously sought out happiness, avoiding anything that destroyed enjoyment or promised suffering. Further, the exercise of the mind itself was a source of happiness: consciousness allowed one to enjoy the intellectual and moral qualities of others and to gain pleasure from being a source of happiness for them. "The consciousness of virtue," Catharine wrote, "which consists in acting for the general good, instead of for contracted selfish purposes, is another source of happiness, while those who witness its delightful results, rejoice to behold and acknowledge it."[44] Good habits that led to virtuous behavior were also a source of happiness and a pleasure that did not dim with time or repetition. Those activities that resulted in bringing good to the self and to others were always a source of enjoyment.

However, happiness did not always mean immediate gratification. There were times when pleasure needed to be deferred for a future and more enduring good. Although long- and short-term goods coincided occasionally, in cases where immediate pleasure was chosen over the greater good the wrong choice had clearly been made. Appearing numb to pain and suffering was not an indication of immoral development if such behavior was aimed at helping another develop habits of benevolence.

Catharine concluded that people were obligated not to cause suffering or to destroy happiness. "For it is the fear of suffering," she wrote, "which is the most powerful restraint, in deterring one mind from interfering with the happiness of others. Both mind and matter are so constituted, that nothing is contrived for the direct purpose of producing pain, which our very susceptibilities of suffering are used as a means of promoting the general happiness."[45]

Attention to the overall good was ultimately what would secure the highest and most enduring happiness. People could be expected to defer or moderate personal pleasure in order to achieve greater ends, since happiness in its highest sense could not always be achieved without sacrifice. "A mind then, which is fitted to secure the object for which it is created, is one that has *formed habits* of acting invariably and constantly for the *general happiness,* irrespective of its own particular share."[46] Only a disordered mind placed immediate gratification and selfish needs ahead of the greater good. Voluntary action for the public good was an ordered state of the mind that was developed and sustained through good habits; such a mental state combined with physical action produced the greatest general happiness.

Education, through the exercise of the mind, thus became a source of pleasure, as did teaching: the benevolent act of helping others secure the happiness of exercising their own minds. These were enduring pleasures, not subject to boredom from repetition. If the discomfort of watching a student struggle to learn did not always result in sympathy from the teacher, this was not an indication of moral failure on the instructor's part. The student was growing in the habits of moral rectitude and benevolence, and the temporary loss of enjoyment was for a noble and greater good. There was reciprocity in the cycle of pleasure from learning, teaching, and seeing right habits develop that would lead to additional happiness.

Experience was the path to three sources of knowledge: personal experience, the experience of others, and reasoning based on experience of the self and others. A fourth source of understanding was revealed knowledge, given to man by God through the experience and testimony of others. Personal experience included primarily what one could learn through sensory means, which was meager compared to what one could learn from the other three sources. If people needed to rely primarily on the experience of others, who were they to trust when they discovered contradictions?

Reasonable individuals, Catharine wrote, would give the most credence "to the testimony of those who are the most *intelligent,* and thus least likely to be deceived; the most *conscientious,* and thus least likely to be in habits of falsehood; and *least interested,* and thus most likely to be freed from prejudice and selfish considerations."[47] If students were to grow in knowledge, they must be conscientious in their work and rely on the greater knowledge and experience of their teachers. Then they, in turn, would become knowledgeable teachers in their own right. It was the well-educated teacher, imbued with moral rectitude, who was intelligent and conscientious, but did not put her own interests before the welfare and happiness of others.

Although Catharine had been zealous at times in seeking the religious conversion of her students, *Elements* suggests that she was no longer convinced of its necessity. This is not to say that she discounted the importance of religion; common wisdom of the day held that the future of the nation relied on the virtue of the people, and *their* virtue depended on religion. Catharine focused on a design that defined salvation in terms of Christian belief coupled with good behavior rather than on the submission of the will to God. Ultimately, happiness was dependent upon one's behavior toward others. Her standard of behavior was stated in the rule *Thou shalt love the Lord thy God, with all thy heart, and with all thy soul, and with all thy mind, and with all thy strength, and thy neighbor as thyself.*[48] Implicit in this, certainly, were faith and belief in the sources of the rule: Jesus as the deliverer of this command and the Bible as the legitimate source of revealed truth.

People, Catharine proposed, had been given a standard of right behavior but needed strong motivation to overcome bad habits. The means to this end were to love God and desire to live in his love: "Love to God, then, is the golden chain to eternal happiness, that is forever to unite in one interest, and in one tide of perfect enjoyment, the Creator and all his holy and infinite family."[49] This kind of love encompassed all levels of happiness and was itself the source of eternal happiness, but it had to be chosen consciously by individuals, as an exercise of free will. Love to God also meant obedience to God and to his commandment to secure the happiness of others.

Of course, people were capable of choosing the wrong path, neglecting to be concerned first and foremost with the happiness of others. But the choice was of great import. She wrote, "[T]he mind is brought to a stand in reference to the great object of existence, in regard to a future state of being, and the question to be decided is, shall happiness be found in gratifying certain other desires, or shall the governing purpose of mind be obedience to God, thus securing the happiness of conscious rectitude, and of being the cause of happiness to others?"[50] Here Catharine makes explicit reference to a "future state of being," linking salvation to mindfulness of the happiness of others and obedience to the commandment *love thy neighbor as thyself.*

She was also explicit as to how this love should be manifested. It was not charitable to accept your neighbor's word that he was in right relationship with God. "The term *charity* is often applied to signify simply 'believing every human being safe and on the way to heaven, who honestly believes what he professes.' But that is not the signification which is warranted by Scripture, where we find it used to express that benevolence enjoined and practiced by the Lord and his Apostles, who declared men to be in darkness and blindness, which was voluntary and guilty, and who went about to seek and save, 'those who were lost.' "[51] At the highest level, then, securing the happiness of others was contingent upon recognizing their moral poverty. Charity, by Catharine's definition, meant loving your neighbors enough to be certain that they were in a right relationship with God, even if that meant pointing out their moral weaknesses. If the tables were turned, she explained, we would expect this kind of love from our neighbors. The proper approach to seeking and saving the lost was not fire and brimstone but "gentleness, kindness, meekness, and benevolence in the heart, but the expression of it, by accommodation to the tastes and prejudices of others, by gentle manners, mild tones of voice, and kind and winning words."[52] Moral poverty was the affliction to be healed, and a successful healing process resulted in the greatest happiness for both giver and recipient.

In line with Catharine's focus on the training of upper-class leaders was the idea that moral poverty pervaded all social classes and crossed all socioeconomic lines. Consequently, locating one's "neighbor" did not necessarily mean working in the streets with the hungry and homeless; benevolence could be exercised within the confines of one's social class. Charity—seeking to alleviate the physical pain and suffering associated with poverty—was different to her and was not a topic taken up in *Elements*. In 1869, Catharine devoted more attention to the right purposes of charity in *The American Woman's Home* and gave the term a broader definition. There she defined the biblical "neighbor" as anyone whose needs are known, anyone who suffers from moral and intellectual poverty, or anyone with immediate physical needs. She cautioned that not as many people needed physical relief as it might seem and that the able-bodied could find work if they were able to develop sufficient virtue. She concluded that it was important to satisfy physical wants, but it was best to help people find a means of support and then concentrate on tending to their spiritual needs.[53]

However insistent Catharine was about moral training, there is no indication that she encouraged her students to have hands-on contact with the physically poor and needy. An announcement that appeared in the *Connecticut Courant* in March of 1826 declared that the new term's courses would offer "occasional opportunities of mingling in good society."[54] Catharine may have tried the patience of many a Hartford father with her revivals and enhanced curriculum, but she did maintain a "respectable" social environment for their daughters. Although Angelina Grimké toured the benevolent institutions of Hartford with Catharine—including the prison, the school for the deaf, and the insane asylum—she did so at her own request. The students perhaps participated in social action from afar by sending bandages to Greece during wartime; they also may have attended one of the public meetings Catharine organized on behalf of Cherokee rights. But there is no evidence that they were active in the community in the way we think of voluntarism today.[55] Catharine's own primary connection to the economically less fortunate of Hartford was through the leaders of benevolent institutions. On Saturday evenings, Catharine gathered these people in her home for religious and literary activities.[56]

Catharine went on in *Elements* to build a stronger case for "good works," dividing humanity into two classes. The first class put precedence on personal gratification and the happiness of friends. These are those unconcerned with the greater good, who observe religion in an outward and superficial way. When the self comes first, Catharine declared, religiosity is often motivated by fear of God. Also in this class were those with disordered minds who made no pretense of concern for the general good. The second class of people live out of love for God, work at correcting selfish habits, and

> regard the temporal interests of themselves, of their children, and of all they hold dear, as of secondary consideration and not ever to be put in competition with the general eternal welfare of their fellow men. They are acting for eternity instead of for time, and in this relation, objects, which to other men are matters of deep concern, are trifles to them. Regarding the rescue of mankind from the evils of selfishness in this and in a future life, as the greatest of all concerns, it is this which interests their thoughts and their efforts, more than the attainment of any earthly good for themselves or for others.[57]

Here again, Catharine directly links good works with eternity, bypassing the issue of conversion.

It was not by profession of faith that the righteous were to be identified, but by their good deeds. "A good tree cannot bring forth evil fruits; wherefore by their fruits ye shall know them." The righteous could be identified in the temporal world by their acts, but ultimately the world—for eternity—would be divided along these lines. "From the laws of mind and from past experience then, we can establish the position, that at some future period, if the mind of man is immortal, the human race will be permanently divided into two classes, the perfectly selfish and the perfectly benevolent."[58]

The break with orthodox Calvinist doctrine is quite clear in Catharine's conception of an eternity defined by benevolent acts. Catharine had always been too much her father's daughter to indulge in a merely temporary revolt. She admired Lyman and was inspired by him, but intellectually she could not accept the necessity of conversion. Benevolence had become her standard, manifested in seeking the greater good and happiness of others, a way to live for now and for eternity. Philanthropy—as voluntary action for the public good, as love, as benevolence—defined the road to eternal life. Education, religion, and the noblest role of woman were united in teaching, made sweet by the reciprocity of the philanthropic act. Teaching—by promoting happiness and the greater good, by working to alleviate the poverty of a soul—was not only a continuing source of happiness but also a route to salvation. Only a noble profession could promise such a noble reward.

REFLECTIONS ON A MORAL EXPERIMENT

Although Catharine's philosophy of education crystallized during these years, her dream of an endowment for Hartford Female Seminary did not. Economics and orthodoxy clashed as Catharine's lectures on mental and moral philosophy drew criticism from members of the Hartford community.[59] Frustrated by the trustees' refusal to pursue endowment, Catharine decided to close the school and go to Cincinnati with her father, who felt that the moral destiny of the nation depended upon educating the generation that would build the West. "Catholics and infidels" already had a start there and he intended to do something about it. Cincinnati, he promised, would supply an excellent opportunity for Catharine to test her theory of moral education.[60]

Catharine's students were not unaffected by her ideas. Angelina Grimké's diary of her days in Hartford tells of students who became teachers out of the desire to be useful, rather than out of financial necessity. Four Hartford graduates had gone on to open a school in Huntsville, Alabama.[61] Two other students of particular note are remembered for activities other than teaching. Sara Payson Willis Parton wrote her humorous essays under the pseudonym Fanny Fern. The champion of the housewife, Parton spoke out in support of women's intellectual equality and against a double standard of morality for men and women. Written in everyday language, her columns sympathized with the ever-present problems of housework and large families. Mary Grew, whose father was a stockholder in Hartford Female Seminary, was an activist on many fronts. As an abolitionist and member of the Female Anti-Slavery Society, she worked alongside Lucretia Mott and Sarah Pugh. During the World's Anti-Slavery Convention in 1840, she and the other female delegates were refused access to the convention floor. That experience inspired more than fifty years of activism on behalf of women's rights, including petitioning for property rights in Pennsylvania and work as the founding president of the Pennsylvania Woman Suffrage Association. Perhaps neither columnist nor suffragette would have fit Catharine's ideal, but like her, Parton and Grew made their stands and left their marks on society as unmarried women. Like Catharine, they believed a better life for women would permanently improve the whole of society. Finally, Catharine's shy and retiring younger sister Harriet was both student and teacher at Hartford. Under Catharine's relentless prodding, she honed her mental and literary skills, growing up to leave her literary mark as the "crusader in crinoline."[62]

Throughout the remainder of her life, Catharine worked to advance the priorities she had outlined in Hartford. She raised funds for female academies and colleges, recruited teachers for the West, and wrote relentlessly to promote the idea of the moral superiority of women in society. In most writing about Catharine, the Hartford Female Seminary years are eclipsed by her subsequent failures—such as the Western Female Seminary (1850–1852)—as well as her arguments against legal rights for women—particularly suffrage—that made her appear reactionary and elitist.[63] But in her days as Hartford's headmistress, she was a visionary who had made her vision a reality. If she continued to preach a message of education for women that led to lives consecrated to teaching moral living, it was because she had seen at Hartford that her system could work.

Catharine Esther Beecher was herself an example of the philanthropic life she encouraged others to lead. At Hartford, her own mind had come to life through preparing to teach. She had developed a curriculum comparable to what was offered young men at the academies of the day and had elevated moral education from its place in extra-curricular activities like religious revival and chapel service, institutionalizing it instead within the lecture hall. In the process of refining and teaching her moral philosophy, she resolved many of her own personal issues with Calvinism and offered her students a moral curriculum for their own teaching. Her own education and teaching, when united with her personal beliefs, gave her life a purpose and meaning that religion alone had not provided. Teaching also allowed her to remain financially independent. At that moment and in her own way, we might say Catharine Beecher both "walked the walk" and "talked the talk." She was training "immortal minds" so that they, in turn, could train others. If Hartford Female Seminary was a laboratory for her personal philosophy of education and teaching, she was perhaps its greatest experiment. Is it any wonder that she returned the gift of this experience by dedicating her life to encouraging others to follow in her path?

NOTES

1. Discussions of education for women in this era can be found in Barbara Miller Solomon, *In the Company of Educated Women: A History of Women and Higher Education in America* (New Haven, Conn.: Yale University Press, 1985), 1–42; Margaret A. Nash, " 'Cultivating the Powers of Human Beings': Gendered Perspectives on Curricula and Pedagogy in Academies of the New Republic," *History of Education Quarterly* 41 (summer 2001): 239–50; Kim Tolley, "The Rise of the Academies: Continuity or Change?" *History of Education Quarterly* 41 (summer 2001): 225–39; and Nancy Cott, *The Bonds of Womanhood: "Woman's Sphere" in New England, 1780–1835* (New Haven, Conn.: Yale University Press, 1997), 101–25.

2. Kathryn Kish Sklar, *Catharine Beecher: A Study in American Domesticity* (New Haven, Conn.: Yale University Press, 1973), 94.

3. The idea that philanthropy and religion were intimately connected permeated social thought throughout the nineteenth century. See Frances A. Goodale, *The Literature of Philanthropy* (New York: Harpers, 1893) and Walton's review of Goodale's book in the introduction to this volume.

4. This definition of education as the transmission of culture is informed by Bernard Bailyn, *Education in the Forming of American Society: Needs and Opportunities for Study* (Chapel Hill: University of North Carolina Press, for the Institute of Early American History and Culture, 1960).

5. Lyman Beecher's evangelical career is discussed in Sklar, *Catharine Beecher,* 3–

77; see also Stephen H. Snyder, *Lyman Beecher and His Children: The Transformation of a Religious Tradition* (Brooklyn, N.Y.: Carlson, 1991), 3–6.

6. Conrad Edick Wright, *The Transformation of Charity in Postrevolutionary New England* (Boston: Northeastern University Press, 1992), 159.

7. Definitions of charity and benevolence are discussed in Wright, *Transformation*, 159–87; Kathleen D. McCarthy, "Parallel Power Structures: Women and the Voluntary Sphere," in *Lady Bountiful Revisited: Women, Philanthropy, and Power*, ed. Kathleen D. McCarthy (New Brunswick, N.J.: Rutgers University Press, 1990), 1–31; and Anne Firor Scott, "Women's Voluntary Associations: From Charity to Reform," in *Lady Bountiful*, ed. McCarthy, 35–38. See also *Oxford English Dictionary*, online edition, 2002, s.v. "benevolence" and "charity." Under these definitions, teaching would not have been considered uncharitable merely because teachers were paid for their services; see, in particular, the discussion of paid services in Wright, *Transformation*, 187.

8. The growth of Protestant benevolent activities is discussed in Wright, *Transformation*, 51–76; Lori D. Ginzberg, *Women and the Work of Benevolence: Morality, Politics, and Class in the Nineteenth-Century United States* (New Haven, Conn.: Yale University Press, 1990), 11; McCarthy, "Parallel Power Structures," 4–8; and Scott, "Women's Voluntary Associations," 35–38. According to Wright, Catholic institutions began to spring up in the 1820s (*Transformation*, 188–89). Jewish benevolent societies that were distinctly separate from the synagogues did not appear prior to the 1840s (Leon A. Jick, *The Americanization of the Synagogue, 1820–1870* [Hanover, N.H.: University Press of New England for Brandeis University Press, 1987], 97–113).

9. Roberta Wollons, "American Philanthropy and Women's Education Exported: Missionary Teachers in Turkey," this volume.

10. Scott, "Women's Voluntary Associations," 37.

11. The philosophy behind separate education for women is discussed in Cott, *Bonds*, 112–25; Solomon, *Educated Women*, 14–26; and Barbara Leslie Epstein, *The Politics of Domesticity: Women, Evangelism, and Temperance in Nineteenth-Century America* (1981; reprint, Middletown, Conn.: Wesleyan University Press, 1986), 45–65. Beecher's years at Sarah Pierce's Litchfield Academy are noted in Cott, *Bonds*, 19; and Sklar, *Catharine Beecher*, 16–18.

12. For discussions of social class in the early 1800s see Stuart M. Blumin, *The Emergence of the Middle Class: Social Experience in the American City, 1760–1900* (New York: Cambridge University Press, 1989), 182–218; Cott, *Bonds*, 123; and Ginzberg, *Women and the Work of Benevolence*, 23–24.

13. Cott, *Bonds*, 123–24.

14. Beecher's catering to financial and social elites is noted in Solomon, *Educated Women*, 24; also Sklar, *Catharine Beecher*, 59–77.

15. Solomon, *Educated Women*, 27–41.

16. Discussion of Beecher's failed conversion and her relationship with Alexander Fisher can be found in Sklar, *Catharine Beecher*, 28–55; see also Snyder, *Lyman Beecher*, 38–50.

17. Quoted in Redding S. Sugg, *Motherteacher: The Feminization of American Education* (Charlottesville: University Press of Virginia, 1978), 44.

18. Sklar, *Catharine Beecher*, 61.

19. Catharine E. Beecher, "Suggestions Respecting Improvements in Education

Presented to the Trustees of the Hartford Female Seminary and Published at Their Request," in *Pioneers of Women's Education in the United States: Emma Willard, Catherine Beecher, Mary Lyon,* ed. Willystine Goodsell (1931; reprint, New York: AMS Press, 1970), 143–63.

20. Ibid., 147.

21. Catharine E. Beecher, "Female Education," *American Journal of Education* (Boston) 2 (April/May 1827), 219–23, 264–69.

22. Sklar, *Catharine Beecher,* 72.

23. Beecher, "Improvements in Education," 152–53.

24. Sklar, *Catharine Beecher,* 61.

25. Beecher, "Improvements in Education," 155.

26. Academic competition in the academies is discussed in Nash, "Gendered Perspectives," 248–49.

27. Catharine E. Beecher, "Essay on the Education of Female Teachers," in Goodsell, ed., *Pioneers,* 172.

28. Catharine E. Beecher, *Educational Reminiscences and Suggestions* (New York: J. B. Ford, 1874), 27.

29. Ibid., 28–29, 35–37.

30. Although Catharine never looked upon the public reading of her journal as an ordeal, as had many of the girls, she may have realized that this system did not encourage honesty. She comments on her disciplinary philosophy in *Educational Reminiscences.* See also Sklar, *Catharine Beecher;* and Nicole Tonkovich, *Domesticity with a Difference: The Nonfiction of Catharine Beecher, Sarah J. Hale, Fanny Fern, and Margaret Fuller* (Jackson: University Press of Mississippi, 1997).

31. Beecher, *Educational Reminiscences,* 46.

32. Mae Elizabeth Harveson, *Catharine Esther Beecher: Pioneer Educator* (1932; reprint, New York: Arno, 1969), 49.

33. Sklar, *Catharine Beecher,* 98.

34. The butter incident is related in Tonkovich, *Domesticity,* 165. See also Richard H. Shryock, "Sylvester Graham and the Popular Health Movement, 1830–1870," *Mississippi Valley Historical Review* 18 (September 1931): 172–83. Beecher discusses the sound-mind-and-body concept and the course of calisthenics in *Educational Reminiscences.*

35. Beecher, *Educational Reminiscences,* 47; Sklar, *Catharine Beecher,* 61.

36. Jeanne Boydston, Mary Kelley, and Anne Margolis, *The Limits of Sisterhood: The Beecher Sisters on Women's Rights and Woman's Sphere* (Chapel Hill: University of North Carolina Press, 1988), 41; Sklar, *Catharine Beecher,* 64, 71.

37. Lyman Beecher, *Autobiography, Correspondence, etc. of Lyman Beecher, D.D.,* vol. 2 (New York: Harper, 1864–65), 63.

38. Sklar, *Catharine Beecher,* 71.

39. Beecher, *Educational Reminiscences,* 51.

40. Beecher's attempt to recruit Zilpah Grant is discussed in Harveson, *Catharine Esther Beecher,* 57–60. See also Sugg, *Motherteacher,* 48.

41. Catharine E. Beecher, *The Elements of Mental and Moral Philosophy, Founded upon Experience, Reason, and the Bible* (Hartford, Conn.: Peter B. Gleason, 1831).

42. Beecher, *Educational Reminiscences,* 52.

43. Beecher, *Elements,* 57.

44. Ibid., 244.

45. Ibid., 245.

46. Ibid., 253.

47. Ibid., 157–58.

48. Ibid., 248

49. Ibid., 279.

50. Ibid., 81.

51. Ibid., 241.

52. Ibid., 413.

53. Catharine E. Beecher and Harriet Beecher Stowe, *The American Woman's Home, or, Principles of Domestic Science; Being a Guide to the Formation and Maintenance of Economical, Healthful, Beautiful, and Christian Homes* (1869; reprint, Hartford, Conn.: Stowe-Day Foundation, 1987), 242–43.

54. *Connecticut Courant*, 20 March 1826.

55. Sklar, *Catharine Beecher*, 99.

56. Ibid., 61.

57. Beecher, *Elements*, 338.

58. Ibid., 357.

59. Snyder, *Lyman Beecher*, 58.

60. Sklar, *Catharine Beecher*, 102.

61. Excerpts from diaries of Angelina Grimké can be found in Sklar, *Catharine Beecher*, 98; and Katharine Du Pre Lumpkin, *The Emancipation of Angelina Grimké* (Chapel Hill: University of North Carolina Press, 1974), 63.

62. Elizabeth Bancroft Schlesinger, "Parton, Sara Payson Willis," and Ira V. Brown, "Grew, Mary," in *Notable American Women, 1607–1950*, ed. Edward T. James, Janet Wilson James, and Paul S. Boyer (Cambridge, Mass.: Belknap Press of Harvard University Press, 1971), vol. 3, 24–25 and vol. 2, 91–92. Harriet Beecher Stowe's years at Hartford are discussed in Boydston, Kelly, and Margolis, *Limits of Sisterhood*, 49–60.

63. See Sklar, *Catharine Beecher*, for discussion of Western Female Seminary, 130–31; endowment of Milwaukee Female College, 223–26; debate over the rights of women, 132–35 and 268–70.

2. Philanthropy and Social Case Work: Mary E. Richmond and the Russell Sage Foundation, 1909–1928

Sarah Henry Lederman

In 1897 Mary E. Richmond, general secretary of the Baltimore Charity Organization Society (and, later, an officer of the Russell Sage Foundation), implored delegates to the National Conference of Charities and Correction to create a "Training School in Applied Philanthropy." She insisted that young people had a right to demand "from the profession of applied philanthropy (we really have not even a name for it) that which they have a right to demand from any other profession; further opportunities for education and development, and, incidentally, the opportunity to earn a living."[1] Many of Richmond's colleagues agreed. Within a year, Dr. Edward T. Devine, general secretary of the New York Charity Organization Society and a professor at Columbia University, invited students to apply for the first official school of social work in the United States: a six-week course at the New York Summer School in Philanthropy.[2]

Richmond's call for a school of social work was motivated in part by her desire to attract talented individuals to the charity organization movement. But she was also motivated by a desire to make charity organization ideals and practice the mainstay of social work education. Richmond saw a widening rift between leaders in the field of philanthropy, a field that included charity organizations, settlement houses, child saving missions, and prison reform campaigns. While settlement house workers, the people who provided classes, health care, and other services to inner-city immigrants, wanted to fight poverty through campaigns for education, public health, and labor legislation, charity organizers, who attempted to fight the problem of urban poverty by helping one individual at a time, insisted that each difficult case required intense, individualized attention. In the late 1890s, Richmond sensed that the former program was proving to be more popular with young people than the latter. Her plea for general training schools in philanthropy reflected her desire to boost the charity organization movement by creating a prestigious social work education program with social case work as the centerpiece of the curriculum. The opening of the New York School in 1898 was followed by the opening of schools of social work, in Boston (1902), Chicago (1903), and St. Louis (1905). Through her regular lectures at these schools, her correspondence with the first generation of teachers, and her preparation of curriculum materials, Richmond exerted extraordinary influence over the emerging profession of social work.

Richmond's ability to shape social work education resulted from her connection with the Russell Sage Foundation. Richmond produced books and periodicals for teachers and students, while she guided Foundation officials in their funding decisions for the schools. Richmond's unique position provided her with an unparalleled opportunity to organize knowledge for an emerging profession. It also won her a host of enemies. The partisan nature of Richmond's approach to social work education alienated many leaders in the field of social welfare, including social scientists Sophonisba Breckinridge and Edith Abbott, settlement house leaders Lillian Wald and Mary Simkhovitch, and Homer Folks, director of the New York State Charities Aid Association. While in recent years a substantial and growing literature has documented the contributions of these figures, the controversies surrounding Richmond during her life have obscured her contribution to the social work profession. One of the few women associated with a large private foundation during this era, Richmond has not attracted the attention of scholars working in the areas of women's history or (unlike her male contemporaries in the foundation world) the interest of scholars bent on forging the critical study of foundation history. Nor has this self-styled educator—a woman who, with only a high school education, spearheaded efforts to provide an educational foundation for social work—received attention from scholars interested in the rise of the helping professions. Indeed, Richmond remains a shadowy figure in the history of American philanthropy and relatively unknown in the history of education. This essay seeks to address these lacunae by examining Richmond's achievements as an employee of the Russell Sage Foundation and assessing her legacy.

Richmond's tenure at the Russell Sage Foundation raises questions about the relationships connecting women, power, and philanthropy. To what extent was Richmond able to use the Russell Sage Foundation to meet her goals? Was her vision of social work implemented at the schools? Did she succeed in organizing knowledge while she balanced the requirements for competent and compassionate case work? The answers to these questions reveal that Richmond's career provides an excellent example of the challenges women faced in the course of engaging in philanthropy and in applying education to philanthropic ends. This essay begins with an examination of Mary Richmond's life and work. It traces the origins of her ideas about social case work and her views of the relationship between philanthropy and education. Mary Richmond—much like an earlier woman educator-philanthropist, Catharine Beecher, whose philosophizing on the connection between philanthropy and teaching in the early 1800s is examined in chapter 1 of this volume—greatly respected the power of education and philanthropy to shape ideas and behavior. For Richmond, the challenge was to articulate the need for systematizing the study of philanthropic practice in social work. In examining Richmond's place within the history of women and philanthropy in education, then, this essay focuses on her ideas and her influence, through her association with the Russell Sage Foundation, on the professionalization of social work.[3]

MARY RICHMOND'S CHILDHOOD AND EDUCATION

The themes of illness, death, and perseverance reverberated through Mary Richmond's early years. Born in 1861 in Belleville, Illinois, to Baltimore natives, Mary was the second of four children and the only one to survive past age two. Henry Richmond, Mary's father, moved to Illinois to work as a blacksmith in a munitions factory. Mary's mother, Lavinia Harris Richmond, returned with Mary to Baltimore before the end of the Civil War. In April 1865, two weeks after Abraham Lincoln's assassination, Lavinia Harris died of tuberculosis. Though Henry Richmond moved back to Baltimore and remarried, Mary remained with her grandmother, Mehitable Harris, an eccentric but inspiring matriarch.

Born in Boston in 1797, Mehitable had moved to Baltimore, married a jeweler and part-time realtor, and borne eleven children between 1820 and 1842. She lost five children in the cholera epidemics of the

1830s and '40s, and lost her husband, William Calendar Harris, when he was prospecting for gold in California in 1848.[4] Endowed with an indomitable spirit, Mehitable Harris joined movements to promote abolitionism, women's rights, and spiritualism. She subscribed to numerous newspapers and substituted committee work for domesticity. Though Harris was nearly seventy when Mary became her ward, the two formed a close attachment. Richmond attended many meetings with her grandmother and even passed the collection basket at a spiritualist convention. Richmond's involvement in her grandmother's work led her to sign her earliest letters "Yours for the Ca[u]se."[5] It is strangely fitting that case work would become *her* cause.

In order to support young Mary and two spinster daughters, Mehitable ran a boardinghouse in a formerly well-to-do section of Baltimore. The house was untidy and disorganized but the atmosphere suited Richmond. Some of the boarders taught her writing, and her aunt, Ellen Harris, taught her elocution. In the 1870s Ellen Harris gained a bit of notoriety as a teacher in a school for African American children, unusual work for a white woman in Reconstruction Baltimore.[6] The political activity of her Harris relatives forced Richmond to consider the plight of marginalized groups, while their dedication to causes infected her with a desire to join a movement.[7]

The combination of Richmond's frailty and Mehitable Harris's disdain for public education prevented Richmond from attending school until she reached age eleven. Up to that time a neighbor appeased Richmond's insatiable appetite for books by lending her volumes on the condition that she return them with thorough written reports. This practice served Richmond well. At age fourteen she passed the highly competitive entrance exams of the elite Eastern Female High School. Though Richmond enjoyed the school's intellectual challenge, she found the social adjustment difficult. Attired exclusively in her aunts' old-fashioned hand-me-downs, she became very self-conscious about her appearance. However, social handicaps did not discourage Richmond from planning for her future. She spoke of her dreams in a graduation speech entitled "Aspirations" and later told friends, "Ambition is a good thing. . . . It has always been a part of any great thing. . . . To feel you are thoroughly useful in this world do your work well. Doing something for others will do as much as anything to bring about happiness."[8] Over the next decade she would combine her desire for success with her altruistic impulse.

Shortly after graduating in 1878 Richmond moved to New York

City, where her Aunt Ellen was employed at a publishing firm. Ellen Harris helped Richmond obtain work at the same firm and then returned to Baltimore. Richmond found herself alone and nearly destitute. During the next two years, she became increasingly ill as she struggled to pay the rent. Finally, loneliness and ill health drove her back to Baltimore. In later years, Richmond confessed that she was glad no "lady bountiful" had tried to rescue her. She insisted, "a woman's best position after all is a certain sense of independence and self-respect."[9] She would later see case work as a tool for cultivating independence and self-respect in others.

In Baltimore, Richmond continued to develop her speaking and writing skills. By day she worked as a bookkeeper in a stationery shop. During the evenings she read and wrote, preparing speeches for a literary club made up of Eastern Female High School alumnae. On weekends she taught Shakespeare to Sunday school students at her Unitarian church, and in 1888 she published an article about Baltimore using a pen name, R. E. Marel. For local newspapers she wrote a weekly précis of the sermons delivered by Charles Weld. Reverend Weld admired Richmond's achievements as a teacher and writer and in December 1888 he urged her to apply for the position of assistant treasurer at the Baltimore Charity Organization Society. Richmond's erudition impressed her interviewers. One Society board member recalled, "she looked pathetically young and she talked like the Ancient of Days!"[10] In January 1889 Richmond embarked on a crash course in philanthropy.

THE CHARITY ORGANIZATION MOVEMENT

The idea of organizing charity was developed by British reformers who were determined to reduce poverty by controlling the distribution of food and money to impoverished people. They established the London Society for Organising Charity to coordinate the work of thousands of tiny relief agencies in the hope that "worthy" families would receive the help they needed. Leaders of the movement aimed to increase donations by issuing effective and uniform financial appeals to the upper classes, while cutting costs by providing a centralized clearinghouse of information for workers in the member agencies. The clearinghouse was designed to prevent one family or individual from obtaining aid from numerous sources.

Two important strains of thought characterized the charity organization movement in America: thrift and service. The notion of thrift appeared prominently in the work of British Presbyterian minister Stephen Humphreys Gurteen, who was a founder of the first charity organization in the United States, in Buffalo, New York, in 1877. Gurteen proclaimed that the primary goal of charity organization was to keep careful records and conduct thorough investigations in order to expose frauds, the "unworthy" poor, while reserving funds for the "worthy" poor. Many civic leaders in Buffalo embraced this brand of charity organization because they believed it would reduce the cost of providing relief. In Buffalo, the idea of thrift and efficiency prevailed over the idea of service.[11]

The precept of service, of providing some kind of help to all people in need, percolated throughout the proceedings of the American Social Science Association (ASSA) and its successor, the National Conference of Charities and Correction (NCCC).[12] In Boston, leaders of organized charity provided service through hundreds of "friendly visitors." Led by Zilpha Drew Smith, Boston charity organizers set out to cultivate relationships between the visitors they enlisted and the families who applied for aid. Smith believed that the friendship between the visitor—either a volunteer or a paid agent (later known as a social case worker)—and the individual or family (later known as a client) was the key to reform.[13]

In preparation for her new job, Richmond spent a week in Boston in January 1889 studying charity organization with Zilpha Smith. Richmond attended case conferences where dedicated upper- and middle-class volunteers and paid agents discussed the problems of each family under their care. These problems included unemployment, low wages, sickness, lack of education, addiction, and homelessness. The committee proposed solutions ranging from jobs to medical treatment to training programs to housing reform. Ideally the solution would be based on plans the case worker had discussed with the client. Under Smith's tutelage Richmond became convinced that sympathy was more important than donations. Understanding the situation in its entirety and enlisting the cooperation of the client were important first steps. The lessons Richmond learned from Smith in 1889, and for the next twenty years as she corresponded with Smith, led Richmond to eschew superficial labels such as "worthy" and "unworthy" poor.[14]

Back in Baltimore Richmond attacked her new job with the zeal of a recent convert. She delivered dozens of speeches exhorting audiences to fight poverty by donating money or by volunteering at the

Baltimore Charity Organization Society (BCOS). "We need a thousand more at once, and to you, the public, we look for recruits. . . . Put out the fires; put out the fires of hopeless misery, of intemperance; of wrong relations of man to man, and plant God's sunlight there in place of them."[15] Richmond astonished her employers with her success at raising funds and recruiting visitors. In 1891 the Society's board members promoted her to the chief executive position, general secretary.

Richmond's commitment to the cause set her apart from BCOS authorities who were less interested in individual cases of need than they were in studying poverty and developing cures. Under the guidance of Daniel Coit Gilman, a longtime member of the American Social Science Association, leaders of the Baltimore Society amplified the original charity organization goals of thrift and service by aiming to provide training for future leaders in philanthropy. As president of Johns Hopkins University, Gilman hoped the BCOS would serve as a laboratory where students of philanthropy, economics, history, and political science could analyze poverty and develop treatments in the same way that the combined hospital and laboratory enabled medical students to study and treat diseases. The first few general secretaries at the BCOS, such as Hopkins Ph.D. Amos G. Warner, soon discovered that the scientific scrutiny of poverty did not yield ready cures. As the men at the BCOS became impatient with the intractable daily problems of destitute families, particularly among Baltimore's large population of African Americans, they retreated to the university. Richmond, a handful of female employees (future case workers), and a cadre of volunteers were left to put BCOS ideals into practice.[16]

Richmond realized she needed to teach case workers to develop sympathetic relations with the individuals who applied for aid and their families. Richmond believed that fledgling case workers could develop constructive relationships if they had the right motive. "The right motive is best stated in the radical meaning of the word charity—love. It may be restated as the desire of every living, human soul to share its best with others. Note the difference between mere giving, which drops the gift and passes on, and generous sharing which lovingly stands by and claims no life apart."[17] For workers with the right motive, professional training would be an important next step. Over time Richmond resolved to provide this training. She read journals and followed developments in numerous professions, especially medicine at Johns Hopkins. She created a periodical to report on and promote BCOS activities. The key to success, she believed, lay in developing and disseminating a standard methodology for charity organizers. In 1896 Charles S. Loch introduced her to the case record forms used at the London COS and to the idea that sympathy could be combined with thorough investigations. It was this methodology— a combination of compassion and intelligence, or "love working with discernment," as Charles Loch described it—that she hoped to refine and promote.[18]

One of the greatest challenges Richmond faced was persuading people that distributing money was detrimental to charity work. The problem intensified during periods of severe unemployment. In depression eras, such as 1893–1895, the workload at the BCOS became unmanageable. Yet Richmond maintained that case workers should refrain from distributing money unless they had conducted thorough investigations and could maintain cordial relations with the family. She constantly reminded her staff that sympathetic relations were impossible when money interfered. How could friendship thrive when the client viewed the charity worker as nothing more than a source of revenue? Meanwhile, contributors to the BCOS expected that poor people could count on the agency to help families when jobs were scarce. Some donors stopped supporting the agency when they learned that it denied many requests for assistance.

Richmond hoped that education, for the general public as well as for her staff, would resolve misunderstandings about the COS mission, and she persisted with her information campaign. As she told one correspondent in 1902, "Charitable societies do not refuse to pay rent as a usual thing because they are so hard-hearted (though this is what I used to think), but because the more they pay back debts of any kind the bigger the debts become and the less the poor are benefitted. . . . It is only after long and bitter experience that I have learned to attack the cause of non-payment (such as lack of work, or thrift or skill, etc.) and let the rent go, except where ejectment would mean suffering to some sick or helpless person."[19]

By the late 1890s Richmond feared that confusion over the role of the case worker was delaying the professionalization of philanthropy. In 1897, in addition to pleading for a school of social work, she prepared a seventy-page manual to guide case workers in their interactions with impoverished families.[20] She wanted to teach case workers to make patient investigations and to weigh evidence objectively. While Richmond hoped the manual would mark the beginning of her formal work as an educator, she sensed that her board of directors at the COS did not support her education objectives. In the spring of 1900 she resigned from the BCOS in order to accept a job as general secretary of the Philadelphia Society for Organizing Charity (PSOC). She hoped her new position would give her time to develop a training program for practical philanthropists.[21]

THE RETAIL METHOD OF REFORM

Richmond was persuaded to move to Philadelphia by several influential women at the PSOC and the Philadelphia Civic Club who promised to support her work in education. She hoped that their intellectual and financial endorsement, coupled with the support of Samuel McCune Lindsay at the University of Pennsylvania, would free her from daily administrative duties and provide teaching opportunities. Her expectations were never realized. During her nine years in Philadelphia, aside from two lectures she delivered at the University of Pennsylvania, "The Basis of Fact in Charity" in 1906 and "Three Stages in the Development of Relief" in 1907, she had little time to establish standards in social work.[22]

In Philadelphia, instead of focusing on education, Richmond found herself battling her agency's great budget deficit. To make matters worse she became caught in a struggle between two groups of PSOC board members. One group wanted "case work development" while another clamored for "community development."[23] Inspired by the reform enthusiasm of the Progressive Era, Richmond steered the PSOC into campaigns to support child labor laws, housing and sanitation reform, and civil service exams. In 1905 she served as the chair of the Committee on Cooperation for the City Party, and she helped elect a reform platform, which put forty women on local school boards. In 1906 Richmond and the City Party were congratulated on handing Philadelphia "one of the most spectacular, far-reaching and significant municipal revolutions ever witnessed in any American city."[24] Richmond neglected social work education for the sake of these achievements. A year later she discovered that poverty persisted despite these campaigns.

Her professional reckoning soon followed. In 1907 thousands of wage earners lost their jobs when a depression struck Philadelphia. The PSOC's resources appeared meager in the face of the desperate requests for assistance that poured into the district offices each week.

Although Richmond had trained a handful of agents in the eighteen districts, only a few provided the level of thorough, compassionate service Richmond demanded. Families in need of aid were turned away by exhausted case workers. As a result the PSOC drew public criticism both for its expenditures on administration and for its failure to attack poverty at its roots.

In response, Richmond introduced a new concept to explain the benefits of social case work. She contrasted social case work, the "retail method" of reform, to the legislative solutions or the "wholesale method" of reform embraced by advocates of social justice.[25] By emphasizing the advantages customized service provided through "retail" reform, Richmond hoped to persuade donors that the service provided by charity organizers was a more reliable form of help than the help that could be rendered through "wholesale" reforms. Regardless of the effort spent by female organizers to pass new laws, Richmond argued, male politicians never appropriated adequate funds to implement the legislation. Politicians, she concluded, were too fickle to be entrusted with matters of human welfare. She longed for a chance to publicize her ideas about case work.

The opportunity presented itself when John M. Glenn—a former board member of the Baltimore COS—became president of the Russell Sage Foundation in 1907. Robert W. de Forest, the driving force behind the Foundation, conspired with Glenn to bring Richmond to New York. De Forest had tried for many years to hire Richmond at the New York Charity Organization Society, where he had been president since 1888. As board member and later vice president of the American Red Cross (ARC) and the Metropolitan Museum of Art— to name only a few of his positions—de Forest had combined his social contacts with his legal acumen to become one of New York City's most influential philanthropists. He served as tenement house commissioner of New York State from 1900 to 1901 and of New York City from 1901 to 1903.[26] When de Forest failed to install Richmond at the NYCOS, he helped arrange the creation of a national publicity agency for the charity organization movement, called the Field Department, and he made Richmond the director. Started in 1905 and funded through the NYCOS publication *Charities* (later *Charities and the Commons*, then *The Survey*), the Field Department fostered the exchange of information between charity organization societies in order for the weaker agencies to learn from the stronger ones.

Richmond welcomed her appointment as director of the Field Department, but she had trouble juggling her work at the PSOC with the responsibility of editing publications for member agencies. The situation grew more difficult after 1907 as relations deteriorated between Richmond and Paul Kellogg, the *Charities* editor. Kellogg found organized charity "old-fashioned" and undemocratic. Determined to attract readers who "felt a sense of wrong," Kellogg shifted his editorial focus away from charity organization work and toward social problems such as immigration, race relations, labor laws, and tenement congestion.[27] De Forest tried to resolve the tension by separating Richmond and the Field Department from Kellogg and *Charities*. He created the Charity Organization Department (COD) of the Russell Sage Foundation to oversee fieldwork, publication, and education related to charity organizing. He and Glenn persuaded Richmond to become the COD's full-time director. She announced her resignation from the PSOC in March 1909.[28] Richmond was delighted to finally have the chance to develop standards for social case work.

THE CHARITY ORGANIZATION DEPARTMENT OF THE RUSSELL SAGE FOUNDATION

In September 1909, Mary Richmond settled into her Russell Sage Foundation office in the Charities Building on East Twenty-second Street. She planned to sponsor research projects, publish results, and train case workers. After the frustrations of her previous positions, Richmond relished the opportunities presented by the Sage Foundation.

In 1907 Olivia Margaret Slocum Sage had founded the Russell Sage Foundation in memory of her husband. Its mission—the "improvement of social and living conditions"—resulted from the close connection between the Foundation's board members and the charity organization movement. Many foundation officials—most notably Sage's lawyer, Robert W. de Forest (who convinced her to create the Foundation), and its president, John M. Glenn—hoped to infuse the emerging profession of social work with the principles of the charity organization movement.

Social work's delayed professional development was due in part to disagreements about the relative merit of the "retail" versus the "wholesale" method of reform. While Richmond and her charity organization colleagues argued that the key to fighting poverty lay in the training of expert case workers, who would lead private social service agencies in restoring families to prosperity one case at a time, leaders of the settlement house movement, including Jane Addams, Lillian Wald, Graham Taylor, Sophonisba Breckinridge, and Mary Simkhovitch, argued that agitation for social justice would provide more long-term benefits to economically disadvantaged groups. While Jane Addams tried to minimize the differences between the two approaches in her 1909 presidential speech at the National Conference of Charities and Correction, entitled "Charity and Social Justice," many of her allies in the settlement movement demanded "justice not charity." Settlement workers scorned what they saw as the paternalistic approach to poverty adopted by Richmond and her colleagues.[29] They campaigned for widows' pension legislation, juvenile courts, and the Children's Bureau.

Up to 1907 Richmond made efforts to bridge the gap between the philanthropic ideas of settlement house leaders and charity organizers. She promoted cooperation between the two groups, insisting they could learn from each other. Her strategy changed after 1907 when she rejected settlement workers' increasingly aggressive calls for welfare legislation. Disillusioned by the political chicanery, corruption, and racial discrimination she had witnessed in the administration of Civil War pensions in Maryland, Richmond steadfastly denied that government grants to individuals could solve the problem of poverty. She believed social case work, conducted by trained experts, would provide poor families with the tools they needed to become self-sufficient. She feared that government intervention would prevent case workers from mediating social relations between members of diverse social and racial groups.[30] Richmond's fears were realized during the campaign for widows' pensions.

The passage of state laws designed to provide cash grants to widows with children marked a turning point in American social welfare history.[31] Organizations supporting the pensions drew thousands of women into politics. These predominantly middle-class women sympathized with the plight of lower-class widows with hungry children. Richmond agreed that single mothers faced hardships, but disagreed with reformers who believed that male legislators would provide adequate funds to enable widows to stop working outside the home in order to focus exclusively on raising their children. While Richmond admitted that the system of charity organization societies had yet to provide a paragon of relief work, she insisted that overworked widows and their children could best be helped through a constructive relationship. According to Richmond, the therapy depended on the sympathy between the case worker and the mother, not on the amount of money distributed.[32]

Between 1909 and 1915, twenty states passed laws providing assistance to some widows and their children. Although Richmond and others at the Russell Sage Foundation had mobilized significant resources to fight the pensions, they lost the battle. Later, as Richmond had predicted, the lack of administrative apparatus created serious problems. Ironically, when thousands of widows applied for pensions, civil servants turned to charity organizers for guidance. Desperate to staff new-born offices for pension distribution, administrators begged many of Richmond's students, some of whom were outspoken opponents of widows' pensions, to supply experienced case workers in order to help evaluate the widows' applications.[33] Richmond advised her colleagues to decline work with state officials because she feared that the failure she anticipated would be blamed on the case workers.[34]

Across the United States, civil servants used some social case work techniques to investigate pension applicants. These investigations aimed to expose weaknesses in the widows' cases and to disqualify the "unworthy poor," as had the early investigations conducted at the Buffalo COS. Richmond's colleagues reported that case workers in the pension offices denied pensions to most African Americans and foreigners.[35] As Richmond feared, poorly trained case workers misunderstood the point of asking questions. Since her 1889 visit to Boston, Richmond had maintained that the purpose of a case worker's questions was to cultivate sympathy between the case worker and the client. Yet the relentless questions to separate the "worthy" from the "unworthy" poor, coupled with the tiny allowances, made the pensions more punitive than helpful, especially when the eligibility rules required these women to resign from any work outside the home. By the early 1920s public officials admitted that the pension legislation yielded disappointing results.[36]

Richmond and her colleagues at the Russell Sage Foundation failed to defeat widows' pension legislation, but they succeeded in making case work a central element of the social work profession. Throughout the tempestuous pension debate Richmond worked to develop and promote standards. *Social Diagnosis,* her 1917 volume on case work methods, proved to be more popular than she anticipated. Despite Abraham Flexner's 1915 claim that social work could not be considered a profession, the field was steadily gaining practitioners who clamored for guidance.[37] At leading schools of social work and in social service agencies, *Social Diagnosis* became the case workers' bible.

The United States' entry into World War I fueled the transformation of social case work from a philanthropic ideal into a widely used technique for mediating social relations.[38] In 1917 the American Red Cross mobilized "Home Service," a division dedicated to providing advice and aid to soldiers' families. In order to train the thousands of division recruits, Red Cross officials (many of whom were former COS administrators) asked Richmond to prepare a pamphlet. Her slim, unsigned volume, *Manual of Home Service,* guided thousands of case workers in advising military families. Between July 1917 and February 1919, the ARC estimated that over five hundred thousand families received advice provided by the manual.[39] Richmond published a less technical book as well—*What Is Social Case Work?*—in 1922. Taken together, this trilogy taught one clear lesson: the successful resolution of a family's or individual's problems rested on the case worker's ability to interpret the problems and develop solutions in cooperation with the client.

While increasing numbers of people embraced social case work theory, those in public agencies found her ideas difficult to realize in practice. Civil servants who embraced her plans soon discovered that Richmond's concept of case work was ill-suited for giant bureaucracies with massive case loads. Her guidelines offered no solutions to widespread unemployment, substance abuse, or homelessness.

By the 1920s the social work profession was fully established, but leading social workers continued to debate the merits of social case work. No event reveals the disagreement more clearly than the controversy over the 1922 presidential election to the National Conference of Social Work (the NCCC was renamed after World War I). Social workers looked forward to celebrating the fiftieth anniversary of the founding of the National Conference in 1923, and therefore special attention was paid to selecting a president who represented all social workers. Both charity organizers and settlement house leaders had served as Conference presidents over the years, including Richmond's fellow charity organizers, Robert W. de Forest (1903), John M. Glenn (1901), and his wife Mary Wilcox Glenn (1915). Richmond's friends tried to have her nominated in 1921 but they did not succeed until the following year. A powerful group of social workers, settlement leaders in particular, objected to Richmond's nomination. When she was nominated in 1922 to serve as president for the 1923 anniversary they prevented her election. Graham Taylor, a settlement house leader from Chicago, objected to Richmond's nomination on the grounds that she was only specialized in one area of social work. Homer Folks, director of the State Charities Aid Association and an advocate of widows' pensions, told the veteran leader of Chicago's Hull House, Jane Addams, that if she did not run again he would pursue the presidency himself, simply to block Richmond. Addams's refusal caused Folks to snatch the honor from Richmond. When he invited Richmond to serve on the 1923 program committee she declined. The negative reaction to Richmond's nomination testifies to the long-term resentment generated by the Russell Sage Foundation's support of social case work.

In 1927 Richmond sent a discouraged note to the Foundation president, John M. Glenn. She complained that leaders in the American Association for Organizing Family Social Work (AAOFSW, the descendant of the Field Department of the COS) were wasting the time of hard-working members by burying them under an avalanche of documents instead of providing direct, practical assistance for case workers in the field. Not only did support of this organization represent a misuse of Foundation funds, according to Richmond, but it also betrayed the original mission of the Field Department. From the beginning Richmond and her colleagues had prided themselves on providing personalized advice to member agencies throughout the United States in order to ensure that case workers in turn provided personalized advice to their clients. Richmond resented the fact that current personnel did not offer this grade of service. In conclusion Richmond urged Glenn to make AAOFSW funding conditional on the improvement of its work.[40]

In his response, Glenn attempted to console Richmond. He defended the AAOFSW leadership (Linton Swift in particular), saying that he had heard much praise for the AAOFSW at the most recent National Conference of Social Work. He advised Richmond to "take the world as it comes and not worry too much if our ideals are not carried out in practice." This was a cruel rebuke to a woman who had dedicated her career to putting ideals into practice. Glenn concluded, "I write you this merely because I think it is unfortunate for your sake that you should feel blue about the growth of your child. I think it is a pretty lusty youngster and growing steadily in a healthy way and you have excellent reason to congratulate yourself and the world at large on what has happened and what is happening."[41] Glenn's paternalistic tone reveals Richmond's impotence. By supporting Linton Swift and at the same time calling the Association Richmond's "child," Glenn portrayed Richmond as an irrational mother fretting about her wayward progeny. More importantly, it shows that Glenn disagreed about the educational role that the AAOFSW, and by extension the Sage Foundation, should play in social work education.

The Russell Sage Foundation empowered Richmond in many ways. Between the start of her tenure at the Foundation in 1909 and her death in 1928, she launched a periodical dedicated to social case work, taught hundreds of charity organizers through her annual month-long Charity Organization Institute, developed a methodology for schools of social work, edited a social work series, and wrote three books on social case work. Under her watchful eye social case work had become the standard course of study in all schools of social work. In 1931 more than 60 percent of graduates from two-year social work programs embarked on careers in social case work, and by 1941 the number had risen to 82 percent.[42] Nevertheless, Richmond's ideas for social case work methods foundered on the shoals of misunderstanding. Elements of Richmond's program were appropriated by the very people—overworked civil servants—she believed were least likely to implement them. Successful case work, in Richmond's opinion, depended on competent and compassionate practitioners. It required as much flexibility and as little bureaucracy as possible. Richmond hoped to educate a generation of case workers in the "art of helping" at privately funded social service agencies. But her view of philanthropy as a relationship that was rewarding to both case worker and client was never realized in an institutional setting.[43] From Glenn's perspective the institutional apparatus that Richmond had created proved the success of social work education. From Richmond's perspective the hollow content of the increasingly mechanical implementation of social case work proved that her work had come to naught.

Mary Richmond's career at the Russell Sage Foundation offers two important lessons. First, her experience demonstrates that foundation personnel could excel in developing and publicizing ideas, but they could not control the implementation of these ideas in the public domain. Just as Abraham Flexner regretted misunderstandings generated by his report on medical education, so Richmond rued the misappropriation of case work by public servants.[44] Second, the case of Mary Richmond shows that the Russell Sage Foundation shared the strengths and weaknesses of other foundations. Foundation leaders could attempt to guide a profession, but they could not control its development in every direction. Richmond could not ensure that competence and compassion became an integral part of professional practice. Just as efforts to professionalize medicine and nursing exalted science at the expense of sympathy, so the codification of social case work emphasized technique over service.[45] Richmond insisted that social case work, or, as she preferred to call it, the "art of helping," was not a science. But Richmond's friends as well as her detractors disagreed. In 1921 Smith College awarded her an honorary master of arts for "establishing the scientific basis of a new profession."[46] In the years following Richmond's 1928 death social case work came to be practiced mainly by poorly paid women in publicly funded bureaucracies. While some of Richmond's protégés, such as Gordon Hamilton and Joanna Colcord, continued to advocate compassionate case work, the onset of the Great Depression and the use of case work methods in large institutions prevented case workers from following Richmond's plans. Despite the expenditure of Russell Sage Foundation resources, Mary Richmond's model for social case work—its implementation by compassionate practitioners in private social service agencies—remained an elusive goal.

NOTES

The research for this project was sponsored in part by a dissertation fellowship and a postdoctoral fellowship from the Spencer Foundation.

1. Mary E. Richmond, "The Need of a Training School in Applied Philanthropy" (1897), in *The Long View: Papers and Addresses by Mary E. Richmond*, ed. Joanna C. Colcord and Ruth Z. S. Mann (New York: Russell Sage Foundation, 1930), 100.

2. Though Edward Devine invited Richmond to lecture in 1898, she delayed until the following year (Edward Devine to Mary Richmond, 24 January and 26 January 1898, Family and Children's Society Records, Johns Hopkins University, Baltimore, Md. [hereafter cited as FCSR]). Richmond used the term *philanthropy* to describe gifts of time, talent, or money. According to Richmond, philanthropists included benefactors such as George Peabody and Andrew Carnegie as well as the lowly widows who eked out a living by working for charity organization societies. She used the word *philanthropy* in the Greek sense, literally "love of mankind," to describe work that would be defined in the twenty-first century as social service.

3. Several important dissertations discuss Richmond. See Muriel Warren Pumphrey, "Mary Richmond and the Rise of Professional Social Work in Baltimore: The

Foundations of a Creative Career" (Ph.D. diss., Columbia University, 1956); Betty Page Broadhurst, "Social Thought, Social Practice, and Social Work Education: Sanborn, Ely, Warner, Richmond" (D.S.W. diss., Columbia University, 1971); Sarah Henry Lederman, "Reluctant Reformer: Mary E. Richmond and the Creation of Social Case Work" (Ph.D. diss., Columbia University, 1994); and Elizabeth N. Agnew, "Charity, Friendly Visiting, and Social Work: Mary E. Richmond and the Shaping of an American Profession" (Ph.D. diss., Indiana University, 1999). Judith Sealander's 1997 book *Private Wealth and Public Life: Foundation Philanthropy and the Reshaping of American Social Policy from the Progressive Era to the New Deal* (Baltimore, Md.: Johns Hopkins University, 1997) has an interesting chapter on Richmond and the Russell Sage Foundation. Her claim that the trio of Sophonisba Breckinridge, Edith Abbott, and Richmond formed an "alliance" to shape the administration of widows' pensions is not supported by documents in the Richmond papers at Columbia University. Richmond's career receives a fair assessment in Roy Lubove, *The Professional Altruist: The Emergence of Social Work as a Career, 1880–1930* (New York: Atheneum, 1965), 22–54.

4. Lederman, "Reluctant Reformer."

5. Mary E. Richmond copybook, May 1872, part I, box 1, folder 8, Mary Ellen Richmond Papers, Rare Book and Manuscript Library, Columbia University, New York (hereafter cited as MERP).

6. Patricia Ann McDonald, "Baltimore Women, 1870–1900" (Ph.D. diss., University of Maryland, 1976), 146.

7. *Afro-American*, 26 May 1900, part IV, scrapbook I, MERP.

8. "Aspirations," in Pumphrey, "Professional Social Work," 23; and report of Mary E. Richmond, talk at the Myrtle Club, 13 February 1891, part IV, scrapbook I, MERP.

9. Richmond to Constance Biddle, 24 February 1908, part I, box 5, folder 87, MERP; and Mary E. Richmond, "Attitude of a Working Woman toward Working Women," 30 April 1897, part I, box 4, folder 55, MERP.

10. Colcord and Mann, eds., *Long View,* 31.

11. Michael B. Katz, *In the Shadow of the Poorhouse: A Social History of Welfare in America* (New York: Basic, 1986), 72–84.

12. The English organization attracted intellectuals such as John Stuart Mill and many politicians. Members included housing reformer Octavia Hill, who believed that the purpose of charity work was to help the wealthy understand the problems of the poor. Other members, such as Bernard Bosanquet, represented the English charity organization societies which defined their work as "concerted action in neighborly service." These ideas about charity and reform spread rapidly through the National Conference of Charities and Correction, founded in 1874 in the United States by the ASSA, which was itself modeled on its British counterpart, the National Association for the Promotion of Social Science (NAPSS). Mary E. Richmond, "Background for the Art of Helping" (1924), in Colcord and Mann, eds. *Long View,* 574–83; Bernard Bosanquet, "The Principles and Chief Dangers of the Administration of Charity," in *Philanthropy and Social Progress: Seven Essays,* ed. Henry C. Adams (New York: Thomas Y. Crowell, 1893), 249; Thomas Haskell, *The Emergence of Professional Social Science: The American Social Science Association and the Nineteenth-Century Crisis of Authority* (Urbana: University of Illinois Press, 1977); and Lawrence Goldman, "A

Peculiarity of the English? The Social Science Association and the Absence of Sociology in Nineteenth-Century Britain," *Past and Present* 114 (February 1987): 133–71.

13. Frank Dekker Watson, *The Charity Organization Movement in the United States: A Study in American Philanthropy* (New York: Macmillan, 1922).

14. Zilpha Drew Smith, "Report of the Committee on the Organization of Charity," *Proceedings of the National Conference of Charities and Correction* (1888), 120–30; and Richmond to Jane Addams, draft, n.d., part I, box 4, folder 70, MERP. (This letter is filed with material from 1899. Though it is undated, it was clearly written in response to Addams's 1902 book, *Democracy and Social Ethics*. Richmond would always favor service over thrift. While the distinction was important to people within the charity organization movement, few people outside the movement understood the tension that existed between the charity organizers who focused on service and those who focused on thrift.)

15. Mary E. Richmond, "The Friendly Visitor" (1890), in *Long View*, ed. Colcord and Mann, 42.

16. Charles Hirschfeld, *A Social History of Baltimore, 1870–1900* (Baltimore, Md.: Johns Hopkins University Press, 1941), 138–39; Hugh Hawkins, *Pioneer: A History of the Johns Hopkins University, 1874–1889* (Ithaca, N.Y.: Cornell University Press, 1960); Mary Jo Deegan, *Jane Addams and the Men of the Chicago School, 1892–1918* (New Brunswick, N.J.: Transaction, 1988), 316–17; Helen M. Thompson to Richmond, 6 November 1892, FCSR; and Broadhurst, "Social Thought," 420–21.

17. Mary E. Richmond, *The Confidential Circular* 10 (1892): 1–2, FCSR.

18. Pumphrey, "Professional Social Work," 326; and Colcord and Mann, eds., *Long View*, 36.

19. Richmond to Mrs. J. C. Winston, 10 June 1902, part I, box 5, folder 74, MERP.

20. Mary E. Richmond, "The Work of a District Agent," 1897, 1900, part I, box 4, folder 60, MERP.

21. The only book Richmond published while at the BCOS was *Friendly Visiting among the Poor* (1899), a handbook for volunteers. In 1915 she told a group of students she wished she could recall every copy (Pumphrey, "Professional Social Work," 428).

22. "Chronology," part I, box 7, folder 134, MERP; Anna Davies to Richmond, 22 February 1900; Helen Parrish to Richmond, 23 February 1900; Susan P. Wharton to Richmond, 3 March and 7 March 1900; all in part I, box 4, folder 50, MERP.

23. Richmond to Annie E. Gerry, 18 July 1917, part II, box 2, folder 29, MERP.

24. Clinton Rogers Woodruff, "Practical Municipal Progress," *American Journal of Sociology* 12 (1906): 190–215; part IV, Philadelphia scrapbook, MERP; Lloyd M. Abernethy, "Progressivism, 1905–1919," in *Philadelphia: A 300 Year History*, ed. Russell F. Weigley (New York: W. W. Norton, 1982), 540–45; and Helen Foss Woods, undated transcript of memorial speech read in Philadelphia, 6, part I, box 7, folder 135, MERP.

25. Mary E. Richmond, "The Retail Method of Reform" (1905), in *Long View*, ed. Colcord and Mann, 214.

26. James A. Hijiya, "Four Ways of Looking at a Philanthropist: A Study of Robert Weeks de Forest," *Proceedings of the American Philosophical Society* 124 (December 1980): 404–18.

27. Robert W. de Forest to John M. Glenn, 23 October 1906, series 1, box 2, folder 11, Russell Sage Foundation Papers, Rockefeller Archive Center, Sleepy Hollow, N.Y. (hereafter cited as RSFP); and Clarke A. Chambers, *Paul U. Kellogg and the Survey: Voices for Social Welfare and Social Justice* (Minneapolis: University of Minnesota Press, 1971), 18–19, 42.

28. Colcord and Mann, eds., *Long View*, 185; and Ada Morawetz to Richmond, 24 February 1909; Alice Higgins to Richmond, n.d.; both in part I, box 5, folder 86, MERP.

29. Lubove, *Professional Altruist*; Allen F. Davis, *Spearheads for Reform: The Social Settlements and the Progressive Movement, 1890–1914* (New York: Oxford University Press, 1967); Lela B. Costin, *Two Sisters for Social Justice: A Biography of Grace and Edith Abbott* (Urbana: University of Illinois Press, 1983); Clarke A. Chambers, "Women in the Creation of the Profession of Social Work," *Social Service Review* 60 (March 1986): 1–33; Katz, *Shadow of the Poorhouse*; Robyn Muncy, *Creating a Female Dominion in American Reform, 1890–1935* (New York: Oxford University Press, 1991); Daniel J. Walkowitz, "The Making of a Feminine Professional Identity: Social Workers in the 1920s," *American Historical Review* 95 (October 1990), 1051–75; Beverly Stadum, *Poor Women and Their Families: Hard Working Charity Cases, 1900–1930* (Albany: State University of New York Press, 1992); Kathryn Kish Sklar, "Who Funded Hull House?" in *Lady Bountiful Revisited: Women, Philanthropy, and Power*, ed. Kathleen D. McCarthy (New Brunswick, N.J.: Rutgers University Press, 1990), 94–115; and idem, "The Historical Foundations of Women's Power in the Creation of the American Welfare State, 1830–1930," in *Mothers of a New World: Maternalist Politics and the Origins of Welfare States*, ed. Seth Koven and Sonya Michel (New York: Routledge, 1993), 43–93.

30. She would articulate this point most clearly in her major book on case work, *Social Diagnosis* (New York: Russell Sage Foundation, 1917), 367–68.

31. Theda Skocpol, *Protecting Soldiers and Mothers: The Political Origins of Social Policy in the United States* (Cambridge, Mass.: Belknap Press of Harvard University Press, 1992); Linda Gordon, *Pitied but Not Entitled: Single Mothers and the History of Welfare, 1890–1935* (New York: Free Press, 1994); and Joanne L. Goodwin, *Gender and the Politics of Welfare Reform: Mothers' Pensions in Chicago, 1911–1929* (Chicago: University of Chicago Press, 1997).

32. Mary E. Richmond, "Motherhood and Pensions" (1933), in *Long View*, ed. Colcord and Mann, 350–64.

33. Richmond to Gertrude Vaile, 1 October 1912, part II, box 25, file 408, MERP; and Helen Glenn to Richmond, 13 January 1916, series 3, box 13, folder 112, RSFP.

34. Richmond to C. C. Carstens, 23 October 1913, part II, box 25, folder 409, MERP.

35. Gordon, *Pitied but Not Entitled*, 48.

36. Frances O'Neill to Richmond, 19 January 1923 and 16 February 1923; and Richmond to O'Neill, 5 February 1923; all three in part II, box 3, folder 51, MERP.

37. Abraham Flexner, "Is Social Work a Profession?" *Proceedings of the National Conference of Charities and Correction* (1915), 576–90.

38. Charity Organization Department Report, 17 December 1917, History of the Charity Organization Department, part II, box 36, folder 621, MERP.

39. [Mary E. Richmond], *Manual of Home Service* (New York: American Red Cross, 1917), part II, box 28, folder 450, MERP; American Red Cross, *The Work of the American Red Cross during the War: A Statement of Finances and Accomplishments for the Period July 1, 1917, to February 28, 1919* (Washington, D.C.: American Red Cross, 1919), 26; and Henry P. Davison, *The American Red Cross in the Great War* (New York: Macmillan, 1919).

40. Richmond to John M. Glenn, 20 April 1927, series 3, box 13, folder 113, RSFP.

41. John M. Glenn to Richmond, 7 May 1927, series 3, box 13, folder 113, RSFP.

42. Philip Klein, *From Philanthropy to Social Welfare: An American Cultural Perspective* (San Francisco: Jossey-Bass, 1968), 226.

43. Harry Specht and Mark E. Courtney, *Unfaithful Angels: How Social Work Has Abandoned Its Mission* (New York: Free Press, 1994); and Leslie Margolin, *Under the Cover of Kindness: The Invention of Social Work* (Charlottesville: University Press of Virginia, 1997).

44. Kenneth Ludmerer, *Learning to Heal: The Development of American Medical Education* (New York: Basic, 1985), 182.

45. Hilary Graham, "Caring: A Labour of Love," in *A Labour of Love: Women, Work, and Caring*, ed. Janet Finch and Dulcie Groves (London: Routledge and Kegan Paul, 1983), 13–30; Berenice Fisher and Joan Tronto, "Toward a Feminist Theory of Caring," in *Circles of Care: Work and Identity in Women's Lives*, ed. Emily K. Abel and Margaret K. Nelson (Albany: State University of New York Press, 1990), 35–62; and Nel Noddings, "The Caring Professional," in *Caregiving: Readings in Knowledge, Practice, Ethics, and Politics,* ed. Suzanne Gordon, Patricia Benner, and Nel Noddings (Philadelphia: University of Pennsylvania Press, 1996), 160–72.

46. Richmond to Helen Wallerstein, 25 June 1921, part II, box 2, folder 45, MERP.

3. Southern Poor Whites and Higher Education: Martha Berry's Philanthropic Strategies in the Building of Berry College

Victoria-María MacDonald and Eleanore Lenington

The closing decade of the nineteenth century and the opening decades of the twentieth century—a period of American history often designated the Progressive Era—witnessed the expansion of southern white women into arenas previously closed to them. Whether by choice or by necessity born of social turmoil in the aftermath of the Civil War, southern white women began to claim the right to effect changes in southern life.[1] Born into this climate of increased expectations and broadened opportunities for women was Martha McChesney Berry (1866–1942), philanthropist and educator. Berry's efforts on behalf of mountain children in northwest Georgia began with Sunday schools and ultimately grew into Berry College of Rome, Georgia. Her life and work expand our understanding of southern women educators during the decades after Reconstruction, a time when education became a vehicle for the regeneration of southern society.

Philanthropy, education, and the American South traditionally have been linked with the work of southern blacks and northern philanthropists. Booker T. Washington's Tuskegee Institute, Samuel Armstrong's Hampton Institute, and the American Missionary Association's network of academies and colleges in the postbellum era all offered an opportunity for education that southern states could not or would not provide to African Americans in the decades following Reconstruction.[2] During this same period, however, parallel work aimed to further educational opportunities for children of rural poor white families. Martha Berry's efforts on behalf of this population illuminate an unexplored aspect of southern history and education. Her donation of personal time and property to those she called her "heirs"—the mountain children—reveals how a white woman whose birthright naturally would have propelled her into a more traditional sphere as homemaker and society woman chose instead to dedicate her life to the less privileged.[3]

Berry's personality, a unique amalgam of convention and radicalism, placed her both in and ahead of her time and sustained her when fundraising took her far from the Georgia hills. Ever the refined, upper-class southern woman, Berry was willing to leave conventional social and geographic spheres of influence in order to enter the very public realm of business and politics where she could further her quest to give mountain children the chance to be "independent, thrifty and self-respecting."[4] Berry brought her philosophies of hard work and perseverance from the small town of Rome, Georgia, to the attention of the early twentieth century's most prominent philanthropists, politicians, and educators.

Martha McChesney Berry was born in 1866 at Oak Hill, the family plantation in Floyd County, Georgia. Although the Civil War had devastated many southern families, including the Berrys, Martha's parents were determined to regain their prewar prosperity. Thomas and Frances Berry also believed it was imperative to lend aid to less-fortunate neighbors; their example would guide their daughter's life and work.

Before the war, Martha's father had risen from the post of shopkeeper's helper to become a successful cotton broker. Primarily a businessman, he distrusted "fire-eater" politicians from North and South, and he hoped their disputes would not lead the nation into conflict. But when the Confederates shelled Fort Sumter in April 1861, he formed an infantry company from his county, one which included Scotch-Irish Highlanders. After the war, in the midst of southern defeat, Berry privately determined to help these loyal Georgians and their families, whose prewar poverty had been exacerbated by the war's destruction.[5]

Thomas did not shield his young daughter from the turmoil of Reconstruction. He often took her with him on his regular trips to provide the Highlanders with food, clothes, and money. According to Martha's recollection, he told her, "These people don't want charity. They want to help themselves. Don't ever forget that, Martha. They're not shiftless by any means. They like to work and work hard, but they don't know how to use their heads. They don't try new methods. They don't improve their lot. It's up to us to help them do that."[6] Just as his northern financier acquaintances had given Berry the means to rebuild his business after the war, he believed in giving others tools to help themselves. He taught this strategy to his daughter. As she developed her own charitable projects, Martha's preferred tool was education.

As life for the Berrys slowly improved after the war, they were able to send Martha to Madame LeFevre's Edgeworth Finishing School in Baltimore in 1883. Martha did not feel comfortable in the sophisticated surroundings of Baltimore, where city girls ridiculed her "country" clothes. She wrote to her father, "I don't belong here and never will. The girls make fun of my wardrobe and shun my company. It is all too, too humiliating, papa. Please may I come home?" Her father replied immediately by wire: "A Berry never forsakes a goal until it is attained. Do not come home. You will be sent back to Baltimore on next train."[7] To ease his daughter's unhappiness, however, he simultaneously wired money to Madame LeFevre—more than enough to provide his daughter with an appropriate wardrobe. Still, Martha sensed that her peers' acceptance of her new, more cosmopolitan appearance was superficial, and the new clothes did not ease her homesickness. She did leave school at the end of the term, but her homecoming was bittersweet; her father had suffered a stroke. And she never forgot the discomfort of having the wrong clothes and being subject to hurtful teasing.

Before Thomas Berry died, he gave Martha a tract of land across the road from Oak Hill. After gently advising her of its value, he cautioned that "no society can survive without land" and counseled her to manage the land and its timber carefully so that she would always have an income. Proud of her "giving hands," he again reminded her, "A person knows very little about the art of living until he learns to give. But just don't hand a man a peck of potatoes, then forget him. That's not the kind of giving that will help him. It's far better to give him seed and tools so that he can grow a patch of his own. That way he can thank you without trading off his pride." The influence of these words would be evident in later years.[8]

After her father's death, Martha spent considerable time working at the family's cotton brokerage in town and at their summer home in Mentone, Alabama. Her mother took over management of Oak Hill and the family's other business interests, and quite often Martha would take her younger brothers, sisters, and cousins to Mentone to escape the hot weather. Here she had the freedom to wander the mountain trails, where she spent time with the Highlanders and learned their language, lore, and traditions. Her associations with these people "outraged the social conventions of the upper-class southerners with whom she had grown up." Even Aunt Martha, informally called "Aunt Marth"—a former slave who had cared for the Berry children before the war and remained to oversee the Berry household servants after emancipation—warned Martha to keep her distance from the "inferior" white mountain children.[9]

Martha was not deterred by such admonitions. In the mountains surrounding Mentone she met Highlanders like those who lived in the north Georgia hills of her home. Like many northern women who came south infused with a missionary spirit, Martha saw opportunities to improve the living conditions of mountain people, particularly through schooling.[10] Education for these children was problematic: at this time schools in rural Georgia were limited and only offered for five months a year. As a result many backwoods children—who lacked transportation or the proper clothes to attend school even when it was in session—were deprived of education.[11] Berry observed that the existing rural public schools were small, isolated, crumbling, and often led by "an old man as tired as the building itself." Furthermore, the curriculum entailed teaching "classic subjects for which the mountaineers had no use."[12] Filtering this lack of educational opportunities through her commonsense approach to life and her growing attachment to the mountain families, Berry came to recognize that her avocation was to "devote her entire time and means to teaching them ways to help themselves."[13]

Through her actions she was carrying out the type of philanthropical work that politically disenfranchised but financially elite southern white women of this era pursued. Frustrated by the lack of governmental provisions for schools, health care, and other matters, Berry responded to this public problem with her own personal solution—to build an institution for this overlooked set of children.[14]

TRANSFORMING IDEAS INTO REALITY

The opening of the Berry Schools form a piece of Georgian folklore—what historian Anne Firor Scott has called an "epic saga."[15] The story—told and retold by many of Martha Berry's admirers, as well as by placards in the Oak Hill Museum on the Berry University campus—tells of a woman of leisure who had a desire to improve the world, yet lacked a mission. The Berry Schools provided that mission. One day twenty-four-year-old Martha Berry was reading comfortably in the log cabin playhouse her father built, now converted into a retreat. Upon observing some young children peering in her window, she invited them in. Shy, nervous, and ready to run, the ragged children entered cautiously. Martha read them Bible stories and gave them apples to eat; when they left, she asked them to return the following Sunday with their siblings and friends. In just a few weeks her impromptu Sunday school had filled the log cabin to capacity. In 1900 she opened her first formal Sabbath School in a larger building on her family's property. In 1902 she deeded her inherited land to the Boys' Industrial School, the first boarding school she would create.

Martha traveled throughout the countryside recruiting boys who were interested in learning and willing to work their way through school. The first group of boys numbered only six, but their number continually increased. For seven years she accepted only boys, believing that they could help more with the construction work necessary for buildings. She acknowledged later, "If I had known how much more they could eat, I would have started with girls!"[16] The townspeople called her students the "biscuit eaters," and socialites wondered if she had lost her head devoting her time and energy to the disparaged poor whites of the region. White Southerners were highly class conscious (a legacy from antebellum slave society); the term "poor white" designated the often propertyless plain people of the South.[17] Although many mountaineers owned their property, they were still stigmatized in the minds of most white Southerners.

In 1909 Berry opened a girls' school, and its pupils—like those of the boys' school—worked at the day-to-day operation of the institution. Each student followed a regular public school curriculum but was also required to devote two hours to chores every day. The Berry Schools received accreditation for high school work in 1923; however, the goal of self-sufficiency was barely being reached. After World War I, education beyond high school became necessary for many jobs in the rapidly expanding industries of the South, but many of Martha's students found the few state universities open to them intimidating and too expensive.[18] As a result, in 1926 she opened a junior college and in 1930 Berry College inaugurated a full four-year program.

The first obstacle Berry had to confront was the reluctance of parents to send their children to boarding school. The usual problems of fluctuating attendance because children were needed to work in the fields or watch younger siblings mingled with more deeply rooted issues of parents' independence and pride.[19] Berry had observed these difficulties when she attempted a day-school arrangement three years prior to opening the Boys' Industrial School. As a strategy to circumvent the problems of spotty attendance, and perhaps as an unconscious reflection of her own class perspective, Berry determined that boarding schools were necessary. Under her constant, watchful eye, attendance could be ensured. Furthermore, like the officials of the Native American boarding schools, she wanted to remove the mountain children at least temporarily from their home environments in order to accustom them to more mainstream southern middle-class culture.[20] In a boarding school she believed that her students would be "surrounded by fine things so that they can absorb them and become part of them."[21]

Unlike administrators of boarding schools for Native Americans, Berry did not seek to stamp out the children's birth culture entirely, but worked to instill pride and preserve part of the children's heritage.[22] The Berry curriculum reflected Martha's belief in an "education of hand and mind, in which one would not be a stranger to the other."[23] The traditional (but not classical) academic curriculum followed that of the public schools and was balanced with industrial training. Boys and girls had separate responsibilities, as was typical of industrial education during the Progressive Era.[24] In the early years the boys spent their two hours doing farmwork and the girls took care of domestic chores. As time progressed and Berry was able to enlarge her schools to accommodate the many would-be students, she also added projects that could prepare students for future occupations. Berry tried to ensure that her students would learn up-to-date procedures, whether for planting crops or canning vegetables. For instance, students were exposed to "scientific agriculture," with its emphasis on crop rotation and soil conservation. U.S. Department of Agriculture specialist W. J. Spillman concurred that the Berry School modeled modern agricultural techniques, writing in 1908, "I do not hesitate to say, after having visited most of the agricultural schools in this country, that you are doing the best work in agricultural education that I have seen anywhere in this country. I regard the success of your school as a critical factor in developing the type of education for our farmers' boys that will open the door of success to them on the farm."[25]

Berry viewed this knowledge as a means to preserve mountain heritage. If students could improve local agriculture they would be less likely to permanently leave the land for the city or other regions of the country. In later years the work schedule was modified, with two days per week reserved for some type of farmwork and four days devoted to class work. Students who so desired could also work exclusively for four months in order to earn eight months of uninterrupted schooling.[26]

Berry's industrial focus was entirely in keeping with educational conventions of the time, although similar efforts had been directed toward African American and Native American populations, rather than toward poor whites.[27] As U.S. industries clamored for more trained workers, vocational education received increased attention in educational circles. Furthermore, progressive educators believed in linking the world of the classroom to real life rather than studying abstract theories and requiring rote memorization.[28] In rural areas such as Floyd County, Georgia, educators called for agricultural training to help students learn "the things to be done in life" and prepare to serve a role "that meets the demands of real community life."[29] For students, the Berry Schools, Junior College (1926), and College (1930) also met a critical need for inexpensive and practical education. Educators and benefactors who supported the Berry Schools saw them as vehicles for creating self-made twentieth-century individuals who, through hard work and opportunity, could rise above their origins.

By the 1920s the Berry Schools had long waiting lists and were receiving the attention and money of philanthropists throughout the country. The persistence, determination, and political savvy that permitted Berry to tap the wealth generated by early-twentieth-century industrialists and entrepreneurs allowed the Schools and College to expand and also attracted national attention to the work school model.[30]

ARISTOCRACY OF WORK

When Martha started her first school in January 1902, she hired a female college graduate as an instructor. Armed with a degree from Stanford College, Californian Elizabeth Brewster trekked across the country to take part in a novel educational experiment in the rural South. In those first years Brewster and Berry performed what we today would call "multitasking." During the day they were teachers, while in the evenings they tried to ease the homesickness of the young boys who were away from family and home for the first time in their lives. These genteel women also made beds, scrubbed laundry, cooked innumerable meals on the school's wood stove, and cleared away underbrush. Berry, like many of her social class in the early twentieth century, believed that some mountain whites were "shiftless" and needed to be taught a healthy work ethic. Daily, she and Elizabeth Brewster lived the philosophy that work was honorable. Early on, though, Berry discovered that this philosophy could run contrary to local cultural values. A near rebellion took place during the first weeks, when the boys discovered they were to perform the "women's work" of laundry and cooking. Berry firmly stepped in to quell the boys' resistance to gender-specific tasks.[31]

Another obstacle the Berry Schools had to overcome was an association between manual labor and African Americans. The legacies of slavery in the South ran deep, decades past the actual emancipation of slaves. The story is told that early in the school's history Martha and her small crew of boys were cutting a new path to the building when a buggy full of townswomen stopped by to "see for themselves . . . the odd things" they had heard were happening on Oak Hill. When the visitors cried out, "You poor things. . . . She has you working like prisoners in a chain gang . . . just like field hands!" the boys dropped their shovels and lowered their heads in "dismay and shame." Berry, knowing exactly what type of racial resentments the women were trying to inflame, scolded them, "Look here. . . . If you women would go around encouraging people to work, the South wouldn't have the poorest farms in America! We wouldn't be crawling with sickness, and we'd have decent farms and taxes paid so we'd have better schools!"[32] Berry's comments reveal her political awareness of the rapidly shifting racial dynamics of the turn-of-the-twentieth-century South. As Grace Hale has explored in *Making Whiteness: The Culture of Segregation in the South, 1890–1940,* southern white women played a pivotal role in shaping the "space" that whites would permit African Americans to participate in after Reconstruction.[33]

Despite the assurances of students and alumni that they did not view themselves as exploited laborers, Martha Berry and her schools would periodically come under fire for relying upon the labor of students rather than paid workers.[34] Rarely did whites make public accusations that blacks or Native Americans in industrial schools were being exploited, and Berry remained vigilant to keep alive what she called the "aristocracy of work. We teach here that the only true aristocrat is the worker—men and women who are doing something for someone, who are helping others in their day work—in the shop, on the farm, in the dairy and in the laundry."[35]

"BEGGING TRIPS"

The work ethic inculcated at the school captured the attention of philanthropists in the early twentieth century. Martha initially believed that between the modest tuition charged for each boy ($40 to $50 annually in the early years) and the labor of the students in constructing new buildings and planting and harvesting their own food, the school could manage to be self-sufficient. As more and more boys enrolled, however, sometimes with only a pig or calf as a donation toward tuition, she realized she would need financial assistance. Local donations from friends and small amounts from philanthropists in Atlanta sustained the school initially. According to school folklore, Martha asked the students to pray for a means to acquire more funds. One night she overheard a boy praying, "I'm wonderin', Lord, whether You ain't showin' the way right now. I read in the paper about some New York people givin' money to schools. Dear God, give Miss Berry strength to get up there and tell them folks how much we need things. Amen."[36]

Although "almost petrified" at the thought of begging for money, Berry headed up to New York in the harsh winter of 1905. With only one or two introductions from former schoolmates, she quickly became discouraged. At last a Presbyterian minister took pity on her and allowed her to speak to his congregation. Not only was she able to arouse some interest in her school, but—more important—she also acquired the names of wealthy Wall Street businessmen. The first significant donation she received in New York was from R. Fulton Cutting for five hundred dollars.[37] In many cases Martha called upon individuals with whom she had no prior acquaintance and invited potential donors to visit the campus. Her first excursion north resulted in a total of $1700 for the school—and a severe case of pneumonia.

Before long Berry became better acquainted with the network of philanthropists who gave money to southern education. In order to educate herself and gain information about potential donors, she attended meetings such as the Conferences on Education for the South and the popular adult-education Chautauqua Institutes. Lacking a high school, normal school, or college degree, Berry taught herself about educational theories through these conferences and spread the gospel of her school. An example of her early success was her acquaintance with George Foster Peabody, a native of Columbus, Georgia, who moved north as a child and became a successful New York banker. He served as treasurer of both the Southern Education Board (SEB) and General Education Board (GEB) in the early twentieth century. The GEB and SEB exerted tremendous influence on southern education, particularly in fostering the idea of industrial education for African Americans.[38] The General Education Board had barely been founded in 1902 when Martha Berry began her appeals to that agency. She persisted in her appeals to the GEB for several decades until her illness and death in 1942.[39] However, it would not send funds to Berry's schools. During its first fifteen years the GEB supported public secondary schools in the South, and worked to encourage taxation for public schools. Private schools such as the Berry Schools were viewed as competitors to the GEB's vision of spreading public education.[40]

Although the GEB did not give funds to Martha Berry and her school, members of the SEB and GEB who were sympathetic to her cause and school donated monies directly. For example, George Foster Peabody contributed to her school's new recitation hall in 1905–1906.[41]

The Berry Schools were fortunate when, in 1906, Robert Ogden, president of the GEB and SEB, announced a plan to bring one of his famous groups of donors to the schools.[42] The year 1906 was also notable because educators from Georgia's Department of Education visited the school to learn and adapt ideas for the creation of agricultural high schools in the state.[43]

In 1907 Martha Berry scored another coup with the acquisition of a grant from the wealthy philanthropist Andrew Carnegie. The steel magnate had proved elusive as a donor; Berry complained to her secretary that it was "impossible to penetrate the web of secretaries at his office." During one of her trips to New York she decided she could not leave the city without speaking to him. According to school lore, she rang the door of the Carnegie mansion one cold evening and, despite the butler's insistence that Carnegie could not be disturbed, she scribbled a note on one of her cards and requested that he give it to the famous philanthropist. A few minutes later she was led into a room where Carnegie was posing for a portrait. With Carnegie as her captive audience, Berry described her school's work. Finally he led her to the next room, asked several questions, and said, "Miss Berry, this is how I do things. Fill out that form in detail, and later if I decide to help, I'll give a certain amount—provided you raise a similar amount from other sources."[44] Shortly afterward she received his pledge for $25,000. Although the precise details of Martha's famous encounter with Andrew Carnegie may never be known, correspondence from Carnegie himself verifies that by 1912 he had already given the Berry Schools over thirty thousand dollars. To John D. Rockefeller, Jr., he wrote admiringly that "Miss Berry's consecration of herself is really sublime."[45] But Carnegie's support did not end with this financial donation. In order to help Berry meet his challenge for the remaining sum, Carnegie invited Berry to accompany him and his wife to a dinner with his fellow philanthropist Mrs. Olivia Sage. Although Berry had already received a small amount from Sage, this luncheon netted her $5,000 toward matching Carnegie's grant. As Ruth Crocker's work in this volume illustrates, Olivia Sage was receptive to schools that promoted practical education, and the Berry Schools became one more of the hundreds of institutions Sage supported.

Martha Berry also pursued funds in the larger cities of the South. Atlanta, only two hours away by train, was becoming the king of the New South cities, and she actively sought out wealthy and influential Atlantans for her cause.[46] Martha not only approached influential men such as governor and then senator Hoke Smith,[47] but she also relied upon assistance from women. Mrs. Frank Inman of Atlanta assisted the Berry Schools through the creation of "Berry Circles" in Atlanta and other southern cities. A member of the nouveau riche in post-Reconstruction Atlanta, Inman invited wealthy women to her home for social gatherings and to "talk Berry."[48] Inman's determination to "let those people up there [Northerners] see that the Southerners were also interested" reveals her regional sensitivity. Like many New South women of the Progressive Era, Louise Inman turned her energies to improving conditions in the South through social and educational welfare voluntarism.[49]

Berry's first national exposure involved the visit of former president Theodore Roosevelt in October of 1910. Several years earlier she had met with Roosevelt in the White House and secured his respect for her combination of practical education, Christian values, and hard work. Roosevelt's concern over the future of the Anglo-Saxon race during decades of heavy immigration to the U.S.—what he called "race suicide"—most likely contributed to his interest in Berry's work for poor white boys. Furthermore, Roosevelt championed the outdoors and the preservation of masculinity, both associated with this rural setting.[50] Before his visit he wrote, "There is not a school in which I have taken more interest than in the Berry School, which is in very fact what its title denotes, a Christian industrial school for country boys."[51] After Roosevelt, Berry secured an audience with every president until her death in 1942.[52]

The mountain background of Berry's students aroused interest among Northerners during the late 1800s and early 1900s. During a time of enormous immigration to the urban Northeast, Appalachian whites became an object of admiration for their alleged Anglo-Saxon racial purity, pioneer stock, independence, and patriotism. Berea College president William G. Frost lauded the craftsmanship of this population through demonstrations at his Kentucky institution.[53] Historian Nina Silber has called this outpouring of interest in mountain whites at the turn of the century part of a "cult of Anglo-Saxonism."[54] Berry highlighted the Anglo-Saxon ancestry of her students in promotional literature, which noted that pupils were recruited "from the descendants of the good old English and Scotch-Irish stock which early peopled the hill-country and the mountain valleys."[55] The interest in poorer southern whites was not exclusively northern. Walter Hines Page's attention to the "Forgotten Man" of the white South in 1902 prompted educational, health, and other reforms aimed at the improvement of poorer whites in the region.[56]

"A PARTIAL RECOMPENSE": BOOKER T. WASHINGTON AND THE BERRY SCHOOLS

World War I presented new challenges to the growing Berry Schools. With the addition of the Girls' School in 1910, enrollment had increased to almost two hundred students. Many students who had not had a chance for formal schooling when they were younger attended Berry in their later teens and early twenties, and the war drew students away from school to the European front. Similarly, many of Martha's advisors and trustees were also called to active service. Regular sources of philanthropy were turned to the war cause, and she was increasingly left on her own to manage the schools' affairs and generate funds from new sources. Although the GEB consistently turned down her requests, she observed that it did fund black private schools, such as the Tuskegee Institute. In 1915 she was presented with an opportunity to learn first-hand about the work of Booker T. Washington's Tuskegee Institute and tap into his network of wealthy donors. Like the Berry institutions, Tuskegee emphasized industrial education, and students worked while also attending classes. John Eagan, another wealthy Atlantan who served on Berry's board of trustees, passed on to Martha a request for scholarship money he had received from Booker T. Washington in January 1915.[57] By the next month Martha had managed to join a group of donors and trustees visiting Tuskegee. Impressed with the extent of involvement and deep pockets of Tuskegee's trustees, Martha determined to market her schools to the same people. She earnestly started a campaign that declared, "We are doing just such a work for the poor white boys and girls of the South as Dr. Washington has done for his race."[58]

Booker T. Washington generously assisted Martha by providing the names and addresses of his trustees and visitors to Tuskegee. He wrote to her in February 1915, "Dear Miss Berry:—as a partial recompense for not calling on you to speak before you left, (and I fully meant to do so but did not know you were going to New York with Mr. Low's party) I am sending you the names of all the visitors with their addresses with the hope that you may interest them in your work." He then pleaded, "Please do not use my name in any use you may make of the list."[59] His letter crossed in the mail one from Martha Berry dated 27 February, in which she thanked him for her wonderful visit to Tuskegee. She also sent him a donation, regretfully adding, "I only wish I could send you what my heart dictates for the work, but as I cannot, I am sending you my 'little mite.'"[60] She immediately replied to Washington when the list of names arrived, writing, "I wish to thank you very heartily. . . . Of course I shall not use your name at all with any of these people."[61]

Booker T. Washington's clandestine support for Martha Berry and her schools sheds further light on this complex man. Biographer Louis Harlan emphasizes his ability to "wear the mask" in the variety of situations in which he found himself as a powerful black man during an era of extreme racism.[62] Washington's theories of hard work espoused in his memoir *Up from Slavery* and put into practice at Tuskegee Institute, an industrial school open to all students with a desire to learn and willingness to work, were shared by Berry. Although they served different clients, Martha's "Gates of Opportunity" at the Berry

Schools and Washington's industrial school both aimed to inculcate the value and promise of hard work in poor white and black southern children alike.[63]

Armed with Washington's valuable list, Berry began a written campaign in 1915 to convince Tuskegee's donors that her efforts should be supported as well. A savvy politician, Berry pointed out how educating rural poor white Southerners helped African Americans. To Miss Adelia Williams of Roxboro, Massachusetts, she argued, "Although this is a school for white mountain people and people from the rural districts—our own neglected Americans—in a way it touches upon the negro question." She continued, "Our mission classes among the boys here are studying the problem of housing of the negroes in the South. They also conduct services in the jails and convict camps. These chaingangs are composed largely of negroes, and what these boys are doing will show the breadth of the Christian training here."[64]

Berry was not completely satisfied with the list Washington initially provided her, and her determination and zeal for her work drove her to secure more names of Tuskegee donors, sometimes through dubious means. In private correspondence with northern friends she confided that she was "very anxious to secure a year book from Booker Washington's school at Tuskegee—I mean the financial year book which they send out to their donors. I saw one at a friend's house for a few minutes; and it was a great temptation to even look between the leaves because I saw some such good names that I should have been glad to have copied so as to send them appeals." She added, "However, I could not, under the circumstances, ask for even the loan of this book—I felt that it would be too delicate a thing to do." Although Martha was reluctant to ask for the book herself, she asked her New York friend Charlotte Young "if, through your friends, you could secure a year book of Tuskegee without letting it be known that it was for me. Of course I would let no one know how I secured the book. If I had it, or reports of other large institutions, I could make good use of them by sending to those addresses some of the literature of our school, which, like the patent medicine men, I believe is a 'cure-all.' "[65]

Although it appears that Martha was only partially successful in securing Tuskegee materials in order to augment her list of donors, the Tuskegee matter provides two insights into this woman and her work. As a woman Berry appears to have been on the margins of "old boy" networks in educational philanthropy and their august cast of wealthy male donors and power brokers. Standing outside the inner circle of these individuals, she resorted to stealth to tap into the network of northern wealth. Second, racial resentment did not appear to undergird Berry's drive for Tuskegee money. She shared with Booker T. Washington a common philosophy about the value of industrial education and believed that southern youth, black and white, could rise above their origins. As was typical of southern progressive reformers, she emphasized to potential donors that her work with poor whites indirectly assisted the cause of African Americans in the South through the eradication of ignorance and the creation of economic prosperity.[66] Booker T. Washington's untimely death in 1915 ended this unusual and unknown alliance between two southern educators of the early twentieth century.

"THE BEST AND PUREST ANGLO-SAXON BLOOD"

Berry's pursuit of funds directed toward institutions of industrial education shifted during the late teens and early 1920s. During these later years of the Progressive Era, Martha capitalized upon patriotic ideology surrounding World War I—including its increased nativism— to bolster support for her schools. Although Georgia, like the rest of the South, sheltered fewer immigrants than most of the country, anti-foreign rhetoric led to the passage of restrictive immigration measures such as the Quota Law of 1921 and the Immigration Act of 1924.[67] The term "Anglo-Saxon stock" creeps into her promotional literature during this period, revealing both her own bias toward the white race and her canny ability to profit from shifting trends in society.

Around 1908 she had discovered the promotional benefits of publishing both a magazine—*The Southern Highlander*—and the *Berry Schools Bulletin,* which contained the course catalog and school announcements. She took copies of this literature—filled with inspirational stories of successful students, ideas for specific donations, letters from grateful alumni, and copies of letters from prominent donors— on what she called her "begging trips." Hundreds of copies of her pamphlets and magazines were purposely left on trains, in waiting rooms and stations, in doctors' offices, in the hands of socialites, and anywhere she felt they might be read by a potential donor.

The 1916 pamphlet *What the Berry Schools Are Doing for America* profiles young men and women who arrived at Berry penniless and illiterate. In these Horatio Alger stories, the Berry experience transforms students from residents of small cabins and farms in the hills of North Georgia into successful teachers, farmers, and homemakers who will return to their communities and "help other poor mountain" folk.[68] The students are portrayed in photographs depicting them both when they arrived as "raw material" and then after they emerged as the "finished products": clean-cut young men and women. Berry exhorts her readers, "In these times the highest patriotism demands that we utilize every resource of our nation. The best material in the world is to be found hidden away among these southern hills. . . . Can we perform a more patriotic service than to educate these boys and girls of the mountains in whose veins flow the best and purest Anglo-Saxon blood?"[69]

Correspondence from donors of this era confirms that some accepted her proclamation about the importance of saving the Anglo-Saxon race. A donor from Brooklyn wanted to donate clothes or money on the condition that the institution assisted be "purely a white school," adding, "I approve of your efforts for the white boys and girls."[70] In the stories of young women who arrive at Berry, Martha notes that they had often received scholarships from the Daughters of the American Revolution, again emphasizing the patriotic and Anglo-Saxon character of the Berry students.[71]

KINDRED SPIRITS

The end of World War I ushered in a new era in philanthropical acquisitions for the schools. Martha's annual "begging trips" finally paid off handsomely in the 1920s when she made the acquaintance of automobile manufacturer Henry Ford and his wife Clara. The Fords developed a warm friendship with Martha and her schools that lasted until the end of her life. According to historian Jonathan Atkins, the values of hard work and opportunity promoted at the Berry Schools struck a chord among wealthy industrialists because they "paralleled their own social assumptions."[72] The first half of the twentieth century was indeed the age of philanthropy, but it also took acumen, persistence, and, in Martha Berry's case, dramatic flair to gain access to individuals or to the gatekeepers of their wealth. The story of how Martha convinced the Fords to visit her campus and eventually secured almost four million dollars exemplifies the strategies and tactics she used with many philanthropists.

For several years Martha had wished to speak with Henry Ford about her school, but she was unsure of how to approach him. He had a reputation for being standoffish and his eccentricities were also well known. Through her friends and donors Thomas Edison and his wife Martha, Berry was finally able to stir Ford's interest in her schools. One day in 1923 she learned through the newspapers that the Fords were traveling through Alabama. According to her former secretary, Martha "dropped everything" and rode directly to the train station, where she sent a note to the Fords in their private car. Ford listened to her discussion of schools that emphasized hard work without charity and, after asking numerous questions, agreed to visit the campus.[73]

The result of Ford's visit surpassed Martha's greatest dreams. Beginning with new dining and residential halls, Ford and his designers recreated an elegant collegiate campus replete with Gothic architecture in the hills of north Georgia. Henry and Clara Ford did not simply give money to the Berry Schools; they adopted them as a special object of philanthropy. For twenty years they visited the campus each year, spending time with Martha and her administrators, making plans for the campus, and enjoying the southern countryside. According to eyewitnesses, Ford felt very much at home on campus. One observer noted that he "shed much of his suspicion, his protective covering against the world." Another associate remarked that the schools "grew deeper and deeper inside the man's heart."[74] Perhaps this is because the Berry campus and its founder, Martha Berry (only three years his junior), tapped into Ford's paradoxical love for the rural premodern world and technological innovation.[75]

Ford's willingness to help Berry is not surprising, particularly when one considers the pragmatic philosophy that guided both of their lives. Berry's emphasis on a utilitarian education struck a chord with the industrialist, and it would be safe to suggest that Ford would also have felt a bond with Thomas Berry, Martha's father. Ford and both of the Berrys held to a steady belief in the ability of practical education to ensure a lifetime of productivity and independence, and they were determined to provide that commodity to the less fortunate. Equipped with such tools, their students could view their futures through the twin lenses of possibility and potentiality.

In 1916, seven years before he would meet Martha Berry, Ford had himself opened a trade school in Michigan. Like Berry, Ford believed that what passed as charity trained "the mind to regard life as a benevolent system of Providence; if you train a boy to look for favours from others instead of looking to his own power to create or command what he needs, then already the seeds of dependence are sown, the mind and will are warped, and life is crippled."[76] The Henry Ford Trade School was governed by three principles: A boy was a student first and was not to be turned into a "premature working man"; an academic education was to be equally combined with an industrial education; and a boy would be trusted with responsibility by being trained on articles which were to be used in actual production.[77] When Ford finally met Berry, he simply found his dream and philosophy transplanted to a rural, southern setting.[78]

With the assistance of Ford money, the 1920s were a heyday for the Berry Schools. Expansion had allowed Martha Berry to admit more students than ever. By the 1920s she had acquired over twenty thousand acres of land, and students numbered in the hundreds. They worked in up-to-date agricultural, cooking, and laundry facilities while securing an academic education. The Berry Schools now included the Mountain School for older men (an early continuing education program) and Faith Cottage, a small school for girls (many of whom were orphans) too young to attend the high school. Among the residents of Faith Cottage in the 1920 census is a two-and-a-half-year-old "adopted" girl born in Arkansas and named Martha Berry. Apparently, the orphans were named after Martha or given another temporary name until they were old enough to reclaim their former names or choose new ones.[79] The academic preparation offered by the schools was also emphasized during this period; the catalog indicated that Berry Schools prepared students for admittance "without examination to the Freshman class of most southern colleges and universities."[80]

However, the success of Martha Berry's schools also aroused suspicion and envy. In the 1920s, for example, attorneys in Rome, Georgia, addressed Georgia's governor in a newspaper article, arguing that money Martha Berry acquired for her schools from outside the state should be taxed. They charged that the schools formed a "wealthy corporation, owning vast holdings of land from which a lucrative revenue is yearly derived."[81] The attorneys also recommended that taxes from the Berry Schools be used to assist Confederate veterans. In response, Berry alumni quoted Joseph Sharp, a Confederate survivor who stated that "veterans would rather give money to the Schools. . . . The Berry Schools are already helping the Confederate veterans in the work they are doing to educate the grandchildren of Confederate veterans."[82]

Another sore spot was Ford's sponsorship, which created a permanent foundation for what would soon become Berry College. In 1926 the Junior College was created and in 1932 it graduated its first four-year class. During the early years of construction on the elaborate Ford buildings, the extent of money and attention given to this project had stirred ill will. Rumors spread that the school was "rich now and it doesn't need my help any more"; "Whatever they want, Ford gives."[83] Although the buildings were in place, the expense of upkeep was not included in Ford's grant, and when the Great Depression hit, the Berry Schools again fell on hard times. By relying on a large network of small donors, the Berry Schools survived, while many other small institutions did not.[84]

At the time of Martha Berry's death in 1942 at the age of seventy-six, Berry College had increased its landholdings to more than thirty thousand acres. Her accomplishments earned her honors still rare for southern white women. In 1924 the Georgia legislature granted her the title "Distinguished Citizen of Georgia." In 1925 the muckraking journalist Ida Tarbell identified Berry as one of America's fifty most influential women. The next year Martha received the Theodore Roosevelt Medal for Distinguished Service. In 1932 the governor of Georgia appointed her the first woman member of the Georgia University System Board of Regents. And in 1934 she received international recognition for her work when she was presented at the court of King George V of England.

Today, Berry College offers both undergraduate and graduate degrees and has been recognized as an outstanding small comprehensive southern college. The institutional mission of the school has not changed greatly from the early 1900s: "Berry College serves humanity by inspiring and educating students. Berry emphasizes a comprehensive, educational program committed to high academic standards, Christian values and practical work experience in a distinctive environment of natural beauty. The college serves all of its students without regard to economic status."[85] As one of the few federally designated work colleges, Berry continues to attract notice nationally and internationally.[86]

The philanthropic work of Martha Berry, evidence of her determination to expand educational opportunities in rural Georgia, constitutes one of the largely untold stories of "the great educational awakening" in the early-twentieth-century South.[87] Contemporary southern educators such as Mary McLeod Bethune, Julia Tutwiler, and Celeste

Parrish have received modest attention in histories of education, but the history of women and higher education in the pre–World War II South remains an untilled field.[88] Beginning in the second half of the twentieth century, historians began a slow and uneven effort first to acknowledge the presence of these women and then to tell their stories.[89] Martha Berry was a leader in southern education whose philanthropic activities altered the educational landscape for thousands of rural white children. As a southern white woman in the first half of the twentieth century, she often had to adapt her strategies to her still marginal position in society. Persistent and creative in her search for funding, she created an enduring institution.

NOTES

1. See Anne Firor Scott, *The Southern Lady: From Pedestal to Politics, 1830–1930* (1970; reprint, Charlottesville: University Press of Virginia, 1995); LeeAnn Whites, *The Civil War as a Crisis in Gender: Augusta, Georgia, 1860–1890* (Athens: University of Georgia Press, 1995); Elisabeth Lasch-Quinn, *Black Neighbors: Race and the Limits of Reform in the American Settlement House Movement, 1890–1945* (Chapel Hill: University of North Carolina Press, 1993); Marjorie Spruill Wheeler, *New Women of the New South: The Leaders of the Woman Suffrage Movement in the Southern States* (New York: Oxford University Press, 1993); Elna C. Green, *Southern Strategies: Southern Women and the Woman Suffrage Question* (Chapel Hill: University of North Carolina Press, 1997); Laura F. Edwards, *Scarlett Doesn't Live Here Anymore: Southern Women in the Civil War Era* (Urbana: University of Illinois Press, 2000); Glenda E. Gilmore, *Gender and Jim Crow: Women and the Politics of White Supremacy in North Carolina, 1896–1920* (Chapel Hill: University of North Carolina Press, 1996); and Michele Gillespie and Catherine Clinton, *Taking Off the White Gloves: Southern Women and Women Historians* (Columbia: University of Missouri Press, 1998).

2. James D. Anderson, *The Education of Blacks in the South, 1860–1935* (Chapel Hill: University of North Carolina Press, 1988); Eric Anderson and Alfred A. Moss, *Dangerous Donations: Northern Philanthropy and Southern Black Education, 1902–1930* (Columbia: University of Missouri Press, 1999); and William H. Watkins, *The White Architects of Black Education: Ideology and Power in America, 1865–1954* (New York: Teachers College Press, 2001).

3. Martha Berry, "Uplifting Backwood Boys in Georgia," *World's Work* 8 (July 1904), 4986–92.

4. Ibid., 4992.

5. General information on Martha Berry's family is obtained from the following tributes to her life and work: Harnett T. Kane with Inez Henry, *Miracle in the Mountains* (Garden City, N.Y.: Doubleday, 1956); Evelyn Hoge Pendley, *A Lady I Loved* (Mount Berry, Ga.: Berry College, 1966); Tracy Byers, *The Sunday Lady of Possum Trot* (New York: G. P. Putnam's Sons, 1932); Joyce Blackburn, *Martha Berry: A Woman of Courageous Spirit and Bold Dreams* (Atlanta, Ga.: Peachtree, 1992), originally

published as *Martha Berry, Little Woman with a Big Dream* (Philadelphia: J. B. Lippincott, 1968); and William L. Stidger, *The Human Side of Greatness* (New York: Harper and Brothers, 1940). See also Victoria-María MacDonald, "Martha Berry," in *American National Biography*, ed. John Garraty (New York: Oxford University Press, 1999). Correspondence and materials relating to the Berry Schools are preserved at the Berry College Archives in Rome, Georgia (hereafter cited as BCA).

6. Blackburn, *Martha Berry*, 19–20.

7. Ibid., 28. Soon after opening her school, Berry decided that standard dress for the students would avoid such problems for them. Boys wore overalls, girls wore gingham dresses.

8. Ibid., 34.

9. Ibid., 37, 43.

10. David E. Whisnant discusses various motivations for becoming involved with rural mountain residents in *All That is Native and Fine: The Politics of Culture in an American Region* (Chapel Hill: University of North Carolina Press, 1983).

11. Dorothy Orr, *A History of Education in Georgia* (Chapel Hill: University of North Carolina Press, 1950), 249–52.

12. Kane with Henry, *Miracle in the Mountains*, 29.

13. Blackburn, *Martha Berry*, 47.

14. See essays in Elna C. Green, ed., *Before the New Deal: Social Welfare in the South, 1830–1930* (Athens: University of Georgia Press, 1999); and the discussion in R. Claire Snyder, "Gendered Radicalism and Civil Society: What Can Democratic Theorists Learn from Southern White Ladies?" *Polity* 34 (spring 2002): 393–407.

15. Scott, *Southern Lady*, 116.

16. Blackburn, *Martha Berry*, 64.

17. Wayne Flynt, *Poor but Proud: Alabama's Poor Whites* (Tuscaloosa: University of Alabama Press, 1989).

18. For information on the early southern state universities open to women, see Amy Thompson McCandless, *The Past in the Present: Women's Higher Education in the Twentieth-Century American South* (Tuscaloosa: University of Alabama Press, 1999).

19. I. A. Newby, *Plain Folk in the New South: Social Change and Cultural Persistence, 1880-1915* (Baton Rouge: Louisiana State University Press, 1989), 426.

20. David Wallace Adams, *Education for Extinction: American Indians and the Boarding School Experience, 1875–1928* (Lawrence: University Press of Kansas, 1995).

21. Kane with Henry, *Miracle in the Mountains*, 29.

22. See Whisnant, *Native and Fine*.

23. Kane with Henry, *Miracle in the Mountains*, 49.

24. Jane Bernard Powers, *The "Girl Question" in Education: Vocational Education for Young Women in the Progressive Era* (Washington, D.C.: Falmcr, 1992).

25. W. J. Spillman to Martha Berry, 9 April 1908, folder 416, box 46, series 1.1, Early Southern Program, record group XX, Rockefeller Foundation Archives, Rockefeller Archive Center, Sleepy Hollow, N.Y. (hereafter cited as RAC).

26. *Berry School Bulletin*, 1921, BCA.

27. Adams, *Education for Extinction*; Anderson, *Education of Blacks*.

28. Lawrence A. Cremin, *The Transformation of the School: Progressivism in American Education, 1876–1957* (New York: Knopf, 1961).

29. *Proceedings of the Conference for Education in the South* (Washington, D.C.: Executive Committee of the Conference for Education in the South, 1900), 247; see also the Conference's 1912 *Proceedings,* 285.

30. Jonathan M. Atkins, "Philanthropy in the Mountains: Martha Berry and the Early Years of the Berry Schools," Georgia History in Pictures, *Georgia Historical Quarterly* 82 (winter 1998): 856–76.

31. The boys reportedly stated, "We don' do no women's work. I ain' never seen no mankind do no washin'" (Kane with Henry, *Miracle in the Mountains,* 60).

32. Ibid., 60–61.

33. Grace Elizabeth Hale, *Making Whiteness: The Culture of Segregation in the South, 1890–1940* (New York: Vintage, 1998), 47.

34. A very public condemnation of Berry by an alumnus appeared in the *New Republic* in the 1930s (Don West, "Sweatshops in the Schools," *New Republic,* 4 October 1933). Alumni and friends of Berry sent over two hundred letters in defense of the schools. See "Response," *New Republic,* 25 October 1933, 292, and a follow-up report, "About the Berry Schools, An Open Letter," *New Republic,* 14 April 1934.

35. Martha Berry, "The Greatest Influence in My Life," undated speech, BCA.

36. Kane with Henry, *Miracle in the Mountains,* 74.

37. Ibid., 77.

38. Anderson, *Education of Blacks,* 86–90.

39. The first correspondence with Berry in the GEB records appears in December 1902 (George Foster Peabody to Berry, 18 December 1902, folder 416, box 46, series 1.1, Rockefeller Foundation Archives, RAC).

40. For a discussion of the GEB's policies during these years see Eric Anderson and Alfred A. Moses, Jr., *Dangerous Donations: Northern Philanthropy and Southern Black Education, 1902–1930* (Columbia: University of Missouri Press, 1999), 85–107.

41. Berry to Peabody, 5 June 1905; and Berry to Peabody, 1 January 1906; both in container no. 1—general correspondence, George Peabody Papers, Library of Congress. In the existing histories of Berry, no mention is made of Peabody's contribution toward the recitation hall.

42. For more information on Ogden, see Anderson, *Education of Blacks,* chapter 3.

43. Orr, *History of Education,* 265–67; and Kane with Henry, *Miracle in the Mountains,* 97.

44. Kane with Henry, *Miracle in the Mountains,* 106–107.

45. Andrew Carnegie to J. D. Rockefeller, Jr., 9 December 1912, folder 416, box 46, series 1.1, Rockefeller Foundation Archives, RAC.

46. Don H. Doyle, *New Men, New Cities, New South: Atlanta, Nashville, Charleston, Mobile, 1860–1910* (Chapel Hill: University of North Carolina Press, 1990).

47. Hoke Smith to Wallace Buttrick, 8 April 1916, folder 416, box 46, series 1.1, Rockefeller Foundation Archives, RAC.

48. Kane with Henry, *Miracle in the Mountains,* 113.

49. Anne Firor Scott, *Natural Allies: Women's Associations in American History* (Urbana: University of Illinois Press, 1993); and Mary Martha Thomas, *The New Woman in Alabama: Social Reforms and Suffrage, 1890–1920* (Tuscaloosa: University of Alabama Press, 1992).

50. Nina Silber, *The Romance of Reunion: Northerners and the South, 1865–1900* (Chapel Hill: University of North Carolina Press, 1993), 143–56.

51. "What One Georgia Woman Is Doing for Poor Children," *Leslie's Weekly,* 27 October 1910, 434 (box 45, BCA).

52. Atkins, "Philanthropy in the Mountains," 865. See, for example, Berry's ability to bring presidential influence to her schools (Woodrow Wilson to Buttrick, 13 April 1916; Wilson to Buttrick, 21 April 1916; and Buttrick to Wilson, 19 April 1916; all three in folder 416, box 46, series 1.1, Rockefeller Foundation Archives, RAC).

53. Whisnant, *Native and Fine,* 64–67.

54. Silber, *Romance of Reunion,* 143.

55. Robert H. Adams, "The Widening Circle," *Southern Highlander,* January–February 1909, 11.

56. Walter Hines Page, *The Rebuilding of Old Commonwealths: Being Essays Towards the Training of the Forgotten Man in the Southern States* (New York: Doubleday, Page, 1902).

57. Booker T. Washington to John J. Eagan, 30 January 1915, correspondence file, BCA.

58. Berry to William G. Willcox, 29 November 1915, correspondence file, BCA.

59. Washington to Berry, 26 February 1915, correspondence file, BCA.

60. Berry to Washington, 27 February 1915, correspondence file, BCA. A subsequent letter from Tuskegee indicates that she had sent five dollars (Washington to Berry, 3 March 1915, correspondence file, BCA).

61. Berry to Washington, 1 March 1915, correspondence file, BCA.

62. Louis R. Harlan, *Booker T. Washington: The Making of a Black Leader, 1856–1901* (New York: Oxford University Press, 1972).

63. Booker T. Washington, *Up from Slavery: An Autobiography* (Garden City, N.Y.: Doubleday, Page, 1927).

64. Berry to Adelia C. Williams, 29 March 1915, correspondence file, BCA.

65. Berry to Charlotte Young, 22 March 1915, correspondence file, BCA.

66. Dewey Grantham, *Southern Progressivism: The Reconciliation of Progress and Tradition* (Knoxville: University of Tennessee Press, 1983).

67. Thomas J. Archdeacon, "Immigration Law," in *The Oxford Companion to U.S. History,* ed. Paul S. Boyer (New York: Oxford University Press, 2001), 365.

68. "Estelle's Story," in *What the Berry Schools Are Doing for America* (1916–17), 6–8, box 215, BCA.

69. Ibid., 8.

70. Letter to Berry from 85 Park Place, Brooklyn, N.Y. (author name illegible), 15 November, circa 1916, box 3, correspondence file, BCA.

71. *What the Berry Schools Are Doing for America.*

72. Atkins, "Philanthropy in the Mountains," 865.

73. Kane with Henry, *Miracle in the Mountains,* 202–203.

74. Ibid., 211.

75. John M. Staudenmaier, "Henry Ford," in Boyer, *Oxford Companion,* 275. See also Anne Jardim, *The First Henry Ford: A Study in Personality and Business Leadership* (Cambridge, Mass.: MIT Press, 1970); and David L. Lewis, *The Public Image of Henry Ford: An American Folk Hero and His Company* (Detroit: Wayne State University Press, 1976). Studies of Ford and his life rarely mention his relationship to the Berry

Schools. Future research at the Henry Ford Archives and Manuscripts Collection in Dearborn, Michigan, will reveal more detailed information on the relationship between the Fords and the Berry Schools.

76. Henry Ford, in collaboration with Samuel Crowther, *Today and Tomorrow* (Garden City, N.Y.: Doubleday, Page, 1926), 178.

77. Ibid., 180.

78. The Fords also developed an interest in the South and provided a community center, reconditioned homes, and a sawmill for Georgia residents outside of Savannah. See Carol Gelderman, *Henry Ford, The Wayward Capitalist* (New York: Dial, 1981), 388–89.

79. United States Bureau of the Census, *Manuscript Population of the Fourteenth Census, 1920,* Floyd County, Ga. (National Archives, Washington, D.C.), 262–63, microfilm reel T625.

80. *Berry Schools Bulletin* 9 (November 1921), 28, BCA.

81. "Berry Schools Alumni Reply to Statement Recently Published Concerning That Institution," *Rome Tribune-Herald,* n.d. (circa 1920s), Berry Schools—Alumni file, BCA.

82. Ibid.

83. Kane with Henry, *Miracle in the Mountains,* 215.

84. David Levine, *The American College and the Culture of Aspiration, 1915–1940* (New York: Oxford University Press, 1986).

85. Berry College, "About Berry College," http://www.berry.edu/about.asp (accessed 8 December 2003).

86. William Stacy Longstreth, "Lamps in the Mountains: American Liberal Arts Colleges with On-Campus Mandatory Student Work Programs" (Ph.D. diss., Claremont Graduate School, 1990).

87. Grantham, *Southern Progressivism,* 246.

88. A notable new exception is McCandless, *Past in the Present.* For bibliographic information on Bethune, Parrish, and Tutwiler, see Maxine Schwartz Seller, ed., *Women Educators in the United States, 1820–1993* (Westport, Conn.: Greenwood, 1994).

89. Glenda Gilmore, "Gender and Origins of the Old South," *Journal of Southern History* 67 (November 2001), 781.

4. Creative Financing in Social Science: Women Scholars and Early Research

Mary Ann Dzuback

The significance and impact of creative financing in the social sciences is evident in the development of the social science disciplines. One case in point is anthropology. American anthropology was fundamentally shaped by the work of Franz Boas and his students, who themselves became leading scholars in their fields. Adequate funds for travel—as well as money to develop collections, pay informants, and publish findings—proved essential, and much of the funding came from individual donors. One donor, herself an anthropologist, was Elsie Clews Parsons. Women anthropologists in the Southwest simply would not have been able to produce scholarly research at the pace they did without Parsons's help. Ruth Benedict, Ruth Bunzel, Esther Goldfrank, Gladys Reichard, Ruth Underhill, Dorothy Keur—as well as Boas himself and other male anthropologists—completed work supported by Parsons. She enabled countless others to conduct fieldwork by financing field schools for the Laboratory of Anthropology in Santa Fe and stipulating that women receive places as researchers in them.[1]

Parsons followed a tradition of women philanthropists who had been supporting social reform for decades before the turn of the twentieth century, often using their wealth to widen women's access to higher and professional education. These philanthropists offered material support coupled with encouragement, or patronage. For example, under the tutelage of M. Carey Thomas, Mary Garrett made a major bequest to the Johns Hopkins University for the establishment of a medical school on condition that women as well as men be admitted as students. Olivia Sage supported the Russell Sage Foundation's program of social research and social reform. Phoebe Apperson Hearst contributed to a number of buildings and programs on the campus of the University of California that benefited male and female students.[2]

The creative financing (given and received by women) explored in this chapter enabled women to further their work as principal investigators and as social science scholars who could define the scope of their own projects. This material support also influenced education within institutions and helped produce external scholarly publications, shaping programs and policies within and among institutions. Colleges might provide time and library materials for women's scholarship, but they rarely offered the necessary financial support to the extent that philanthropists did.

Analyzing strategies women used to gain financing for their research projects helps us to understand the nature and impact of the research those strategies produced. Financing for women's research in higher education comes from three kinds of sources: fellowships, private sponsorship, and foundations. Funds from these sources overlapped within institutions and time periods and influenced scholarship in different ways; however, I will discuss them in the order in which they first became available to social science researchers.

The first option, fellowships, included woman-generated support through organizations. For example, many women graduate students applied for fellowships from the Association of Collegiate Alumnae (later the American Association of University Women or AAUW). This kind of support was available throughout the twentieth century, but became somewhat less significant as women found limited access to more prestigious fellowships, like those from the Social Science Research Council, in the 1920s and 1930s. However, because most university graduate fellowships were granted to male students, AAUW fellowships continued to provide crucial support for women pursuing graduate study, as did fellowships provided by women's colleges for their graduates. Both the individual scholar and her academic advisor's expertise and interests shaped the research funded by these fellowships, although the questions pursued tended to fall squarely within those valued by the leading scholars in the disciplines—in part to assure the legitimacy of the research, in part to obtain male support for it, and in part to suggest that women could apply as much painstaking rigor as men did in dominant research areas. Yet AAUW and college fellowships offered some autonomy to women scholars in pursuit of doctorates, enabling them to explore graduate programs in the United

States and abroad and to begin research on projects that emerged from their undergraduate work.[3]

The second source of financing developed for faculty women; individuals and families supported both short-term projects and ongoing research. This kind of patronage began as early as the turn of the century and continued over the next five decades, but—like fellowships—it became a less salient and respected source of support as the large foundations increasingly sustained academic social science research beginning in the 1920s. Nevertheless, private support was critical for much of women scholars' work in the first half of the twentieth century. Before 1920, such funding enabled women to complete graduate work and pursue research that they chose as significant. Between 1920 and 1940, as philanthropic funding increased but focused on men's projects in research universities that employed few women scholars, funding from individuals continued to be essential for women scholars. Studies financed in this way tended to be shaped by the scholar herself, in conjunction with the giver's concerns (often similar or shared) and with the program goals and emphases of the researcher's home institution. Such autonomy allowed women to pursue their work even when prominent male social scientists and foundation officials did not consider their questions and methods central to the developing disciplines. Parsons's support of anthropology, for example, furthered disciplinary research that was still considered marginal in many institutions, particularly in its focus on North America. Thus, patronage by individuals helped to shape emerging science disciplines and women's contributions to them, despite the relatively smaller scale of funds involved.[4]

The third source of philanthropic support for women was the large foundations. For example, the Laura Spelman Rockefeller Memorial focused on developing social science inquiry at research universities. However, most women faculty of the period had appointments at the women's colleges, not research universities; moreover, the principal investigators of research projects typically were men well connected in the academic world, where women struggled against marginalization as scholars. Despite these problems, women obtained access to some of these foundation funds as staff and faculty associated with university research institutes and in social work and home economics graduate programs. Projects financed in this way and involving women tended to be shaped by the rare woman scholar entrusted with administration or by male faculty who invited women students and colleagues to contribute to the larger effort. Women at the School of Social Service Administration at the University of Chicago had access to Rockefeller funding for dissertation and other projects in the 1920s and 1930s, but this was atypical. Such funding, which granted both stature and the stamp of high-level disciplinary academic approval, was key to promoting particular questions and research methodologies in the social sciences and in particular institutions.

Each of these funding sources helped shape both the focus of scholarly research and the ways it was conducted by women social scientists in the first half of the twentieth century. Although I will touch on the fellowships and foundation research funds that women provided, sought, and received, this chapter will emphasize "creative financing" women obtained by tapping into less institutionalized sources. If we only examine the large foundations that financed social science research in the first third of the twentieth century, we miss two important aspects of the development of the social sciences. One is the ways that women academics used their networks of friends and colleagues to garner financial support for their efforts to influence social and economic research and (less directly) local, state, and national policymaking. The other aspect that might be missed is the large body of often interdisciplinary, grounded research that academic women conducted into the kinds of problems they considered important and the often subtle ways they contributed to theoretical and empirical formation of the disciplines. Without creative financing, much of the most interesting and valuable work women social scientists accomplished would have been nearly impossible—there simply was no other source of funding for it.[5]

The personal characteristics of women academics in this period may have affected their ability to secure creative financing: before the 1940s, most were white, middle-class, and Protestant. They came from small-town, urban, and occasionally rural families. They typically had parents who had completed some formal education, up to or including college, and at least one parent who strongly supported his or her daughter's further education. Exceptions to this profile included Jewish and African American women, women from wealthy and occasionally poor families, and women who lacked parental approval of their educational choices. All of the women in my study were confident of and committed to their own and often other women's full intellectual development in spite of women's marginalization in academe. In many cases, the donor-recipient relationship was formed within social networks already established. In others, it was formed in networks taking shape as more women pursued graduate degrees and became social science researchers, meeting each other in graduate programs, in social reform organizations, and in higher education institutions as faculty and members of boards of trustees.

SUPPORT FOR WOMEN'S RESEARCH IN THE EARLY TWENTIETH CENTURY

An early example of grounded, woman-defined research emerging out of such networks was a study conducted by the Association of Collegiate Alumnae (ACA). This study, completed in 1885, was designed as a direct response to Edward Clarke's *Sex in Education* (1873). Clarke argued on the basis of a few anecdotal examples that intellectual pursuits depleted women's physical health and robbed them of their capacity to reproduce. In response, researchers in the Association surveyed over 1200 women college graduates and found that their responses contradicted Clarke's "evidence."[6] The study results supported ACA members' determination to provide both graduate and undergraduate opportunities, so that women could do "the hardest kind of intellectual work," add "to the world's stock of knowledge," and join the ranks of teachers and scholars increasingly sought by colleges and universities.[7] To foster these kinds of opportunities, the Association determined to provide women with fellowships to study in graduate programs in Europe and the United States. The ACA was the first organization to recognize and finance the work of American women scholars; it began doing so as early as 1890 with its annual European Fellowship for overseas graduate work. Over the years, the ACA and then the AAUW became the principal national-level organization to which individuals and groups donated funds to support fellowships and scholarships for women. The contributions of the AAUW to developing social science knowledge cannot be ignored; fellowship funds enabled dozens of women social scientists to pursue graduate study before 1940 and launched them on their academic careers.[8]

Clearly, however, the AAUW's fellowships for graduate students represented a drop in the bucket. Some colleges, including Vassar and Bryn Mawr, provided graduate fellowships for alumnae to study at European institutions. Most graduate institutions also provided in-house fellowships, but women received few of these in the first half of the twentieth century, and before the 1920s money was scarce for both men and women as principal investigators on research projects of their own. Some funding was available in this period: John D. Rockefeller, Edward S. Harkness, and James B. Duke supported higher education institutions; the General Education Board, the Rosenwald Fund, and the Jeanes Foundation helped finance the construction of public schools in the South; and local and national philanthropies raised funds for relief efforts before and during World War I. But philanthropic foundations did not begin giving generously to social science research until the 1920s. When they did, the money was targeted toward producing scientific data that would support the organization and management of what Guy Alchon calls a "technocorporatist state." In other words, funders wanted to promote cooperative management of capitalistic growth by both public and private organizations, with the ultimate goal of reducing class friction, unemployment, and other socioeconomic ills that had emerged by the turn of the century with the expansion of industrial capitalism.[9]

Several philanthropies supplied some funds for survey research, industrial studies, and investigative reports before the 1920s. The most notable, the Russell Sage Foundation, began financing studies in 1907, but research was only one of several funding priorities, and the studies were designed to furnish "disinterested" statistical and other kinds of information for voluntary associations, government offices, and legislators attempting to address large social problems at the municipal and state levels. Academic researchers received some of the Russell Sage funds, but most of the support stayed within the foundation for internally led studies or was administered through local charity organization societies, of the kind conducted by Mary Richmond in Philadelphia and New York, as Sarah Lederman illustrates in this volume.[10]

But these institutional grants were exceptions; male and female social scientists in the early 1900s relied largely on individuals or families to support projects. Women carried this pattern forward into the 1920s and 1930s, often using the funds to develop and maintain cooperative and multidisciplinary projects that explored social economic and social welfare problems. Two cases illustrate this form of support: the social economy research program at the University of California, Berkeley, and the Council of Industrial Studies at Smith College. I focus on these two programs because they capture emerging fields within the study of economics and economic history. In addition, they demonstrate how critical noninstitutional grants were in supporting women's efforts to develop new social science knowledge, particularly in the interwar period. Finally, the Berkeley and Smith programs suggest the kinds of contexts in which women were able to elicit and use such support. The former program emerged in a university that was transforming its identity from a teaching to a research institution; the latter developed in a women's college, where graduate students were scarce and monetary resources for supporting faculty research were almost nonexistent.

THE UC BERKELEY SOCIAL ECONOMY RESEARCH PROGRAM

The social economy research program at Berkeley was developed largely by one faculty member: Jessica B. Peixotto, the first woman appointed full-time to the University of California faculty. She had received her Ph.D. (the second awarded to a woman at Berkeley) in political economy in 1900 after completing a dissertation entitled "The French Revolution and Modern French Socialism" under Bernard Moses. In 1904 she became the economics department's lecturer in socialism. Promoted to assistant professor in socialism (1907), then associate professor (1912), and eventually professor in social economy (1918), she built a steady record of research and service at the local and national levels. By the late 1910s, Peixotto had established social economy as one of the department's three programs, something of a distinction in a department among the earliest to name itself a Department of Economics. Peixotto used the social economy program to bring more women into this department at Berkeley, one of the few in the country to hire women as instructors and, in time, as tenure-track faculty.[11]

After completing service during World War I as a member of the Council of Defense Subcommittee on Women and Children, Peixotto began enlarging her earlier research program by conducting a study for the California Civil Service Commission that investigated cost of living issues among clerical, wage-earning, and executive state employees. From this study, Peixotto concluded that annual pricing of family and household budgets could be theoretically interesting if she expanded the criteria typically used to examine the decision-making processes in household spending.

It was this work that captured Clara Hellman Heller's interest and drew her financial support. Heller was a close friend of Peixotto's; both women had come of age in the upper echelons of San Francisco's merchant elite and shared similar progressive political views. Peixotto's father Raphael had moved to the city when Jessica was a child and raised his large family there as he expanded his business interests. Heller's father, Isaias Hellman, was a banker who migrated north from Los Angeles and developed both business and real estate holdings in the city. Her husband, Emanuel S. Heller, a lawyer with a lucrative practice, was a University of California alumnus and himself a philanthropist. But it was largely Clara Heller's money that supported Peixotto's work. She was a generous benefactor of the university and the Democratic Party as well as such San Francisco institutions as the San Francisco Opera, the Symphony Association, the Museum of Art, and the Children's Hospital.[12]

Heller's ongoing grants for Peixotto's work were targeted to help expand the research capabilities of women in social science at Berkeley. They contributed significantly to the development of consumer economics in a critical period. And her faith in the nature and quality of the research moved her to continue supporting the Heller Committee for Research in Social Economy under the leadership of Emily Huntington, who took over after Peixotto retired in 1935. By 1943, Heller's annual grants totaled $63,050, and when she died, her son (who was on the university's board of regents) continued to finance the committee until his death in 1961.[13]

Heller expected the committee to conduct "studies of problems in Social Economics with special reference to conditions in the State of California." Peixotto used this broad mandate to become a major influence in developing the theoretical and empirical sophistication of the field of consumer economics. The Heller studies can be divided into three groups: quantity and cost budgets, published annually; income and expenditure studies; and special studies. The first two comprised cost of living studies and bore some relationship to the third, which encompassed investigations into such areas as care for the dependent aged and children, unemployment relief and the unemployed, California's labor market and problems of re-employment, the nutritive value of diets among particular population groups, and standards and methods of relief.[14]

The quantity and cost budget studies began with a straightforward premise. In perusing the cost of living research, Peixotto discovered that not enough distinction was made between the ways families in various social and economic groups spent their money in relation to their incomes. Beginning in 1923, the committee conducted price surveys in the San Francisco Bay region to determine the living costs for families of wage earners, clerks, and professionals. By 1929, Peixotto could claim that the budgets were "used in wage arbitrations, by union and business officials, charity workers, the Labor Bureau, Inc., the State Bureau of Labor Statistics, and other agencies." In 1932–1933, the committee added a fourth budget, to cover dependent families on relief. A fifth was added in 1939; it investigated single working women's living costs.[15]

One innovation in the committee's approach was the wide range of items priced—from food to household furnishings to recreation activities—and the incorporation of concerns about other household management costs. This work was modified and revised whenever the committee pursued an income and expenditure study that contributed new insights into the substance and methods of the budget surveys. The result, as Peixotto claimed in 1933, was a rare effort "to measure [the changing standards of living] in quantitative terms," involving tracking the "increasing proportion of income that is being spent for the so-called 'miscellaneous' items—including automobiles, recreation, in fact all expenses other than food, clothing, and shelter." The index published by the Bureau of Labor Statistics did not reflect the typical expenses of salaried professionals—including domestic service and automobile upkeep—and applied the clothing expenditures for wage earners to middle-class earners. Peixotto suggested in 1935 that "the interest in these budgets continues, particularly since no other agency in the country prices a complete set of detailed budgets at regular intervals." Moreover, the attention to detail regarding how families spent their incomes, as opposed to how economists thought they probably spent it, expanded the categories examined and made the studies more reliable.[16]

Another innovation was Peixotto's challenge to the taboo of violating that "romantic and shadowy domain of home life, 'hopelessly private,' 'sacred,' " in which families had been "shut away" making their budgetary decisions. Introducing psychologically and sociologically informed explanations of consumer choice, she presented a case for "the American standard of living" reflected in professionals' desires and actual decisions, a standard that represented a kind of ideal annual household income for all "standard" families consisting of a husband, a wife, and "two growing children." She developed what she called the " 'comfort' standard," of about "$7,000, the sum needed to satisfy a set of desires for goods and services, desires that at the present time influence widely and profoundly the way men earn their money and the way they spend it." Moreover, she brought this "hopelessly private" life, in which middle-class women played an increasingly dominant role, into public discussion by publishing the research and encouraging its use in the making of public policy. By using as a guiding principle "the unswerving faith of our time in the social value of a rising standard of living; the growing belief especially among wage earners in a universal 'right' to a comfort standard," she succeeded in placing economic decisions at the household level squarely within a widely shared social vision of American middle-class life. No doubt Peixotto's personal experience, including the eleven years she devoted to domestic and charitable occupations between high school and college to satisfy her father's paternalistic concerns, helped to shape her understanding of these issues. But so, too, did the changing conditions of social and economic relationships in families and in society; the age of advertising and consumption framed the ways families, and often women, made decisions about household budgets.[17]

The Heller Committee program of the late 1920s and early 1930s reflected Peixotto's success in connecting the committee's research and distribution activities to other local agencies, including the YWCA, welfare associations, unions, and school boards. Under Huntington, the most significant larger-scale special studies of the middle to late 1930s were an indication of the committee's effort to place the local findings in a national context, in light of New Deal efforts to respond to unemployment and poverty. By insisting that the committee remain in the economics department, governed by faculty members appointed by the chair, Peixotto and Heller assured that the work would have an impact on the character of the department, as well as on the larger social economic research and policymaking community. As many of the researchers actually associated with Heller Committee work were women Ph.D. students and faculty in economics and home economics, the committee created a safe and respected haven for women social scientists at the University of California in the very years the university was expanding both its research and its teaching commitments in the state. Further, the Heller annual donations were among the university's earliest sources of outside funding for social science research. When the university agreed to begin financing the committee's work, Heller's donations decreased proportionally. When the university's commitment slackened under the presidency of Robert Gordon Sproul in the 1930s because the research itself was considered less significant than other kinds of social and economic research and theory making, Heller's donations increased in order to sustain the committee's work, still in demand by such agencies as the Brookings Institution.[18]

Why is this case significant in a collection of studies of women and educational philanthropy? First, the University of California was a land-grant institution. Accordingly, until the 1920s most public funding for research went to projects in the sciences and to studies related to agriculture and food production, major contributors to the state's economy. Consumer economics was not a priority of the state, nor was labor economics until the middle to late 1920s. The Heller grant provided seed money, or an opening for the university to help finance the research. Second, the funding and the program transformed the department's activities and faculty representation. The Berkeley Department of Economics was among the very few then extant to appoint not just one woman, but eventually four in positions that led to tenure; three became full professors in economics and the fourth a full professor in the law school. Still other women were appointed to faculty research and assistant positions for varying periods of time. Third, the social economy program was unusual in its full integration into the department's teaching and research. The Heller funding raised the profile of Peixotto and the work of her social economy colleagues and students among members of the university community. And it served the university well in the 1930s. When President Sproul received inquiries regarding the university's response to the Depression, he could point to the work in the department. Heller's support was critical to creating and maintaining these distinctive characteristics in Berkeley's economics department for four decades. Fourth, the grant enabled women to direct research into areas that were avoided or overlooked by male economists. Because this research focused on households and used women as informants about budgetary decision making, they were less likely to be funded by foundations seeking to support the more "objective" and "scientific" domains of male economists' work.[19]

THE SMITH COLLEGE COUNCIL OF INDUSTRIAL STUDIES

The Smith College Council of Industrial Studies offers a different example of creatively funded research. Supported largely by a single donor to further the work of women social scientists on the Smith faculty, the Council conducted research that could not have been done otherwise. In the 1920s and 1930s, Smith College occasionally provided faculty with leaves of absence and small stipends in order to foster faculty development. Although hiring of women faculty expanded in most colleges in the 1920s, funding for "extras" like research was not plentiful. By the 1930s, colleges were hard-pressed even to hire new faculty. Small stipends were available to faculty with strong proposals (they were typically used for travel, books, or research assistance), but completing social science research projects was often difficult and expensive in colleges located in relatively rural areas. Thus, women faculty at Smith's Northampton, Massachusetts, campus felt the effects of isolation, the struggle for access to libraries, the need for clerical assistance to complete statistical research, and a heavy teaching load. As an economist herself and a member of the faculty, donor Dorothy Wolff Douglas recognized these difficulties.[20]

Douglas was appointed instructor in the economics department at Smith in 1924, just before she finished her Ph.D. at Columbia in French economic history and theory. She had been married to economist Paul H. Douglas, who relinquished his position at the University of Chicago to teach at Amherst in order to keep his household and family intact and encourage his wife's academic career. By 1930, when Smith promoted her to assistant professor, Douglas was divorced, caring for four children, and sharing her house in Northampton with her domestic partner Katherine D. Lumpkin. She had inherited a good deal of family money and contributed generously to social and political causes, particularly those supporting organized labor. By the 1930s she was exploring female and child labor and labor legislation. One result was *Child Workers in America* (1937), co-authored with Lumpkin. Her politics and her own research shaped her belief that contemporary policy discussions, particularly regarding labor issues, had to be informed by economic history. Her contributions to establish the Council of Industrial Studies at Smith arose out of these concerns and commitments.[21]

On condition that it remain independent of the economics department and include an interdisciplinary advisory board of faculty from Smith's economics and history departments, Douglas provided a grant of $3,500 to Smith College to establish and develop the Council in 1932. She believed the focus should be on the Connecticut River Valley region and suggested that the college contribute up to $1,500 beginning in the second two years, after which her support would end and the college could decide whether to continue the Council's work.

William A. Neilson, Smith's president, appointed Katherine D. Lumpkin to serve as the Council's first director (1932–1939) on a half-time basis. Lumpkin had done some master's-level work in sociology at Columbia, participated in a YWCA effort toward interracial student organization in her native South, finished a Ph.D. at the University of Wisconsin in 1929, and taught at Mount Holyoke for one year. This was followed by a research fellowship from the Social Science Research Council to study families in New York seeking public assistance, and then by involvement in a project with the Bryn Mawr Department of Social Economy and Social Research.[22]

The work of the Council represented a concerted effort to make this a coordinated enterprise—to utilize the expertise of faculty at a number of colleges in the region, to offer research support to graduate students from other institutions working on their dissertations, and to envision the projects as a series of related studies that would yield a coherent body of work about the valley. The grant was designed to accomplish two additional goals. One was to capture the region's historical and economic transformations over the course of the nineteenth and twentieth centuries. The other was to collect and preserve whatever documentary evidence existed in the various industrial and social agencies in the valley. Both of these, Douglas hoped, would also result in some collaboration with businesses, agencies, and individuals in the region, helping to popularize the idea of research within local communities.[23]

Two directors, first Lumpkin and then Constance McLaughlin Green, headed the Council's program from 1939 to 1948. The chair throughout the 1930s and 1940s was Esther Lowenthal, professor of economics at Smith. Douglas, Lumpkin, and Lowenthal originally hoped that the committee's research would explore why industries that had long been located in the valley were abandoning "valuable property" to undertake "new investment" outside of western Massachusetts. But because some industrial leaders would not open their papers and decision-making processes to Smith's researchers, the Council settled on exploring the impact "of plant abandonment" on families, institutions, government, and other economic activity when a major industry pulled up stakes and left town. By the early 1950s, the Council had produced studies exploring the development and decline of transportation systems, trade practices going back to the colonial period, agricultural practices in the nineteenth century, women workers in local war industries, and the rise and decline of a number of industries in the Holyoke and Springfield areas. The studies were all carefully co-ordinated to increase understanding of the region's transformation historically and as it was actually taking place by the middle of the twentieth century. The second Douglas donation of $3,500 was de-pleted by 1936, and the Smith College board of trustees agreed to support the Council's work on a year-by-year basis, with a reduced budget, until Green resigned after her husband's sudden death in 1948. By then, the Council had produced a significant body of research and uncovered and helped to preserve a large collection of pri-mary materials that otherwise would have been lost to subsequent researchers.[24]

The Smith case presents an important form of creative financing by and for women. For Lumpkin and the Smith faculty, the Council offered resources for pursuing work in economic history and labor economics during the Depression, when private and public funding for social science research was harder to obtain than it had been in the 1920s. This was particularly the case for women doctoral students at the dissertation stage. By 1938, five of approximately seven projects conducted by the fellows were being used for dissertation studies. Smith College faculty were able to work with doctoral-level students, a rarity at the women's colleges, where most women academic social science scholars were employed. In addition, the studies produced in-valuable archival materials: diaries, collections of correspondence, oral histories, industrial publications going back to the colonial period, and a variety of business papers and town records. These materials were catalogued and preserved by the Council's researchers. Finally, the studies were coordinated in an unusually rigorous way for social science research. The Council's projects offered the opportunity to examine the impact of the immediate economic situation on the valley; by fo-cusing on the region, Douglas, Lowenthal, and Lumpkin ensured that as each project was defined it fit within the larger scope of the grant, contributed to the other studies, and extended and enriched the body of work the Council produced. And in the process of creating this work, both the knowledge and the networks of the women increased. The fellows often overlapped in their stay at Smith and were able to share work with each other, while benefiting from faculty oversight. The scholarship produced was impressive; many of the studies were published in *Smith College Studies in History*.[25] Thus, as in the Social Economy program at Berkeley, targeted, private funding had a measur-able impact on social science research by women at Smith.

FOUNDATION SUPPORT: THE UNIVERSITY OF PENNSYLVANIA CASE

Beginning in the 1920s the third type of funding—foundation grants—became available when women academic social scientists were able to access funds already allotted to male colleagues. The University of Chicago's Local Community Research Committee, Harvard's Bureau of International Research, and the University of Pennsylvania's Department of Industrial Research are examples of programs that received such funding. (An exception was a $7,000 grant Emily Huntington secured from the Rockefeller Foundation to augment Heller funds for a study of unemployment and re-employment in California in 1937; she remained the principal investigator and controlled the grant.) The situation at Penn nicely illustrates how women scholars made use of foundation money.

Penn's Department of Industrial Research was initially financed by the Carnegie Corporation, the Philadelphia Association for the Discussion of Employment Problems, and the university under the direction of Joseph Willits in 1921, who co-founded the department with Anne Bezanson and appointed her as his assistant director. In 1928–1929, after the Carnegie Corporation ended its support, the department received a five-year grant from the Laura Spelman Rockefeller Memorial (LSRM), effectively tripling the budget for that period. The grant was given on condition that the university increase its support over the same period.[26]

Bezanson, who did not initially have a faculty appointment at Penn despite her Ph.D. in economics from Harvard (1929), became co-director in 1934, after Willits left to act as dean of the Wharton School. In 1939, when Willits left for the Rockefeller Foundation, Bezanson became director. The department was established to offer courses in industrial relations and to pursue "co-operative industrial research in the Philadelphia community." As funding increased in the late 1920s, its purposes expanded to include building social science research within the community. Another emergent goal, that of conducting "fundamental studies of the economic and human problems and phenomena of industry," gave the faculty and research associates considerable latitude in designing projects. This latitude was always tempered by the idea that the research itself would be conducted in a coordinated fashion rather than by lone scholars in isolation.[27]

The Rockefeller support for Penn's Department of Industrial Research continued into the middle 1940s, although at a reduced level.

As a result of this financing, approximately one-third of its total budget over two decades, the department created an enormous body of research. This encompassed work in personnel and labor relations; the hosiery, upholstery, textile, and bituminous coal industries; and community labor studies that included examinations of labor market trends, personnel relations, wages, and transportation. Under Bezanson and Willits, the department hired several women to conduct research, including Eleanor Lansing Dulles, who contributed a number of studies, and Gladys Palmer, who directed the research after Bezanson's retirement. These appointments occurred at a time when the University of Pennsylvania hired no women to its social science faculty.[28]

In the early twentieth century, women scholars in the social sciences turned to a number of sources in their quest for research funding. Individual and family donor support for research was highly valued in certain kinds of institutions into the 1920s, including colleges and universities in the early stages of redefining themselves as research institutions in the social as well as other sciences. This was largely because few other external sources of funding existed for these research interests. Such support continued to be important into the 1930s and 1940s for maintaining research programs that otherwise would not have received any outside funding. However, in the 1920s philanthropic foundation support had surpassed this earlier kind of funding both in quantity and in its ability to accord status to the receiving institutions. The experience of the Industrial Research Department at the University of Pennsylvania illustrates what large allocations of research funds made possible for scholars in institutions fortunate enough to benefit from them. For women social science scholars who did not have access to these funds, the best means of gaining financing and controlling their own projects was by securing the first and second kinds of support: fellowships for investigator-initiated projects, and grants from private individuals to support programs and research projects in the institutions in which women academics worked—typically four-year colleges, often women's. By the 1930s, both of these kinds of financing offered women far less prestige and recognition in the social sciences than foundation support granted to a named principal investigator, but both were critical to keeping women in the academic social sciences and funding their work.

When women were the beneficiaries of foundation support in programs such as Penn's, they were not usually able to translate that support into career advancement strategies at the pace and rate of men. They rarely were granted principal investigator status or appointed to the research universities most prominent in social science research. Emily Huntington at Berkeley, Anne Bezanson at Penn, and a few others were exceptions. Given this lack of professional visibility and recognition, the extent to which women were able to carry on their research programs is truly remarkable. The support these scholars received was largely due to their sharing research and reform goals with wealthy donors, carefully cultivating these donors and aligning with them in commitment to women as researchers and the kinds of knowledge needed for municipal and state social reform, and determinedly pursuing continued and new funding.

This resourcefulness and persistence were set against a variety of difficult limitations throughout the first half of the twentieth century, including institutional discrimination—which relegated most women academic Ph.D.s in social sciences to teaching colleges—as well as a system of philanthropic financing that favored male rather than female leadership in social science research. The constraints women researchers faced make all the more clear how important creative financing was for women social scientists in the 1920s and 1930s, the decades when increasing numbers of women were completing Ph.D.s and entering academe. Situated in the women's colleges, these scholars not only lacked access to foundation support for research in the 1920s, but were also not as well protected as their male research university colleagues from the budgetary reductions higher education institutions suffered in the 1930s.[29]

The women I have discussed here brought to their work a commitment to understanding the impact of economic change on social organizations and relations at the state and community levels, combining the most recent methodologies (in statistical and ethnographic research) with the questions they identified as critical. Peixotto's work in social economics at Berkeley yielded new theoretical perspectives, while Lumpkin and the Council of Industrial Studies at Smith—and, to some extent, Bezanson and the Penn Industrial Relations Department—enlarged understanding of the regional effects of historical economic changes. In examining what Bezanson accomplished with large-scale funding from the LSRM, one cannot help but wonder what kind of impact Peixotto's and Lumpkin's research might have had on the social science disciplines and public policy had they had access to similar support.

Much of the work of these research enterprises was in high demand by federal and local agencies, and the demand increased throughout the Depression. As Nancy Folbre suggests, women economists (and social economists, particularly) braved the masculine world of academic economics—the basic premises of which were designed to protect patriarchal interests in economic theory and research—in order to promote research questions that granted women an active place in the productive economy. Folbre focuses on Edith Abbott's and Sophonisba Breckinridge's struggles to frame the discipline and influence public policy, but her conclusions also apply to the cases of Peixotto and Lumpkin. Peixotto's efforts to explore how household earnings and consumption functioned in relation to each other, and Lumpkin's efforts to understand local regional economic transformation, were unlike most kinds of research financed by large funding organizations in that period. Nevertheless, these studies produced important findings for policy makers and others seeking to offer municipal, state, or philanthropic intervention in an unstable economic period. Their studies continue to be important to anthropologists seeking to understand the sociohistorical transformations that shaped the physical and cultural contexts of the populations they investigate. Further, the value of those studies today is inestimable for economists who, rather than relying primarily on rational choice models to explain economic activity, are seeking to understand how the discipline developed and to place economic activity in broader and more complex social contexts.[30]

NOTES

My thanks to Peter Best, Peter D. Hall, Andrea Walton, and the contributors to this volume for their critical readings of different versions of this chapter, and to the Spencer Foundation for its generous support of the larger project of which this is a part.

1. Margaret Rossiter argues that "creative" philanthropy was also "coercive," used to pressure institutions to accept women graduate students and appoint women faculty (*Women Scientists in America: Struggles and Strategies to 1940* [Baltimore, Md.: Johns Hopkins University Press, 1982], 39). For information about Parsons, see Louis A. Hieb, "Elsie Clews Parsons in the Southwest," in *Hidden Scholars: Women Anthropol-*

ogists and the Native American Southwest, ed. Nancy J. Parezo (Albuquerque: University of New Mexico Press, 1993), 63–75; Desley Deacon, *Elsie Clews Parsons: Inventing Modern Life* (Chicago: University of Chicago Press, 1997), chapter 10; and Andrea Walton, "Rethinking Boundaries: The History of Women, Philanthropy, and Higher Education," *History of Higher Education Annual* 20 (2000): 29–57. Kamala Visweswaran analyzes the financing women anthropologists obtained in " 'Wild West' Anthropology and the Disciplining of Gender," in *Gender and American Social Science: The Formative Years,* ed. Helene Silverberg (Princeton, N.J.: Princeton University Press, 1998), 86–123.

2. Helen Lefkowitz Horowitz, *The Power and Passion of M. Carey Thomas* (New York: Knopf, 1994), chapter 12; and David C. Hammack, "A Center of Intelligence for the Charity Organization Movement: The Foundation's Early Years," in *Social Science in the Making: Essays on the Russell Sage Foundation, 1907–1972,* ed. David C. Hammack and Stanton Wheeler (New York: Russell Sage Foundation, 1994), 1–33.

3. Susan Levine, *Degrees of Equality: The American Association of University Women and the Challenge of Twentieth-Century Feminism* (Philadelphia: Temple University Press, 1995), 8–9. On the dominant lines of research in social sciences before 1920, see Dorothy Ross, *The Origins of American Social Science* (Cambridge: Cambridge University Press, 1991).

4. Thanks to Andrea Walton for helping me to clarify this point. On funding for women in the sciences, see Martin Bulmer and Joan Bulmer, "Philanthropy and Social Science in the 1920s: Beardsley Ruml and the Laura Spelman Rockefeller Memorial, 1922–29," *Minerva* 19 (autumn 1981): 347–407; Lawrence K. Frank, "The Status of Social Science in the United States," 1923, file 679, box 63, series III, Laura Spelman Rockefeller Memorial Archives, Rockefeller Archive Center, Sleepy Hollow, N.Y. (hereafter cited as LSRMA); and Rossiter, *Women Scientists in America: Struggles and Strategies,* 39, 46–50, 205–206.

5. Rosalind Rosenberg, *Beyond Separate Spheres: Intellectual Roots of Modern Feminism* (New Haven, Conn.: Yale University Press, 1982); Ellen Fitzpatrick, *Endless Crusade: Women Social Scientists and Progressive Reform* (New York: Oxford University Press, 1990); and Robyn Muncy, *Creating a Female Dominion in American Reform, 1890–1935* (New York: Oxford University Press, 1991). On the importance of female networks in securing support, see Lynn D. Gordon, *Gender and Higher Education in the Progressive Era* (New Haven, Conn.: Yale University Press, 1990).

6. See Edward H. Clarke, *Sex in Education; or, A Fair Chance for the Girls* (Boston: James R. Osgood, 1873); and Sue Zschoche, "Dr. Clarke Revisited: Science, True Womanhood, and Female Collegiate Education," *History of Education Quarterly* 29 (winter 1989): 545–69.

7. Christine Ladd Franklin, quoted in Ruth W. Tryon, *Investment in Creative Scholarship: A History of the Fellowship Program of the American Association of University Women, 1890–1956* (Washington, D.C.: American Association of University Women, 1957), 5.

8. Marion Talbot and Lois Kimball Mathews Rosenberry, *The History of the American Association of University Women, 1881–1931* (Boston: Houghton Mifflin, 1931); Levine, *Degrees of Equality;* and Rossiter, *Women Scientists in America: Struggles and Strategies to 1940,* 39–40. For the period after 1940, see Linda Eisenmann's chapter on continuing education for women, this volume; and Margaret W. Rossiter,

Women Scientists in America: Before Affirmative Action, 1940–1972 (Baltimore, Md.: Johns Hopkins University Press, 1995).

9. Guy Alchon, *The Invisible Hand of Planning: Capitalism, Social Science, and the State in the 1920s* (Princeton, N.J.: Princeton University Press, 1985), 5. On fellowship allotment, see Rossiter, *Women Scientists in America: Struggles and Strategies to 1940*, chapter 10; and Rosenberg, *Beyond Separate Spheres*. See also Robert H. Bremner, *American Philanthropy*, 2nd ed. (Chicago: University of Chicago Press, 1988), chapters 7 and 8; and Theresa Richardson and Donald Fisher, "Introduction: The Social Sciences and Their Philanthropic Mentors," in *The Development of the Social Sciences in the United States and Canada: The Role of Philanthropy*, ed. Theresa Richardson and Donald Fisher (Stamford, Conn.: Ablex, 1999), 3–21.

10. John M. Glenn, Lilian Brandt, and F. Emerson Andrews, *Russell Sage Foundation, 1907–1946*, vol. 2 (New York: Russell Sage Foundation, 1947), 678. Leah Feder, a doctoral student in social economy at Bryn Mawr College, received funds for her thesis research and writing ("Unemployment Relief in Periods of Depression"): see student files, School of Social Work and Social Research Papers, Bryn Mawr College Archives, Canaday Library, Bryn Mawr College, Bryn Mawr, Pa. (hereafter cited as BMCA); and Mary Ann Dzuback, "Women and Social Research at Bryn Mawr College, 1915–1940," *History of Education Quarterly* 33 (winter 1993): 579–608. On the goals of the Russell Sage Foundation, see Hammack, "Center of Intelligence"; Guy Alchon, "The 'Self-Applauding Sincerity' of Overreaching Theory, Biography as Ethical Practice, and the Case of Mary van Kleeck," in *Gender and American Social Science*, ed. Silverberg, 293–325; and Sarah Henry Lederman, this volume. On Sage, see Ruth Crocker, "Margaret Olivia Slocum, 'Mrs. Russell Sage': Private Griefs and Public Duties," in *Ordinary Women, Extraordinary Lives: Women in American History*, ed. Kriste Lindenmeyer (Wilmington, Del.: Scholarly Resources, 2000), 147–59; and Crocker's chapter about Sage's involvement in philanthropy for higher education, this volume.

11. Most economics study was conducted in economics and sociology departments or political economy departments that included political science programs; see Mary E. Cookingham, "Social Economists and Reform: Berkeley, 1906–1961," *History of Political Economy* 19 (1987): 47–65. The other two programs in the Berkeley department were in business economics and labor economics. On Peixotto: Jessica B. Peixotto Papers, Bancroft Library, University of California, Berkeley (hereafter cited as BL); Henry Rand Hatfield, "Jessica Blanche Peixotto," in *Essays in Social Economics in Honor of Jessica Blanche Peixotto* (Berkeley: University of California Press, 1935), 5–14; Clarke A. Chambers, "Peixotto, Jessica Blanche," in *Notable American Women, 1607–1950*, vol. 3, ed. Edward T. James, Janet Wilson James, and Paul S. Boyer (Cambridge, Mass.: Belknap Press of Harvard University Press, 1971), 42–43; "Jessica Blanche Peixotto," *In Memoriam* (Berkeley: University of California Press, 1941), 24–25; Mary Ann Dzuback, "Peixotto, Jessica Blanche," in *American National Biography*, ed. John Garraty (New York: Oxford University Press, 1999); and Clark Kerr, interview with author, 14 May 1996, Berkeley, Calif.

12. William R. Roberts, archivist at the University of California, Berkeley, was most helpful in searching for more information on the Hellers. See "Rites Today for Clara H. Heller," *San Francisco Chronicle*, 18 August 1959, 41; and "Heller Millions to 3 Grandchildren," *San Francisco Chronicle*, 25 August 1959, 36.

13. For the reports of the committee, see Heller Committee, University of California Presidents' Papers (CU-5 series 2) for Campbell and Sproul, University Archives, BL. (University of California Presidents' Papers are hereafter cited as PP, with the then president's name and the year of the item in question.) For the committee under Emily Huntington, see her "The Heller Committee for Research in Social Economy," 20 January 1943, PP (Sproul), 1943: 471. Heller's annual support varied over three decades, beginning at $4,000 per year throughout the 1920s, decreasing to $2,400 per year in the 1930s, when the university began allocating research funds to the committee, and increasing to $3,600 in 1935 and to $4,800 in 1940.

14. Jessica B. Peixotto, "Annual Report on the Heller Fund for Research in Social Economics" (hereafter cited as HC Annual Report), 1, PP (Campbell), 1924: 1388.

15. Peixotto, HC Annual Report (1929–30), 4, PP (Sproul), 1930: 248. See also Huntington, "Heller Committee," 471. Some of this work was completed in cooperation with the university's Department of Home Economics; see Maresi Nerad, *The Academic Kitchen: A Social History of Gender Stratification at the University of California, Berkeley* (Albany: State University of New York Press, 1999).

16. Peixotto to Julius Wangenheim, 7 June 1933, PP (Sproul), 1933: 471; and Peixotto, HC Annual Report (1935), 3, PP (Sproul), 1936: 471.

17. Jessica B. Peixotto, *Getting and Spending at the Professional Standard of Living: A Study of the Costs of Living an Academic Life* (New York: Macmillan, 1927), vii, viii.

18. Emily H. Huntington, *Unemployment Relief and the Unemployed, 1929–1934* (Berkeley: University of California Press, 1939), 1, 3.

19. A. O. Leuschner to Dean C. B. Lipman, 29 October 1930, PP (Sproul), Economics/Heller Committee: 1930: 248. On Peixotto's contributions to economics, see Joseph Dorfman, *The Economic Mind in American Civilization*, vol. 5 (New York: Viking, 1959), 570–78; and Elizabeth Hoyt, *The Consumption of Wealth* (New York: Macmillan, 1928). See also Nancy Folbre, "The 'Sphere of Women' in Early Twentieth-Century Economics," in *Gender and American Social Science*, ed. Silverberg, 35–60.

20. Social Science Research Council, "Summary of the Conference on Research in the Social Sciences in Colleges," 12 and 13 December 1931, 8–10, Marion Edwards Park Office Files, 1922–1942, box 28, BMCA.

21. On Douglas, see Faculty Biographical Files, Dorothy Douglas, Smith College Archives, Northampton, Mass. (hereafter cited as FBF). On Douglas and Lumpkin, see Daniel Horowitz, *Betty Friedan and the Making of the Feminine Mystique: The American Left, the Cold War, and Modern Feminism* (Amherst: University of Massachusetts Press, 1998), chapter 3.

22. "Suggested plan," n.d. (circa 1932), box 38, Office of the President, William A. Neilson Papers, Council on Industrial Studies Files, box 38, SCA (hereafter cited as WAN). On Lumpkin, see FBF, Katherine Du Pre Lumpkin; Jacquelyn Dowd Hall, " 'To Widen the Reach of Our Love': Autobiography, History, and Desire," *Feminist Studies* 26 (spring 2000): 230–47; idem, "Open Secrets: Memory, Imagination, and the Refashioning of Southern Identity," *American Quarterly* 50 (March 1998), 109–24; and Katharine Du Pre Lumpkin, *The Making of a Southerner* (New York: Knopf, 1946).

23. Katherine D. Lumpkin, "Report of the Director of Research of the Council

of Industrial Studies," *Bulletin of Smith College, President's Report Issue*, 1933, 49–57, SCA.

24. Esther Lowenthal, "Foreword," in Katharine Du Pre Lumpkin, *Shutdowns in the Connecticut Valley: A Study of Worker Displacement in the Small Industrial Community, Smith College Studies in History*, vol. 19, April–July 1934, 141, SCA. See also correspondence on Council of Industrial Studies, boxes 398 and 38, WAN.

25. Katherine D. Lumpkin, "Brief Resume of the Work of the Council of Industrial Studies, 1932–1938," box 398, WAN; and idem, "Report(s) of the Director of Research of the Council of Industrial Studies," in *Bulletin of Smith College, President's Report Issue*, 1933–1938, SCA. See also vols. 19, 21, 23, 24, 26, 28, 33, 37, *Smith College Studies in History*.

26. The Carnegie Corporation shifted support from research institutes to popular education in the middle to late 1920s (Ellen Condliffe Lagemann, *The Politics of Knowledge: The Carnegie Corporation, Philanthropy, and Public Policy* [Middletown, Conn.: Wesleyan University Press, 1989]). On the LSRM grant: Josiah H. Penniman to Beardsley Ruml, 13 June 1927, and other materials in file 792, box 75, series III, LSRMA. The university's obligation increased from $10,000 (1928–29) to $40,000 (1931–32); the LSRM's decreased from $50,000 (1927–28) to $10,000 (1931–32).

27. *University of Pennsylvania: The Wharton School of Finance and Commerce, Announcement, 1922–1923* (Philadelphia: University Press of Pennsylvania, 1921), 66; and *Announcement, 1934–1935*, 26, University Archives, University of Pennsylvania, Philadelphia, Pa. According to Steven A. Sass, LSRM funding increased the budget to over $110,000 (*The Pragmatic Imagination: A History of the Wharton School, 1881–1981* [Philadelphia: University of Pennsylvania Press, 1982], 208).

28. The Rockefeller Foundation appropriated $50,000 over two years in 1932 and $75,000 over five years in 1935 ("Minutes," 9 May 1932 and 17 April 1935, box 5, file 78); in 1939, the Foundation gave $11,000 for two specific projects (Norma S. Thompson to Alfred H. Williams, 25 October 1939, box 8, file 112); and in 1940, $105,000 for three years ("Minutes," 17 May 1940, box 5, file 78); all in Rockefeller Foundation Archives, record group 1.1, series 241, Rockefeller Archive Center.

29. See, for example, Frederick Rudolph, *The American College and University: A History* (1962; reprint, with an introduction and bibliography by John R. Thelin, Athens: University of Georgia Press, 1990), 465–69; and Rossiter, *Women Scientists in America: Struggles and Strategies*, chapters 6 and 7.

30. Folbre, " 'Sphere of Women,' " 54; Alan Swedlund, University of Massachusetts, conversation with author, August 1993; and David Hogan, formerly of the University of Pennsylvania, conversation with author, July 1993. See also, for example, Marianne A. Ferber and Julie A. Nelson, eds., *Beyond Economic Man: Feminist Theory and Economics* (Chicago: University of Chicago Press, 1993); and Helene Silverberg, "Introduction," in *Gender and American Social Science*, ed. Silverberg, 3–32.

5. Considering Her Influence: Sydnor H. Walker and Rockefeller Support for Social Work, Social Scientists, and Universities in the South

Amy E. Wells

Through the largesse of the Laura Spelman Rockefeller Memorial, higher education experienced a unique era of institution-building during the 1920s. Established in 1922 by John D. Rockefeller, Sr., to honor his wife and "support certain welfare activities in which she was interested," the Laura Spelman Rockefeller Memorial (LSRM) later assumed a distinct objective: to advance the social sciences. The Memorial's overall program dispersed an unprecedented twenty million dollars, usually in the form of fluid research funds to social science research institutes in universities. Recipient institutions in the United States included Harvard, Columbia, Yale, Stanford, and the Universities of Chicago, North Carolina, Virginia, and Texas; the London School of Economics and universities in Stockholm and Berlin also received funding. While the Memorial existed for only seven years before being absorbed by the Rockefeller Foundation (RF), it contributed to "notable progress" in the field. In particular, it helped persuade university administrators and trustees that social science research deserved facilities, time, and money and that the "non-academic world" was hungry for the "results of scholarly investigation."[1]

Foundation historians and scholars have previously considered the significance of the LSRM,[2] especially how the Memorial's plans related to the ambitious leadership of its director, Beardsley Ruml.[3] However, very little is known about those who worked with him. Sydnor Harbison Walker was one of his associates. An LSRM research associate who later became an acting director of the division of social sciences in the Rockefeller Foundation, she was one of few female program officers in a major foundation during the late 1920s and 1930s. This study assembles the first biography of Walker and then considers her influence upon southern higher education through her relationships with grant recipients and through her funding decisions.

Exploring a biographical portrait of Sydnor Walker as a triple lens for discovery in the three related areas of women's history, the history of philanthropy, and higher education history, this chapter draws heavily from the research and analysis of a larger study of southern scholars and emerging universities in the South from 1920 to 1950.[4] However, source materials from the institutions where Walker worked, as well as data gleaned from her own scholarship—her master's thesis, dissertation, books, and articles—also inform this chapter. No autobiographical or oral history artifacts are available about Walker. Admittedly, then, this analysis errs on the side of "officializing" her by drawing on work-related correspondence and the few personnel records available, records that do not capture the many interpersonal interactions that occur beyond the official gaze.

Who was Sydnor Walker? And what was her influence upon southern social scientists and southern universities? Margaret Rossiter's scholarship about women scientists through the 1940s provides a valuable framework for understanding Sydnor Walker as a talented intellectual who used foundation employment to earn a living and to advance her views of research and the social sciences.[5] As she allocated funds first from the LSRM and later from the Rockefeller Foundation, Walker demanded, by requiring matching grants, that southern universities increase their financial support for research, and she often decided the level of support that southern scholars and universities could seek from the foundation—or whether they should seek it at all. Thus, Walker exerted tremendous influence upon southern social scientists and universities just as they were taking on more complex university missions.

In addition to demonstrating the type of influence that foundation personnel had on developments within higher education, a study of Walker's life and work can contribute new and complicated detail to our somewhat limited historical understanding of daily work in foundation philanthropy, especially for women. To southern social scientists, Walker was more than a gatekeeper. In her, they gained a confidante, a caretaker of regional plans for university recognition, and an insider willing to educate them in the intricacies of foundation giving.

In return, southern social scientists validated Walker's intellect and expertise by seeking her counsel and publishing her research. In this way, Walker's relationships with grant recipients and applicants evidenced mutual warmth and respect.

That said, Walker also exercised prudence in her decision making. In the 1930s, she decidedly curtailed funding to southern social scientists and universities that she (and Rockefeller funding) had nurtured in the prior decade.[6] Even though Walker's disposition evinced this curious mix of "heart and head" suited to foundation philanthropy and despite the fact that she advanced within the Rockefeller organization, the balance of her research and responsibility fell within prescribed gender roles and expectations. Whether Walker noticed these limitations or felt frustrated by them remains uncertain. Perhaps Sydnor Walker never felt the weight of her pioneer status even as she earned an unrecognized place within the foundation's history.

WHO WAS SYDNOR WALKER? HER EDUCATION AND WORK WITH THE LSRM

While the Laura Spelman Rockefeller Memorial appointed Beardsley Ruml as its director when Ruml was twenty-six, Sydnor Walker took her position with the Memorial in June 1924 at age thirty-three. Previously employed by the American Friends Service Committee on European Relief (1921–1923), Walker might appear to have had the kind of resume she later described as customary for social work in her time—i.e., a bachelor's degree from a women's college (Vassar, 1912) and a desire to "get into the midst of things."[7] Upon closer inspection, however, Walker's credentials and resume include academic and business experience less common for women involved in social welfare work. After graduating from Vassar with honors, Walker briefly taught English and Latin in secondary schools in Louisville, Dallas, and Los Angeles.[8] While in Los Angeles, she completed a master's degree in economics at the University of Southern California; her thesis traced the origins of the general strike to European "Syndicalism" and assessed its "practicability" for improving American labor conditions.[9]

In 1917, Walker returned to Vassar as an instructor in economics. One of her colleagues, historian Mabel Newcomer, eulogized Walker by noting her popularity in the hall where she lived with students. Newcomer asserted that Walker's "quick wit and gaiety" extended to her teaching, along with her "clarity of thought and expression." However, Newcomer warned that Walker could also be "sharply critical of the careless and dilatory."[10]

This aspect of Walker's personality possibly explains why, after just two years of teaching at her alma mater, Walker sought "practical experience." She turned to personnel work, first for the Scott Company and then for Strawbridge & Clothier in Philadelphia. Walker's short tenure at the Scott Company, a "pioneering firm of industrial relations," resulted in a lifelong relationship with Beardsley Ruml, who later recruited her to the LSRM and served as a co-executor of her estate upon her death.[11]

Walker's next move took her overseas for one year of relief work in Vienna and another in Russia as part of the American Friends Service Committee. This introduction to private philanthropy made a lasting impression upon Walker and greatly influenced her future analysis of social "case work" methods. About her responsibility for overseeing the feeding and clothing of thousands each week, Walker reported, "Our work is done on an individual basis, which we think to be the soundest, not only from a social point of view, but because we believe that method essential for the creation of a spirit of international good-will."[12] This "practical experience" in personnel and relief work, and the tour abroad, prepared Walker for her next five years' work with the LSRM and for her subsequent fourteen-year term with the Rockefeller Foundation.

Walker's employment with the LSRM in 1924 as a "research associate" of Beardsley Ruml reflects the employment opportunities available to unmarried women scientists in universities, government, and industry of the 1920s and 1930s. Rossiter explains that the ascendancy of the "female research associate" resulted from the coalescence of various "intellectual, technological, financial, and social forces that were transforming science into an increasingly team-oriented enterprise in those very years that women were seeking to enter it." Instead of gaining the professorial appointments given to men with similar academic credentials, women with Ph.D.s were a boon to institutions expanding their research efforts because they willingly filled associate positions, with proportionately lower salaries.[13]

Familiar with Walker from their days together at the Scott Company in Philadelphia, Ruml recruited her to the LSRM in 1924 to assist him in promoting scientific research, standardization, and professionalism in the social sciences. This increased emphasis on "sci-

entific" approaches for solving problems in the fields of sociology, psychology, anthropology, political science, economics, and even history
remained a fundamental or guiding principle of the LSRM plan for
the advancement of the social sciences. Through the Memorial, Ruml
institutionalized a belief that workers in the social fields needed the
concerted and cooperative effort of social scientists to generate "widely
accepted generalizations as to human capacities and motives as to the
behavior of human beings as individuals and in groups."[14] Thus, in his
quest to make the social sciences more "scientific," Ruml also copied
the ascendant model for conducting research in universities by hiring
the unmarried Walker as a "research associate." Walker, like women
scientists who garnered the sponsorship of female-supportive male
professors overseeing research laboratories,[15] gained a valuable sponsor
in Ruml.

Walker earned her Ph.D. in economics from Columbia (1926)
while working for the LSRM, and her dissertation, "Social Work and
the Training of Social Workers," was published by the University of
North Carolina Press in 1928. In many ways, Ruml and other Rockefeller Foundation officers supported Walker's scholarship. For example, in the preface to her study, Walker reveals that Ruml and Edmund
E. Day, the new director of the Rockefeller Foundation Division of
Social Sciences, gave her their "interest and counsel" during its preparation.[16] Walker also used her work time and responsibilities to her
academic advantage. The notes from meetings with grant applicants
and officers of various social welfare agencies and professional organizations clearly provide the content and organization of her study.[17]

However, the support given to Walker by Ruml, Day, and even
the economics department at Columbia fell within the fields and research interests often deemed appropriate for women scientists at the
time.[18] Like those of women scientists in the field of home economics,
Walker's research and job responsibilities safely involved the female-
dominated field of social work. At first glance, the topic of Walker's
dissertation study—social work—might appear to reflect the rich tradition of social service work upheld by many women college graduates,
a tradition illustrated by the stories of other women in this volume.
However, a closer reading of Walker's scholarship belies this assertion.

Walker's thesis on social work displays little passion for the subject,
congruent with the underlying assumption that knowledge is gained
best through objective, nonparticipant observation—the standard of
research the LSRM advocated for the overall improvement of the so-

cial sciences.[19] Like Abraham Flexner's Carnegie-supported study of medical education in the United States and Canada, which he conducted as a layperson and wrote for a general audience,[20] Walker's study employed a research design of site visits to social work schools and attendance at meetings of the National Conferences for Social Work. Comparatively less exhaustive than Flexner's study (because of the smaller number of social work schools) and recipient of much less fanfare, Walker's study and the job responsibilities it reflected appropriately involved the female-dominated field of social welfare work. More important, her conclusion that professional training in social work should be carried out by universities ultimately provided a necessary rationale for declining future grants to applicants who lacked university training.

Like many academics, Walker identified primarily with her discipline. As an economist, she framed her thesis on social work as part of her interest in the field of "private philanthropy."[21] If indeed Walker displays any zeal in her volume on social work, it is in her discussion of the role of private philanthropy in the economy. In this discussion, Walker shows her ideological alignment with Ruml and other Rockefeller philanthropists, who have been characterized by Donald Fisher as "sophisticated conservatives."[22] As such, Walker desired to solve the problems of capitalist systems without fundamentally changing the socioeconomic structure.

Drawing from her master's thesis on American labor, Walker contrasted supporters of social welfare work with organized labor, describing the former as "persons who believe that existing conditions are subject to improvement without radical departure from present institutions and customs" and the latter as comparable to those who demand "action through the machinery of government."[23] Sharing Ruml's "deep and abiding faith in the potential of social science knowledge for putting things right,"[24] Walker believed that there was little wrong with the American economic system that an organized, scientific, comprehensive social science plan could not fix. Offering social welfare as a "corrective for the present somewhat faulty system of distribution of the national income," Walker assigned social workers the task of caring for those unable to support themselves "under a capitalist—and probably under any other—economic system." Walker reasoned that time and the scientific organization of industry would eventually mitigate the need for assistance.[25]

Walker's intellectual understanding of the economic purpose of social welfare went beyond the altruism typically ascribed to lay workers in the field. She parlayed her academic knowledge, backed by Rocke-feller monies and work responsibilities, into "expert" status. In the fall of 1929, she received an invitation to participate in some meetings of President Hoover's Research Committee on Social Trends and con-tributed an impressive chapter on privately supported social work to the resulting publication.[26]

Surveying the field of social work in her day, Walker recognized the trend toward state control of welfare functions formerly handled by private agencies.[27] Because the state tended to be "more conserva-tive and less flexible than private organizations in its methods," Walker expected private philanthropy to take the lead in assisting the state with proper management and "setting standards for tax-supported wel-fare activities."[28] More important, as Walker wrote about this leader-ship role for private philanthropy, she lived it.

As a foundation expert in partnership with other social scientists and the state,[29] Walker adopted the type of approach to or strategy of giving that Marxist critics of philanthropy have generally characterized as the state-foundation alliance for the redistribution of wealth and, in this case, government resources.[30] Assuredly, Walker would have been offended by this assessment of her involvement. However, as an economist, Walker recognized the problem of concentration of cor-porate wealth in private hands and valued private philanthropy and state welfare assistance as vehicles for redress.[31]

Yet within the LSRM and Rockefeller Foundation leadership structure, Walker's expert status came gradually and evolved with her job responsibilities. During her years of work with the LSRM (1924–1929), Walker's responsibilities centered on social science work in uni-versities and social welfare work in larger cities, endeavors often de-scribed as "social technology."[32] Accordingly, she met and corre-sponded daily with social scientists and social workers from all over the country. She also attended the meetings of various academic and professional associations. Walker often visited universities and social welfare agencies to monitor the progress of grant recipients, to identify good work and encourage prospective applicants, and to evaluate and make recommendations about current applicants. The Memorial's principle and policy statements and regular communication with Ruml and other officers guided Walker in her work.

In 1929, the LSRM consolidated with the Rockefeller Foundation, and Walker joined the Foundation as assistant director of the Division of Social Sciences, which was led by Dr. Edmund Day. The diary of notes from Walker's appointments shows that in her early years, she carried on with many of her work responsibilities from the LSRM.[33] However, in the mid-1930s, Rockefeller Foundation officers became disillusioned with the Memorial's tradition of support for institutional research centers and switched instead to funding individual projects in the concentrated areas of international relations, social security, and public administration.[34] Walker was promoted to associate director in 1933 and acting director from 1937 to 1939, and her areas of expertise changed along with the foundation's program to include international relations.[35] This transformation is also depicted in her diaries for the years 1933 through 1940, when the diary concludes.[36]

The analysis that follows is one snapshot of Sydnor Walker's work with Rockefeller-supported philanthropy. By investigating only her relationships with and decisions involving southern social scientists and southern universities, we can draw a speculative portrait of her influence as a foundation program officer. The next section begins with background information on the LSRM regional plan for social science support; the chapter concludes by returning to what is known about Walker's life during her final years at the Rockefeller Foundation and her return to Vassar.

THE REGIONAL PLAN FOR SUPPORT OF THE SOCIAL SCIENCES

In a number of memoranda and policy statements, LSRM officers reasoned that the "best auspices for research is the university" and granted resources to universities primarily for use by academics at their own discretion. Seeing in universities a certain stability, permanence, and opportunity for training future researchers through graduate and undergraduate instruction, the LSRM depended upon scholars to produce research immediately useful to various practitioners in the social field. Imagining collaboration between university researchers and community agencies, the Memorial set its sights on solving problems related to the elderly, children, occupations, leisure, immigration, race, and poverty.[37]

The specifics of the LSRM plan for institutional support of the social sciences first involved funding outstanding institutional centers of research and advanced training at Harvard, Chicago, Columbia, the University of North Carolina, and the Brookings Institution in Washington, D.C.[38] Over time, concerns mounted about the dominance of

Chicago and northeastern universities in Rockefeller-funded social science efforts.[39] To alleviate these concerns, the University of North Carolina's Howard Odum and several others advocated funding social science research in southern universities.

Odum, a promising sociologist and director of UNC's School of Public Welfare, attracted national attention in 1922 by launching the journal *Social Forces*. In fact, Odum originally thought of developing a university institute for social science research.[40] In 1924, North Carolina's Institute for Social Science Research (later to become the Institute for Research in the Social Sciences, or IRSS) opened and was immediately boosted by a three-year grant from the LSRM for $32,500 annually.[41] Hence, Howard Odum became the primary point of contact for Rockefeller-supported social science research in the region. His central position is confirmed by the lore of southern social scientists[42] and the fact that Odum's endorsement of Wilson Gee, professor of rural economics and rural sociology at the University of Virginia, eventually landed funding for Virginia's own institute in February 1926, with a five-year grant of $27,000 annually.[43] Odum's regional role was legitimized further as the IRSS took on the mission of conducting research pertinent to the entire southern region, while in contrast the Virginia institute's scope of study was limited to problems within the state.[44]

Another institute—the University of Texas Bureau of Research in the Social Sciences (BRSS)—was established in 1927, taking shape nearly as the LSRM's work was coming to a close. Implemented to focus on Texas's social problems, the BRSS received a sizeable grant of $250,000 ($50,000 annually) with a sophisticated dollar-for-dollar matching scheme employed in the grant's last three years.[45] LSRM grant documents cited the state's "abundant natural resources," especially its mineral wealth, as first among reasons for selecting Texas. The Memorial believed that the state's wealth would allow it to nourish its university with healthy appropriations when other southern state universities were starving for support.[46]

During the years the LSRM and the RF were supporting institutional grants for research in the social sciences, Sydnor Walker presided over grants to the Universities of North Carolina, Virginia, and Texas totaling $1,165,500—the sums of $518,000, $242,500, and $405,000 were allotted to each respectively. Adjusted for inflation, today these grants would be valued at nearly $14 million. Remember, these funds were granted to boost research efforts and were not intended for social science faculty salaries, equipment, or facilities. In most cases, follow-up grants required matching contributions for research either from the university's general budget or from legislative appropriations. (The exceptions to this pattern prove interesting and illustrate Walker's influence as a foundation program officer.) Nevertheless, the Rockefeller monies, combined with university and state contributions at North Carolina, Virginia, and Texas, brought momentum to these state universities precisely when they needed it to bolster their research efforts.[47]

MATTERS OF THE HEART: A GLIMPSE INTO WALKER'S RELATIONSHIPS WITH GRANT RECIPIENTS

In her extensive survey of the field of social work, Walker described numerous ways that social welfare programs were implemented, such as the "community-chest" approach, in which cities centrally collected donations or tax contributions and dispersed them to needy organizations. Walker's in-depth discussions of various options for benevolence reveal some of her expectations for beneficial relationships between donors and recipients. The community-chest movement was spurred by a desire to make community agencies more businesslike and efficient, but she criticized it, lamenting a possible loss of interaction between donors and recipients. Proclaiming interaction as a necessary "spark" for making "charity more than a duty," Walker warned, "If the economy, the efficiency, and the thoroughness of the community-chest method are stressed at the expense of the human interest side of welfare work, support may in time come grudgingly, or only from a desire for social approbation and advancement."[48]

Walker obviously heeded her own words in foundation work, because she gave much time and energy to her relationship with Howard Odum. Apparently, Walker and Odum thought similarly about society, the nature of individuals, social work, and the social sciences. For example, Odum read and edited Walker's dissertation, eventually publishing it as a monograph in UNC's Social Studies Series. Then he required the book as a text in his teaching. Odum also sponsored Walker's participation in the President's Research Committee on Social Trends, and her chapter precedes his in the resulting publication. The two corresponded regularly—although admittedly Odum carried the lion's share of this burden, sometimes sending two or three letters a day to Walker and other officers.[49]

At first, Odum's enthusiasm is puzzling. Some may argue that he finessed Walker in order to gain more Rockefeller funding. My reading of Odum's papers in the UNC library suggests that Odum's relationship with Walker was central to him and his work.[50] He often sought her counsel on substantive matters. In contrast, a close reading of Walker's diaries and documents at the Rockefeller Archive Center show that to Walker, Odum was one of many grant recipients, although she astutely comprehended his strengths and weaknesses, always maintaining respect and appreciation for the sociologist. I contend that this difference in perspective demonstrates how effectively Walker maintained her "spark" for building and maintaining caring donor relationships.

Sometimes Walker simply listened as Odum shared frustrations. For example, in one 1929 letter Odum disparaged those who blamed southern social scientists and southern universities for not solving the region's various social problems. Odum wrote,

> I am reminded much of certain added responsibilities which southern social science folk have in the smaller universities. I think no one would ordinarily hold the professors of the University of Chicago responsible for Big Bill's fundamentalism or the gang warfare of Chicago, or the Columbia professors for strikes, East Sides and difficulties in New York. And yet, as you probably know, our constant stream of inquiry implies that the University of North Carolina professors *could not* be very progressive or else they wouldn't *let* so many things happen at Gastonia and elsewhere.

Indicating that he expected no reply from Walker, Odum closed his letter by asking his confidante to "jot down" his frustrations "simply as a little conversation across the table."[51]

At other times, Walker nurtured Odum's optimism. For example, in 1933, upon his return from a Georgia Press Institute and Emory University Institute of Citizenship, Odum confided to her about his southern colleagues, "It is almost pathetic to see the eager enthusiasm of our southern institutions to go forward."[52] Later that year, Odum noted the often "paradoxical and contradictory nature" of his statements, when he confessed to Walker that "the outlook here and in other parts of the South is very promising and it is very gloomy. We have here an admirable set-up, and we are on the brink."[53]

Yet on other occasions Walker challenged Odum, giving the full weight of her professional opinion. Noting to Odum that meetings had been taking place in New Orleans about a new social work department at Louisiana State University, Walker told him that she was skeptical of the plan. She scrutinized his endorsement:

> I cannot say that I share your confidence that a School or Department of Public Welfare Administration can be developed at Louisiana State University without treading on the toes of the Tulane school. It is difficult to imagine their going far with their plans without developing an outlet in New Orleans for field work. In view of the past record of Louisiana State University I am inclined to think that they would not be respectful of Tulane's prerogatives. Perhaps you can convince me otherwise.[54]

Through their correspondence Walker and Odum created a mutually beneficial relationship. Walker was confidante and steward of Odum's dream to promote research excellence in the social sciences in the South, while Odum affirmed her intellect and provided information about southern universities.

Even as Walker fostered Odum's vision of research excellence, she was aware of his negative habits and the University of North Carolina's limited resources. Although admitting he was diligent in his work, Walker assessed the sociologist's efforts as "scattered," sometimes complaining that he spread himself "too thin."[55] Often Odum's dreams were bigger than the university's ability to support them with outright appropriations—a key consideration for future grants from the LSRM and the RF. Thus, Walker had the task of reining in the enthusiastic academic when he sought additional funding.

At least twice Odum put himself in a precarious position with Walker. In 1929, for example, Odum traveled to New York to request funding for his School of Public Welfare, which needed additional resources to attract an outstanding scholar as its director. Believing the university had made a commitment for salary and the Rockefeller Foundation a commitment for program funding, Odum witnessed his scheme evaporate as foundation officers informed him that the university had made "no such commitment!" Walker and the other program officers sternly chastised Odum for "trying to 'cover the earth' " instead of focusing on a few initiatives.[56] Follow-up correspondence from Walker confirmed her position:

> I hardly know what to say which should be characterized as advice. I, too, should dislike seeing the School of Public Welfare lapse but it is a hard alternative for you to give up a number of things in

which you are interested. I feel one thing clearly, and that is that you should not be driven to sacrifice everything else for the school. If, as you say, writing is the thing now, you shouldn't abandon it. Don't forget that south of the Mason and Dixon line there is an equivalent of the Puritan conscience which is not necessarily an enlightened guide. . . . I am sorry you are in such a quandary but sympathy is all I have to offer.[57]

Later that summer at a social science conference, Odum faced further jeopardy when he "overstated things a bit" regarding the university's support for the IRSS. At the conference, Odum claimed that the university would give $10,000 to the IRSS—when $4,500 was all it had to contribute.[58]

Today, Walker's chastisement and correspondence might be regarded as "tough love." Colloquialism aside, I suspect that practitioners of foundation philanthropy might confirm that strong donor relationships require reasonable measures of challenge and support. Yet the continued Rockefeller funding for the North Carolina IRSS, despite the university's persistent failure to contribute matching funds for research, suggests that Walker's strong relationship with Odum advantaged the institution in her funding decisions. Setting aside Walker's relationships or "matters of the heart," I now turn my discussion to some of her funding decisions.

MATTERS OF THE HEAD: A GLIMPSE INTO WALKER'S FUNDING DECISIONS

Walker critiqued the community-chest movement in social welfare for sometimes sacrificing the quality of donor relationships in the drive to make community agencies more efficient.[59] Clearly, Walker understood the importance of establishing and maintaining strong relationships with grant recipients. However, her push to make programs sustainable by requiring matching research grants from universities sometimes sacrificed program effectiveness to program efficiency and fiscal strength. A comparison of North Carolina's IRSS and Texas's BRSS, which received nearly equal amounts of Rockefeller funding, illustrates this point.

RF program evaluation documents penned by Walker in 1932 confirm that although the Texas BRSS began with an appropriate plan of action in 1927, the social science faculty soon strayed from its focus during the Bureau's early years because of a change in university administration. Lacking organization and purpose, for a few years BRSS faculty conducted research with little concern over its relevance to the social sciences. Walker's project notes further verify that instead of functioning as intended—as an interdisciplinary, cohesive institute overseeing individual research projects—the institute at one point stooped so far as to merely distribute monies pro rata among departments, including Home Economics and Education.[60]

By 1929, Walker reported, the situation had improved under the leadership of a new university president and because of the appointment of sociology professor Warner Gettys as the new BRSS director.[61] However, her optimism overlooked significant deficiencies. For example, the Bureau often carried over large balances from the previous year, a sure sign that it had more money than it could use.[62] Also, in the years 1933 through 1940, it tallied only twenty-one studies. While a few studies from this period merit attention, e.g., "The Economic and Social Condition of the Mexican in Texas," "The Administration of Justice in Texas with Special Reference to Factors of Race, Class, and Sex," and "United States–Mexican Boundary Problems with Special Reference to the Distribution of Water," the Bureau failed to deliver on its potential to solve problems related to the "relative sparsity of population, vast distances, and the complexity of racial adjustments among white, Mexican, and negro populations." Unfortunately, Walker's decisions regarding Texas leave the impression that the Bureau received increased funding simply because the university successfully matched the Rockefeller grants.[63]

The case of the University of North Carolina and its IRSS stands in stark contrast to that of Texas. Where Texas's state government and university provided generously for social science research, the Depression hit North Carolina particularly hard, eliminating a sizeable portion of the university's appropriations for 1929 and 1930.[64] Under these circumstances research became an unaffordable luxury rather than a priority. As a result, Odum's ambitious plans and requests for Rockefeller grants in 1927 and 1931 were curtailed significantly, because the University could contribute only limited amounts to the Institute for Rockefeller monies to match.[65]

Despite depleted coffers, however, North Carolina's record of achievement is striking. By the end of the IRSS's first decade (1934), the Institute had published 162 research report manuscripts and volumes.[66] Included among these studies was some of the most substantive research in race and race relations that can be attributed to Rockefeller-supported institutes in the era.[67] Also by 1934, the UNC

Department of Sociology was one of only two programs in the South cited for eminence by the American Council on Education's Committee on Graduate Instruction.[68]

Yet North Carolina's success in sociology also frustrated Sydnor Walker and Edmund Day, who were displeased with the "make-up of the Institute," finding "sociologists too numerous and the sociological approach too prevalent."[69] Odum felt Walker's dissatisfaction and expressed his anxiety repeatedly in their meetings and through his correspondence.[70] Walker's decision to withhold funding from North Carolina because she did not believe it could match the grants constrained the Institute and diminished its achievements, illustrating that when there is an abundance of academic talent, there is really never enough money.

In sum, Walker's funding decisions regarding Texas and North Carolina yield an interesting finding related to program permanence and matching grants—the strategy vigorously employed by the LSRM to prevent the Memorial from becoming the primary supporter of any project it did not control.[71] Not long after the Rockefeller Foundation redirected support from university centers to individual projects, the Texas BRSS folded. However, the North Carolina IRSS flourished, later winning "the first National Science Foundation science development grant awarded in the social sciences."[72]

Of course, in presenting this analysis of Sydnor Walker's funding decisions, the danger remains that some may attribute her actions to gender without considering the demands of her role. The truth is that the decisions of few individual program officers have undergone equal scrutiny. This analysis benefits from time, a luxury not afforded to Walker when she considered grant applications. Should she be faulted for her short-sightedness or for funding inadequate research? No. Perhaps a rigid idealist, Walker was not a bystander. Her decisions had consequence for the social sciences in the South and southern universities.[73] Only time and further research can measure the extent of her influence.

WHO WAS SYDNOR WALKER? RETIREMENT FROM THE ROCKEFELLER FOUNDATION AND RETURN TO VASSAR

In November of 1930, the Rockefeller-funded General Education Board reconsidered its interest in colleges for women. GEB officers determined that "Miss Walker of the Rockefeller Foundation might visit some of the more important colleges for women" to assist with their project.[74] Essentially, this early request from GEB officers presaged Walker's candidacy for "the presidency of a prominent college for women."[75] Her status as a presidential prospect was heightened at the end of her term as acting director of the RF's Division of Social Sciences (1939), when the Vassar faculty voted her a member of their board of trustees. But Walker's extensive leadership experiences were not to culminate in a presidential appointment. In October 1941, Walker suffered a spinal infection and the beginning of a traumatic, paralytic illness.[76]

Walker's friends later asserted that she "rejected the idea of permanent immobility," but they claimed that the ordeal of surgeries, "mistaken diagnoses," and clinical rehabilitation eventually signaled to Walker that she would not fully recover.[77] When she resumed her public intellectual life in 1945 by editing a volume on the atomic age for the Woodrow Wilson Foundation,[78] her friends were pleased. And three years later, when Walker's work life recommenced with her appointment as the assistant to Vassar's president, Sarah Blanding, one friend called the opportunity "God-given."[79] Of course, the dilemma for the researcher is that Walker's own reflections about her illness and return to work are absent from the personnel records and press releases available. Very little can be discerned about Walker's work life after her return to Vassar. It is known that she served as secretary to the Mellon Committee and chair of the Lectures Committee and the Committee on the Library.[80] On occasion, she represented the president and the board to the press.[81] She held her position for nine years, retiring in 1957.[82]

Born to Walter and Mary Sydnor Perkins Walker in Louisville, Kentucky, on 26 September 1891,[83] Sydnor Walker mentioned home infrequently in her correspondence. Usually unsentimental, Walker once confessed to Howard Odum that "the thought of Louisville at Easter had a pulling effect."[84] However, in her later years Vassar College became Sydnor Walker's home; like her science and teaching cohorts who retired and settled near their campuses to live out their days,[85] Walker retired to a "large colonial house, reminiscent of her native Kentucky," in Millbrook, New York. There, on 12 December 1966, Walker died at age seventy-five.[86] Her bequest of ten thousand dollars to Vassar College gave lasting testament to her affection.[87]

Sydnor Walker's life and work as a research associate and later program officer for the Laura Spelman Rockefeller Memorial and the

Rockefeller Foundation constitute a new and important chapter in the history of women, philanthropy, and higher education. In Walker's experience two important trends coalesce: increased employment for women scientists in universities, government, industry, and foundation-related work; and a unique era of Rockefeller-funded institution-building in the social sciences in the 1920s and 1930s. Her life was that of a foundation pioneer who not only earned her livelihood through philanthropy, but who also advanced her views of research, social work, and the social sciences in concert with foundation principles. Her work—especially her relationship with Howard Odum and her funding decisions regarding southern social science institutes—illustrates the origins of influence: the mix of challenge and support required in strong donor relationships, and the problematic consequences of matching-grant strategies. Her death bears witness to the notion of *alma mater* as home and safe harbor for a generation of women scientists and teachers somewhat marginalized by the academy.

NOTES

1. Raymond B. Fosdick, *The Story of the Rockefeller Foundation* (Long Acre, London: Odhams, 1952), 212–30.

2. Ibid. See also Donald Fisher, *Fundamental Development of the Social Sciences: Rockefeller Philanthropy and the United States Social Science Research Council* (Ann Arbor: University of Michigan Press, 1993); and Robert Shaplen, *Toward the Well-Being of Mankind: Fifty Years of the Rockefeller Foundation* (Garden City, N.Y.: Doubleday, 1964).

3. Fisher, *Social Sciences*, 31–32. Ruml graduated with a Ph.D. in psychology from the University of Chicago in 1917. He studied with James Rowland Angell, an experimental psychologist, and produced a thesis on the reliability of mental testing.

4. See Amy E. Wells, "From Ideas to Institutions: Southern Scholars and Emerging Universities in the South, circa 1920–1950" (Ph.D. diss., University of Kentucky, 2001).

5. Margaret W. Rossiter, *Women Scientists in America: Struggles and Strategies to 1940* (Baltimore, Md.: Johns Hopkins University Press, 1982).

6. During the late 1930s, the foundation became disillusioned with the results of its support for university social science centers and decided to fund, instead, specific projects in international relations, social security, and public administration (Fisher, *Social Sciences*, 179). See also "Proposed Social Science Program of the Rockefeller Foundation," 13 March 1933, folder 13, box 2, series 910, record group 1.1, Rockefeller Foundation Archives, Rockefeller Archive Center, Sleepy Hollow, N.Y. (hereafter cited as RAC); and "The Social Sciences Statement of Program Presented at Special Trustees Meeting," 15 December 1936, folder 14, box 2, series 910, record group 1.1, Rockefeller Foundation Archives, RAC.

7. Sydnor H. Walker, *Social Work and the Training of Social Workers* (Chapel Hill: University of North Carolina Press, 1928).

8. "Office of Public Relations, Vassar College," March 1951, College Archives, Special Collections, Vassar College Libraries, Poughkeepsie, N.Y. (hereafter cited as Vassar Special Collections).

9. Sydnor H. Walker, "The General Strike with Particular Reference to Its Practicability as Applied to American Labor Conditions" (master's thesis, University of Southern California, 1917).

10. Winifred Asprey, Josephine Gleason, Clarice Pennock, and Verna Spicer, "Memorial Minute," n.d. (1968?), Vassar Special Collections.

11. Ibid. See also "Office of Public Relations," Vassar Special Collections; and "Sydnor Harbison Walker," Rockefeller Foundation Biography Files, Rockefeller Foundation Archives, RAC. This information about Walker's estate is provided in "Lived in Millbrook: Miss Walker's Will Makes Gift of $71,500," *Poughkeepsie Journal,* 8 January 1967, Vassar Special Collections.

12. Asprey et al., "Memorial Minute."

13. Rossiter, *Women Scientists in America: Struggles and Strategies,* 204–205.

14. "Memorial Policy in Social Science: Extracts from Various Memoranda and Dockets," from a General Memorandum, October 1922, folder 10, box 2, series 910, record group 3, Rockefeller Foundation Archives, RAC.

15. Rossiter, *Women Scientists in America: Struggles and Strategies,* 209.

16. Walker, *Social Work,* preface, n.p.

17. Notes from a meeting with Frank J. Bruno, Washington University and the Association of Schools of Professional Work, outline points made in Walker's book. See Sydnor Walker officer's diary, 31 December 1925, record group 12.1, Rockefeller Foundation Archives, RAC.

18. Rossiter, *Women Scientists in America: Struggles and Strategies,* 237.

19. "Memorial Policy."

20. Abraham Flexner, *Medical Education in the United States and Canada* (New York: Carnegie Foundation for the Advancement of Teaching, 1910).

21. "Release, Office of Public Relations, Vassar College," n.d., Vassar Special Collections.

22. Fisher, *Social Sciences,* 32–34.

23. Walker, *Social Work,* 74–75.

24. Fisher, *Social Sciences,* 32–34.

25. Walker, *Social Work,* 74–75.

26. Sydnor H. Walker, "Privately Supported Social Work," in *Recent Social Trends in the United States,* ed. President's Research Committee on Social Trends (New York: Whittlesey House, 1934), 1168–1223.

27. Walker, *Social Work,* 178.

28. Ibid., 43.

29. Fisher, *Social Sciences,* 8–20. Fisher explains that to social scientists the foundations were an important conduit to the state whereby they received public recognition and expert status.

30. Clyde W. Barrow, *Universities and the Capitalist State: Corporate Liberalism and the Reconstruction of American Higher Education, 1894–1928* (Madison: University of Wisconsin Press, 1990), 3–7.

31. Walker, *Social Work,* 74–75.

32. "Rockefeller Foundation Newsletter," n.d. (1967?), Vassar Special Collections.

33. Sydnor Walker officer's diary, vol. 1 (28 October 1925–14 December 1928), record group 12.1, Rockefeller Foundation Archives, RAC.

34. "Social Sciences Statement." The first ideation of the change in program occurred in 1933, with the establishment of the new focus areas "economic structure and process, international relations, and social organization and procedures, with special reference to problems of community organization and planning." See "Proposed Social Science Program."

35. "Rockefeller Foundation Newsletter," Vassar Special Collections.

36. Sydnor Walker officer's diary, vol. 2 (1 February 1929–5 September 1940), record group 12.1, Rockefeller Foundation Archives, RAC.

37. "Memorial Policy."

38. "The Social Sciences under the Laura Spelman Rockefeller Memorial, 1923–1928," 11 April 1933, folder 12, box 2, series 910, record group 3, Rockefeller Foundation Archives, RAC.

39. This dominance was exacerbated by the make-up of the Rockefeller-funded Social Science Research Council (SSRC). See Fisher, *Social Sciences,* 203.

40. Guy Benton Johnson and Guion Griffis Johnson, *Research in Service to Society: The First Fifty Years of the Institute for Research in Social Science at the University of North Carolina* (Chapel Hill: University of North Carolina Press, 1980), 13, xii. Odum earned a Ph.D. in sociology from Columbia and a Ph.D. in psychology from Clark University, where he studied under the direction of G. Stanley Hall, Clark's president.

41. Harry W. Chase to Beardsley Ruml, 8 August 1924, folder 781, box 74, series III, sub-series 6, Laura Spelman Rockefeller Memorial Archives, RAC.

42. Howard Odum's influence within the region and with Rockefeller-funded philanthropies is noted in a letter from W. C. Binkley (Department of History and Political Science) to Chancellor J. H. Kirkland, Vanderbilt University, 3 May 1933, Vanderbilt University Special Collections and University Archives, Nashville, Tenn.

43. Howard Odum to Ruml, 28 January 1926; and Edwin Alderman to Ruml, 8 February 1926; both in folder 812, box 78, series III, sub-series 6, Laura Spelman Rockefeller Memorial Archives, RAC.

44. "The New Institute for Research," editorial, *The Daily Progress,* 30 October 1926, Charlottesville, Va., folder 812, box 78, series III, sub-series 6, Laura Spelman Rockefeller Memorial Archives, RAC.

45. "University of Texas—Research—Social Sciences Grant Action," 13 April 1932, folder 38, box 4, series 249, record group 1.1, Rockefeller Foundation Archives, RAC.

46. Ibid. For details on Texas's wealth compared to that of other southern states, see Howard W. Odum, *Southern Regions of the United States* (Chapel Hill: University of North Carolina Press, 1936), 181–85.

47. Wells, "Ideas to Institutions," 38–60. Today the grants to North Carolina, Virginia, and Texas would equal approximately $6,100,000, $2,900,000, and $5,000,000, respectively. For inflation conversions see Robert Sahr, "Inflation Conversion Factors for Dollars 1665 to Estimated 2013." Available online: http://oregonstate.edu/dept/pol_sci/fac/sahr/sahr.htm (accessed 2 March 2004).

48. Walker, *Social Work,* 42.

49. Johnson and Johnson, *Research in Service*, 343.

50. See the Howard Washington Odum Papers (#3167), Southern Historical Collection, Wilson Library, UNC.

51. Odum to Sydnor Walker, 29 October 1929, folder 113, box 9, series 236, record group 1.1, Rockefeller Foundation Archives, RAC.

52. Odum to Walker, 13 February 1933, folder 306, Odum Papers.

53. Odum to Walker, 18 April 1933, folder 314, Odum Papers.

54. Walker to Odum, 9 December 1932, folder 122, box 10, series 236, record group 1.1, Rockefeller Foundation Archives, RAC.

55. "Memorandum of Interview," 8 March 1927, folder 777, box 74, series III, sub-series 6, Laura Spelman Rockefeller Memorial Archives, RAC.

56. Johnson and Johnson, *Research in Service*, 105.

57. Walker to Odum, 18 November 1929, folder 113, box 9, series 236, record group 1.1, Rockefeller Foundation Archives, RAC.

58. Johnson and Johnson, *Research in Service*, 105–106.

59. Walker, *Social Work*, 42.

60. "University of Texas—Project Record," 9 February 1932, folder 38, box 4, series 249, record group 1.1, Rockefeller Foundation Archives, RAC.

61. Ibid.

62. "Interviews: SHW (Benedict)" and "Interviews: SHW (Gettys and Miller)," both 29 February 1932, folder 38, box 4, series 249, record group 1.1, Rockefeller Foundation Archives, RAC.

63. See Wells, "Ideas to Institutions," 53–60. For the University of Texas, the matching-grant strategy was incredibly successful. President Benedict went to great lengths to guarantee that the BRSS received the full amount offered each time. A series of letters between Benedict and Walker and between Benedict and Edmund Day in the academic year 1933–34 convey Benedict's enthusiasm and success in the pursuit of more money. See Benedict to Day, 5 January 1934, 8 January 1934, and 13 February 1934, all in folder 39, box 4, series 249, record group 1.1, Rockefeller Foundation Archives, RAC.

64. William D. Snider, *Light on the Hill: A History of the University of North Carolina at Chapel Hill* (Chapel Hill: University of North Carolina Press, 1992), 208–209. See also Tyre Taylor to Frank Porter Graham, 3 January 1931; and Mrs. D. F. Harris to the editor, 17 January 1931; both in the Frank Porter Graham Files, 1930–1932 (#40006), series 5: business and finance, Records of the Office of the President, University Archives, Wilson Library, UNC.

65. Graham to Day, 22 March 1932, box 24, sub-series 6, Robert Burton House Series, Records of the Office of Chancellor, University Archives, Wilson Library, UNC. See also "University of North Carolina–Institute for Research in Social Science," folder 130, box 11, series 236, record group 1.1, Rockefeller Foundation Archives, RAC; and "University of North Carolina," folder 125, box 10, series 236, record group 1.1, Rockefeller Foundation Archives, RAC.

66. Johnson and Johnson, *Research in Service*, 54.

67. "Staff Conference," 14 January 1930, folder 17, box 3, series 904, record group 3, Rockefeller Foundation Archives, RAC.

68. George Brown Tindall, *The Emergence of the New South, 1913–1945*, vol. 10

of *A History of the South,* ed. Wendell Holmes Stephenson and E. Merton Coulter (Baton Rouge: Louisiana State University Press, 1967), 498.

69. Sydnor Walker officer's diary, 9 March 1938.

70. "Memorandum of Interview."

71. Jerome D. Greene to members of Rockefeller Foundation, 22 October 1913, folder 163, box 21, series 900, record group 3, Rockefeller Foundation Archives, RAC.

72. Frank J. Munger, foreword to *Research in Service,* ed. Johnson and Johnson, ix.

73. For example, following Walker's lead the foundation did not support programs in rural social work. In the predominantly rural South, this hindered the professionalization of social work (except in New Orleans). In 1929, the University of Alabama successfully entered negotiations for its own School of Social Work. See Sydnor Walker officer's diary, 4 April 1929. In another example, at Walker's recommendation the University of Georgia's request for support of an Institute of Public Affairs and International Relations was declined in 1930. See "The Rockefeller Foundation Activities under Consideration," 1 September 1930, folder 18, box 18, series 904, record group 3, Rockefeller Foundation Archives, RAC.

74. "Officers' Conference, General Education Board," 15 January 1931, folder 8, box 1, series 904, record group 3, Rockefeller Foundation Archives, RAC.

75. Asprey et al., "Memorial Minute."

76. Ibid. See also "Sydnor Harbison Walker."

77. Asprey et al., "Memorial Minute."

78. Sydnor H. Walker, ed., *The First One Hundred Days of the Atomic Age* (New York: The Woodrow Wilson Foundation, 1945).

79. Untitled document, n.d., Vassar Special Collections. Walker's appointment as assistant to the president and assistant secretary to the board of trustees was announced in "Release, Office of Public Relations," Vassar Special Collections.

80. "S. Walker Assists President Blanding," n.d., Vassar Special Collections.

81. "Doubt Change at Vassar to Co-Ed School," *Newburgh New York News,* 3 October 1956, Vassar Special Collections.

82. Asprey et al., "Memorial Minute."

83. "Miss Sydnor Walker Dies; Former Trustee at Vassar," 13 December 1966, Vassar Special Collections.

84. Walker to Odum, 22 April 1925, folder 776, box 74, series III, sub-series 6, Laura Spelman Rockefeller Memorial Archives, RAC.

85. Rossiter, *Women Scientists in America: Struggles and Strategies,* 20–22.

86. "Miss Sydnor Walker Dies."

87. "Lived in Millbrook." Rossiter describes many women scientists and teachers who left similar bequests to women's colleges (*Women Scientists in America: Struggles and Strategies,* 22).

6. Brokering Old and New Philanthropic Traditions: Women's Continuing Education in the Cold War Era

Linda Eisenmann

Foundation support of American women's collegiate education was insignificant and generally undirected before the early 1960s.[1] During the Cold War, however, women attracted foundation attention for an instrumental reason: they had become potential "womanpower" for perceived shortages in the professional and technological labor force. The Carnegie Corporation provided the first concentrated boost to woman-oriented philanthropy when it supported a small group of "continuing education for women" programs in the early 1960s. Although this was not a large effort, Carnegie money proved to be prestigious, newsworthy, and fertile, kindling a women's continuing education movement that would produce over a hundred similar programs by 1965.[2] From this modest beginning, the continuing education movement and the philanthropy behind it paved the way for larger, more radical, and longer-lasting developments in women's education in the 1970s and 1980s—much of which was supported by foundations. This later growth in women's studies, women's research institutes, and women's resource centers found its origins in the little-explored continuing education movement of the early 1960s.

This chapter, which is part of a larger project, examines the origins of women's continuing education at three Carnegie-funded programs: those of the University of Minnesota (1960), Radcliffe College (1960), and Sarah Lawrence College (1962).[3] These pioneers parlayed their Carnegie connection into national influence, propelling a movement to return to the educational mainstream women who had halted their educational careers in response to the prevailing postwar domestic ideology. However, foundation support was not the only form of philanthropy that ignited this movement. An older tradition of women supporting women helped these early programs as well as subsequent dozens that replicated the initial ideas. The University of Michigan program (1964) exemplifies endeavors built not with foundation funding but through the dedicated philanthropy of alumnae and local female supporters.

Thus postwar women's continuing education is significant for two reasons. First, through Carnegie support, it spurred an efficacious combination of a new female-oriented foundation philanthropy with an older tradition of women's local fundraising. Second, an examination of these pioneer programs demonstrates the groundwork laid for larger, more sustained foundation support in the 1970s and 1980s, when the women's movement and gender equity concerns interested and motivated a broader segment of the nation.[4]

AMERICAN WOMEN'S POSTWAR SITUATION

World War II produced considerable economic and professional gains for women. The wartime dearth of men had opened up opportunities and energized women, propelling them into many previously closed business, government, and academic posts. Women made up 45 percent of all college students during the war, they earned 57 percent of master's degrees and 19 percent of Ph.D.s by 1946, and they held 28 percent of college faculty posts. However, postwar America did not so eagerly support women's continued professional participation. The influx of G.I. Bill veterans—nearly one-half of all students in 1946 and 1947—overwhelmed collegiate women, and women's gains waned as they were eased out in favor of bright, usually younger, men.[5]

A new domestic ideology urged women into family roles and valued them more as wives and mothers than as professionals. Popular stereotypes like the television families on *Father Knows Best* and *Leave It to Beaver* suggest that postwar mothers were white, middle-class females who rarely worked outside the home, and, if they had prepared for a career, were content to let that training lie idle while they devoted themselves to family.

In fact, recent scholarship reveals that women abandoned neither jobs nor education to the extent popularly believed. The frequently assumed large dip in the postwar female labor force did not occur.

Alice Kessler-Harris notes a net female labor force *gain* of 16 percent between 1940 and 1950, and she shows that women worked in greater numbers in 1960 than in 1940. Further, the largest gains occurred among married and older women.[6] In higher education, too, the overall trend has been upward. Although women's *proportion* as college students dipped in the G.I. Bill era, their actual *numbers* increased annually from 1947 to the 1980s, with exceptions only in 1950 and 1951. In other words, contrary to the general impression, the long-term trend for women's participation in both college and the labor force has been steadily upward.[7]

These differences between expectations and behavior provoked tensions for postwar women caught between competing ideologies. To be patriotic citizens, they were urged to stay home and defend the country, one household at a time, against communism and domestic disruption. To be ideal economic citizens, women became a reserve labor pool, working only when necessary, subordinating their status and pay to men. Culturally, women's domesticity was valued, as were their volunteer contributions in civic and family organizations. Psychology, too, supported motherhood. The era's strong Freudianism argued that women would be satisfied primarily through accepting their reproductive role and rejecting competition and ambition.[8]

HIGHER EDUCATION CONSIDERS THE FEMALE STUDENT

Mary Ingraham Bunting, who as president of Radcliffe College in 1960 created one of the first continuing education centers, described these conflicting postwar demands as a "climate of unexpectation" for women.[9] People accepted, or even assumed, that a well-trained woman would cede her job when marriage or motherhood called. Similarly, a woman student might hear a mild sigh from her dean or professors if she abandoned college for marriage, but she would find ready understanding among her parents and classmates.

A short-term view predominated in the 1950s, with many women—including some educators—focusing on the immediate appeal of marriage and motherhood and ignoring the longer-term possibilities of education and career. Anecdotal evidence suggested that women were turning their backs on higher education in favor of marriage. The president of Mills College organized an entire analysis around such a complaint: "On my desk lies a letter from a young mother a few years out of college: 'I have come to realize that I was educated to be a successful man and now must learn by myself how to be a successful woman.' The basic irrelevance of much of what passes as women's education in America could not be more compactly phrased."[10]

Yet many educators worried that foreshortening expectations would lead both to labor market problems and to dissatisfied middle-aged women. A few 1950s groups championed a different approach to women's education. Most notably, the American Association of University Women (AAUW) and the National Association of Women Deans and Counselors (NAWDC) devoted both money (in the form of fellowships) and discussion (through conferences and sharing of information) to women's concerns.

But the most scholarly attention was paid by the Commission on the Education of Women, sponsored by the American Council on Education (ACE) from 1953 to 1961. Many female Commission appointees were also members of the AAUW and NAWDC. The Commission was created through a philanthropic gift by Kathryn Sisson Phillips, a founding member of NAWDC. Phillips lamented the state of women's education and persuaded her husband to contribute $50,000 from their family foundation to begin the work. The Commission fostered research on the condition of women in higher education, encouraged pilot studies, and publicized work on behalf of collegiate women.[11]

The ACE Commission actually represents an example of postwar lack of philanthropic interest in women. Phillips intended her $50,000 as seed money for support by bigger foundations, as happened with most ACE projects. However, the records of the Commission's first four years detail a Sisyphean effort to secure support. Commissioners spent every early meeting honing their mission statement for presentation to a foundation. Commission director Althea Hottel (dean of women at Penn), chair Esther Lloyd-Jones (professor at Columbia Teachers College), and ACE president Arthur Adams approached the Ford, Rockefeller, Russell Sage, Guggenheim, Kellogg, and Mellon Foundations, as well as the Carnegie Corporation, all without success. They sustained the project only through careful stewardship of the Phillips money and small infusions of ACE funding.

The effort finally succeeded in 1956 when the Carnegie Corporation—after declining to support the larger Commission program—contributed $9,000 for "a conference to assess the present status of research on the education of women." This gathering produced a strong volume, *The Education of Women: Signs for the Future.*[12] More good news followed. Although the Lilly Foundation is scarcely mentioned in the minutes, ACE announced in 1957 that Lilly had provided $75,000 for three years. Although the Commission finally had help, Carnegie and Lilly together provided less than $100,000, considerably shy of the million dollars Commission members had budgeted for their research agenda.

CONTINUING EDUCATION PROVIDES AN ANSWER

The research analyzed by the ACE Commission demonstrated a disjunction between expectations for women's lives and women's later actual performance in education and at work. Over time, as families grew, women who had seen college as irrelevant found more time and energy for work, increased volunteer opportunities, and re-engagement with the world of ideas.

Educators and researchers advanced a "life-cycle" understanding of women's lives which acknowledged that women moved through roles sequentially. Postwar women revealed different demographic characteristics than their mothers or grandmothers:

> By the time they reach twenty, half the women in the country are married. Their last child is born by the time they are twenty-six years old. So, it's a thirty-two year old mother who takes her youngest child off to first grade. When this same last child graduates from high school, twelve years later, his mother is forty-four years old.[13]

Not only were these forty-four-year-old mothers virtually child-free, but they were also likely to join the work force. Nearly one-third of all women worked in the late 1950s, and almost half of them were wives or mothers.[14] By outlining the contours of the average woman's experience, educators accentuated the fact that rearing children occupied only part of a woman's lifespan. Two educational implications resulted. First, while in college women should be better informed about their likely futures and encouraged to plan for a complicated life cycle. Second, women who had abandoned college because of its presumed irrelevancy should be encouraged to return when older to finish degrees or retrain for a different future.

The continuing education movement developed out of these two concerns, suggesting that women should not be ignored because of their early decisions about college. Rather, they should be encouraged to resume education. Before the movement, women who left college were often simply written off, and the brave soul who returned found little support, no special programming, and many barriers. Schools did not routinely allow part-time study, especially at the graduate level, and part-time students rarely qualified for fellowships. Women who had moved, usually to support a husband's profession, found it hard to win collegiate credit for work done elsewhere. Although today's notion of "continuing education for women" can connote rather low-profile programs, in the early 1960s this movement was quite radical, pushing for institutional change in response to women's needs.[15]

FOUNDATIONS DISCOVER WOMEN'S POTENTIAL

The key to winning foundation support for continuing education was educators' recognition of the manpower implications of the pool of returning female students. Increasingly, labor force analysts had called for "womanpower" to supplement the trained workforce. In 1954, Dael Wolfle published *America's Resources of Specialized Talent* for the Rockefeller-supported Commission on Human Resources and Advanced Training. Wolfle emphasized women's potential; further, he encouraged colleges and universities to find better ways to attract both women and minorities to science and technology fields, proving quite sophisticated in his understanding of how cultural and economic assumptions inhibited their full participation.[16]

A second study of American labor force needs was conducted by the National Manpower Council, funded by Ford. Like Wolfle, NMC analysts had not planned to highlight women, but added them to their agenda fairly early. In its 1957 *Womanpower*, the Council declared that "women constitute not only an essential but also a distinctive part of our manpower resources," and devoted the entire report to the development of womanpower (in schools, colleges, and private sector programs), the effective utilization of female employees (in hiring and promotion), and the enhancement of knowledge about women (through increased research).[17]

Joining Ford and Rockefeller in support of the womanpower trend, Carnegie developed a funding stream for the "better use of human resources." Its 1960 annual report noted, "Many studies indicate that, numerically at least, the greatest wastage of human resources in the United States today is the under-utilization of intelligent women. Part—and perhaps a major part—of this waste is unnecessary.[18]

THE FIRST CONTINUING EDUCATION FUNDING

Once educators recognized the connections between their students and national womanpower needs, they found an easier fit with foundation interests. Carnegie led the support of womanpower through the continuing education programs. The first to win its attention was the Minnesota Plan for the Continuing Education of Women, which in 1960 became the first nationally prominent program designed specifically for older women returning to college.

The Plan was a hybrid of ideas developed by two women, Virginia Senders and Elizabeth Cless. Senders, a lecturer in psychology, worried about women who left college to marry. For several years she had pushed innovative programming for women, sparked by earlier experiences at Antioch and Mount Holyoke Colleges. Senders envisioned women returning to school part-time while still playing their family role, and she hoped that college-age women could be influenced to see more value in education.[19] Meanwhile, Elizabeth Cless, in Minnesota's General Extension Division, was creating liberal arts courses for community women not ready to attend college full-time. She experimented with "New Worlds of Knowledge" seminars to update women on changes in science and the humanities. Senders and Cless joined their ideas in a creative plan that caught Carnegie's attention.

Fully employing manpower language, the educators matched women to the nation's needs in outlining two goals for their new program:

> It is widely recognized that the United States urgently needs to develop and utilize all possible resources of trained or trainable manpower, and particularly needs to make use of its gifted and high-ability individuals. . . . The principal objective of the program proposed here is to make possible the full utilization of our resources of able and educated womanpower. A second objective, complementary rather than competitive with the first, is an increase in the personal happiness and satisfaction of many individual women.[20]

The Minnesota Plan proposed a three-pronged approach to serving undergraduate and community women simultaneously. First, for traditional-aged undergraduates, the Plan provided "orientation to the multiple roles of later life so that realistic preparation can be made for them." The second component—whose popularity surprised its planners—was targeted to young homemakers with family responsibilities. These women received special curricula, along with strong counseling. Finally, for "the mature woman whose formal education is already far behind her," the Plan offered special courses and guidance in using the university's wide resources.

The Plan's efforts to develop opportunities at this large, land-grant institution particularly appealed to Carnegie. While the foundation valued the Plan's programming, it also emphasized the importance of embedding the program within existing local resources. Making the Plan a part of the overall university from the beginning would aid in its seamless absorption into the institution when Carnegie pilot funding expired.[21]

WHY THE CARNEGIE CORPORATION?

Three elements help explain why the originators of the Minnesota program approached Carnegie. First was Senders's previous role as a Mount Holyoke student under the tutelage of John Gardner, who later become Carnegie's president. Senders had done independent study work with Gardner and stayed in touch, sending him her ideas about women's education.[22] A second reason was the clear—and carefully crafted—match between the Plan and Carnegie's interest in "better use of human resources." A third factor was the active involvement of a key Carnegie player: Florence Anderson, secretary of the Corporation.

Anderson was very influential at Carnegie.[23] She joined the foundation in 1934, a fresh college graduate working as an actual secretary. She advanced through the ranks (the only woman to do so) from administrative assistant (1937–1947) to assistant secretary (1947–1957), associate secretary (1951–1954), and then secretary of the Corporation in 1954. Her responsibilities ranged widely, but in 1955 Anderson's personal interest in women's issues drew her to a meeting of the ACE Commission on the Education of Women while Carnegie considered its funding request. Several continuing education pioneers identified Anderson as the linchpin of Carnegie's involvement. Cless noted that the "practical and tenacious" Anderson "returned academic proposals in this field over and over again, until they were rewritten in such a way that they could stand on their own." Historian Margaret Rossiter recognized Anderson's influence when few women sat in the inner circle of foundation decision making. "An astute applicant for a possible grant would quickly discover," she noted, that Anderson "in fact handled most of the proposals and played an important role in the foundation's ambiguous collective decision making."[24]

The histories of the three Carnegie-funded continuing education pioneers—Minnesota, Sarah Lawrence, and Radcliffe—record increasingly close correspondence with Anderson as the representative of Carnegie interests. At Minnesota, Anderson and the directors were soon on a first-name basis. Of the 1963 program report, Anderson wrote, "I was particularly pleased to note the many ways in which this program has been made an integral part of the University rather than a tangential activity."[25] The extension of the Sarah Lawrence program beyond the "tangential" similarly enjoyed Anderson's support. At that small, experimental, single-sex college, dean (and later president) Esther Raushenbush instigated continuing education efforts that differed considerably from Minnesota's, but appealed to Carnegie's wish to spark innovation and provide models.

Raushenbush investigated older women's concerns by talking with alumnae and the mothers of her students. Noting how easily older women's needs were set aside, she explained, "The trouble is that we have generally evaded the hard task of helping [women] accomplish what we have said they should accomplish, as soon as the simple line of continuous education has been broken."[26]

In 1958, Raushenbush created special continuing education seminars, and with president Paul Ward, she tried to secure funding from the Ford Foundation. She was disappointed, even indignant, when Ford rejected her idea as too traditional, too focused on curricular tinkering, and insufficiently experimental. Raushenbush countered that her effort was, in fact, experimental in three important ways: she was investigating the "intellectual potential" of women on whom little attention had been focused, she was creating a research and planning function to study their progress, and she was providing new curricular formats seldom offered to mature students.[27]

Still smarting from Ford's rejection, Raushenbush and Ward jumped on the lead of Minnesota's success at Carnegie. After an initial rejection, Raushenbush worked closely with Florence Anderson to craft an appealing program. In fact, in her initial rejection letter to President Ward, Anderson noted, "since this is an area in which I have a personal interest, I should enjoy discussing the plan with Mrs. Raushenbush at her convenience."[28] Anderson's "personal interest" paid off: Carnegie gave Sarah Lawrence $76,000 in 1961. When coupled with a $15,000 anonymous contribution from a Sarah Lawrence alumna, the Carnegie grant allowed the school to fund both operations and physical plant for its new Center for Continuing Education in 1962.

Unlike Minnesota, which moved its continuing education students into the mainstream, Sarah Lawrence created a parallel track where students took special seminars under the watchful care of hand-picked faculty. After the first year, Sarah Lawrence stretched its mission in a new direction. Taking advantage of its metropolitan New York City setting, the college created partnerships with area universities that allowed students to pursue graduate training. The first collaboration, in 1963, was for a master's degree in education with the NYU School of Education, and shortly thereafter, a master's degree in social work. With both programs, a key was the opportunity for part-time field and class work; another was willingness to grant credit for previous classes and experience. A third, less successful, program in library science was created with the Pratt Institute.[29]

Carnegie liked this new direction, and the Corporation funded the joint programs with nearly $300,000. Since graduate schools had rarely welcomed part-time or older female students, this seemed a new avenue for tapping into womanpower. In her oral history, Raushenbush told of her first meeting with John Gardner. Florence Anderson had warned Raushenbush that Gardner was "willing to talk to you, but he's not excited about it." In their meeting, Gardner was cordial but told Raushenbush that her continuing education program wouldn't do much long-term good since the graduate schools would be uninterested in older female college graduates. Raushenbush responded that she would just have to work on the graduate schools. "So he laughed," she remembered. "He had a little gleam in his eye, and he said, 'Oh well, if you're going to crack the grad schools, then that's different then. Maybe we'll give you the money.' "[30]

Between funding Minnesota in 1960 and Sarah Lawrence in 1961, the Carnegie Corporation also made a grant to the Radcliffe Institute for Independent Study, a third pioneer that addressed a quite different clientele. Where the other centers served women still earning degrees, the Radcliffe Institute believed that women already holding the Ph.D. represented an ideal lever for change. The program created by President Bunting provided fellowships, a research center, office space, access to Harvard faculty and libraries, and uninterrupted time for women whose careers had slowed due to family responsibilities. Radcliffe's only requirements of fellows were to work on a project and to present their work at a public colloquium.[31]

Bunting's ideas did not develop in a vacuum. Besides discussing plans with Raushenbush, Bunting also was no stranger to Florence Anderson. In her oral history, Bunting describes fellow Brooklynite Anderson as an old friend with whom she had enjoyed horseback riding.[32] Further, by the early 1960s, Bunting was one of the nation's best-known women educators. She served on several national boards, becoming chair of the ACE Commission on the Education of Women in 1959. Her scientific training (a Ph.D. in bacteriology from the University of Wisconsin) made her a frequent choice for technical committees, such as the National Science Foundation's Advisory Committee to the Office on Scientific Information and Research. There, Bunting learned the manpower utilization language that helped sell her educational ideas. She also astutely connected her plan to the concept of equal and excellent education that John Gardner had trumpeted.[33]

Bunting appreciated Gardner's work, especially his notion that "we get the excellence we value" and his sensitivity to including women in educational planning. In her appeal for Carnegie funding, she told him, "There is something about the education of women in this country that reminds one of plants cultivated under conditions permitting excellent early vegetative growth but few flowers and less fruit."[34] Apparently convinced, Carnegie provided a five-year grant of $150,000 for fellowships.

In the foundation game, Bunting was even more successful than her Minnesota and Sarah Lawrence colleagues. Her work attracted interest from Laurance Rockefeller, who invited her funding appeal. The Rockefeller Brothers Fund provided $250,000, and both Laurance Rockefeller and staff member Nancy Hanks served on the Radcliffe Institute's advisory board.[35]

SHORT- AND LONG-TERM EFFECTS OF FOUNDATION SUPPORT

Although Rockefeller actually surpassed Carnegie in its start-up gift to Radcliffe, it was the intentionality of the Carnegie grants that drew national attention to continuing education. In selecting a range of projects, Florence Anderson wished to disseminate both information and models. With the initial trio, she had picked a large public university, a small liberal arts college, and a medium-sized women's college attached to a prestigious research university.

Selection by Carnegie brought benefits beyond the financial. Both Sarah Lawrence and Radcliffe won prominent coverage in the *New York Times;* Raushenbush and Bunting relate how their switchboards were swamped with phone calls the morning after favorable articles by education editor Fred Hechinger appeared in the paper. The leaders of the three programs were frequent conference speakers, they were invited to tout their work in the October 1961 *Educational Record,* they received broad publicity in Carnegie materials, and they corresponded with dozens of educators hoping to establish continuing education programs.[36]

In the short run, then, Carnegie support was influential for these programs and for the continuing education movement. In the longer term, Carnegie's decision to tie women's programming into its scheme for "better use of human resources" paved the way for increased interest by other foundations—notably Ford—in the subsequent stages of the women's movement.

Ford showed little interest in women's issues during the early 1960s.[37] In the 1970s, however, Ford would lead the way in national support of women's studies. Rosa Proietto has characterized five phases of Ford's support through the 1980s: a fellowship program for individuals, beginning in 1972; funding for fifteen women's research centers; support of a national journal (*Signs*) and a national research council; curriculum mainstream projects throughout the 1980s; and, in the late 1980s, funding for women's programs outside the United States.[38]

Carnegie's early contribution to women's continuing education paled in comparison to Ford's later support; in addition, continuing education was never a huge part of Carnegie's agenda. Throughout the 1960s, Carnegie support of women's programming never exceeded 3 percent of its total U.S. grants.[39] Nevertheless, continuing education leaders, with the help of Florence Anderson, leveraged Carnegie money and influence to sustain a movement that grew from 20 programs in 1963, to 100 in 1966, to 376 by 1971, and that modeled foundation involvement in women's education.[40]

AN ALTERNATIVE STREAM OF SUPPORT FOR WOMEN

Foundation funding clearly played a major role in the new programs at Minnesota, Sarah Lawrence, and Radcliffe. However, foundation money tells only part of the story of how leaders built the continuing education movement. In fact, given foundations' limited role, an older tradition of women giving to women was needed to spark and sustain the movement. Contributions by local women's groups, alumnae, and individual benefactors all supplemented foundation funding, extending an old tradition in higher education.

Although women's financial contributions have not always been well recognized, local female philanthropy made all the difference in opening colleges to women. Such philanthropy created female institutions, opened schools previously limited to men, supported women students with fellowships and housing, and funded teaching posts specifically for women. Educational history provides scattered stories of female philanthropy, but seldom has it emphasized the significance of the whole effort.[41] The continuing education movement provides another example in the long story of women supporting women.

Two of the three pioneers in continuing education for women used female philanthropy to supplement foundation funding. Although Minnesota managed solely on Carnegie and university funding, both Radcliffe and Sarah Lawrence raised money from individuals. Sarah Lawrence welcomed a "timely" gift of $15,000 from an anonymous local donor who refurbished a campus building for the new center. At Radcliffe, Bunting had been told to fund her project with outside money, and she secured several individual gifts, including $50,000 from Agnes Meyer of the *Washington Post*.

LOCAL SUPPORT CREATES THE UNIVERSITY OF MICHIGAN CEW PROGRAM

Although the pioneers had enjoyed Carnegie support, newer programs found the foundations less interested in supporting the movement as it grew. The history of the center at the University of Michigan exemplifies a successful program that raised its entire budget through the older approach to supporting women's education. Michigan's Center for the Education of Women (CEW) opened in 1964, just two years after Carnegie funded Sarah Lawrence. In that short time, many educators had studied the pioneers, hoping to borrow the most relevant methods for meeting their local women's needs. Michigan modeled itself most closely after the Minnesota Plan, which emphasized opening institutional resources and advocating for women on a large public campus. Michigan developed a tripartite mission of advocacy, service, and research, with particular focus on providing information to students wishing to resume education, guiding those students toward appropriate local resources, and—most importantly—"working with the administration and faculty to achieve further flexibility in university programs and requirements."[42]

In appeals to foundations, the Michigan program attracted little interest. Perhaps its approach seemed too similar to that of the model schools. Louise Cain, Michigan's co-founder, visited Carnegie while still in her planning stage. However, Cain recalled in a later interview that she had not devoted much time to raising outside funds, citing only one unsuccessful overture to the Kellogg Foundation. Generally, Cain asserted that unless the university itself was willing to support the center financially, it would not be able to attract outside funding.[43]

Instead, founders of the Michigan program turned to local options, directing the first fundraising appeal to alumnae. Michigan's women had a long history of supporting female students and faculty. In 1890, local women had funded the Michigan League, a women's social center, as a counterpart to the all-male Michigan Union. A women's dormitory and gymnasium also were built through local philanthropy. When Louise Cain and Vice President for Academic Affairs Roger Heyns approached the Michigan Alumnae Council about funding the new center, the alumnae were already raising money on behalf of the long-dormant Alice Freeman Palmer Professorship.

Despite their devotion to the Palmer effort, the alumnae responded positively, especially after they won Heyns's agreement to match any money they raised. In September 1964, the alumnae committed to raising $15,000 annually for three years. Their commitment was a huge one: they assumed a total obligation of $45,000 for a venture that had been operating less than three weeks.

The alumnae's success in raising CEW money involved careful planning and hard work. Louise Cain worked with an alumnae Committee on Continuing Education that shared reading lists, distributed a survey, and prepared a public relations blitz on behalf of the new Center. Alumna Jean Cobb single-mindedly focused on raising money, spending nearly four years heading the effort.[44] Cobb's work, the committed support of Heyns, alumnae publicity to the city's women's clubs (including the American Association of University Women and the

Business and Professional Women's Club), and the excellent reports of the center's initial accomplishments all combined—after a rocky start—to help the club reach its goal.

Over time, Michigan was notably successful raising outside money for its research program, which was considerably stronger than those of most of the early programs. Initially, however, Michigan distinguished itself as the only center to support itself completely through the combined contributions of its alumnae and its home university.

Continuing education programs from the early 1960s may appear timid compared to the exuberant women's movement that hit campuses only a half-decade later, generating women's studies programs, women's research centers, and resource centers for women's needs. In addition, the limited philanthropic support of Carnegie and Rockefeller may seem insignificant compared to Ford's later robust contributions to women's studies. Yet, in their modest aims and unpretentious means, the continuing education programs were suited to their era, when women were often seen as "incidental students" on their own campuses. As Esther Raushenbush explained their approach, the leaders employed a "respectful way of working within the system" that merely asked for a fair share of resources and a recognition that women could make contributions.[45]

Yet the long-term accomplishments of these programs should not be overlooked. In asserting women's place in collegiate settings, continuing education programs were early institutional efforts at gender equity. Born in an era of little encouragement for women, the centers organized around women's needs as students, and many remained viable by adapting their missions when the women's movement subsequently burst onto campuses. Continuing education also laid groundwork for later, more focused women's programming by recognizing women's nascent needs that would grow over time. The leaders' advocacy and calls for research drew attention to women, even if the time was not yet ripe to address them fully.

In drawing foundation support to women's programming—even at a modest level—continuing education efforts paved the way for larger woman-oriented foundation agendas in the 1970s and 1980s. At the same time, the history of this movement reveals an older educational tradition of women helping women. As such, continuing education offers a significant case study wherein a legacy of old-style female philanthropy combined with a new and powerful funding source on behalf of women's education.

NOTES

1. Although some foundations supported women's education (e.g., the Laura Spelman Rockefeller Memorial with child study and the General Education Board with collegiate buildings), no significant funding program for women students appeared before the 1950s. See Andrea Walton, "Rethinking Boundaries: The History of Women, Philanthropy, and Higher Education," *History of Higher Education Annual* 20 (2000), 29–57; and Kathleen D. McCarthy, ed., *Lady Bountiful Revisited: Women, Philanthropy, and Power* (New Brunswick, N.J.: Rutgers University Press, 1990).

2. Elizabeth L. Cless, "The Birth of an Idea: An Account of the Genesis of Women's Continuing Education," in *Some Action of Her Own: The Adult Woman and Higher Education,* ed. Helen S. Astin (Lexington, Mass.: Lexington, 1976), 15.

3. See Linda Eisenmann, *Higher Education for Women in Postwar America, 1946–1965: Reclaiming the Incidental Student* (Baltimore, Md.: Johns Hopkins University Press, forthcoming).

4. See Mariam Chamberlain and Alison Bernstein, "Philanthropy and the Emergence of Women's Studies," *Teachers College Record* 93 (spring 1992): 556–68; and Rosa Proietto, "The Ford Foundation and Women's Studies in American Higher Education," in *Philanthropic Foundations: New Scholarship, New Possibilities,* ed. Ellen Condliffe Lagemann (Bloomington: Indiana University Press, 1999), 271–84.

5. For college women, see Thomas D. Snyder, ed., *120 Years of American Education: A Statistical Portrait* (Washington, D.C.: U.S. Dept. of Education, Office of Educational Research and Improvement, National Center for Education Statistics, 1993); and U.S. Bureau of the Census, *Historical Statistics of the United States, Colonial Times to 1970,* 2 vols. (White Plains, N.Y.: Kraus International Publications, 1989). For postwar women, see Alice Kessler-Harris, *Out to Work: A History of Wage-Earning Women in the United States* (New York: Oxford University Press, 1982); and Margaret W. Rossiter, *Women Scientists in America: Before Affirmative Action, 1940–1972* (Baltimore, Md.: Johns Hopkins University Press, 1995). For the G.I. Bill, see Keith Olson, *The G.I. Bill, the Veterans, and the Colleges* (Lexington: University Press of Kentucky, 1974).

6. Kessler-Harris, *Out to Work;* and Claudia Goldin, *Understanding the Gender Gap: An Economic History of American Women* (New York: Oxford University Press, 1990).

7. See Snyder, ed., *120 Years of American Education.*

8. Linda Eisenmann, "Educating the Female Citizen in a Post-war World: Competing Ideologies for American Women, 1945–1965," *Educational Review* 54 (June 2002): 133–41.

9. Mary Ingraham Bunting, "Radcliffe Institute for Independent Study," *Educational Record* 42 (October 1961), 279–86.

10. Lynn H. White, Jr., *Educating our Daughters* (New York: Harper and Brothers,

1950), 18. For the era's debates on women, see Paula S. Fass, *Outside In: Minorities and the Transformation of American Education* (New York: Oxford University Press, 1989).

11. See records of the Commission on the Education of Women, American Council on Education, series B-22, Schlesinger Library, Radcliffe Institute, Harvard University.

12. Opal David, ed., *The Education of Women: Signs for the Future* (Washington, D.C.: American Council on Education, 1957).

13. From "To Be Continued," a script by the Minnesota Plan for the Continuing Education of Women as part of the public television series *Freedom to Learn,* broadcast in 1962. Probable authors were Virginia Senders and Elizabeth Cless. In "Publicity" folder, box 1, Minnesota Women's Center collection, University of Minnesota Archives, Minneapolis (hereafter cited as UMA).

14. Goldin, *Understanding the Gender Gap,* 17.

15. For a contemporary discussion emphasizing women's "educational track," see Mary I. Bunting, "A Huge Waste: Educated Womanpower," *New York Times Magazine,* 7 May 1961. For a discussion of issues facing 1950s collegiate women, see Linda Eisenmann, "Advocacy, Research, and Service for Women: The Pioneering Origins of the Center for the Education of Women at the University of Michigan," Research Report of the Center for the Education of Women, University of Michigan, February 2001.

16. Dael Wolfle, *America's Resources of Specialized Talent* (New York: Harper and Brothers, 1954).

17. National Manpower Council, *Womanpower* (New York: Columbia University Press, 1957), 9.

18. Carnegie Corporation of New York, *1960 Annual Report,* 42.

19. Donald L. Opitz, *Three Generations in the Life of the Minnesota Women's Center: A History, 1960–2000* (Minneapolis: Minnesota Women's Center, 1999), 4.

20. Proposal for the Minnesota Plan for the Continuing Education of Women, 1, in "Women's Continuing Education, 1960–1966," box 16, collection 951, General Extension Division, UMA.

21. See Opitz, *Three Generations;* and Virginia Senders, "The Minnesota Plan for Continuing Education: A Progress Report," *Educational Record* 42 (October 1961), 270–78.

22. Senders discusses her relationship with John Gardner in an oral history interview with Donald Opitz, 8 January 2000, available in UMA.

23. In her history of the Carnegie Corporation, Ellen Lagemann stresses that, as president, John Gardner gave considerable authority to his staff, encouraging them to help formulate policy (Lagemann, *The Politics of Knowledge: The Carnegie Corporation, Philanthropy, and Public Policy* [Middletown, Conn.: Wesleyan University Press, 1989]).

24. Cless, "Birth of an Idea," 7–8; and Rossiter, *Women Scientists in America: Before Affirmative Action,* 251. See also Barry Dean Karl, "Going for Broke: The Historian's Commitment to Philanthropy," in *Philanthropic Foundations,* ed. Lagemann, 288–89.

25. Florence Anderson to Vera Schletzer, 24 October 1963, in "Women's Continuing Education, 1960–66," box 16, collection 951, General Extension Division, UMA.

26. Esther Raushenbush, "Unfinished Business: Continuing Education for Women," *Educational Record* 42 (October 1961), 264. For a discussion of her growing interest in continuing education, see Raushenbush's oral history interviews (1973 and a 1974 addendum), Oral History Office, Columbia University, New York City.

27. Esther Raushenbush to Elizabeth Pascal, Fund for Advancement of Education, 31 May 1961, in Esther Raushenbush folder, box 1, Center for Continuing Education, Sarah Lawrence College Archives, Bronxville, N.Y.

28. Anderson to Paul Ward, 18 April 1961, "Carnegie Corporation, 1961–1964," box 1, Center for Continuing Education, Sarah Lawrence College Archives.

29. Melissa Lewis Richter and Jane Banks Whipple, *A Revolution in the Education of Women: Ten Years of Continuing Education at Sarah Lawrence College* (Bronxville, N.Y.: Sarah Lawrence College, 1972), 58.

30. Raushenbush 1973 oral history interview, 478–79.

31. The best source for a discussion of Radcliffe is Bunting, "Radcliffe Institute."

32. Raushenbush describes a chat between the two educators when they served on a Middle States Evaluation accrediting team. See her 1973 oral history interview, 15. Bunting mentions Anderson on page 97 of her oral history memoir with Jeanette Bailey Cheek, 1978, Radcliffe College Archives, Schlesinger Library, Radcliffe Institute, Harvard University, Cambridge, Mass.

33. Bunting refers frequently to Gardner in her oral history, including 68, 93, 97. For Gardner's ideas, see Rockefeller Brothers Fund, *The Pursuit of Excellence* (Garden City, N.Y.: Doubleday, 1958); and Gardner's *Excellence: Can We Be Equal and Excellent Too?* (New York: Harper and Brothers, 1961).

34. Mary Bunting to John Gardner, 11 October 1960, Records of the Bunting Institute, series 6-1, Radcliffe College Archives.

35. Bunting oral history interview, 97.

36. Fred Hechinger, "Radcliffe Plans Institute to Aid the Gifted Woman," *New York Times*, 3 November 1960, 1; and "Sarah Lawrence Plans New Center," *New York Times*, 11 January 1962, 35.

37. Ford did fund a prior continuing education effort by Bunting during her deanship of Douglass College. There, Bunting created a small program for older women interested in returning to school to pursue mathematics. See her 1973 oral history interview, 71–74. On the development of Ford's interest in women's issues, see Susan M. Hartmann, *The Other Feminists: Activists in the Liberal Establishment* (New Haven, Conn.: Yale University Press, 1999), esp. chapter 5.

38. Proietto, "The Ford Foundation," 274–76. Proietto notes that Ford gave $9 million to women's studies from 1972 to 1981 (282).

39. Data gathered from *Annual Reports of the Carnegie Corporation*, 1959 through 1969.

40. Helen S. Astin, "Adult Development and Education," in *Some Action of Her Own*, ed. Astin, 49.

41. See Walton, "Rethinking Boundaries"; Linda Eisenmann, "Creating a Framework for Interpreting U.S. Women's Educational History: Lessons from Historical Lexicography," *History of Education* 30 (fall 2001): 453–70; and Merle Curti, *Philanthropy in the Shaping of American Higher Education* (New Brunswick, N.J.: Rutgers University Press, 1965).

42. "Proposal for CEW," 1964, in box 6, CEW collection, Bentley Historical

Library, University of Michigan, Ann Arbor. For the Michigan center, see Eisenmann, "Advocacy, Research, and Service for Women."

43. Louise Cain, Jean Campbell, and Jane Likert, joint interview by Ruth Bordin for CEW's twenty-fifth anniversary in 1989. Tape is available in the CEW collection, University of Michigan.

44. Unprocessed papers of the alumnae Continuing Education Committee are available in the CEW collection, University of Michigan. See also Eisenmann, "Advocacy, Research, and Service."

45. Raushenbush, 1973 oral history interview, 27.

PART II.
WOMEN'S PHILANTHROPY AS AN AGENT OF
SOCIAL AND EDUCATIONAL CHANGE

7. American Philanthropy and Women's Education Exported: Missionary Teachers in Turkey

Roberta Wollons

Throughout the nineteenth century, women from the United States traveled both alone and with their husbands to remote regions of the world under the auspices of missionary work. One of the largest of the missionary organizations was the American Board of Commissioners for Foreign Missions (ABCFM), originating in Boston, Massachusetts, in 1810. The ABCFM, along with other missionary organizations, not only gave women the respectability and institutional support they needed to travel, but also placed them in situations of unprecedented autonomy. Missionaries have generally been conceptualized solely within the framework of their Christian identity and evangelical goals, and their actions are commonly interpreted as cultural imperialism.[1] This essay recontextualizes those ideas, focusing on individual women missionaries as philanthropists, educators, and social reformers, formed in the same mold as the settlement workers who flocked to poor urban immigrant neighborhoods in the late nineteenth century. In this case, however, they were placed in the politically and religiously tumultuous region of Ottoman Turkey.

The women I discuss here were educated at women's colleges in the United States and in turn became the founders of educational institutions for women and girls in Turkey. Missionaries were prohibited by the Turkish government from proselytizing among Muslims and concentrated their efforts among Greeks, Armenians, and other minorities within the borders of the Ottoman Empire. As founders of schools for women and girls, missionaries were engaged not only in the central missionary enterprise of religious conversion, but also in reformulating concepts of womanhood, in understanding the political context of education and national identity, and in navigating tensions among powerful and competing religious ideologies.

This essay focuses on the interplay of education, evangelism, and adventure that motivated women to choose missionary work. It further explores the tangled interaction between the missionaries and the people they came to "save," under the pressure of a polarizing political climate that led them inevitably to take sides. American missionaries by design became bilingual and, in the process, deeply bicultural. Over time, they accommodated themselves to local religious practices and to the limitations placed on both Muslim and Christian women. The women missionaries I present here, the Ely sisters in Bitlis, Turkey, and Ellen Stone in Macedonia, were shaped by the Mount Holyoke model of women's education, traveled as single women, and were involved in founding or directing schools for girls. Located in small towns and villages, they became pivotal figures between warring religious and political factions and in the process experienced their own conversion from evangelists to educators, and from educators to political partisans.

The religious revival that took place in the United States in the early nineteenth century gave rise to two major movements that continued into the twentieth century. First was the missionary crusade to spread the gospel throughout the world, and second was the advancement in higher education for women.[2] The two movements came together in the missionary enterprise of the American Board of Commissioners for Foreign Missions. In the early years of America's Second Great Awakening (1800–1830), an evangelistic movement arose in response to a perceived decline in religious uniformity. The revival was linked to other antebellum reform movements, including abolitionism, women's rights, and temperance. The revivals of the period spread to college campuses, inspiring four students at Williams College—in what came to be called the "Haystack Prayer Meeting"—to petition the state of Massachusetts to form a society solely to support foreign missions.[3] Deeply committed to the principles of evangelism, they formed the American Board of Commissioners for Foreign Missions in 1810. While the founders were Congregationalist, the ABCFM did not have a specific denominational agenda. The group was emboldened, rather, by three religious-intellectual ideas: the biblical injunction to "go ye into all the world and preach the gospel to every creature" (Mark 16:15);[4] the conviction that America had a special and disproportionately large role in God's saving plan for humankind; and the vivid and horrible notion of millions of heathen perishing yearly without Christ.[5] The idea took hold, and the ABCFM sent its first missionaries abroad in 1812.[6]

Equally inspired by the New England revivals, educator Mary Lyon—building on the ideas of Emma Willard in Troy, New York; Zilpah Grant in Ipswich, Massachusetts; and Catharine Beecher in Hartford, Connecticut—formulated the Mount Holyoke model for the education of women. Along with a classical curriculum, Lyon encouraged charitable service as defined by the New Divinity concerns for piety and benevolence.[7] While charity and philanthropy were broadly conceived Christian values, "Christian self-sacrifice," as Amanda Porterfield notes, "was one arena in which American women in the nineteenth century could compete with men and win."[8] Missionary work not only celebrated self-sacrifice, however; it also allowed for self-expression and social activism. As the aggressive evangelical movement swept through the colleges and universities, it attracted the women of Mount Holyoke as it had the men of Williams. Once animated by the idea of missionary work, Mary Lyon loyally supported the American Board. Each year, a stream of missionaries came through Mount Holyoke to talk about their experiences in Japan, Africa, India, and Asia Minor (Turkey) and to recruit new missionaries. She brought to campus Dr. Rufus Anderson, the Board's energetic secretary, and Fidelia Fiske, the legendary missionary to Persia, who enthralled Mount Holyoke students with their stories of exotic adventure and salvation.[9] In 1843, Mary Lyon alone raised $900 to support Fiske,[10] and when Fiske finished her missionary career, she returned to teach at Mount Holyoke. After the Civil War, missionary work was not only permitted for women, but, along with teaching, nursing, and writing, was actively encouraged by the presidents of women's colleges, particularly by Mary Lyon at Mount Holyoke in Massachusetts and Anna Peck Sill at Rockford Female Seminary in Illinois. Interestingly, a disproportionate number of the Turkish educational programs for girls and women founded by the American Board traced their lineage to Mount Holyoke.[11]

An increasing call for single women missionaries came from male American missionaries in the field who saw the need for women to do the work among native women. They were frustrated by customs that prohibited girls from studying with male teachers or in the company of boys. Emily White Smith, second president of the Women's Board (1871–1906) and Mount Holyoke graduate, argued, "The most definite reason for organizing women's boards to do women's work for women was the existence of millions of women who were so secluded in Zenans [India] and Harems [Turkey] that only a Christian woman could reach them with the message of salvation."[12]

The connections between the Protestant commitment to serve and the rising acceptance of women's education gave women an unprecedented opportunity to devote themselves to a life of service and extraordinary adventure. During the period 1837–1888, a total of 178 Mount Holyoke graduates enlisted in the foreign missions, a considerable percentage of the school's alumnae.[13] Bess Vickery, historian of Mount Holyoke missionaries, pointed out the enormity of the decision to serve:

> Naive and inexperienced, the majority of these young women had traveled less than fifty miles from their places of birth before embarking for societies that were nearly incomprehensible within the aegis of their upbringing. Often, in addition, the people they met were generally hostile to the aims of the missionary movement of which they were a part.[14]

The motives propelling women missionaries were complex and often idiosyncratic, but they stemmed in great part from their Christian and classical education, which instilled both a deep appreciation for the importance of education for all women and the call to philanthropic, charitable service. The Mount Holyoke Missionary Association was founded in 1879, and in 1888 members pledged to identify themselves with the organized missionary effort as an auxiliary to the Hampshire County Branch of the Woman's Board of Missions. In doing so they made official the college's commitment to promoting missionary work among the students. While the actual effect of their encounters abroad is difficult to evaluate, missionary women actively promoted female literacy, commitment to the necessity of monogamy and marital affection, and the well-being of children.[15] These ideas, well embedded in Western thought and assumed to be natural by educated American women, were perceived in Turkey as revolutionary and, by the 1930s, women missionaries in Turkey presented a challenge to prevailing notions of womanhood and were described as militants.[16]

In the early years of the ABCFM, the Protestant emphasis on individual salvation and reading the Bible required that women first become literate and learn enough history, geography, mathematics, logic, and science to interpret the Bible according to Protestant teachings. The perceived importance of educating indigenous women was growing, and because missionary wives were not always trained as teachers the ABCFM reconsidered its policy prohibiting the recruitment of single female teachers. In 1868, the Women's Board was formed to support and oversee the work of single women.

The spread of women's missionary societies has been called the largest mass women's movement in the late nineteenth century,[17] with an estimated membership of more than three million by 1915. These societies, together with the women's club movement and the Women's Christian Temperance Union (WCTU), constituted the forerunners of women's activism in social reform during the Progressive Era. Noriko Ishii, historian of the women's boards of the ABCFM, argues that in the same spirit as the club movement, after 1868 women organized and joined separate women's boards for foreign missions because they wanted to "do more, to exert some influence on the world around them."[18]

Several separate women's boards for foreign missions were organized across denominations during and after the Civil War.[19] The first two ABCFM boards, the Women's Board of Missions (WBM) in Boston and the Women's Board of Missions of the Interior (WBMI) in Chicago, were organized in 1868. In 1873, the Women's Board of the Pacific (WBMP) separated from the WBMI and became one of the three women's boards of the ABCFM. The formation of the boards contributed substantially to the ABCFM's overall fundraising. By 1899, receipts from the women's boards constituted over 40 percent of ABCFM revenue.[20]

In addition to becoming an essential economic force in the mission movement, the separate women's boards opened up the possibility that single women might seek careers as foreign missionaries. The prevailing nineteenth-century attitude was that unmarried women needed protection; therefore, the few single women who traveled alone were widows. As mission historian R. Pierce Beaver observed, "somehow . . . if the women were widows, it was all right to send them out single."[21] The person responsible for supporting the women's boards was Rev. N. G. Clark, newly appointed foreign secretary of the ABCFM in 1866. Unlike his predecessor, Rufus Anderson, who had opposed the formation of women's boards, Clark recognized the importance both of women's education and of women's work among native women abroad. Clark came from a family of educated women and served on the board of trustees for both Mount Holyoke and Wellesley Colleges, ultimately serving as president of the Wellesley board of trustees from 1888 to 1893.[22] During his tenure as foreign secretary, in addition to supporting the development of the women's boards, he presided over the founding of colleges for women in Turkey and elsewhere.

Unlike the ABCFM men, who viewed their relationship to non-Christian men from the position of American and Anglo-Saxon superiority, the women who formed the women's boards included in their rhetoric the coexistence of dual concepts: that American women were superior to the native women in mission fields, but that the two groups could unite as women despite their cultural differences. The WBMI believed their superiority lay in Christianity, and therefore felt they could elevate the less fortunate women by extending Christian education to them. Education and evangelism were linked in the minds of the women missionaries from the beginning. On this issue, the ABCFM and the WBMI sharply diverged, as the ABCFM maintained a strong prejudice against education in evangelical work. It would be a long struggle for the ABCFM to redefine and elevate education on a par with evangelism for men. This difference in attitude toward education demonstrated the fundamental differences between the background and training of the men and women who made up the gender-divided boards. The leaders of the two women's boards were college-educated, sympathetic to the political and legal changes coming for women, and committed to reaching "native" women through education rather than evangelism. The women who chose to become missionaries in foreign fields were educated at Mount Holyoke, Rockford College, Wellesley, and Smith; they were schooled in social amelioration, and their classmates became settlement workers in New York, Boston, and Chicago. The men, however, largely came to missionary work through religion and the ministry and distrusted higher education in their quest for "civilizing" non-Protestant Christians. These differences were clear in the women's focus on reproducing their education abroad, and in the men's discomfort with and suspicion of the growing autonomy of the women who were teaching secular curricula in educational institutions in Japan, Turkey, China, and Africa.[23]

From the beginning, the women's boards operated on three fundamental principles: "the work was for their own sex; they would send single women only as their missionaries; and they would consider the establishment and support of girls' boarding schools as of primary importance."[24] By 1903, sixteen collegiate institutions in nine countries were closely connected to the American Board, of which four were already under a separate board of trustees. Of the remaining twelve, four were women's colleges—two in Ottoman Turkey, one in Spain, and one in Japan.[25] The WBMI founded the first boarding school for girls in Japan, which became Kobe College, and took over three others: the Central Turkey College for Girls in Marash, the school for girls in Samokov, Bulgaria, and the newly formed North China Union Women's College, all of which they believed could be classed as colleges.[26]

At home, the WBMI employed several strategies to secure support. Its members reached local networks of women through churches and women's seminaries. Using strategies that emphasized personal relationships, they raised interest in missionary work by creating what the WBMI called a "sense of immediateness."[27] This was an effort to directly link lay supporters to the women missionaries in foreign fields. They promoted missionary interest among children and accepted very small donations so that even women of small means could participate. In these ways, the women's boards increased the number of local auxiliaries much more quickly than the ABCFM. They organized the locals into state associations, which linked to the national association. By 1872, when only four years old, the WBMI had organized 208 chapters in the Midwest alone, and by its ten-year anniversary the number had increased to 669, including 150 children's "mission bands" and branches in women's seminaries. At the end of thirty years, in 1898, there were 2,692 societies, including junior and children's organizations. Individual societies supported individual missionaries, giving the societies a sense of connection and immediacy. Collecting "tiny gifts from hired girls in farmhouses throughout the land,"[28] casting widely across class and region, the WBMI was able to raise funds to support its missionaries. Nevertheless, despite its financial support for the ABCFM, women missionaries' salaries were less than half those of men, and support for the women's schools, hospitals, and other endeavors was consistently less than that given to the men. For years, women of the WBMI chafed under this unequal support, argued for better pay for teachers and greater support for buildings and supplies, and meanwhile did what they could to ensure the education of the women in their mission fields.

Following the formation of the women's boards, the numbers of single, educated American women who went to Turkey rose. While each missionary professed her desire to bring the word of Christ to the "heathen" of Turkey, the Turkish government had banned the teaching of Christianity among Turkish Muslims, thus limiting potential converts to Armenians, Jews, Nestorians, and other religious minorities within the Turkish realm. Under these conditions, the missionaries stationed in the minority villages were unavoidably caught up in struggles over religious and political control.

Two early missionary travelers to Turkey were Mary and Charlotte Ely, graduates of Mount Holyoke and models of American female culture. They were, as Vickery described, equally romantic and committed to the missionary ideals as presented to them by visiting missionaries in the parlors of Mount Holyoke. Once in Turkey, however, they found themselves in a place that was not only profoundly alien but hostile to their sincerest aims. Over time, the sisters were able to fashion an American-style education for women, symbolically and concretely, while adapting to the limits set by the political, cultural, and religious forces shaping their students' lives.

Although Mary and Charlotte were born respectively in 1841 and 1839, the Ely sisters graduated together in 1861. The sisters grew up in Connecticut with their minister father, Reverend Judah, and mother Caroline, an Englishwoman from Bath, Bristol County. Their father died when the sisters were young and they were raised by their mother, a devout Christian who supported missionary causes. The sisters taught briefly after graduating from Mount Holyoke, then in 1865 went to visit family and to study in Europe for a year. Charlotte studied music and Mary studied French and German. On their return voyage, they happened to meet aboard ship the Reverend George and Alzina Knapp, who were just beginning a furlough from their missionary station in the Armenian village of Bitlis, Turkey. For the duration of the voyage, the sisters sat mesmerized on a Turkish rug with the Knapps, listening to their tales of travel and adventure.[29] At the end of the voyage, the Knapps invited both Mary and Charlotte to Bitlis to work with them, an offer that neither sister was prepared to accept.

Missionary activities began in Turkey with the arrival in 1820 of Levi Parsons and Pliny Fisk, who found themselves drawn to the region. "[I]n historical, archeological, and Biblical interest no lands compared with Asia Minor, Syria, and Egypt."[30] A printing press was set up in Malta to publish the Bible in vernacular languages, and in 1831 the first permanent station was established in Constantinople (modern Istanbul). Of all missionary activities, educational undertakings would prove to be the most influential, widespread, and long-lasting. Under the directorship of William Goodell, the first American Bible school was established in 1831, and a girls' school followed in 1834. Goodell and those who came after him envisioned literacy as a way to enable the Bible to be read more widely. By the 1840s, the first theological seminary had been founded by Cyrus Hamlin for the training of future pastors and teachers. Odul Bozkurt, historian of missionaries in Turkey, argues that a central aspect of the period was the introduction of female education on a large scale. The schools expanded significantly after the formation of the women's boards, and by the 1890s missionaries had established twenty secondary schools for girls in the Ottoman Empire. From the beginning, with the restrictions against proselytizing among Muslims (Kurds and Turks) and little interest among Jews and Gregorian Armenians, the missionaries located in eastern Turkey focused their attention largely on the communities of Protestant Armenians. For the Ely sisters, this would prove to be a painful political alliance.

The Knapps had arrived at their missionary station in the ancient city of Diarbakir on the Tigris River in eastern Turkey in 1856. Two years later, Rev. Knapp was advised to spend some time in the nearby mountains of Bitlis for his health. Bitlis is situated on a mountain plateau at five thousand feet, rising from a narrow river valley into the mountain slopes. An ancient mountain castle dominates the town, with houses cut from lava blocks terraced into the hills. In the nineteenth century, it was the capital of a semi-autonomous Kurdish principality, with a population of thirty thousand Armenians, Kurds, and Turks. Here, the air was fresh and cool, and Bitlis was considered to be one of the most picturesque and healthy towns.

Upon their arrival, the Knapps—the first Protestants and only Americans in town—proceeded to spread the word of the gospel. In 1860, they were joined by a second missionary couple, the Rev. and Mrs. Lysander Burbank, who established a Bible class for men. Despite an edict from Constantinople declaring religious freedom in the Empire, the Burbanks faced resistance from the local Armenian church hierarchy in Bitlis, which forbade Armenian children from going to the Protestant schools. After the Knapps protested to the British ambassador, Armenian church leaders took a less confrontational but more competitive approach, opening up free schools for both boys and girls right across from the Protestant chapel, thereby temporarily undermining the Protestant enterprise.[31]

The Knapps and Burbanks pressed on with their work and by 1866, with the help of a missionary widow from Harput, they were able to open a school for girls. It was their hope, however, to recruit a teacher and principal from the United States to run a boarding school.[32] That year, both the Knapps and the Burbanks, tired and in ill health, took a lengthy furlough from their work and returned to the United States. It was on the last leg of their trip, aboard the ship from Liverpool to New York, that they crossed paths with the Ely sisters. Of the two, Charlotte was most attracted to the Knapps' stories, and upon her return to the U.S. she contacted her college classmates from Mount Holyoke to find a volunteer for the Bitlis station. Charlotte was unsuccessful in finding a recruit for Bitlis, but the idea stayed with her for the next year and a half until she was visited again by the Knapps toward the end of their furlough. When the Knapps renewed their offer, Charlotte had already decided to go, and Mary agreed to join her.

The Knapps and Burbanks were not the first missionaries with whom the Ely sisters had had contact. At Mount Holyoke they met Fidelia Fiske, one of the first single women to go to the Middle East as a missionary in 1843, and other experienced missionaries also taught at Mount Holyoke by then, including Dr. Justin Perkins, who had been in the Middle East for thirty years. Moreover, the Elys' own mother, Caroline, had as a girl wanted to become a missionary to the South Sea Islands, but was thwarted by fragile health. Instead, she married an American Presbyterian minister and moved to Philadelphia from her native England. A bit of wanderlust may have been in the Ely women's blood.

The underlying motivation of these single women missionaries to travel to remote lands and alien cultures intrigues us today, and it also worried the ABCFM's board of examiners. In responding to the Elys' applications, the board's foreign secretary wrote of his concern that they were guided by sentimental, romantic wishes to see an exotic country. Notwithstanding their hurt protestations in response, surely Mary and Charlotte were as drawn to the unknown as they were sure of their commitment to their Christian faith and the missionary purpose. In fact, historian Barbara Merguerian argues that adventure and romance were compelling draws for the Ely sisters.[33] Like many of the women who chose missionary work, they brought with them a concept of privilege and service that had been cultivated by Mary Lyon at Mount Holyoke. Educated at the highest level available to American women, they were imbued with equally strong lessons of philanthropy and civic responsibility that defined Lyon's concept of Christian charity. It was a singularly female model, which both preserved women's sphere and at the same time elevated that sphere through literacy and the training of the mind. It is particularly significant that, like all the missionary women who traveled to Turkey in this period, the Ely sisters and other single women coming out of women's colleges were offered an opportunity to start schools in their own image.

Once arrived, Mary and Charlotte Ely optimistically named the new school "Mount Holyoke in Bitlis," a tribute to their alma mater and their hope for the women and girls of their village. Over time, the school's curriculum grew with the increased demand for education in the village. They reproduced the "Mount Holyoke plan," which meant that the students were responsible for domestic work. The purpose of education was not only to impart knowledge, but also to shape and mold their character. In keeping with the principles of the American Board, Mount Holyoke in Bitlis was to retain as much as possible the native customs of the students and avoid "Westernizing" or "modernizing" them in a way that would separate them from their families and villages. In a letter written in 1869, the sisters said of their students,

> We are fully persuaded it is best to train them in keeping with the condition of the people—not to raise their general habits of living so far above the ways of the nation at large as to make any distinction of class and thus enfeeble their influence with their own people. In a word, our aim is to teach them the Gospel, not civilization.[34]

Implied in this assessment is their belief in Western cultural superiority, and that Western education and religion had the power to uplift the students, independent of the local culture. These dual concepts, intrinsic to the missionary mind and unwittingly patronizing, were blinders that made the resistance of the Turkish government to the Christian missionary presence difficult for the missionaries to comprehend. At the same time, however, these two ideas also allowed common ground between the modernizing desires of parents and the philanthropic impulse of the missionaries. A Western-style education for girls appealed to growing numbers of parents, who easily welcomed its benefits without adopting the missionaries' form of Christianity.

Over time the curriculum expanded, following Mary Lyon's stress on science along with arithmetic, grammar, astronomy, physiology, and eventually the full range of the classical curriculum. In 1870, in a dramatic act symbolizing the bringing of Western education to Bitlis, Charlotte Ely had a Steinway piano imported from Boston so she could teach singing. The piano reached the port of Trabzon, whence it was carried over two hundred miles by porters south across mountainous eastern Turkey to the hill town of Bitlis, "sustaining surprisingly little damage."[35]

Along with education, the Ely sisters communicated a Protestant theology that valued the individual's autonomous relationship to God and community. Over time, they altered the curriculum to suit the ideas and needs of the community and altered the Western practice of Protestant Christianity to accommodate the practices of the local Armenians and their mixture of Christian and ancient pagan traditions. While much of their original vision changed, Mary and Charlotte held to their belief in the education of girls and women, despite opposition rooted in local traditions of early marriage and the devaluation of girls in favor of boys. Little by little, the Ely sisters became only occasional travelers to America, having shifted their cultural center to some location halfway between who they had been and whom they now served.

In 1895, the town of Bitlis was one of the targets for a wave of Muslim attacks on Armenians. Eyewitness accounts listed five hundred dead in Bitlis alone, leaving hundreds of orphans in the hands of the Ely sisters and the school. Missionaries around the region wrote to the regional governors for help, but to no avail. Nor did the government either protect the missionaries or assist the Armenians. The Ely sisters were asked to leave Turkey, which they did temporarily, but they returned again in 1897 to help rebuild the village. The school continued on with new missionary arrivals and some hope until the outbreak of World War I. In 1913, as the sisters were about to celebrate forty-five years in Bitlis, Mary became ill with a heart condition and died at the American hospital in Beirut at the age of 72. Charlotte stayed on in Bitlis without her lifelong companion until war broke out between Russia and Turkey in the fall of 1914. A general uprising of the Kurds against the government had brought Turkish soldiers into the city, and then in 1915 another final round of massacres by the Turkish military began in the villages surrounding Bitlis. Charlotte Ely fled to nearby Van, while Armenians were massacred or led on marches out of their homes. Devastated by her incomprehensible losses, Charlotte Ely died in Van in July 1915.

The Ely sisters did not abandon their belief in American exceptionalism, but they did shift their work from purely philanthropic and evangelical goals to a focus on the singular importance of education for girls. They turned their lives over to the world they created at Mount Holyoke in Bitlis and in the end could do little as their town crumbled around them.

One of the most compelling factors sustaining the international missionary enterprise, and the one most vulnerable to modification over time, was the belief in American exceptionalism. In his book on the missionary experience in China, Lian Xi argues that the missionary ideology relied on traditional binary distinctions between civilization and barbarism, light and darkness. For some missionaries, however, a growing belief in the worth of local cultural traditions threatened the distinctions that were required to sustain pure dedication to Christian evangelism.[36] While the Ely sisters met the culture halfway, Ellen Stone abandoned those distinctions and came to identify with the local culture.

In the 1870s and again in late 1895, missionaries across Turkey were witnesses to a systematic program of hostilities toward Bulgarians and Armenians carried out by Turkish soldiers and nationals in countless villages. Ellen Stone, an American missionary working in a Bulgarian village in Macedonia, was one of those witnesses. Like the Ely sisters in eastern Turkey, Stone became wholly committed to her life in the outposts of the Ottoman Empire. And, like the Ely sisters, she could not have foreseen how local politics and centuries-old internecine struggles would affect her directly.

On 3 September 1901, Ellen Stone was taken captive by a band of brigands. She and a small entourage of teachers from the local Protestant primary schools were traveling along a remote mountain path between Bansko and the Razlog region of Macedonia. Stone was in Bansko to conduct a two-week training and refresher course for local teachers in the Protestant primary schools and for "Bible women," who worked under the auspices of the missionary station at Salonika. A few hours outside of Bansko, the brigands surprised and surrounded them. Brandishing knives and shouting in what sounded to the teachers like poor Turkish, they immediately separated Stone from the group. In keeping with social norms that would not permit a woman to travel alone in the company of men, they singled out Katerina Tsilka, a young Bulgarian teacher, to be her companion. Madam Tsilka was married to an Albanian Christian minister who watched helplessly as the two women were taken off into the mountains. She was six months pregnant at the time.

Ellen Stone was an unlikely captive. Born in Roxbury, Massachusetts, in 1846, she taught school in Chelsea, Massachusetts, before joining the editorial staff of the *Boston Congregationalist*. In 1878, at the age of thirty-two, Stone made the decision to dedicate herself to missionary service and applied for foreign service with the Board. Her first assignment was with the girls' school in Samokov, Bulgaria, and she was reassigned to Plovdiv in 1883. In accordance with Board practice, she studied the Bulgarian language in preparation for her work.

Much of the next ten years was spent visiting Protestant Bulgarian women in their homes, teaching reading, science, and rudimentary hygienics while propagandizing for Protestant Christianity. Stone also began to train a corps of native Protestant women to perform similar work. She took charge of the Plovdiv Girls' School for a time and also traveled to Sofia during 1885 to minister to the casualties of the Serbian-Bulgarian war. In 1898 she was assigned to the Salonika Mission Station and placed in charge of evangelical work for women in the area. Her new job required much touring throughout Protestant communities in Macedonia, most of them isolated in rural mountainous areas.

Katerina Stefanova Tsilka was Bulgarian by birth and had been educated in America at the Northfield Seminary, later graduating from the training school for nurses at the Presbyterian Hospital in New York City. Two years before, she had met and married the Reverend Gregory Tsilka, an Albanian by birth who was completing his studies at the Union Theological Seminary in New York. Both had studied at the missionary schools in Monastir and Samokov before going to America, and both were fluent in English and Bulgarian. The summer after their marriage, they returned to Macedonia to devote their lives to Christian work in their homeland. Katerina Tsilka had relatives in Bansko, whom she had been visiting when the incident occurred.

Prior to the kidnapping, according to Ellen Stone's memoir in *McClure's Magazine*, she had a few trifling brushes with the bandits plaguing Macedonia.[37] These encounters made her conscious of the dangers of touring, but as she had traveled the road from Bansko to Gorna Dzhumaia many times, she did not fear the trip. In fact, her facility with the language and familiarity with the people of the area gave her a distinct feeling of security.

The decision to seize Ellen Stone was not an easy one for her captors. She was, after all, a woman of fifty-five who might not survive the difficult and hazardous flight through the mountains. However, they believed that the Turkish government would ransom her quickly to avoid international complications. In this they misjudged both Ellen Stone's fortitude and the Turkish government's compliance.

The identity of Ellen Stone's captors was suspected shortly after her capture. They were the latest warriors in a five-hundred-year-old struggle of the Bulgarian people against the Ottoman Empire. It was only since the mid-nineteenth century that Bulgarians had experienced a cultural revival of language, religion, and literary tradition, resulting in the establishment of schools and a Bulgarian church. International powers pressured Turkey to grant civil and religious rights to the Christians in its Balkan territories, but with little effect. The April Uprising of 1876 that resulted in the massacre of Bulgarian Christians by the Turks, which occurred just prior to Stone's arrival, prompted the European powers to discuss the fate of Bulgaria.

Russia recommended creating an autonomous Bulgarian state, but England, fearing that such a state would have disproportionate power because of its size and location, recommended creating two smaller states. Russia accepted the compromise, but the suggestion was unilaterally rejected by the Ottoman government, and Russia declared war. Russia swiftly occupied all the northern territories of the Ottoman Empire, threatened Constantinople, and in 1878 the Turks conceded an autonomous Bulgarian principality. The Treaty of Berlin, signed in July 1878, divided the Principality of Bulgaria into three regions, but did not include Macedonia, which remained within Turkish borders, laying the groundwork for the revolutionary movement.[38] Formal demands for reforms that would protect the religious and civil rights of Bulgarians in Macedonia did not move the Turkish government. Because of tight censorship of newspapers published in the Ottoman Empire and the illegality of political activity in Macedonia, the people's demands for reform were publicized only in the press of the Bulgarian principality and in the *Zornitsa*, a Bulgarian-language newspaper published in Constantinople by American missionaries. It was certainly through this newspaper that Ellen Stone, fluent in Bulgarian, followed the ongoing discontents and the hopes of the Bulgarian Christians in Macedonia.

Turkish propaganda demanding that Bulgarians take up Serbian nationality and accept the authority of the Greek patriarch further inflamed Bulgarian national pride. In 1896, a small Macedonian Revolutionary Movement (IMRO) was formed, dedicated to the full political autonomy of Macedonia. Money, however, was a constant problem. Robberies, extortions, and kidnappings were all considered as expedients, despite swift and generally violent reprisals by the Turkish government. Over the next few years, the movement suffered from lack of organization, bungled robberies and kidnappings, and on-again, off-again relations with Bulgaria, which wished both to assist and to control the Macedonian Bulgarian movement. By the summer of 1901, the organization, desperate for money to fund training and propagandizing in villages, decided to kidnap a wealthy Turkish leader. Before the kidnapping could take place, however, the targeted man suffered a debilitating stroke. At that point, Yane Sandansky and Khristo Chernopeev headed to Bansko to construct a new plan.

The town of Bansko had both a thriving Protestant church and an active chapter of IMRO. Dimitur Lazarov, chairman of the local revolutionary committee, was also an active member of the Protestant church. Protestants, it was said, were more zealous than their orthodox counterparts. The new kidnapping target was Dr. John House, a missionary in Sofia who was planning a trip to Bansko. But House refused to travel in the area, believing it to be too dangerous. However, Sandansky and Chernopeev learned that an American missionary was in Bansko at that very moment preparing to travel. It is not clear who suggested kidnapping a missionary,[39] but the links between the revolutionary movement and the Protestant community were apparent to those closest to the kidnapping. In the first few weeks of her capture, Ellen Stone was suspected by journalists and local officials of not only being aware of the revolutionary goals, but of possibly being a co-conspirator.[40] Fearing Turkish reprisals, the bandits tried to deflect suspicion from themselves by wearing Turkish military uniforms and speaking in Turkish. They further hoped that waiting to act until the entourage was out of town would spare the village from harm by angry Turkish militia.

Within hours of the kidnapping, messages were sent to the American consul general in Constantinople and to the State Department in

Washington, D.C., alerting both the ABCFM and the American government. Local Turkish authorities reacted swiftly, but had little success tracing the kidnappers or learning their identities. Turkish government officials were immediately suspicious that the Protestants had worked together with the revolutionaries in planning the kidnapping. Within days the Bulgarian government closed its borders with Macedonia to prevent the kidnappers from crossing it. Few were fooled into thinking that the kidnappers were Turkish.

On September 24, the kidnappers finally sent a ransom note, in Ellen Stone's handwriting, demanding 25,000 lira, or $100,000, in payment for the release of the two women. Stone described them as merciless and their situation desperate, though her own memoir would later say that she and Tsilka were treated quite well, despite being moved continually.[41] The letter went to Reverend H. C. Haskell at the American School in Samokov, who carried it immediately to Constantinople. Speculations about the kidnappers were rampant. The Bulgarian press supported the theory that the group was composed of Turkish soldiers, while the Turkish government and the American minister to Constantinople believed that Bulgarians had organized in Bulgaria for the purposes of kidnapping Stone for ransom. Missionaries were convinced that the kidnapping had political as well as monetary motives. According to this theory, the bandits were aided by the Macedonian revolutionary committee in Bulgaria. The missionaries also believed the kidnapping was revenge for their failure to support the Macedonian cause in the past and that it was intended to provoke foreign intervention in Macedonia's plight. One more theory, held by some Turkish officials, was that Stone and Tsilka had had a hand in their own kidnapping, either because of their sympathies for the Macedonian revolutionaries, or because they expected a large part of the ransom for themselves.

The Ellen Stone story captivated the American imagination. She was the first known American woman captured outside the continental United States and a representative of a powerful religious segment of the American population.[42] It is not surprising that her dramatic plight became a national *cause célèbre*, championed by the American government. While the State Department sent out press releases and warned the Turkish government about possible consequences if she were killed, they did not agree to pay a ransom. Nor did the American Board of Foreign Missions, for fear of setting a precedent. The Bulgarians insisted that the crime took place in Turkey and was therefore the responsibility of the Turkish government, whereas the Turks believed the brigands were Bulgarians and so also refused to pay. On October 3, a month after the abduction, the acting secretary of state recommended to the foreign secretary of the American Board that the money be raised by private donations. The secretary of state assured the Board that the American government would make every effort to secure money from the government found responsible for the kidnapping, or, at the very least, urge Congress to reimburse the contributors. With these assurances, a committee of Stone's friends, her brother Charles, and the employees of the *Christian Herald*—the voice of the ABCFM—began a campaign across the nation to raise money for her release. Within days they had set up an account for contributions and notified the State Department that the money would be raised. By October 26, the committee had raised an astonishing $66,000 for the ransom of Ellen Stone.[43] This rapid mobilization of resources doubtless reflected the national network of women's auxiliaries the women's boards had developed to support the missionary work abroad. With thousands of local branches linked to missionary activities, it is possible to imagine the outpouring of concern for Ellen Stone and the immediate response to the request for donations to free her from captivity.

What followed was a series of complicated and arcane negotiations among representatives of the State Department, the governments of Bulgaria, Russia, Turkey, and England, and finally the kidnappers themselves. During this interminable period, Stone and Tsilka were moved from place to place in the Macedonian mountains with winter approaching and Tsilka nearing childbirth. The ransom had been collected in October, and no one involved would have predicted that the captivity would drag on through the winter. Tsilka gave birth on 2 January 1902.[44] Both women later presented vivid and dramatic accounts of their primitive accommodations, the places they were taken, and the drama of Tsilka's childbirth in captivity. Never in their memoirs, however, do the women identify their captors, nor do they criticize the cause for which they were held in captivity. In the letters written by Stone pleading for the government to meet the ransom demands and save her life, she signed her name using the Bulgarian form, Ellenova. She never says whether that signature was coerced or chosen.

In the end, the kidnappers were never identified or caught, and only revealed their identities by choice many years later. While the missionaries and American and Turkish government officials were convinced the kidnappers were part of the Macedonian movement, they had no tangible evidence and neither Stone nor Tsilka was very helpful in providing information that could have led to their capture. In interviews with police immediately upon their release, as in the accounts in *McClure's*, Stone reported the brigands were "unquestionably Turkish subjects," despite their fluency in the Bulgarian language and failure to follow Muslim traditions of food or prayer. While she probably told no outright lies, Stone "could not remember" much of what she was asked about.[45] The Ottoman government suspected that the plan had been carried out with the knowledge and agreement of the Tsilkas, who were Christian Bulgarians. Journalists at the time reported that most people did not suspect that Stone was a willing participant in her own kidnapping, but they did suspect her of not telling the whole truth. It is possible that Stone's captors threatened her and Katerina Tsilka, whose family lived in Bansko, within easy reach of the Macedonian revolutionaries. Perhaps Stone chose to protect Tsilka's family, or to preserve the interests of the Protestant mission; perhaps she deliberately protected her captors.[46]

Stone did not reveal any incriminating information about the band once she returned to the United States. She may have provided more information in a book she was writing, but the manuscript was destroyed in a fire at her home in Massachusetts in 1908.[47] She did, however, become an ardent and open supporter of Macedonian independence and the leading exponent of Ottoman responsibility for the affair. In a series of lectures across the United States in 1903 and 1904, Stone described Turkish atrocities in Macedonia and preached the necessity of freeing Macedonia from the Ottoman Empire. At the end of the 1902 memoir in *McClure's*, she summarized her position:

> Had Turkey ever fulfilled her promise, made twenty-four years ago in the Treaty of Berlin, to introduce reforms for the betterment of the various Christian nations ruled over by her, Macedonia might not be overrun and terrorized as now it is by brigands and this strange spectacle of women kidnapped by them and held in the heart of the Balkan peninsula for an exorbitant ransom might never have happened.

Stone's lectures led many missionaries to strongly censure her for "singing too much the song of the brigands themselves,"[48] and the American Board finally warned her that they would have to disassociate themselves from her if she continued her anti-Turk, pro-Macedonian lectures.

Over the next few years, Stone petitioned the government to re-imburse each of the more than 2,200 individuals who had contributed to her ransom. From 1905 to 1908, she pressed the State Department to secure repayment from the responsible government, but the State Department could not determine whether the claim should be pressed against Turkey or Bulgaria. Unsatisfied, Stone took the matter to Congress, which was responsive, having been notified by the secretary of state that the assurances of repayment had been "instrumental in enabling Miss Stone's friends to secure the sum of $66,000." Between 1908 and 1912, the Senate four times passed legislation authorizing repayment of the money raised to ransom Ellen Stone, but the bill never passed the House of Representatives. Finally, on 21 May 1912, Congress passed a bill enabling the secretary of state to return to contributors who filed a claim within two years of the passage of the bill "the money raised to pay the ransom for the release of Miss Ellen M. Stone, an American missionary to Turkey who was abducted by brigands on September third, nineteen hundred and one."[49]

What happened to Ellen Stone? What led to her transformation from a New England Congregationalist missionary to a spokesperson for the Macedonian revolutionary cause? We can assume that the missionary Ellen Stone did not intend to become the Patty Hearst of her day. The plight of the Bulgarian Christian community undoubtedly influenced her attitudes up to the moment of her capture in 1901, and her support for the Bulgarian cause is unexpected but understandable. Perhaps by then Stone believed her calling was not only to teach and uplift, but also to assist in the political liberation of an oppressed Christian minority. Surely Stone could not have predicted her own transformation from a traveling missionary educator in remote Macedonian villages to the centerpiece of an international political kidnapping.

Stone came to Macedonia with a level of education still unusual among American women and a deep Protestant conviction of the inviolability of the individual in relation to God. She found herself the guest of a government hostile to the people she came to serve, in a period of international political alignments, when she knew of and even witnessed brutal acts by the Turkish government against the Protestant Bulgarians. In concert with the long-standing universal missionary practice of learning the vernacular language, Stone was fluent in Bulgarian, not Turkish. Her educational goals for women and children, her Protestant religious convictions, her belief in republican freedoms, and her years of intimate familiarity and friendship with, and concern for, the people among whom she worked are possible reasons for her decision to publicly support the Macedonian cause after nearly six months in captivity. Stone never told us why she adopted her views, but upon her return, she publicized them, clearly and often, to the alarm of the American Board.

The transformation of Ellen Stone is a study in her evolution from educator and evangelist to advocate for the political rights of a Christian minority. While she went abroad with the conviction that she could promote Protestant Christianity, education, and respect for women, she departed as a political prisoner and partisan for the Macedonian liberation movement. Stone redirected the impulse for philanthropy and education to a lifetime commitment to political reform. In this way, she is not unlike her college classmates who became settlement workers and advocates for social change. In the process, she abandoned the binary distinctions that defined "other" as inferior and misguided, and replaced them with a view of the people of Macedonia as oppressed equals.

"In all mission fields," Merguerian argues, "the American schools were popular with the indigenous populations, but not always for the reasons intended by the board. American schools became a vehicle for the acquisition of a Western education by students who often had no interest in the Protestant religion."[50] Indeed, this proved to be the case in Turkey. Why, then, did missionaries continue to go to these unrepentant lands, generation after generation, and why did they stay? Missionaries were educators, adventurers, and reformers of a particular sort, who shared some commonalities. They were middle class, well educated for their day, and had not ventured beyond their own regions before taking off alone into a challenging and often dangerous unknown. In addition to their commitment to Christian service, they were captivated by the stories told by missionaries on furlough, individuals who fueled their imaginations with images of exotic places and wild adventures. It is not surprising that the American Board commissioners worried about their motivations.

Missionary status both allowed women to travel alone and defined the parameters of their experiences. It was work that required a level of commitment and confidence unasked-for in other work they might have chosen. The missionaries in the field did not stay because they were successful at bringing the heathen to Christ. At this they were decidedly unsuccessful. They stayed because they became bilingual, bicultural, and embedded in the daily lives of their communities. Each was deeply committed to the education of girls and women, and to the improvement of the lives of individuals. The missionaries who stayed were able to maintain high standards of education, while incorporating the fundamental values of local cultures. Ellen Stone could teach Bible studies and support a political insurrection against her host country. And the Ely sisters, dramatically importing a Steinway piano from Boston to their mountain village in eastern Turkey, did not convert many Armenians to Protestantism, but did teach girls to read and write and offered them the chance to be teachers as well as wives. The missionaries presented here, and many others like them, were as profoundly changed by their experiences as they were agents of change for the people of their adopted towns and villages.

NOTES

Research for this chapter was made possible through a generous grant from the Spencer Foundation. I would also like to acknowledge sabbatical and Faculty Fellowship support from Indiana University Northwest and the office of Indiana University International Programs.

1. See, for example, Arthur Schlesinger, Jr., "Missionary Enterprise and Theories of Imperialism," in *The Missionary Enterprise in China and America,* ed. John King Fairbank (Cambridge, Mass.: Harvard University Press, 1974); William R. Hutchison, *Errand to the World: American Protestant Thought and Foreign Missions* (Chicago: University of Chicago Press, 1987); and Albert K. Weinberg, *Manifest Destiny: A Study of Nationalist Expansionism in American History* (1935; reprint, Chicago: Quadrangle, 1963).

2. This idea is developed by Barbara J. Merguerian in "Mt. Holyoke Seminary in Bitlis: Providing an American Education for Armenian Women," *Armenian Review* 43 (spring 1990): 31–65.

3. For an account of the founding of the American Board of Commissioners for Foreign Missions, see William Ellsworth Strong, *The Story of the American Board: An Account of the First Hundred Years of the American Board of Commissioners for Foreign Missions* (1910; reprint, New York: Arno, 1969), 7–9; and Fred Field Goodsell, *You Shall Be My Witness: An Interpretation of the History of the American Board, 1810–1960* (Boston: ABCFM, 1959), 5–10.

4. See Lian Xi, *The Conversion of Missionaries: Liberalism in American Protestant Missions in China, 1907–1932* (University Park: Pennsylvania State University Press, 1997), 7.

5. The history of the ABCFM is vast and complex, encompassing missionary enterprises in Japan, China, the Ottoman Empire, Africa, India, Burma, Bulgaria, and the American West. The most complete archival holdings for the ABCFM are in the Houghton Manuscript Library of Harvard University, including the years from its founding in 1810 to 1967. The majority of the primary material for this chapter comes from the ABCFM archive of the Houghton Library.

6. The first missionary was sent to India in 1812, and the second to the Sandwich Islands (Hawai'i) in 1819 (Frank A. Stone, "Mt. Holyoke's Impact on the Land of Mt. Ararat" [reprinted in *The Muslim World: A Quarterly Review of History, Culture, Religions, and the Christian Mission in Islamdom* 66 (1976): 44–57]). Emma Bliss, the wife of one of the ABCFM founders, Reverend H. J. Van Lenney, was a Mount Holyoke graduate and the first woman to perish in service to Turkey, one year after her arrival there in 1834, becoming a martyr and heroine of the new missionary agenda.

7. The most comprehensive analysis of the Mount Holyoke tradition and its relationship to the missionary movement is in Amanda Porterfield, *Mary Lyon and the Mount Holyoke Missionaries* (New York: Oxford University Press, 1997). See also Bess Vickery, *Mount Holyoke Courageous: A Call to the Near East* (New York: Carlton, 1994); and Merguerian, "Mt. Holyoke Seminary in Bitlis."

8. Porterfield, *Mary Lyon*, 5.

9. Eager for women's support of mission work, Anderson nevertheless opposed sending single women missionaries abroad; he also opposed the formation of the women's boards. It was not until his retirement in 1866 that the women's boards were approved under the leadership of Rev. N. G. Clark, who succeeded Anderson and supported women's missionary work from the beginning of his appointment.

10. Stone, "Mt. Holyoke's Impact," 47.

11. Ibid.

12. Quoted in Noriko Kawamura Ishii, "American Women Missionaries at Kobe College, 1873–1909" (Ph.D. diss., George Washington University, 1998), 48. As early as 1834 Rev. David Abeel, a missionary in China, had appealed to Christian women in the U.S. and England to evangelize among the degraded native women in India and China (47).

13. Between the years 1837 and 1940, a total of almost four hundred Mount Holyoke graduates were appointed overseas, of whom some sixty served in the four American Board missions in Turkey (Stone, "Mt. Holyoke's Impact," 47).

14. Vickery, *Mount Holyoke Courageous*, xxii.

15. For an excellent study of the impact of missionary education on Turkish women in the early twentieth century, see Odul Bozkurt, "The Making of Young Women at an American Missionary School in Early Republican Turkey: A Study Based on the Life Histories of the 1928–1940 Graduates of the American Collegiate Institute for Girls in Izmir" (master's thesis, Bogazici University, Turkey, 1995).

16. See Louise Porter Thomas, *Seminary Militant: An Account of the Missionary Movement at Mount Holyoke Seminary and College* (South Hadley, Mass.: Department of English, Mount Holyoke College, 1937).

17. Patricia R. Hill, *The World Their Household: The American Woman's Foreign Mission Movement and Cultural Transformation, 1870–1920* (Ann Arbor: University of Michigan Press, 1985), 2–3, 8.

18. Ishii, "American Women Missionaries," 44.

19. Ibid., 45. The Woman's Union Missionary Society was organized in 1861. Formation of the ABCFM Women's Board was followed by Methodist, Presbyterian, Baptist, and Episcopal women's boards.

20. Ishii, "American Women Missionaries," 46. In 1889, the total revenue from the American Board in the Interior District was $93,164, of which $45,701 came from the WBMI.

21. R. Pierce Beaver, *All Loves Excelling: American Protestant Women in World Mission* (Grand Rapids, Mich.: Eerdmans, 1968), 63.

22. Ishii, "American Women Missionaries," 58.

23. The ABCFM closed down the women's boards in 1927. For a full discussion, see Ishii, epilogue, 304–31.

24. Goodsell, *You Shall Be My Witness,* 162.

25. Ishii, "American Women Missionaries," 42.

26. Their idea of a collegiate curriculum was largely comparable to that offered at Mount Holyoke.

27. Ishii, "American Women Missionaries," 74.

28. Ibid., 79.

29. Anna Edwards Alumnae Biographical File, Mount Holyoke College Archives and Special Collections, South Hadley, Mass.

30. Bozkurt, "The Making of Young Women," 19.

31. Merguerian, "Mt. Holyoke Seminary in Bitlis," 33–34.

32. Prior to 1868, wives of missionaries, although they had "assistant missionary" status, were not given much responsibility, nor were they often trained as teachers. They were largely expected to support the work of their husbands, organize meetings for women, and visit homes. In Turkey, the customary separation of women from men made the role of the missionary wives more important.

33. Merguerian, "Mt. Holyoke Seminary in Bitlis," 35.

34. Ibid., 39.

35. Ibid., 44.

36. Lian Xi, *Conversion,* 9–10.

37. Ellen Stone, "Six Months among Brigands," *McClure's Magazine,* May 1902, 3.

38. The non-Muslim population of Macedonia was diverse, including Greeks, Serbs, Albanians, Bulgarians, Jews, and Gypsies, with each group feeling vulnerable to the Turkish government.

39. Laura Beth Sherman, *Fires on the Mountain: The Macedonian Revolutionary Movement and the Kidnapping of Ellen Stone* (Boulder, Colo.: East European Monographs, distributed by Columbia University Press, 1980), 22.

40. Eugene P. Lyle, Jr., "An American Woman Captured by Brigands," *Everybody's Magazine,* January 1902, 44–55.

41. The details of their days in captivity, the consideration shown to them by their captors, the discomforts of their daily existence, and the cold of winter were published in a six-part series in *McClure's Magazine,* May to October 1902.

42. Sherman, *Fires on the Mountain,* 37.

43. Ibid., 49. There were 2,261 donors to the Ellen Stone fund.

44. Katerina Tsilka's detailed account of the conditions under which her daughter was born appeared in *McClure's Magazine,* August 1902.

45. Sherman, *Fires on the Mountain,* 88.

46. Ibid., 89–90.

47. Ibid., 89.

48. Ibid., 90.

49. Actually, $77,432 was contributed to the ransom fund (House Committee on Claims, *Repayment of Ransom of Ellen Stone,* 62nd Cong., 2nd sess., 1912, H. Rept. 807, 2–3, 5).

50. Barbara Merguerian, "The Beginnings of Armenian Women: The Armenian Female Seminary in Constantinople," *Journal of the Society for Armenian Studies* 5 (1991): 117.

8. Sisters in Service: African American Sororities and Philanthropic Support of Education

Marybeth Gasman

African American sororities have long been one of the major arenas for black self-help and educational advancement. Their rise can best be understood within the context of black women's advances within education and the professions in the early twentieth century. Faced with the challenges of racism and sexism, African American women had few career options in the early 1900s. They were refused entry into most professions other than domestic work,[1] encountering substantial barriers to entry even into the so-called women's careers, such as nursing, social work, and teaching.[2] Despite these considerable obstacles, African American women sought out education as a way to move beyond a life of servitude and to acquire the "greater quality of life and status derived from professional work."[3]

The progress that black women achieved in education and the professions in the late nineteenth and early twentieth centuries was felt not on the level of the individual but in the growing consciousness of black women as a group. Indeed, progress in education and the professions led to the development of several black women's organizations between the late 1800s and the mid-1920s, among them the National Association of Colored Women and the National Republican Colored Women's League. The era also saw black women increase their participation in established organizations that spoke to their life circumstances, such as the National Association for the Advancement of Colored People (NAACP), the National Urban League, and the Young Women's Christian Association (YWCA).[4] And, during this same period, black female students began to organize and founded black sororities on college campuses. Through these venues, black women learned "how to identify issues needing to be addressed, how to mobilize their sisters, how to develop persuasive arguments and how to fight for the survival and well-being of their families and communities."[5]

This chapter illuminates the philanthropic efforts of black sorority women to support and further education—both formal and informal—as a means of serving their communities and working toward social justice. Such an exploration of black women's work in sororities can deepen our historical understanding of the range and significance of black women's civic leadership and contributions to public life. Although this aspect of history is too often overlooked, black women were influential players before and during the Civil Rights movement.[6] Women "organized and operated the structures of the movement, the groups that got things done, while men were spokespersons who interacted with white male leadership." The church, specifically, provided black women with opportunities to lead the masses and "share the tribulations they encountered on the job and at home while providing them the means and faith to triumph and overcome their trials and tribulations."[7] According to Laverne Gyant, this communal experience in the church led to a desire for similar coalitions in educational arenas as well as in the professions.[8] Black sororities are an example of the coalitions to which Gyant refers.

Despite their important contributions to education, philanthropy, and civil rights, however, African American sororities have received scant coverage by historians. This is due in large part to the secretive nature of these organizations. Several of the sororities have not opened their records to the general public; as a result, interested parties must piece together information through oral histories, house histories, and small collections of documents at various colleges across the country. In recent years, two authors have examined the history of the black Greek system; both are "insiders." Lawrence C. Ross, Jr., has provided a basic overview of the nine most prominent fraternities and sororities, one that summarizes their goals and activities.[9] Paula Giddings has looked more intensely at one group, crafting a well-documented portrait of Delta Sigma Theta that situates the sorority nicely in the political, social, and economic contexts in which it developed.[10] Other scholars have explored the experiences of individual black sorority members who have led prominent lives.[11] However, the literature in this area lacks an explicit discussion of sorority membership and participation as a means of philanthropic action. Likewise, although Darlene Clark Hine, Kathleen Thompson, and Evelyn Brooks Higginbotham look at the role of African American women in shaping the church and society, they do not focus their discussions on philanthropy per se.[12] This study seeks to set the history of black sororities in a broader context of education and action for social justice.

Like their white counterparts, black sororities were founded by college women "with the idea of creating social bonds or a sense of sisterhood among [their] members."[13] These young women were initially interested in transforming the individual sorority member into a "finer woman," but given the important societal issues receiving greater notice at the turn of the century, their purposes came to include women's and civil rights issues.[14] According to Giddings, sorority leadership shaped the members to be "agents of change": leaders educated members about the political and legislative issues of the time, including the suffrage movement and the racial climate for blacks.[15]

Greek life is, in limited respects, similar for African American and white women. Both groups' organizations have an esoteric culture that is rich with ritual and symbols and subject to charges of exclusivity. Each has membership criteria and some sort of "intake" procedure,[16] and members in each organization form social bonds with similarly minded students.[17] While membership is lifelong in both systems, in the case of African American sororities, women generally make a lifetime commitment to volunteerism, philanthropic giving, and the support of the African American people.[18]

Membership in a black sorority historically has been considered a sign of commitment to one's scholarly pursuits and a "mark of academic distinction."[19] The emphasis on scholarship served two main purposes. First, it was proof of the intellectual capabilities of black women in a society that doubted their ability to succeed in the academic environment. Second, it signaled the sororities' efforts to increase black women's access to education, as part of the racial obligation to "graduate and reach back to uplift others."[20] In this sense, the goals of black sororities were much closer to those of honor societies like Phi Beta Kappa than they were to those of their white counterparts. According to Lawrence Otis Graham, "[black] sororities . . . are a lasting identity, a circle of lifetime friends, [and] a base for future political and civic activism."[21]

This chapter will explore the contributions of African American sororities to education, especially with regard to women's education in the twentieth century. It will consider the sororities' funding of scholarships, schools, and colleges, as well as their support of specific causes related to education, such as desegregation and civil rights. The chapter will also demonstrate the sororities' efforts to educate a cadre of future professionals. As this effort was often subject to charges of elitism and exclusivity,[22] the chapter will discuss the complex social and economic factors involved in the development and maintenance of these organizations.

ESTABLISHED WITH A FOUNDATION OF PHILANTHROPY

Ethel Hedgeman, a student at Howard University, developed the idea of forming a sorority in the summer before her junior year. Hedgeman told her friends about her plan to "form an association of women students through which the talents and strengths of these students could be organized for the mutual benefits of all."[23] Ethel's friends began working to create a formalized structure; within a week of solidifying their idea, the young women approached the Howard University administration to apply for official organizational status on the black college campus.[24] Shortly afterward, in 1908, the university conferred this status on the organization, named Alpha Kappa Alpha (AKA). The nation's first white sorority, Alpha Delta Pi, had been established fifty-seven years earlier.

At first glance, AKA appeared to be mimicking a white cultural tradition. However, its members were dedicated to community activism and service to the African American community and saw the formalized student organization as a way to accomplish their goals.[25] According to the preamble of AKA's 1909 constitution, the sorority was established to "cultivate high scholastic and ethical standards, improve the social stature of the race, and promote unity and friendship among college women."[26] In the words of AKA's twenty-third Supreme Basileus (president) Mary Shy Scott, sorority leaders took their founding charter seriously: "Every president has tried to emulate the preamble and to make sure that under her watch there's a print that shows that she's been there."[27]

With the success of the Howard chapter, AKA members soon decided to expand to other college campuses. This required some changes in organizational structure—such as legal incorporation. But a group of younger members pushed for more extensive changes. They questioned the meaning of the sorority's name, noting that it was a mere offshoot of their male counterpart, Alpha Phi Alpha (established 1906). Motivated by the feminist movement of 1912, the young women wanted to move AKA in a more political direction nationally.[28] Part of their inspiration also came from the emergence of strong black intellectual leaders such as W. E. B. Du Bois.[29] Unable to reach consensus, the membership divided; those advocating broader changes established Delta Sigma Theta on 13 January 1913.[30]

The Delta members pledged to work to establish a sorority that was "not only a social group but a working group," with each young woman committed to helping her own community.[31] They sought to use "their collective strength to promote academic excellence and to provide assistance to persons in need."[32] Although the Delta mission is similar to that of AKA, the organization considers itself the first and only black sorority founded specifically on the principle of service—thus, to the Delta members, service was a mark of status.[33]

It would be seven more years before another black sorority would form on the Howard University campus. Zeta Phi Beta (Zeta) was founded by five women on 16 January 1920.[34] According to one modern Zeta history, "These women dared to depart from the traditional coalitions for black women and sought to establish a new organization predicated on the precepts of Scholarship, Service, Sisterly Love and Finer Womanhood."[35] However, this "daring" mission appears quite similar to that of the AKAs and the Deltas. Perhaps, as Lawrence Otis Graham suggests, the Zetas' need to create a new sorority was due to ideological or class differences within the existing sororities.[36]

Several years later, on 12 November 1922, seven young women organized another sorority—Sigma Gamma Rho (Sigma)—that emphasized service and achievement. What differentiated it from previous sororities was its location on a predominantly white campus: Butler University in Indianapolis, Indiana. The founders had a straightforward mission: in accordance with their motto "Greater Service, Greater Progress,"[37] they sought "to promote and encourage high scholastic attainment."[38]

GROOMING FOR MEMBERSHIP

As the sororities grew, so did their reach into the community. For example, AKA Supreme Basileus Mary Shy Scott was groomed for this leadership position by her sixth-grade piano teacher: "She was an excellent person to emulate. She was determined that I would be an

Alpha Kappa Alpha." As an undergraduate, Scott attended Spelman College, which did not allow sororities on campus at the time—so she joined after graduation. Scott's experience highlights a key difference between black and white sororities. Many African American women join a graduate sorority chapter instead of joining during their under-graduate years. Scott explained, "We are structured differently from other sororities. We have undergraduate chapters and graduate chapters. This makes us unique and keeps our members involved."[39]

Like Scott, Sibyl Avery Jackson was groomed from birth to be a member of Delta Sigma Theta. In her words, "All the women in my family are Deltas. My mom had a Delta paddle that she kept visible in our house. . . . I didn't even think about which sorority to join. I was raised on public service and excellence and that's what Delta Sigma Theta embodies."[40] Another AKA member, Zenda Bowie, joined the sorority while attending Talladega College. Her mother was an AKA member, as were most of the women in her family. According to Bowie, "AKA is a service organization that is specifically interested in doing whatever we can to enhance the community and lift up our people. This organization is about empowering and education. Education empowers people."[41] Giddings has noted that the "challenge of the sorority . . . is to maintain that sense of sisterhood while striving, organizationally, for a more general purpose: aiding the Black community as a whole through social, political, and economic means."[42] These black women had many reasons for joining a sorority, but many of those reasons were shared, including their interests in education, their desire to cultivate future professional women, and their support of desegregation and civil rights activities.

SUPPORTING EDUCATION THROUGH PHILANTHROPY

Large-scale activism and philanthropy began among black sorori-ties with the involvement of Delta Sigma Theta members in the 3 March 1913 march on Washington on behalf of women's suffrage. The Deltas marched with women of all backgrounds and ethnicities and endured taunts and insults from an angry crowd. According to the *Baltimore Afro-American,* "The women, trudging stoutly along un-der great difficulties, were able to complete their march only when troops of cavalry from Fort Myers were rushed into Washington to take charge of Pennsylvania Avenue."[43] By participating in the march, the Deltas were acting in defiance of the Howard University administration and, in many cases, against the wishes of their parents.[44] Participation in the Woman's Suffragette March was the beginning of the Deltas' enduring commitment to service.

Black sororities fulfilled their stated commitment to education in a variety of ways. In the 1940s, the Grand Basileus of Zeta Phi Beta, Lullelia Harrison, initiated the Prevention and Control of Juvenile Delinquency project. The Zeta sisters were cognizant of increasing problems with juvenile delinquency and wanted to launch a national effort to provide young people with an alternative to crime. In conjunction with U.S. Attorney General Tom Clark, the Zetas designed neighborhood-specific programs to aid youth.[45] Involvement with children, especially young girls, has been a cornerstone of Zeta activities. For example, the Manhattan alumnae chapter in New York City, chartered in 1950, formed a cohesive partnership with Gompers High School in the Bronx. In cooperation with the school's administration, the Zeta volunteers taught reading, math, and science to African American and Hispanic girls in after-school programs. Over time, the sorority's volunteer efforts grew to include an emphasis on writing, which culminated in scholarship competitions. From the onset of their scholarship program, the Zetas tracked the recipients, inquiring as to their success after college, and many times brought them into the sorority as undergraduate or graduate members.[46] By stressing academics, the Zetas encouraged women to strive for greater achievement in education, especially in nontraditional areas.

Because there were very few college-educated women during the early years of the black sororities, the members of Alpha Kappa Alpha became role models for many youth. This role was formalized at the AKA's fifteenth anniversary Boule (annual meeting) in Baltimore, Maryland, in 1923. Following Booker T. Washington's "practical approach" to education, the sorority decided to formally support what it called "vocational education" for children. But the AKA program also encompassed skills that went beyond the menial work often associated with industrial or vocational education.[47] The AKA women wanted to "help students qualify for entrance into . . . [the] professions."[48]

During their 1937 national convention, the sisters of Delta Sigma Theta launched a nationwide library project. Their efforts addressed an urgent need in the black community—especially in rural areas—for reading education. Of the nine million African Americans living in the South, two-thirds were without public library services and thus had little or no exposure to books.[49] The national chapter of Delta

Sigma Theta asked all of its chapters to donate a minimum of ten books, worth approximately $2.50 each. Each local chapter was equipped with a "book basket with a lock and key to facilitate the transportation of the books."[50] The project was aided by the contributions of Delta member Mollie Lee, who held teaching positions at Atlanta University and North Carolina College. Lee advised the library project and asked local teachers and principals to help by assisting with the distribution of books. Perhaps one of the most innovative aspects of the program was the emphasis on providing books about black history and black achievement to people in rural communities, a strategy that gave African American children a glimpse of the past and of the possibilities that lay ahead. After the first year of the program, many teachers and parents wrote to the Deltas to proclaim their appreciation for the library project. Even more significant, several of the rural towns continued the sorority's efforts by creating permanent libraries.[51] In areas that could not support the infrastructure of a library, the Deltas offered help—sometimes providing furniture, film projectors, and trained personnel.[52] The Deltas were also instrumental in lobbying state legislatures in Georgia, North Carolina, and Alabama for library funds, and when none were allotted they provided bookmobiles with librarians.[53]

PHILANTHROPIC EFFORTS IN HIGHER EDUCATION

In a letter to me dated 29 August 2001, AKA member Joanne Jackson Jones remarked, "Our sorority has placed an emphasis on education by offering scholarships to students who are academically worthy and to students who demonstrate a financial need." Her words exemplify the black sororities' commitment to higher education, specifically scholarships for African American women. At their fifth Boule, for example, the AKAs established a fund "to be used as a revolving loan for members who needed financial aid to further their education and made long-range plans for the establishment of graduate awards for foreign study." A form of self-help, this fund strengthened the black female economic base by helping women to attain higher degrees and enter higher-paying professions.[54] According to Supreme Basileus Mary Shy Scott, the AKAs "support education first because the ladies who started the sorority were students at Howard University and realized two things: that there were black women coming into Washington, D.C., who needed support and help and that there were black children coming in who needed support, help, and education."[55]

Alpha Kappa Alpha did much to support women and children with their Summer School for Rural Negro Teachers program, which was developed in 1934.[56] Through this program, AKA volunteers sponsored classes in early child development, art, music, social sciences, and other topics that served the needs of the rural teachers. This was especially important to African American female teachers in the South because they rarely had opportunities for professional development.[57] Moreover, additional training for teachers had a significant impact on the education of children living in rural areas.[58]

Within the ranks of AKA, there were many role models for young women. One of the most influential AKA women was founder Lucy Diggs Slowe. A nationally known educator, Slowe started as a teacher at Armstrong High School in Washington, D.C., in 1915, and later was asked by the board of education to organize the first junior high school in the area.[59] She served as principal of the school for three years and then secured a position as the first dean of women at Howard University.[60] In addition to her duties as dean, Slowe created the National Association of College Women and served as the organization's president. A visionary, Slowe "began in 1933 [to] emphasize the importance of education for all women and [to] advis[e] that Black women, in particular, study economics and government so as to have the necessary knowledge to improve social conditions for Black people."[61] According to biographer Linda M. Perkins, "Unlike many who often discussed educating women for the 'uplift' and benefit of the race, Slowe wanted to prepare black women for the 'modern' world"— a world in which economic stability was crucial.[62] Slowe's ideas were consistent with those of prominent black sociologists of her day, specifically Charles S. Johnson and W. E. B. Du Bois.[63] Both men called for economic stability as a way to gain equality.

In addition to individual economic autonomy, the women of Alpha Kappa Alpha promoted financial stability for black colleges. On a grand scale, they supported the efforts of the United Negro College Fund (UNCF), as did the other three sororities. The UNCF was an example of African Americans working together to pool their fundraising efforts in order to aid institutions that did not have access to prominent philanthropists.[64] Individual chapters and the national chapter have contributed funds to the UNCF annually from its inception in 1944 to the present. Further, the leadership of AKA publicly supported the efforts of the UNCF leadership.[65]

Individual Alpha Kappa Alpha chapters and coalitions of chapters worked together to support individual black colleges. According to AKA historian Marjorie Parker, "They support[ed] 'their' [black colleges] through financial support, community and public relations efforts, [and] recruitment of students."[66] The focus on black colleges has been a major tenet of the AKA's mission from its beginnings. In particular, the sorority has paid attention to first-generation college students and transfer students coming from community colleges to the four-year setting. Sorority members also placed special emphasis on encouraging HBCU students who have "majored in the areas of science or technology to go on to graduate school."[67] This is another example of black sorority efforts to reshape women's education to include fields that traditionally have been dominated by men.

POLITICAL ACTIVITY, CIVIL RIGHTS, DESEGREGATION, AND PHILANTHROPY

Given their support of social and economic equality through education, it is not surprising that black sororities also promoted legal equality through their philanthropic efforts in the area of desegregation and civil rights issues.[68] The 1954 *Brown v. Board of Education* decision was the impetus for much change and activity among black sororities. The women of Zeta Phi Beta, for example, showed their support by opening leadership roles in the sorority to non–African Americans. They also began to affiliate with and financially support the National Council of Negro Women and the National Congress of Christians and Jews. Individual members of the sorority did their part in the civil rights movement as well. Prior to the well-publicized Woolworth sit-ins, Clara Luper worked "to integrate the eating establishments of Oklahoma City, Oklahoma and ultimately was successful."[69] Likewise, in the late 1950s, the women of Zeta Phi Beta gave both verbal and financial backing to the nine high school students who attempted to integrate Little Rock Central High School. To support the students, the sisters drafted a formal citation at their Dallas Boule and donated $500 to the students in honor of their efforts.[70]

The women of Alpha Kappa Alpha solidified their role in national political change under the leadership of Supreme Basileus Barbara Phillips. According to Mary Shy Scott, Phillips "pulled a committee together internationally—one representative from every region—and they planned how [AKAs] as a group could support the political rights of our people first, and second, look at candidates and educate our people on how to vote."[71] This political force was a bi-partisan effort that focused on education and civil rights. According to AKA member Zenda Bowie, "the sorority places an emphasis on educating blacks so that they become more active and able to participate in race relations issues."[72]

Of course, this was not the first time that the AKAs had come together in an effort to lobby for civil rights and changes in education. Under the leadership of Norma Boyd in 1938, the AKAs formed the Non-Partisan Lobby for Economic and Democratic Rights. Boyd's lobbying efforts concentrated on the alleviation of police brutality, the attainment of the minimum wage for laundresses, and access to education for blacks. However, after much internal discussion, the Non-Partisan Lobby was renamed the American Council on Human Rights and grew to encompass most of the black sororities and fraternities.[73] Parker writes that the "invitation to other Greek letter groups to share that unity and cooperative action was a significant trend of the times, and, in this unprecedented action, AKA once again blazed a trail toward a new level of cooperation among fraternities and sororities."[74]

Sigma Gamma Rho concentrated its civil rights efforts on monetary support of the NAACP and President Johnson's Anti-Poverty Program;[75] however, Delta Sigma Theta took a more frontline approach to making change. For example, after a violent outbreak of police bullying during the Selma to Montgomery march in 1965, Delta member Lynnett Taylor helped students rally support for the civil rights movement at Alabama State University. Likewise, the Delta chapter at South Carolina State University sponsored parties at which it raised money for bail bonds for student activists. Further, much like their sisters in Zeta Phi Beta, the Deltas supported the efforts of the Little Rock nine. They gave $300 to the students and additional support to Daisy Bates, the president of the Little Rock NAACP, who led the students in their efforts. When Bates's NAACP newspaper the *State Press* was in danger of going under because advertisers were afraid to continue support, eighty-three Delta chapters banded together and purchased ads so the paper could continue to serve as a much-needed information source for blacks.[76] In the words of Giddings, "In the fifties, before the sit-ins, before the national press gave sanctions to defying state authorities, before going to jail or losing one's job became a badge of honor, before, even, the NAACP had become entirely 'comfortable' with Bates's methods of direct challenge, Delta had supported Bates when few others did."[77]

In a 1959 incident, Petersburg, Virginia, officials tried to prevent fifty-seven black seniors from graduating from high school. Rather than comply with the Supreme Court's mandate to integrate the schools, officials shut them down. To aid the students, Delta Sigma Theta raised scholarship money so that students could attend schools elsewhere and graduate on time. In 1961 and 1962, the Deltas supported students trying to desegregate schools in McComb, Mississippi, and Albany, Georgia. According to Giddings, these events "signified a less conventional posture of the sorority." Unlike some of the other groups, Deltas were willing to support efforts that "confronted authorities with direct-action campaigns."[78]

CREATING PROFESSIONAL WOMEN

Black sororities have trained, supported, and funded African American women to help them pursue their career goals. According to Walter M. Kimbrough, membership in black Greek organizations is "valued overwhelmingly among members, [and] provide[s] them with more and earlier opportunities for leadership development than [do] White-dominated student groups [and local organizations]."[79] With this leadership experience comes more pressure to be responsible and take care of the less fortunate among the race. Darlene Clark Hine and Kathleen Thompson note that "the more educated [the women] were, the greater the sense of being responsible, somehow, for the advancement of the race and the uplift of black womanhood. They held these expectations of themselves and found them reinforced by the demands of the black community and its institutions."[80]

Each black sorority has developed and fostered programs to aid women in their pursuit of leadership roles. Zeta Phi Beta, for example, has focused on economic and career development programs. Interested in creating entrepreneurs among black women, each local chapter provided mentors and resources to young women. Even more important, the Zetas emphasized careers for women in nontraditional areas such as space exploration, architecture, contracting, and engineering. Zeta women also have been prominent leaders in the field of education. For example, Elizabeth Koontz was the first black president of the National Education Association (1968–1969) and Deborah Wolfe served as the United States education chief (1958–1965).[81]

Through affiliations with the National Council of Negro Women (NCNW), which was founded by Delta member Mary McLeod Bethune, Delta Sigma Theta also provided leadership opportunities for African American women. Bethune "wanted black women to be able to be independent, and to have the means to make it possible for others to be so as well." In addition, she "knew the value of jobs and their connection to the power and independence black women could have if they commanded extensive government and private resources."[82] As president of the Deltas, Dorothy Height worked for the same goals that Bethune had set forth for women. In 1944, Height initiated the Delta Jobs Project to "expand black women's opportunities beyond the fields of teaching, nursing, and social work. . . . And to keep Delta members abreast of national and international issues, Height involved people [in national conventions] who were not directly tied to race issues."[83] Height's leadership in Delta Sigma Theta would eventually lead her to the presidency of the NCNW, a position in which Height would have even more influence on the future of black women. Height broadened the organization's membership and brought in celebrity personalities like Lena Horne to chair membership drives. In addition to Height and Bethune, Delta Sigma Theta boasted many other leaders in the area of education, including Mary Church Terrell, a teacher and founder of the National Association of Colored Women (NACW). As president of the NACW, Terrell led efforts to increase services for mothers and children. She was also instrumental in desegregating Washington, D.C., restaurants in 1953.[84]

In the 1960s, Alpha Kappa Alpha solidified its efforts to assist women in the pursuit of leadership roles with the establishment of the Leadership School and Fellows Program. Annual workshops, which were held throughout the country, focused on political action, economic development, and cultivating future leaders among young women. Women were also given opportunities to participate in internships in government, nonprofit, and corporate settings. Perhaps what was most significant about the Leadership Program is that many of the women who participated in the early years later returned to teach and prepare a new generation of young women.[85]

ELITIST OR PHILANTHROPIC?

Although founded on philanthropic service and academic excellence, black sororities have become "a magnet for not just the intellectual elite but also the economic elite, who looked at the groups as a way to distinguish themselves from nonmembers who could not afford the membership fees or pay for the kinds of clothes, parties, and automobiles that were de rigueur for members."[86] Of course these charges of elitism are also leveled at white sororities, but since those organizations generally are tied to undergraduate experience only, the effect is less significant. African American sociologist E. Franklin Frazier (1957) and African American newspaper publisher Claude A. Barnett (1925–1966) have offered the most scathing critiques. In Frazier's words,

> The weekly accounts in the Negro press of the activities of Negro "society" are invariably stories of unbridled extravagance. These stories include a catalogue of the jewelry, the gowns, and mink coats worn by the women, often accompanied by an estimate of the value of the clothes and jewelry, and the cost of the parties which they attend. One constantly reads of "chauffeured" Cadillac cars in which they ride to parties and of the cost of the homes in which they live. . . . For these top "social" and intellectual leaders, the fraternities and sororities represented their most serious interest in life.[87]

Frustrated with this "black elite," Frazier wrote that membership in exclusive organizations served to "differentiate the black bourgeoisie from the masses of poorer Negroes."[88] He claimed that Washington, D.C., the very place where three of the four sororities were established, was the center of black "society." It was here that the black professional class was largest and that Howard University, the hallmark of black education, stood. According to Frazier, "The Negro 'society' which developed in Washington was composed of the upper-class mulattoes who, in fleeing from persecution and discriminations in the South, brought to Washington the social distinctions and color snobbery that had been the basis of their ascendancy in the South."[89]

Prior to World War I, family background and skin complexion were important components of selection for elite organizations, especially black sororities. However, black social mobility and physical migration after the war led to changes in the requirements for membership. "Family background and color snobbishness based upon white ancestry" became less important for membership among social elites.[90] Instead, occupation and education became the keys to admission into elite organizations. This transition, according to Frazier, brought on a black obsession with income level and professional stature. He pays homage to the volunteer work and philanthropy undertaken by the black elite but points out that in many cases they spent extravagant amounts of money creating an atmosphere in which to raise money. Frazier gives the following example, which appeared in a 25 February 1954 issue of *Jet* magazine: "There appeared . . . under the section labeled 'People Are Talking About,' the statement that $1,500 was raised by a group of . . . society women who wore over $500,000 worth of furs and gowns."[91] Frazier looked at the community service of female elite organizations, including sororities, as a justification for their exclusive nature, which he claimed resulted from their members' being shunned by the white middle class.[92]

Like Frazier, Claude A. Barnett was also highly critical of black sororities. Barnett was the president of the Associated Negro Press (ANP), which was the largest black press service in the United States.[93] Founded by Barnett in 1919, the ANP supplied news stories, opinion columns, essays, and book and movie reviews to black newspapers throughout the country. The ANP not only provided news to black communities but also "helped to heighten black self-esteem long before the civil rights revolution of the 1960s."[94] In 1951, Barnett sent a letter to Zeta Phi Beta Grand Basileus Nancy Bullock McGhee, informing her that he would no longer publicize events that were exclusively social. Barnett wrote similar letters to the leaders of the other black sororities, warning them that the tradition of merely celebrating social accomplishments was over.[95]

Although the types of criticism lodged by Frazier and Barnett have existed throughout the history of black sororities, the scope of these organizations' philanthropic efforts have helped to offset the negative image such criticism creates. Further, sororities have consciously worked to change this reputation and portrayal of their organizations. Black sororities have undergone a "constant redefining of the meaning of class and achievement within [their] own ranks."[96] According to Delta Sigma Theta member Tiffany Franklin, "Our founders saw a need for a black women's organization that would be more than just a social organization, sitting around sipping tea and being an arm piece to a male fraternity. They saw an organization that would recognize social injustices of the time and fight to correct them as well as trying to uplift the black community."[97]

As the black sororities emerged historically, they strove to be more than social clubs and as a result developed into dedicated service organizations. They have been involved in virtually all aspects of African American social, political, educational, and economic advance, either through direct action or through philanthropic support. Black sororities make little distinction between what is political and what is philanthropic. Born of a racial climate that discouraged serious education for blacks, and particularly black women, these organizations and their philanthropic efforts remain inherently political.

Through the years, the charge of classism has been lodged against many elite organizations, including Greek fraternities and sororities, regardless of their racial make-up. However, to apply this charge uniformly to black and white sororities is to ignore the unique leadership role the African American groups have had in the advancement of black education through philanthropic means. In the black community an expectation exists that is not necessarily present in the white community: "once you make it, you must reach back and pull a sister up."[98] This expectation is even more pronounced among black women, who arguably have the most difficulty achieving success in a nation that has not placed faith in their abilities. Seen in this light, the sororities' achievements have been quite remarkable. By opening their organizational papers to historians of education and philanthropy, black sororities may deflect some of the suspicions that have always been held about elite social groups. Until then, they will be open to greater criticism and their efforts will continue to be overshadowed by those of more mainstream philanthropic and voluntary organizations.

NOTES

1. Bettye Collier-Thomas, "The Impact of Black Women in Education: An Historical Overview," *Journal of Negro Education* 51 (summer 1982): 173–80.

2. The following sources discuss the role that black women have played in shaping education: Mary Frances Berry, "Twentieth-Century Black Women in Education," *Journal of Negro Education* 51 (summer 1982): 288–300; Jacqueline Jones, *Labor of Love, Labor of Sorrow: Black Women, Work, and the Family from Slavery to the Present* (1985; reprint, New York: Vintage, 1995); and Dorothy Sterling, ed., *We Are Your Sisters: Black Women in the Nineteenth Century* (New York: W. W. Norton, 1984).

3. Paula Giddings, *In Search of Sisterhood: Delta Sigma Theta and the Challenge of the Black Sorority Movement* (New York: William Morrow, 1988), 6.

4. Deborah Gray White, *Too Heavy a Load: Black Women in Defense of Themselves, 1894–1994* (New York: W. W. Norton, 1999); Bettye Collier-Thomas and V. P. Franklin, *Sisters in the Struggle: African American Women in the Civil Rights–Black Power Movement* (New York: New York University Press, 2001); and Sibby Anderson-Thompkins, "Lugenia Burns Hope: Black Clubwoman and Progressive Reformer" (unpublished class paper, Georgia State University, 2002, in author's possession).

5. Darlene Clark Hine and Kathleen Thompson, *A Shining Thread of Hope: The History of Black Women in America* (New York: Broadway, 1998), 245.

6. Constance Carroll, "Three's a Crowd: The Dilemma of Black Women in Higher Education," in *All the Women Are White, All the Blacks Are Men, But Some of Us Are Brave: Black Women's Studies,* ed. Gloria T. Hull, Patricia Bell-Scott, and Barbara Smith (New York: Feminist Press, 1982), 115–28.

7. Hine and Thompson, *Shining Thread of Hope,* 200; and Laverne Gyant, "Passing the Torch: African American Women in the Civil Rights Movement," *Journal of Black Studies* 25 (May 1996), 637.

8. Gyant, "Passing the Torch."

9. Lawrence C. Ross, Jr., *The Divine Nine: The History of African American Fraternities and Sororities* (New York: Kensington, 2000).

10. Giddings, *In Search of Sisterhood.* See also Felecia Carter Harris, "Race, Gender, Mentoring, and the African American Female College Experience: A Case Study of the Delta Sigma Theta Sorority" (Ph.D. diss., North Carolina State University, 1994).

11. See Linda M. Perkins, "Lucy Diggs Slowe: Champion of the Self-Determination of African-American Women in Higher Education," *Journal of Negro History* 81 (autumn/winter 1996): 89–104; White, *Too Heavy a Load;* and Audrey Thomas McCluskey and Elaine M. Smith, eds., *Mary McLeod Bethune: Building a Better World* (Bloomington: Indiana University Press, 1999).

12. Hine and Thompson, *Shining Thread of Hope;* and Evelyn Brooks Higginbotham, *Righteous Discontent: The Women's Movement in the Black Baptist Church, 1880–1920* (Cambridge, Mass.: Harvard University Press, 1993).

13. Giddings, *In Search of Sisterhood,* 6.

14. Sorority constitutions are located at Delta Sigma Theta, 1707 New Hampshire Avenue NW, Washington, D.C. 20009; Alpha Kappa Alpha, 5656 S. Stony Island Ave., Chicago, Ill. 60637; Zeta Phi Beta, 1734 New Hampshire Ave. NW, Washington, D.C. 20009; and Sigma Gamma Rho, 8800 South Stony Island, Chicago, Ill. 60617.

15. Giddings, *In Search of Sisterhood,* 6.

16. Mary Shy Scott, member of the National Black Pan-Hellenic Council and twenty-third Supreme Basileus, Alpha Kappa Alpha, interview by author, Atlanta, Ga., 5 October 2001.

17. Giddings, *In Search of Sisterhood.*

18. Alexandria Berkowitz and Irene Padavic, "Getting a Man or Getting Ahead: A Comparison of White and Black Sororities," *Journal of Contemporary Ethnography* 27 (January 1999): 530–57; and Valerie Smith Stephens, "A Historical Perspective of

the Influence of African-American Sororities in Higher Education" (Ph.D. diss., Rutgers University, 1998).

19. Giddings, *In Search of Sisterhood*, 18; and White, *Too Heavy a Load*.

20. Giddings, *In Search of Sisterhood*, 19.

21. Lawrence Otis Graham, *Our Kind of People: Inside America's Black Upper Class* (New York: HarperPerennial, 2000), 85.

22. E. Franklin Frazier, *Black Bourgeoisie: The Rise of a New Middle Class in the United States* (1957; reprint, New York: Free Press Paperbacks, 1997); Graham, *Our Kind of People;* and William B. Gatewood, *Aristocrats of Color: The Black Elite, 1880–1920* (Bloomington: Indiana University Press, 1990).

23. Ethel Hedgeman quoted in Marjorie H. Parker, *Alpha Kappa Alpha through the Years, 1908–1988* (Chicago: Mobium, 1990), 9.

24. The founders of AKA were Hedgeman, Beulah Burke, Margaret Holmes, Lillie Burke, Marjorie Hill, Marie Taylor, Lucy Diggs Slowe, Anna Brown, Ethel Lyle, and Lavinia Norman (http://www.aka1908.com/aka/history/founders.htm [accessed 8 December 2003]).

25. AKA founders' histories, Alpha Kappa Alpha Papers, Moorland-Spingarn Collection, Howard University, Washington, D.C. (hereafter cited as AKA Papers). Histories of the founders of Sigma Gamma Rho, Delta Sigma Theta, and Zeta Phi Beta are located at the national headquarters of each sorority.

26. Scott, interview.

27. Ibid.

28. Giddings, *In Search of Sisterhood*.

29. Ross, *The Divine Nine*.

30. The founding members of Delta Sigma Theta were Winona Alexander, Madree White, Wertie Weaver, Vashti Murphy, Ethel Black, Frederica Dodd, Osceola Adams, Pauline Minor, Edna Coleman, Edith Young, Marguerite Alexander, Naomi Richardson, Eliza Shippen, Zephyr Carter, Myra Hemmings, Mamie Rose, Bertha Campbell, Florence Toms, Olive Jones, Jessie Dent, Jimmie Middleton, and Ethel Watson (Delta Sigma Theta Sorority, "Delta History," http://www.deltasigmatheta.org/d_history/index.htm [accessed 8 December 2003]).

31. Bertha Campbell quoted in Helen G. Edmonds, "The History of Delta Sigma Theta Sorority," unpublished manuscript in Delta Sigma Theta Headquarters, 1954, 33; and Naomi Richardson, interview by the Mid-Hudson Alumnae Chapter, New York, 1976, quoted in Giddings, *In Search of Sisterhood*, 53.

32. Delta Sigma Theta Sorority, "Delta History."

33. Sibyl Avery Jackson, Delta Sigma Theta, interview by author, Atlanta, Ga., 13 August 2001.

34. The founders were Pearl Neal, Viola Tyler, Fannie Pettie, Myrtle Tyler, and Arizona Cleaver (Ross, *The Divine Nine*), 213–43.

35. Zeta Phi Beta, "Heritage," http://www.zphib1920.org/heritage/index.shtml (accessed 8 December 2003).

36. Graham, *Our Kind of People*, 83–100.

37. Ross, *The Divine Nine*, 213–43; the motto is quoted on the sorority's Web site at http://www.sgrho1922.org/index2.html (accessed 8 December 2003).

38. Sigma Gamma Rho Sorority, "National History," http://www.sgrho1922.org/history.html (accessed 8 December 2003). Sigma Gamma Rho's founders were

Mary Lou Little, Nannie Mae Johnson, Dorothy Whiteside, Hattie Mae Redford, Cubena McClure, Bessie Downey Martin, and Vivian Marbury.

39. Scott, interview. All sorority members interviewed for this project noted this distinction.

40. Jackson, interview. A paddle is a souvenir of the initiation process; it is given by both white and black Greek organizations to their members.

41. Zenda Bowie, AKA member, interview by author, Atlanta, Ga., 5 September 2001.

42. Giddings, *In Search of Sisterhood*, 10.

43. *Baltimore Afro-American* quoted in Giddings, *In Search of Sisterhood*, 58.

44. Ross, *The Divine Nine*, 213–43.

45. Organizations material 1945–77, Tom C. Clark Papers, series IV, Tarlton Law Library, Jamail Center for Legal Research, University of Texas School of Law, Austin, Tex.

46. Ross, *The Divine Nine*, 257.

47. Washington believed that blacks should be committed to economic improvement and eventually civil rights would follow. Economic improvement would come through a steadfast commitment to hard work and the ownership of property. See Booker T. Washington, "Atlanta Compromise," a speech given at the Cotton States and International Exposition, September 1895, Atlanta, Ga., contained in the Booker T. Washington Papers, Tuskegee University Archives, Tuskegee, Alabama (there are copies of it on display); Louis R. Harlan, *Booker T. Washington: The Making of a Black Leader, 1856–1901* (New York: Oxford University Press, 1972); and idem, *Booker T. Washington: The Wizard of Tuskegee, 1901–1915* (New York: Oxford University Press, 1983).

48. Parker, *Alpha Kappa Alpha*, 181.

49. Giddings, *In Search of Sisterhood*, 27–45; Charles S. Johnson, *Patterns of Negro Segregation* (New York: Cronwell, 1943), 52–56.

50. Giddings, *In Search of Sisterhood*, 183.

51. Ibid.

52. AKA Papers.

53. Mary Elizabeth Vroman, *Shaped to Its Purpose: Delta Sigma Theta—The First Fifty Years* (New York: Random House, 1964), 15–17.

54. Parker, *Alpha Kappa Alpha*, 164.

55. Scott, interview.

56. Collier-Thomas and Franklin, *Sisters in the Struggle*, 28–29.

57. Darlene Clark Hine, "'We Specialize in the Wholly Impossible': The Philanthropic Work of Black Women," in *Lady Bountiful Revisited: Women, Philanthropy, and Power*, ed. Kathleen D. McCarthy (New Brunswick, N.J.: Rutgers University Press, 1990), 70–93.

58. White, *Too Heavy a Load*, 158–59.

59. Lucy Diggs Slowe, AKA founders' histories, located at national headquarters, Chicago.

60. Jana Nidiffer, *Pioneering Deans of Women: More Than Wise and Pious Matrons* (New York: Teachers College Press, 2000).

61. AKA historical documents, located at national headquarters, Chicago.

62. Perkins, "Lucy Diggs Slowe," 89. See also Geraldine J. Clifford, ed., *Lone*

Voyagers: Academic Women in Coeducational Universities, 1870–1937 (New York: Feminist Press, 1989); and John M. Faragher and Florence Howe, eds., *Women and Higher Education in American History* (New York: W. W. Norton, 1988).

63. Marybeth Gasman, "W. E. B. Du Bois and Charles S. Johnson: Differing Views on the Role of Philanthropy in Higher Education," *History of Education Quarterly* 42 (winter 2002): 493–516. See also W. E. B. Du Bois, *Black Reconstruction in America, 1860–1880* (1935; reprint, New York: Touchstone, 1962); and Charles S. Johnson, *Shadow of the Plantation* (1934; reprint, Chicago: University of Chicago Press, 1966).

64. Lea E. Williams, "The United Negro College Fund in Retrospect," *Journal of Negro Education* 49 (autumn 1980): 363–72; and William Trent, Jr., "Cooperative Fund Raising for Higher Education," *Journal of Negro Education* 24 (winter 1955): 6–15.

65. AKA to William Trent, Jr., 1958, endorsement of UNCF campaign 1944–58, microfiche 1905, United Negro College Fund Papers, Woodruff Library, Clark Atlanta University, Atlanta, Ga.

66. Parker, *Alpha Kappa Alpha*, 172.

67. Ibid., 173.

68. Black sororities were also involved in anti-lynching activities; however, a discussion of their efforts is beyond the scope of this chapter.

69. Ross, *The Divine Nine*, 248.

70. Ibid., 247–49.

71. Scott, interview.

72. Bowie, interview.

73. One fraternity chose not to belong to the Council: Omega Psi Phi.

74. Parker, *Alpha Kappa Alpha*, 241.

75. Sigma Gamma Rho Sorority, http://www.sgr1922.org/sgrgeninfo.htm (accessed 13 July 2001).

76. Giddings, *In Search of Sisterhood*, 244–45.

77. Ibid.

78. Ibid., 256–57.

79. Walter M. Kimbrough, "Self-Assessment, Participation, and Value of Leadership Skills, Activities, and Experiences for Black Students Relative to Their Membership in Historically Black Fraternities and Sororities," *Journal of Negro Education* 64 (winter 1995), 63–74.

80. Hine and Thompson, *Shining Thread of Hope*, 221.

81. Ross, *The Divine Nine*, 244–74.

82. White, *Too Heavy a Load*, 191–92.

83. Ibid., 192.

84. Ross, *The Divine Nine*, 164–212.

85. Parker, *Alpha Kappa Alpha*, 43–46.

86. Graham, *Our Kind of People*, 86.

87. Frazier, *Black Bourgeoisie*, 202–203.

88. Ibid., 195.

89. Ibid., 198.

90. Ibid., 198.

91. Ibid., 206.

92. White, *Too Heavy a Load,* 217, 251.

93. Claude A. Barnett Papers, W. E. B. Du Bois Institute, Harvard University, Cambridge, Mass.

94. General Information Guide, Claude A. Barnett Papers, Chicago Historical Society, Chicago, Ill. (hereafter cited as Barnett Papers).

95. White, *Too Heavy a Load,* 187–89; see also folders 332–33, series G, Philanthropic and Social Organizations 1925–1966, Barnett Papers.

96. Giddings, *In Search of Sisterhood,* 20.

97. Tiffany Franklin, Delta Sigma Theta member, interview by author, 15 August 2001, Atlanta, Ga.

98. Scott, interview; see also Marybeth Gasman, "An Untapped Resource: Bringing African Americans into the University Giving Process," *CASE International Journal of Educational Advancement* 1 (winter 2002): 280–92.

9. "Valuable and Legitimate Services": Black and White Women's Philanthropy through the PTA

Christine Woyshner

In 1928, when Cornell professor of education Julian Butterworth finished his study of white parent-teacher associations, he concluded, "It is not the responsibility of the parent-teacher association to finance the schools." That women in such groups spent so much of their time raising money was proof to him that they did not understand "the basic principles of public school financing, as now generally accepted by progressive thinkers."[1] Butterworth's study not only revealed a typical educator's opinion that volunteer involvement by women was usually officious and uninformed; it also acknowledged the overwhelming commitment of women's associations to philanthropy in local schools. Had he conducted a similar study in the segregated schools of the South during this era, he would have found an even more striking example of educational philanthropy on the part of black teachers and community members.

Historians of education generally argue that the proliferation of parent-teacher associations in public schools during the first half of the twentieth century was a reaction by citizens to the bureaucratization of public education and the professionalization of teaching.[2] William J. Reese exemplifies this interpretation in his explanation that parent-teacher groups "helped break down the isolation of institutions whose increasingly professionalized and centralized nature threatened to drive them far away from the life of the average citizen."[3] However, this argument does not take into account women's beneficence through widespread networks of women's clubs and associations, in part because these scholars conflate the notions of "mother" and "parent" in their analyses. When we examine the development of home-school associations within the context of the women's club movement, a different picture emerges. Therefore, in this chapter I maintain that women's organized interest in public education through school improvement societies, parent-teacher associations, and women's clubs was as much an extension of the rapidly growing women's club movement as it was a reaction to the rise of the education professions and the reorganization of school administration.[4] The theory of municipal housekeeping—the notion that women's legitimate activities in the "home sphere" included caring for the civic community—provided the justification for women's associations to take to the schools and fulfill a much-needed munificent role.[5] In a contemporary chronicle of clubwomen's extensive efforts in municipal settings, Mary Ritter Beard observed in 1915 that women's associations contributed significantly to the schools, so much so that the schools were becoming "one huge settlement with a thoroughly democratic basis in place of a philanthropic foundation."[6]

Prior to the 1920s, women's organized philanthropy in schools was both a local phenomenon and a national movement directed by groups like the General Federation of Women's Clubs, the National Congress of Mothers, and the National Association of Colored Women (NACW). For most of the 1910s, the extensive educational reform efforts of women's associations were coordinated through the National Education Association's (NEA's) Department of National Women's Associations.[7] By the mid-1920s, however, when gender-segregated reform activities had largely lost their appeal,[8] women's activism in public education became less intrusive in school affairs and was subsumed under the direction of the National Congress of Mothers, which in 1924 changed its name to the National Congress of Parents and Teachers (or National PTA). Though the name change reflected PTA leaders' desire to represent fathers as well as mothers, male membership in the white PTA was negligible.[9] At this same time, a segregated PTA—the National Congress of Colored Parents and Teachers—was organized in the South by African American women teachers. In the 1920s the membership of the white PTA began to grow exponentially; by 1930 it had a paid membership of one million in forty-nine states and territories.[10] Enjoying a larger percentage of male leaders and members—though a smaller proportion of the black population—the Colored Congress merged with the white PTA in

1970. Despite the existence of a black membership, the National PTA has remained a white, middle-class women's association in the public consciousness.

This chapter focuses on the philanthropy of black and white women through parent-teacher associations and analyzes the complications that arose as a result of these women's beneficence. In this context, I view most PTA activities as philanthropic, including the material contributions that women's groups made to schools in the form of donations and fundraisers, as well as time spent volunteering at local schools. (Admittedly, some of the other purposes of PTAs, such as sponsoring parent education workshops and coordinating social hours, are not philanthropic and thus fall outside my purview.)[11] Viewing PTA work through the lens of philanthropy highlights women's contributions to education and foregrounds the power they wielded through voluntary networks; it also redirects other scholars' analyses away from a focus on the parent-teacher relationship, orienting it instead toward gender and race complications in school improvement endeavors.[12] Prior to the 1920s, black and white women's associations can be given much of the credit for purchasing books and materials, providing school lunches and nurses, working for better teacher wages, and ensuring that schools were built or renovated. After the 1920s, black PTA philanthropy continued to a marked degree out of necessity. The philanthropic efforts of black and white PTA women formed a web of support for public education that changed as schools' needs changed; their adaptability to local needs was a strength.

White and black women's PTA efforts, while beneficial to local schools and generally welcomed by school leaders, nevertheless remained a threatening prospect due to gender and racial dynamics. Most PTA women felt that *because* they were women, they possessed special qualities that had the potential to influence society for the better; therefore, their educational philanthropy was legitimate work in the public realm. However, this kind of municipal housekeeping challenged the rising male administrative hierarchy of schools, posing a threat to the power structure that sought to manage and control women through parent-teacher associations and women's clubs.[13] For example, in Denver in 1897, the women of the mothers' clubs were "denounced as 'faddists'" for their support of kindergartens and nature study. Denver's male school administrators were so threatened that they "led a successful smear campaign against the 4,000 women in the city's educational union in the 1890s, causing it to disband."[14]

In turn, the growing number of black parent-teacher associations in segregated schools in the first half of the twentieth century presented a threat to white PTA women, who attempted to monitor the segregated associations' activities and who ironically criticized their overreliance on fundraisers and other acts of beneficence. In contrast to white women's experience, black women's school improvement associations and clubs were more localized and were usually organized by women teachers, so they did not necessarily pose a threat to black school leadership.[15] However, they did at times challenge the white school boards and community leaders who were in charge of disbursing funds to segregated schools. A pecking order of racial and gender hierarchies was thereby established in which those with more power sought to control the philanthropic activities of those with less. That is, male administrators sought to manage and direct white women's PTA beneficence, while white PTA women after 1930 criticized black PTA women for not adhering more closely to the dictates of the white PTA, which placed fundraising secondary to educational activities. This criticism failed to recognize the needs of segregated schools in the South that depended upon the "double taxation" of its community members to survive.[16] In what follows, I outline the various manifestations of PTA philanthropy and analyze the roles of gender and race in the philanthropic work of white and black PTA women.

THE PHILANTHROPY OF PARENT-TEACHER ASSOCIATIONS

As the beneficent work of parent-teacher associations intensified in the first two decades of the twentieth century, and as women played a greater role in shaping public education, principals and other school administrators noted that their "material contributions . . . have been commendable."[17] The philanthropy of the PTA and local women's clubs included both monetary (fundraising) and nonmonetary activities. The monetary contributions helped fund schools or school renovations and additions, purchase materials for schools, provide uniforms for sports teams, and serve hot lunches. According to Butterworth, providing cash donations was by far the most extensive work of parent-teacher associations, accounting for more than fifty percent of all activities ranked in his 1924–1925 study.[18] When nonmonetary contributions are taken into account, the percentage of material contributions climbs significantly higher.

Noncash contributions were just as essential and pervasive as monetary beneficence and affected entire school systems as well as particular programs within schools.[19] These contributions helped enact curricular reforms such as kindergartens, vacation schools, and vocational education programs; they also improved teachers' pay and benefits and provided for school lunches. Donations of time allowed for greater decision-making power among clubwomen, who successfully lobbied for school suffrage and women on school boards. Black and white PTA women also worked to improve school facilities by initiating health inspections and promoting playgrounds, better ventilation, and sanitary measures such as drinking fountains. When schools were sufficiently renovated, clubwomen turned to philanthropy in the aesthetic and patriotic arenas by purchasing artwork and flags for schools. Examples of women's philanthropy through groups and associations are many and varied; oftentimes PTA women would hold fundraisers and use the money to purchase materials for classrooms or institute new programs personally.

While these efforts were almost universal around the United States, regional differences allowed women to address specific needs. Butterworth's study found that poorer communities relied more heavily on PTA philanthropy, "either because a reasonable tax rate does not bring in enough or because the citizens are more reluctant to raise funds for school purposes."[20] The three southern states in his study—North Carolina, Texas, and Virginia—ranked the highest in percentage of time spent by PTA women providing money for schools.[21] Conditions for white schools in the South during the early decades of the twentieth century were indeed dire, and women's associations helped gather the capital for establishing educational institutions. In James L. Leloudis's study, local units of North Carolina's white Woman's Association for the Betterment of Public Schools (WABPS) raised the tax revenues to build an average of one school a day between 1902 and 1910.[22]

Once schools were built, PTAs did not disband, but rather moved on to the next phase of philanthropy, contributing supplies and materials. This evolution was noted by contemporaries like Mary Ritter Beard, who commented, "The movement for sanitary school buildings in which women have sometimes led, instigated officials to lead, helped personally, or inspired janitors to act, has been followed up by the decoration of the buildings."[23] For example, at the turn of the twentieth century in Illinois, a white PTA provided better ventilation and sanitary conditions in schools and introduced innovations such as "bubble fountains and proper toilets for boys." Two decades later, the health renovations completed, the association renamed itself the School Beautiful Committee and turned its attention to school aesthetics and encouraging the arts. Projects in the 1920s and 1930s included landscaping and running photo competitions for students.[24] This attention to aesthetics reflected white middle-class women's belief that attractive schools would translate to an ideal educational setting, thereby imbuing schools with the "cultural conventions of middle-class life."[25]

Transportation to and from school stood as a major challenge to both white and black communities, especially with the widespread consolidation of rural schools at the turn of the twentieth century. For example, in the early 1900s, white Iowa clubwomen addressed the transportation issue by "band[ing] themselves together and . . . provid[ing] a covered vehicle [to carry] the little ones to school."[26] In segregated schools, transportation was a major function of black PTAs, since these schools were overlooked in the pupil transportation movements of the 1920s and 1930s. In Vanessa Siddle Walker's study of the Caswell County Training School in North Carolina, parents coordinated rides to school for the African American students and even drove them to various extracurricular activities. During the Depression, as the need for a school bus became ever greater and white school boards were unrelenting, the local black PTA raised funds to purchase a bus and donated it to the state so that students would have transportation.[27]

Though the amount of time spent on philanthropic activities by white parent-teacher associations was significant, it was nonetheless surpassed by black teachers and community members in the segregated schools of the South. Theirs was a philanthropy of necessity. For black communities the "primary purpose of the PTA was to provide for the financial needs of the school."[28] Black parents typically built the schools they wanted for their children or matched funds from white boards of education. Donations by black parents often increased after schools opened, since the work of education had just begun and community groups needed to raise money for books and materials.[29] These differences between white and black women's PTA philanthropy in education can be attributed to general patterns in white and black women's giving. White women generally worked to reform institutions and gain political power while black women worked locally. Elisabeth Clemens argues that the more conservative white women's associations opted to continue voluntary contributions while the more radical white women's groups worked for cash contributions to get political power.[30] White PTA women used both strategies; they volunteered their time and they raised money, and as a result white women in PTAs challenged the authority of male administrators in schools more than the average taxpayer ever could. White PTA women's influence far exceeded taxpayer power because they were organized and typically worked from inside a school. Their meetings were usually held in school auditoriums and classrooms and the focus of their work was on school improvement. In response, male administrators began to question whether such extensive philanthropic work was the best use of volunteers' time. I now turn to an examination of the role that gender played in white women's school philanthropy.

GENDER AND PTA PHILANTHROPY

White women's PTA philanthropy in the first half of the twentieth century changed over time as it traversed two phases in the development of public education. The first phase included the consolidation of rural school districts and the creation of public school systems in urban settings, extending roughly from the 1890s to the 1920s. The second phase, after 1930, was one in which the white PTA simultaneously became a household name and grew less involved in the establishment and renovation of schools. Its role at this time was supportive, though philanthropy continued to be a central activity of local units. During the first phase, local associations gave significant aid to public schools in rural as well as urban settings and ensured that such programs as affordable lunches and school nurses were taken over by school management by the 1920s.[31] Most of the money that PTAs raised came from sponsorship of entertainment programs, donations, and sales.[32]

Generally, white PTA women did not intend to continue their contributions for the long term. Through their municipal housekeeping in the Progressive Era, clubwomen sought to "transform public policy, to move from personal and private encounter to state action, to bring about compulsory legislation of one sort or another."[33] And this understanding carried over to their school improvement endeavors. As with wider social welfare legislation reforms, PTA women enacted reforms that they believed school authorities and boards of education should eventually assume. For example, vacation schools that were begun in Chicago in the 1890s by a women's club were turned over to the board of education to manage in 1911. In Minnesota by that same year, the school medical inspector and nurse were no longer provided by the women's clubs, but by the school system.[34] In California in 1916, clinics started by the California Congress of Mothers were taken over by the schools.[35] As reforms were taken over by professionals, white PTAs declared success and sought new issues to address. For instance, after health inspections were implemented in Massachusetts, the women "turned to other work, including vocational training and vocational guidance, particularly of girls."[36]

Inasmuch as PTA women attempted to remake society according to white, middle-class standards—a well-established argument in the history of education literature—they faced gender barriers due to a growing hierarchical school administration that excluded them from decision making and sought to place them under the watchful eye of male principals, superintendents, and school board members. If these male administrators clashed among themselves over control of the schools, they were at least united on one issue: white women's power in matters of school decision making was threatening, even if their efforts improved schools at the local level. The National PTA's involvement in legislation to support mothers' pensions and the Sheppard-Towner Maternity and Infancy Act was a testament to their potency and certainly made school administrators think twice about giving them any license to enact school reforms independently.[37]

Mary Ritter Beard referred to this gender dynamic when she noted that through parent-teacher associations "women participate on equal terms with men, where they do not direct the aims and activities themselves."[38] This is evidenced in the NEA's Department of National Women's Organizations, which represented approximately 900,000 members in 1908. As one clubwoman boasted, they were able to wield power through "their standing committees [that] receive[d] impulse and instruction quickly and systematically from center to circumference."[39] This sizeable membership—representing white women's efforts on behalf of public education—dwarfed the nearly all-male membership of the NEA, which at that time stood at roughly five thousand. If educational leaders had not recognized the ascendancy of women's associations in public education to this point, they surely could not overlook their representation in the NEA. The potential of so many women to influence matters in public education after they had been subordinated so neatly in their roles as classroom teachers was expressed by Elmer Ellsworth Brown, U.S. commissioner of education. Speaking at a Department of Women's Organizations meeting, Brown complimented the clubwomen on the selfless work they had undertaken, but suggested that they take direction from male educational leaders through referenda.[40]

Educators' concerns continued throughout the next several decades as they sought to distinguish men's authority and money-managing duties from women's voluntary contributions. In the 1920s, two scholars studying the National PTA successfully created a division between volunteer work and fundraising by making a distinction between the educational functions of PTAs and volunteers' monetary contributions. Elmer Holbeck of Teachers College claimed that white women's PTA activities focused inappropriately on "the purchase of school equipment, . . . the arrangement of [fundraising] entertainments, and . . . other non-educational activities."[41] Julian Butterworth argued that the PTA could endanger schools if the associations continued their policies of raising and giving money as they saw fit. However, Butterworth was careful not to completely advise white PTA women to cease all philanthropic activities, lest the schools lose this important source of support. He noted that his recommendation to focus on educational endeavors did not "preclude the parent-teacher association from engaging in certain types of activities to finance the school more adequately."[42]

Holbeck and Butterworth also represent the male administrators who, by the 1920s, sought to regulate PTA activities by backing the commonly held notion that philanthropy by women should not focus on raising money. Proposing acceptable ways for PTAs to continue their beneficence, Butterworth drew up parameters for raising funds only "under special conditions": PTAs should provide "the desired facilities" in the poorest school districts that did not have adequate tax money to cover costs. Other than that, he explained "it is preferable for the parent-teacher organization to create public recognition of the need for better standards than to raise the money through its own efforts."[43] When other acts of beneficence were pursued, such as instituting hot lunches or building cafeterias, Butterworth suggested that PTAs get superintendent or school board approval first. Other legitimate activities, in his view, included raising money for an association's own operating expenses. The most egregious offense in parent-teacher association philanthropy, according to Butterworth, was the use of money to raise a teacher's salary "contrary to the salary schedule of the school."[44] Additionally, fundraising that provided paid work for its members was patently unacceptable. The reason for these reservations is alluded to by Holbeck, who argued that fundraising strengthened the association locally and nationally, thereby affording white PTA women "a greater opportunity to influence policies, legislation, and educational practice."[45]

By the mid-1920s, white PTA women were accused of being out of touch with the latest educational developments and contributing to schools as though they were still "in the days of the 'little red schoolhouse.'"[46] While clubwomen's philanthropy was painted as quaint and obsolete, in truth PTA women's contributions challenged the newly institutionalized means of funding for public education. This tension was reflected in comments by male principals and superintendents concerned by the "meddling attitude" of the PTA women, and who began to wonder whether it was easier to manage groups of women or individual women volunteers.[47] Nonetheless, by the end of the decade, educational leaders had been successful in confining PTA women to their own "legitimate field" of work, which did not emphasize raising and distributing funds.[48]

The women's club movement also began to wane during this period, and the political and economic upheavals of the late 1920s and 1930s brought with them a retreat from radical support of social welfare legislation by white PTA women.[49] Julia Grant notes that the maternalist argument that fueled municipal housekeeping became outdated as an ideological framework, and more politically radical women turned to other justifications for their work in the public arena.[50] Sheila Rothman speaks to this "broad disillusionment with reform activities in the post–World War I period," attributing it to a social emphasis among white, middle-class women on romantic marriage over motherhood as a uniting ideology and the fact that the reforms of the Progressive Era did not "enhance opportunities for women in structural ways."[51] By 1930, the Department of National Women's Organizations of the NEA had long been dissolved and the National PTA became a public school auxiliary, as white women's intrusive school philanthropy finally was mitigated and controlled by educational administrators. This next era of the white PTA was characterized by its exponentially increasing membership through the post–World War II years and its increasing visibility as a conservative lobby for the child, home, and family. During this time, the well-established leadership of

the white PTA expended considerable energy developing and moni-
toring its authority over the National Congress of Colored Parents
and Teachers, much as male administrators had scrutinized the white
PTA. The white organization's attempts to control its black counterpart after 1930 are the focus of the next section.

RACE AND PTA PHILANTHROPY

Black women's school philanthropy experienced localized development after the Civil War. As Darlene Clark Hine argues, "unlike
impersonal institutional forms [of white philanthropy], . . . black philanthropy and charitable giving usually assumed the form of small-
scale, personal assistance and involvement."[52] For black clubwomen,
social change—rather than social control—was an important goal, as
was individual improvement.[53] If, according to Hine, the NACW represented "the institutionalization of black women's voluntarism and
philanthropy . . . [that] mandated an end to all racial and gender discrimination,"[54] this work was carried into the public schools in large
part by a growing network of black parent-teacher associations. The
black PTA movement did not gain significant momentum nationally
until the late 1920s; PTA organizers in segregated schools wished to
maintain as much control as they could over black children and black
schools by having their own local associations instead of joining with
the white National PTA.[55] As historian Gerda Lerner argues, "since
Reconstruction days the schoolteacher in her one-room schoolhouse
was sustained by the fund-raising committees of black church ladies'
auxiliaries long before she was the beneficiary of white philanthropy."[56]

Lacking an organized system of schools in the South, black community members and educators worked to build schools during the
first third of the twentieth century.[57] The establishment of schools for
African American children depended almost exclusively on the philanthropy of black school improvement associations, many of which
later became parent-teacher associations. For many southern blacks,
the "immediate problem in most communities . . . was to get something resembling a school."[58] Black schools were especially dependent
upon community resources, including the support of women's clubs,
due to poor funding from state and local governments and the reluctance of local white school boards to finance black education. A black
PTA worker from West Virginia reported that the "[m]ajor emphasis

[of the black PTA in that state] was placed on securing the school equipment and supplies that boards of education either would not or could not provide."[59]

As with the white PTA, the history of the black PTA's organizational structure and activities can be parsed into two phases in the first half of the twentieth century. In the first phase, roughly 1900 to 1930, black PTA philanthropy remained localized, characterized by strong local activism and weaker national ties. Local associations gave rise to state associations in the first two decades of the twentieth century. What national direction existed came not from the National PTA, which proclaimed that it would not discriminate based on "race, color, or condition,"[60] but from the National Association of Colored Women, whose membership during these years enjoyed a significant proportion of teachers and which focused on public education. The National Congress of Colored Parents and Teachers, or black PTA, was officially organized in 1926 by women teachers and club leaders in the black community. By this time, the appeal of allying with the nationally known and politically powerful white PTA took precedence over black educators' local activism and desire for autonomy.[61] Therefore, from 1926 until 1970, the PTA was a segregated association. While the two associations had the same goals and guidelines, each was managed by separate local, state, and national officers.

In the early decades of the twentieth century, the number of African American parent-teacher groups and school improvement societies began to increase and the National PTA encouraged their development, either from PTA headquarters in Washington, D.C., or through representatives sent to attend organizational meetings.[62] As one black PTA historian observed, "The efforts of the National Congress of Mothers to organize a congress of Negro mothers was [sic] having its effect in the South. Parents, teachers, and welfare workers of both races . . . set about to organize similar associations in a number of Negro schools."[63] For example, the white PTA of Georgia donated ten dollars in the early 1920s toward the founding of the Georgia State [Black] Council of Parents and Teachers.[64] However, a major impetus to organize came from the Jeanes Foundation (also known as the Negro Rural School Fund), which was established in 1907 and sent supervisors to rural territories. A primary goal of Jeanes supervisors was to organize school improvement leagues and enlist community members' help in building and renovating schools.[65]

Selena Sloan Butler, the founder of the National Congress of Colored Parents and Teachers, had long been active in PTA work in Atlanta and helped orchestrate the founding of the Georgia Colored Parent-Teacher Association in 1921. An educator, clubwoman, and graduate of Spelman Seminary, Butler convened the National Colored Congress of Parents and Teachers in 1926 to "function only in those states where separate schools for the races were maintained."[66] Deeply committed to race work, Butler nonetheless dissented from the black PTA's focus on fundraising because she feared the "real spirit of the work for children would be lost if the organization converted into a purely money-raising machine."[67] In this apparent instance of capitulation to the guidelines of the white PTA—despite the fact that "many changes" to those very guidelines already had been made by the black PTA leadership—Butler repeats the sentiments of Butterworth and Holbeck: PTA work should not focus on fundraising, lest it detract from more legitimate educational purposes.[68] As in the white PTA, black national leaders promoted educational goals (read: nonphilanthropic) while local units sought to respond to local needs through significant fundraising work.

Ironically, black PTA national officers had few funds to work with and little to give to members in need. One black PTA history summarized years of financial struggles at the local, state, and national levels:

The question of finance has long been a problem for the National Congress [of Colored Parents and Teachers] as well as for its state branches and local units. As is often the case with budding organizations, many local units were prone to borrow too much time from their programs for children for fund-raising projects. Little of the money they raised, however, was converted into parent-teacher dues and often the expense of carrying out the work of the Congress exceeded the dues forwarded to the national treasury by the state congresses. Some local units, too, were poor and needed to look to the National Congress for aid, financial and otherwise, which it was not in a position to give. If the Congress had been better financed it could have given more attention to the needy areas.[69]

Unlike the white PTA, which enjoyed financial solvency due to an endowment fund established by its second president, Hannah Kent Schoff, in the early 1900s, the black PTA struggled to secure funds that would enable it to provide leadership to its local units. Yet despite such challenges—and much like the schools it supported—the black PTA managed to remain a viable organization even on a lean budget.

Thus began the second phase of school-building and beneficence after 1930, as an interstate network of black leaders and educators generated political and moral support for their endeavors in public education. Unlike white PTA women, black women were joined by men in school philanthropy, making their beneficence more a function of race than gender. Racial uplift was a major theme of educational work, as black community members donated time, money, and materials for the education of their children. As Grant argues, African American women "did not clearly distinguish between their educational and social-reform efforts and civil rights, which differentiated them from most white female reformers."[70]

During these years the black PTA faced the challenge of following the white PTA's program while attending to the specific needs of its own constituency. In a 1929 report by the Extension among Colored People Committee of the white PTA, chairperson Mrs. Fred Wessels revealed the patronizing attitude of the white national leadership toward its black counterpart. She expressed concern that black PTA leaders could not be trusted to follow the program of the PTA: "The work done by local colored parent-teacher associations should be along the same lines as those pursued by our own parent-teacher associations and in our capacity as advisors, we should see that nothing detrimental to the welfare of home, school, community, and church be undertaken by their associations."[71]

By July 1932, the Extension committee was discontinued as other issues during the Depression took on a greater significance for the white PTA.[72] Over the next several decades, however, different committees were created in an attempt to manage and monitor the efforts of the black PTA. Mrs. Charles Center, chair of the Committee on Cooperation with the Colored Congress, attended the black PTA's annual meeting in 1936. She noted, "In hearing their reports we found the most urgent need for a simplified program material and a simplified outline for a health program."[73] From this point to the merger in 1970, an ambiguous relationship was established between the two PTAs. White and black leaders periodically held interracial meetings that seemed to serve two general purposes: white PTA leaders sought to manage the black PTA program and black PTA leaders attempted to work toward racial understanding in these groups.[74] During this time, the white PTA adopted the argument made by white male school administrators that fundraising was less desirable than and should be separate from educational activities in PTAs.

This point is highlighted by a study undertaken in the early 1950s in Missouri, which still had a segregated educational system. As part of her master's thesis, white state PTA officer Marguerite Taylor surveyed Missouri's seventy-five local units—representing roughly 3,400 members—affiliated with the black PTA. Taylor hoped to "propose or recommend ways or means of improving the programs of the units of the Colored Parent-Teacher Association."[75] She examined the activities of these local units and compared them to the approved activities of the white PTA, noting in her conclusions that activities deemed secondary by the white PTA were quite primary for black units, especially fundraising. Fundraising often was accomplished through entertainment programs such as the popularity contests that Walker describes in her study of Caswell County High School in North Carolina.[76] Yet Taylor ultimately overlooked the centrality of fundraising activities to the very existence of schools for African Americans; she concluded, "Although entertainments and money making devices often contribute valuable and legitimate services to the school and the community, care [should be] exercised to keep such activities in proper relationship to the real purpose for which the organization is structured—the welfare of children."[77] By this time, white PTA women had the luxury of holding fundraisers to purchase extra materials that school boards could not or would not provide, while black communities knew that their own fundraising was crucial for necessities such as buildings and books.[78] For black PTA members, education and monetary philanthropic efforts were inseparable.

The post–World War II era brought an increased radicalization among African Americans and the concomitant rise of the civil rights movement. This third and final phase of the black PTA involved more aggressive race work as the association worked toward greater educational opportunities for black children, culminating in the demise of the black PTA in 1970 when it integrated with the white PTA. In sum, the early decades of the twentieth century were marked by the extensive philanthropy of white and black parent-teacher associations, which were largely responsible for the building and renovating of schools and for the institution of health and educational programs. In the segregated schools of the South, black PTA beneficence was connected to racial uplift as community members funded their own schools and continued to support them through voluntary contributions.

In 1934, Elmer Holbeck wrote that the "efforts of the local [PTA] units were directed into money-raising activities and other fields which had no connection with the original need which had brought the organization into being."[79] The original need—child welfare—was indeed a rally point for the National Congress of Mothers and other women's associations of the Progressive Era. Holbeck, like other male administrators, was hesitant to allow white women's clubs power and influence in schools through their philanthropy. If white women's philanthropy were accepted as central to educational work, it might confer power on women outside the school management hierarchy. To counter this threat, male administrators successfully separated fundraising from what they considered to be true educational work, thereby assuring male administrators control of public education. By 1930, white women's philanthropy was contained, as PTA women were relegated to an auxiliary role in the public schools through local parent-teacher associations that emphasized "cooperation." Ironically, even as the power of the PTA's philanthropy was palliated, the association grew exponentially and a thriving segregated association was organized. In submission, the white PTA found success, as well as a new focus: supervision of its black counterpart.

The Congress of Colored Parents and Teachers, like the white PTA, considered child welfare a central goal that required significant attention to fundraising and other forms of philanthropy. Just as the power of white women's philanthropy was contained by the ideological separation of money from educational work, the white PTA applied a similar line of reasoning to its oversight of black parent-teacher associations. However, white women's power was not potent enough to entirely control the philanthropy of black PTAs.

PTA women's philanthropy resided within the charged political context of schools and society; it challenged notions of responsibility for public education materially and administratively. Butterworth's early admonitions regarding overreliance on fundraising and other forms of beneficence are echoed by today's historians, who often downplay PTA women's contributions to public education. On the one hand, many scholars who examine the early PTA either focus on its more radical contributions to social welfare reform or overlook its political efforts in education altogether.[80] On the other hand, even historians of education have characterized the day-to-day contributions of local PTAs as "mundane."[81] Yet the commonplace activities of the PTA formed an unmistakable network of philanthropy that contributed to the advancement of popular education in tangible and significant ways. In short, emphasizing the more radical and overt acts performed by women in public education has led historians to undervalue the small, everyday, and seemingly ordinary philanthropy of women in school associations. Their efforts, repeated time and again in schools across the nation, were very much like waves lapping on the shore: they produced long-term impacts more significant than those perceptible at first glance.

NOTES

This research was supported in part by Temple University and the Radcliffe Grant for Graduate Women. While some of the research was conducted for the Civic Engagement Project at Harvard University, interpretations and any errors are my own.

1. Julian E. Butterworth, *The Parent-Teacher Association and Its Work* (New York: Macmillan, 1928), 52.

2. David B. Tyack, *The One Best System: A History of American Urban Education* (Cambridge, Mass.: Harvard University Press, 1974), 6–7, 14, 24, 146; William J. Reese, *Power and the Promise of School Reform: Grassroots Movements during the Progressive Era* (Boston: Routledge and Kegan Paul, 1986), xxi; and William W. Cutler III, *Parents and Schools: The 150-Year Struggle for Control in American Education* (Chicago: University of Chicago Press, 2000), 3–4.

3. William J. Reese, "Between Home and School: Organized Parents, Clubwomen, and Urban Education in the Progressive Era," *School Review* 87 (November 1978), 3.

4. Works on the women's club movement that speak to education include Karen J. Blair, *The Clubwoman as Feminist: True Womanhood Redefined, 1868–1914* (New York: Holmes and Meier, 1980); Anne Ruggles Gere, *Intimate Practices: Literacy and Cultural Work in U.S. Women's Clubs, 1880–1920* (Urbana: University of Illinois Press, 1997); Anne Meis Knupfer, *Toward a Tenderer Humanity and a Nobler Womanhood: African American Women's Clubs in Turn-of-the-Century Chicago* (New York: New York University Press, 1996); and Anne Firor Scott, *Natural Allies: Women's Associations in American History* (Urbana: University of Illinois Press, 1992). Prior to the publication of *Natural Allies,* Scott outlined phases of women's philanthropy through clubs and associations in "Women's Voluntary Associations: From Charity to Reform," in *Lady Bountiful Revisited: Women, Philanthropy, and Power,* ed. Kathleen D. McCarthy (New Brunswick, N.J.: Rutgers University Press, 1990), 35–54.

5. Blair, *Clubwoman,* 34–35.

6. Mary Ritter Beard, *Woman's Work in Municipalities* (New York: D. Appleton, 1915), 39. She further remarked that "[a]lmost every hamlet and town has felt the

influence of women in that direction" (36–37). More recently, in his study of urban women's contributions to public education, William J. Reese has argued that club-women influenced every important change in education from 1890 to 1920 (*Power and the Promise,* 40).

7. While Reese describes these reforms as grassroots efforts, I argue that women's national networks played a strategic role in organizing local associations.

8. Kathleen D. McCarthy, "Parallel Power Structures: Women and the Voluntary Sphere," in *Lady Bountiful Revisited,* ed. McCarthy, 6.

9. In a 1934 study, Elmer Holbeck of Teachers College (Columbia) found that on average 10 percent of the members of local white PTA associations were men (Holbeck, *An Analysis of the Activities and Potentialities for Achievement of the Parent-Teacher Association with Recommendations* [New York: Teachers College Bureau of Publications, 1934], 58).

10. Civic Engagement Project, directed by Theda Skocpol and Marshall Ganz (Cambridge, Mass.: Harvard University, 1998), data in possession of author.

11. For an examination of the parent education efforts of the PTA see Steven L. Schlossman, "Before Home Start: Notes toward a History of Parent Education in America, 1897–1929," *Harvard Educational Review* 46 (August 1976): 436–67. For a study that investigates philanthropy and parent education, see Steven L. Schlossman, "Philanthropy and the Gospel of Child Development," *History of Education Quarterly* 21 (fall 1981): 275–99.

12. Studies that focus on tensions between parents and teachers include Barbara Finkelstein, "In Fear of Childhood: Relationships between Parents and Teachers in Popular Primary Schools in the Nineteenth Century," *History of Childhood Quarterly* 3 (winter 1976): 321–25; Geraldine Jonçich Clifford, "Home and School in Nineteenth-Century America: Some Personal History Reports from the United States," *History of Education Quarterly* 18 (spring 1978): 3–34; Lawrence A. Cremin, "Family-Community Linkages in American Education: Some Comments on the Recent Historiography," *Teachers College Record* 79 (May 1978): 683–704; and Cutler, *Parents and Schools.*

13. For a discussion of the gender hierarchy in public education during this era, see David Tyack and Elisabeth Hansot, *Learning Together: A History of Coeducation in American Schools* (New Haven, Conn.: Yale University Press, 1990).

14. Reese, "Between Home and School," 13.

15. Christine Woyshner, "The PTA and the Origins of the National Congress of Colored Parents and Teachers" (paper presented at the annual meeting of the American Educational Research Association, New Orleans, La., 2000).

16. James D. Anderson, *The Education of Blacks in the South, 1860–1935* (Chapel Hill: University of North Carolina Press, 1988), 183–84. Double taxation is the term Anderson uses to describe the condition of southern blacks who, because their taxes went to white schools, voluntarily contributed additional funds to support their own local public schools from approximately 1900 to 1935.

17. Butterworth, *Parent-Teacher Association,* 1.

18. Ibid., 9–11.

19. This discussion synthesizes data from extensive primary sources such as PTA minutes, histories, and state reports as well as archival materials of the General Federation of Women's Clubs. All PTA data are located at the national PTA Historical

Collection, Chicago, Ill. My analysis echoes the findings of historians of education such as William J. Reese, James L. Leloudis, and Vanessa Siddle Walker, but builds on these localized studies by demonstrating that PTA philanthropy was a widespread national phenomenon.

20. Butterworth, *Parent-Teacher Association,* 15.

21. Ibid., 15–16. According to Butterworth, Virginia spent 74.4 percent of its activities on providing money for schools, with North Carolina and Texas following with figures of 64.4 percent and 60 percent, respectively (table 9, 126–27). Butterworth surveyed only white parent-teacher associations.

22. James L. Leloudis II, "School Reform in the New South: The Woman's Association for the Betterment of Public School Houses in North Carolina, 1902–1919," *Journal of American History* 69 (March 1983): 903. See also chapter 5 of James L. Leloudis, *Schooling the New South: Pedagogy, Self, and Society in North Carolina, 1880–1920* (Chapel Hill: University of North Carolina Press, 1996). In 1919, the Woman's Association for the Betterment of Public Schools became the North Carolina PTA.

23. Beard, *Woman's Work,* 36.

24. Dorothy Sparks, *Strong Is the Current: History of the Illinois Congress of Parents and Teachers, 1900–1947* (Chicago: Illinois Congress of Parents and Teachers, 1948), 18–19.

25. Leloudis, "School Reform," 896.

26. Iowa Congress of Parents and Teachers, *A History of the Iowa Congress of Parents and Teachers, 1900–1941* (Des Moines: Iowa Congress of Parents and Teachers, n.d.), 25.

27. Vanessa Siddle Walker, *Their Highest Potential: An African American School Community in the Segregated South* (Chapel Hill: University of North Carolina Press, 1996), 36–38, 69.

28. Ibid., 72.

29. Ibid., 75.

30. Elisabeth S. Clemens, "Organizational Repertoires and Institutional Change: Women's Groups and the Transformation of American Politics, 1890–1920," in *Civic Engagement in American Democracy,* ed. Theda Skocpol and Morris P. Fiorina (Washington, D.C.: Brookings Institution Press, 1999), 92.

31. Reese, *Power and the Promise;* see especially the discussion in chapter 6, "Vacation Schools, Playgrounds, and Educational Extension." For PTA work in suburbia, see Claudia Keenan, "P.T.A. Business: A Cultural History of How Suburban Women Supported the Public Schools, 1920–1960" (Ph.D. diss., New York University, 2002).

32. Holbeck, *Activities and Potentialities,* 43.

33. Sheila M. Rothman, *Woman's Proper Place: A History of Changing Ideals and Practices, 1870 to the Present* (New York: Basic, 1978), 135.

34. "Summary of State Reports of Joint Committees and Affiliated Organizations [to the Department of School Patrons], 1910–1911," *National Education Association Proceedings* (Chicago: University of Chicago Press, 1911), 1098, 1101.

35. "Secretary's Minutes, Department of School Patrons," *National Educational Association Proceedings* (Chicago: University of Chicago Press, 1916), 799.

36. "Summary of State Reports of Joint Committees and Affiliated Organizations [to the Department of School Patrons], 1911–1912," *National Education Association Proceedings* (Chicago: University of Chicago Press, 1912), 1344. For women's voca-

tional education, see Jane Bernard Powers, *The "Girl Question" in Education: Vocational Education for Young Women in the Progressive Era* (London: Falmer, 1992).

37. Also known as the Federal Act for the Promotion of the Welfare and Hygiene of Maternity and Infancy, the Sheppard-Towner Act supported educational programs and free clinics for mothers beginning in 1921. It was repealed in 1929. For fuller discussions of these reforms, see Theda Skocpol, *Protecting Soldiers and Mothers: The Political Origins of Social Policy in the United States* (Cambridge, Mass.: Belknap Press of Harvard University Press, 1992); Robyn Muncy, *Creating a Female Dominion in American Reform, 1890–1935* (New York: Oxford University Press, 1991); and Molly Ladd-Taylor, *Mother-Work: Women, Child Welfare, and the State, 1890–1930* (Urbana: University of Illinois Press, 1994).

38. Beard, *Woman's Work*, 40.

39. Mrs. O. Shepard Barnum, "Women's Work in the Socialization of the Schools," *National Education Association Proceedings* (Chicago: University of Chicago Press, 1908), 1236.

40. Elmer Ellsworth Brown, "The Work of Women's Organizations in Education: Suggestions for Effective Co-operation," *National Education Association Proceedings*, 1908, 1220–21.

41. Holbeck's study, published in 1934, relied on Butterworth's data and replicated his findings. Holbeck concluded that the energies of local white PTAs "were directed into new and in many ways less important fields" (Holbeck, *Activities and Potentialities*, 14).

42. Butterworth, *Parent-Teacher Association*, 54.

43. Ibid., 64.

44. Ibid., 66.

45. Holbeck, *Activities and Potentialities*, 44.

46. Ibid., 28.

47. Butterworth, *Parent-Teacher Association*, 68–69. This interpretation challenges Cutler's argument that male school administrators found clubs and associations easier to manage than individual parents or families. The fiscal power of PTA philanthropy led some administrators to adopt a divide-and-conquer strategy when dealing with women's voluntary groups.

48. Ibid., 74.

49. See Muncy, *Creating a Female Dominion*, chapter 5.

50. Julia Grant, *Raising Baby by the Book: The Education of American Mothers* (New Haven, Conn.: Yale University Press, 1998), 39. For sources on maternalism, see Seth Koven and Sonya Michel, eds., *Mothers of a New World: Maternalist Politics and the Origins of Welfare States* (New York: Routledge, 1993); Lynn Y. Weiner, "Maternalism as a Paradigm," *Journal of Women's History* 5 (winter 1993): 96–130; and Ladd-Taylor, *Mother-Work*.

51. Rothman, *Woman's Proper Place*, 187–88.

52. Darlene Clark Hine, "'We Specialize in the Wholly Impossible': The Philanthropic Work of Black Women," in *Lady Bountiful*, ed. McCarthy, 71.

53. See also Marybeth Gasman's chapter on black sororities, this volume.

54. Hine, "Wholly Impossible," 81.

55. The "white PTA" was the name used by the leaders of the National Congress of Colored Parents and Teachers to refer to the National PTA.

56. Gerda Lerner, "Community Work of Black Club Women," in *The Majority Finds Its Past: Placing Women in History* (1979; reprint, New York: Oxford University Press, 1981), 84. See also Gerda Lerner, ed., *Black Women in White America: A Documentary History* (New York: Vintage, 1972), especially pages 435–37.

57. Anderson, *Education of Blacks*, 18. Many other works illustrate the importance of education as a central theme in black history. For example, see Donald G. Nieman, ed., *African Americans and Education in the South, 1865–1900* (New York: Garland, 1994); and Darlene Clark Hine and Kathleen Thompson, *A Shining Thread of Hope: The History of Black Women in America* (New York: Broadway, 1998).

58. National Congress of Colored Parents and Teachers, *Coral Anniversary History* (Dover, Del.: National Congress of Colored Parents and Teachers, 1961), 65.

59. National Congress of Colored Parents and Teachers, *Coral Anniversary*, 72–73. See also Scott, *Natural Allies*, 150.

60. National Congress of Parents and Teachers, *Golden Jubilee History, 1897–1947* (Chicago: National Congress of Parents and Teachers, 1947), 38.

61. Christine Woyshner, "Toward a History of a Black Parent-Teacher Movement" (paper presented at the annual meeting of the History of Education Society, San Antonio, Tex., October 2000).

62. This evidence challenges the claims of historians who have implied that black parent-teacher associations did not form until the 1920s. For example, Ladd-Taylor claims that "separate 'colored' mothers' clubs and parent-teacher associations appeared during the 1920s" (*Mother-Work*, 58). Similarly, Nancy Cott asserts that "[t]he founding in 1926 of a National Colored Parent-Teachers Association indicated black women's similar concerns for their children's welfare" (*The Grounding of Modern Feminism* [New Haven, Conn.: Yale University Press, 1987], 87). Such claims are curious, given the extensive efforts of the National Association of Colored Women's clubs in prior decades. Scott's research on women's organizations in U.S. history reveals that black women "had been organized for many decades to deal with the social needs of their own people" (*Natural Allies*, 90). See also Lerner, ed., *Black Women in White America*.

63. National Congress of Colored Parents and Teachers, *Coral Anniversary*, 7.

64. Georgia Congress of Colored Parents and Teachers, *Golden Anniversary History* (Atlanta: Georgia Congress of Colored Parents and Teachers, 1969), 10. For another study that analyzes black and white relations in the South, see the chapter by Victoria-María MacDonald and Eleanore Lenington, this volume.

65. The Jeanes Foundation provided funds to hire field supervisors who worked to maintain and improve school plants, provide parent and teacher education, address health and curriculum concerns, and promote interracial solidarity. See National Association of Supervisors and Consultants Interim History Writing Committee, *The Jeanes Story: A Chapter in the History of American Education, 1908–1968* (Atlanta, Ga.: Southern Education Foundation, 1979), 26; Anderson, *Education of Blacks*, 86, 153; and Valinda Littlefield, "'To Do the Next Needed Thing': Jeanes Teachers in the Southern United States, 1908–1934," in *Telling Women's Lives: Narrative Inquiries in the History of Women's Education*, ed. Kathleen Weiler and Sue Middleton (Philadelphia: Open University Press, 1999), 130–45.

66. National Congress of Colored Parents and Teachers, *Coral Anniversary*, 9.

67. Ibid., 10.

68. National Congress historians do not detail any of the "many changes" made to white PTA guidelines in order to adapt them to the needs of the black PTA (National Congress of Colored Parents and Teachers, *Coral Anniversary*, 12).

69. Ibid., 83.

70. Grant, *Raising Baby*, 96.

71. National Congress of Parents and Teachers, *Proceedings of the Thirty-Second Annual Meeting* (Washington, D.C.: 1929), 177.

72. See *Child-Welfare Magazine* (official publication of the National Congress of Parents and Teachers, Washington, D.C.), July 1932, inside back cover.

73. National Congress of Parents and Teachers, *Proceedings of the Forty-First Annual Meeting* (Washington, D.C.: 1937), 351.

74. A discussion of race relations in the PTA is beyond the scope of this chapter. Certainly, there were white allies in the PTA who worked toward equality in the organization and in education and society, just as there were black PTA members who saw separatism as a worthwhile strategy.

75. Marguerite Smith Taylor, "Evaluation of the Program of the Colored Parent-Teachers Association in Missouri" (master's thesis, Lincoln University, 1954), 9.

76. Walker, *Their Highest Potential*, 76–77.

77. Taylor, "Evaluation," 27–28.

78. See Walker's extensive discussion of PTA fundraisers in *Their Highest Potential*, especially chapter 3.

79. Holbeck, *Activities and Potentialities*, 19.

80. Ladd-Taylor, *Mother-Work;* Susan Crawford and Peggy Levitt, "Social Change and Civic Engagement: The Case of the PTA," in *Civic Engagement*, ed. Theda Skocpol and Morris P. Fiorina, 249–96; and Robert D. Putnam, *Bowling Alone: The Collapse and Revival of American Community* (New York: Simon and Schuster, 2000).

81. Cutler argues that while the National PTA leadership focused on child labor, the local "affiliates focused on more mundane issues like lunchrooms, libraries, and health clinics" (*Parents and Schools*, 73).

10. Women's Philanthropy for Women's Art in America, Past and Present

Karen J. Blair

This essay examines the efforts of American women who have believed that women artists and audiences have been woefully underserved by men's philanthropic contributions to art museums—institutions largely administered by men and featuring works of art created by men. Women donors past and present have taken issue with the inference that viewers should revere this art exclusively as the best representation of civilization's creativity. Let us dissect two eras when women's rights activism ignited women's enthusiasm to rectify the gender imbalance they observed in the art world. The women donors under our scrutiny are not individuals, but rather groups of women who cooperated to create new arts venues for the exhibition of women's works of art. Beyond their obvious success in educating audiences to respect art made by women, these donors increased their own knowledge, learning to evaluate the arts, create institutions, and shape the values of their culture.

The feminist movement of the 1970s indisputably launched an era of change in U.S. women's political, economic, and social lives, providing opportunities and advancements for women in government, the workplace, and their personal lives. This era also brought new gains in the arts; notably, there was a blossoming of arts institutions created for the work of women. Many of these facilities were founded by women acting collectively—by donors who shared a respect for the creativity of women, observed that resources for women in the arts were meager, challenged the canon of white male worthies, and sought to offer exposure and respect to women's works of art. The impact of their efforts has been measurable, but not unique: modern goals and gains resemble efforts of turn-of-the-century American women's rights activists. Despite the passage of over half a century, the parallels between women philanthropists of women's creativity at the beginning and the close of the twentieth century are striking.

Examples abound of contemporary women who founded facilities to enhance arts opportunities for women and educate the broader public to their value. One such benefactor is Wilhelmina Cole Holladay, who in the 1980s founded the National Museum of Women in the Arts in Washington, D.C. Wife of a self-made real estate developer and publishing entrepreneur, Holladay contributed a collection of paintings by women and refurbished a 1907 Masonic temple using millions of her own money and that of her friends. Today, the museum stands only a few city blocks from the Smithsonian museums and other venerable arts institutions in the nation's capital. Its exhibitions of paintings by such artists as Angelica Kauffman, Anna Peale, Suzanne Valadon, and Alice Neel challenge the male-dominated canon of art on display down the street in such illustrious exhibition halls as the National Gallery of Art. Holladay's alliance with other donors provides a useful case study of women's philanthropic giving.

In addition, we can examine the success of contemporary quilt museums created by women donors in cooperation with one another. Perhaps in modern times no creative work by women has fared better than quilting, a craft that has won the respect both of feminists who applaud the long history of women's work and expressive culture and of traditionalists who continue to embrace productive work within the home over efforts to establish women in male-dominated occupations. In recent years, several museums dedicated to the exhibition of antique and contemporary quilts have made their debuts. The oldest of these is the American Museum of Quilts and Textiles in San Jose, California, founded in 1977 by members of the Santa Clara Valley Quilt Association. In Golden, Colorado, a Denver suburb, Eugenia Mitchell founded the Rocky Mountain Quilt Museum and donated one hundred quilts to its permanent collection. The museum opened its doors to the public in 1990. The following year, Meredith Schroeder and her husband Bill (a publisher of guides for hobbyists and collectors) donated ninety-one quilts to the collection of their brand-new American Quilt Society Museum in Paducah, Kentucky. In 1988, Mennonites Merle and Phyllis Good, with Merle's in-laws Rachel and Kenneth Pellman, established a quilt museum as one component of the People's

Place Cultural Center located in Intercourse, Pennsylvania, a center point for Mennonite and Amish communities. Still another enterprise is the New England Quilt Museum, opened in 1988 in Lowell, Massachusetts, under the ambitious sponsorship of local quilt guilds. Institutions like these five museums have launched hundreds of exhibitions of heirloom and recently created textile art, inspiring new quilters and enlightening the general public.

It is not insignificant that the vision for these galleries has largely come from women or that education for all participants has emerged as a pattern in the process of institution-building. Clearly the donors of these arts institutions have distinguished themselves as unusual nurturers of women's creativity, who reject self-aggrandizement in favor of broad transmission of knowledge. But their efforts also illustrate another noteworthy phenomenon in philanthropy. These women supporters are far removed from the traditional stereotype of the philanthropist as a rich industrialist who writes fat checks for a pet arts project and proceeds to fashion an institution based on a personal vision and intended to impress peers within an elite social circle. Instead, these donors reflect an impressive movement to create a supportive environment for women artists in self-consciously collaborative ways. They have sought to involve many individuals in their goals, educating them about the possibilities of shaping culture through museum-building. They have demonstrated considerable success in developing a broad base of women funders for women's arts institutions, women willing to donate as part of founding efforts and as ongoing partners in facility maintenance. Finally, they have prioritized popular education as a goal, seeking to educate great numbers of women and men about the value of previously overlooked forms of expressive culture. One of my goals here is to examine the ways that women's forms of collaborative philanthropy have had both positive and negative effects on two of the new institutions devoted to the visual arts: the National Museum of Women in the Arts and the New England Quilt Museum.

But if we imagine these modern founders have been groundbreaking in their efforts to forge wide partnerships for giving, we are unaware of their antecedents from the turn of the twentieth century. American women in the early nineteen hundreds likewise developed philanthropy, arts, and education values in conjunction with a vital women's suffrage and temperance movement; furthermore, they embarked on a similar mission: to champion the creative work of women by seeking to sustain and promote it, using ingenious alliances to achieve their collective goals. Accordingly, I also wish to review efforts by women's amateur arts societies in the Progressive Era to develop an environment that would foster the creative work of women artists, with the aim of providing delectation and education for a broad public. This activity foreshadowed commitment to women's art in the 1980s. We can observe considerable similarities between recent and earlier patterns of partnership for philanthropic activity, despite major differences over seventy years of history.

THE NATIONAL MUSEUM OF WOMEN IN THE ARTS

The National Museum of Women in the Arts (NMWA), opened in 1988, has enjoyed considerable publicity as the first art museum in the world to dedicate itself completely to the exhibition of women's work. The gallery's founder, Wilhelmina Cole Holladay, has received much (and deserved) attention for her ingenuity and generous financial donations. Holladay contributed to the acquisition of a historic building in Washington, D.C., assembled and donated a collection of paintings by European and North American women, and secured considerable corporate support for a somewhat controversial enterprise. Some critics, for instance, have argued that the pieces she shows—created by women who have not generally enjoyed recognition in traditional art museums—are not really "art." Others have complained that her institution smacks offensively of feminism, foisting assertions of women's equality on the arts-loving public. Additionally, some women artists have been known to reject NMWA's "ghettoization" of their work, refusing to permit their paintings or sculpture to be exhibited in a separate, all-women's arts institution. Nevertheless, Holladay has managed to attract funding from a healthy panel of corporate donors—including Philip Morris, AT&T, Martin Marietta, and Dupont—in order to create a formidable space for women's art.

Let us examine a heretofore unexplored dimension of the NMWA: the institution's eagerness to attract support, financial and otherwise, from a broad base of women. This brand of philanthropy has been initiated by the institution's leadership rather than emerging from the grassroots, as it has in quilt museums. But part of Holladay's genius lies in her ability to link her institution with modern women's consciousness of women's auxiliary status, past and present. Her strides in winning support of the museum on these grounds are considerable.[1]

For example, a visitor to the NMWA will immediately observe a large book at the reception desk. This book—seen long before any painting comes into view—holds the names of all charter members who contributed $25 when the facility was only an idea. Holladay invited multitudes of women to assist her in funding the museum, soliciting help from women she located on five mailing lists (museum catalog buyers, upscale catalog shoppers, female members of professional arts organizations, supporters of cultural programs, and members of women's rights organizations). With persistence, she collected small checks from eighty-five thousand women, enabling her to boast that the museum's membership list trails behind only those of the revered and established Metropolitan Museum of Art and Art Institute of Chicago. Today, the bound list of charter NMWA members is fondly and steadily perused by museum guests who have traveled from distant places to view the results of their support. The prominent book reminds them that the effort to build this unique women's arts institution was a shared one. They hunt for their names and those of their friends, proud to see that they have made a mark on the institution that has managed to dignify the creative work of women.

An intensive appeal for charter members was only one of Holladay's innovative ways of building a foundation for her new institution. One of the most successful strategies has been to invite each state to form a committee of women that will generate a show of local contemporary women's art and fund the show's exhibition at the national museum. The plan has had wide appeal, for it taps the pride of women volunteers, artists, and individual and corporate sponsors even (and perhaps especially) in states far from Washington, D.C. To date, numerous states have formed committees, and several of these have assembled shows for the NMWA.[2]

Let us examine the work of the women in the state of Washington, who formed a committee in July 1987 and raised about $80,000 in two years. The committee sent a juried show of forty-three pieces (oil, watercolor, photography, glass, computer graphics, ceramics, and sculpture) to the nation's capital, representing fifteen women artists.[3]

It was an artist, Nellike Langout-Nix, who blended the interests of women donors and women artists in Washington State. She organized a survey of women artists in the state and urged women to submit their work. Over 668 artists responded. The fundraising chairperson, Ruth Gerberding (whose husband was president of the University of Washington), arranged receptions for women who had been supporters of art in the Northwest and who were willing to associate themselves with a woman-focused museum. Among the $500 donors were Anne Gould Hauberg—founder of the Pilchuck School for Glass and patron of Dale Chihuly—and Betty Hedreen, supporter of the Seattle Art Museum. Still, only twenty donors offered five hundred dollars; additional funds were needed to hold the competition, assemble the show, crate and insure the exhibition pieces, transport the show to and from Washington, D.C., print a catalog, and fly the artists to a gala opening attended by their senators, congressmen, and governor.[4] To raise more support, lecturers toured state universities, senior centers, women's clubs, and other public forums with a slide show of women's art. Towns and cities in the state came forth with small amounts of money after the exhibit was committed to tour in several local communities.[5] The Washington State Committee also won support from local businesses that did not generally support women or the arts. They were attracted by the opportunity to champion northwestern contributions in the nation's capital. Money came from such improbable sources as the Deep Sea Fisherman's Union, Olympia Brewery, the Washington State Apple Commission, Arbor Crest Winery, Puget Power and Light, Tree Top (apple juice) Cooperative, Boeing Aircraft, Kaiser Aluminum, and Weyerhaeuser. The effort was enormous, but it was successful. A museum in Washington, D.C., was publicized throughout Washington State; fifteen Washington women artists were featured in their home state and in the nation's capital; local sponsorship touted the Northwest on the East Coast; and local women's arts supporters expanded organizational skills they had developed in other voluntary church, civic, and social welfare projects.

This case illustrates a key element of donor cooperation: the involvement of many sponsors bolstered the new institution, however far away it might be. As in the nineteenth-century efforts of ladies' aid societies, hospital guilds, and female auxiliaries of benevolent and charitable enterprises, the National Museum of Women in the Arts was strengthened by inviting women's personal and financial investment in its success.

In addition to a broad base of financial support, the NMWA exhibitions also enjoyed and encouraged a new and broader audience. Here was a different audience than that enjoyed by traditional art museums. Women supporters alerted their neighbors, their networks, and members of other woman-centered voluntary organizations to the project, encouraging them to see, enjoy, and absorb the artwork on display. Audiences arose from such constituencies as Girl Scouts, women's studies students, and members of the National Organization for Women, extending women's art well beyond the world of art historians and collectors.

THE NEW ENGLAND QUILT MUSEUM

Perhaps the ultimate expression of women's cooperative philanthropy lies in the creation of the New England Quilt Museum (NEQM) in Lowell, Massachusetts. It opened its doors in June 1987 to exhibit traditional and contemporary quilts to visitors to the City of Spindles. The historic mill town today attracts tourists by reflecting on and representing its association with the textile industry.[6]

In 1991, the museum's collection was much bolstered by a generous contribution of thirty-five antique quilts by Crayola Crayon heiress and quilter Gail Binney-Winslow. Also a collector of quilts, she had circulated part of her collection nationally through the Smithsonian Institution's SITES program in 1985. The show, "Homage to Amanda," toured cities throughout the United States. Binney-Winslow chose to make her gift—including some of the quilts that had enjoyed national exposure—to a budding institution in her own area.

For all her generosity, the new quilt museum was not bankrolled by a major donor. Instead, it was funded by an ambitious alliance of home quilters, united through the New England Quilter's Guild (NEQG). As a member of the Cranberry Quilters Guild of Cape Cod, Binney-Winslow was also allied with the NEQG, which formed in 1976 to meet the needs of modern quilters. In 1981, eager to view as many quilts as possible but stymied by the lack of attention that local fine arts museums gave to quilts, officers of the NEQG voted to embark on the founding of a quilt museum. Six years later, the organization's membership had raised $45,000 and opened the doors to its museum.

The story of the fundraising is complex. In the absence of a primary benefactor, the museum exists because many women believed it was important. The membership of the New England Quilter's Guild—in the late 1980s, two thousand individual quilters and members of fifty affiliated guilds—pooled their energies and finances. Dozens of quilt clubs, with memberships ranging from a handful to a few hundred, used their meetings not only to trade quilting techniques, sew crib quilts for AIDS babies and battered women's shelters, and attend instructional workshops, but also to devise methods for raising museum contributions. Strategies were many and varied. The Narragansett Bay Quilters sent $7,650 over ten years, money raised by auctioning off donated quilts. Members of Hands across the Valley Quilters Guild in Amherst, Massachusetts, sent profits from the quilt they raffled at their own quilt show. Individual members simply wrote checks. Some groups coaxed other women's voluntary associations to contribute, as when the Connecticut Federation of Women's Clubs was persuaded to contribute $25 by Connecticut quilters. Some guild members preferred sending needlework over donating cash. They crafted items for sale at the museum gift shop for the museum's profit.

The guild's work to pay museum bills was and continues to be arduous. A flood from burst pipes in 1991 did not damage the collection but necessitated considerable fundraising for a move to a more reliable building, at 18 Shattuck Street, where the museum reopened in July 1993. In addition to money, volunteers have provided time: they give tours, hang exhibits, organize the library, sell admission tickets, and entertain at openings. In return, volunteers expect to have a voice in the operational decisions of the museum, a situation that has contributed to the problem of turnover among museum directors over the years. But the involvement of thousands of New England women in the founding of the institution also provides a foundation of support, a sense of ownership, and a pool of creativity that is impressive. The effort of so many women who insisted on bringing a traditional but neglected art form to the attention of the public overcomes an omission in the professional art world and dignifies the history of women's creative efforts. As in the case of the National Museum of Women in the Arts, the New England Quilt Museum creators have attracted and educated viewers through the dignity and accessibility their institution has lent to quilting. Furthermore, their lectures, workshops, classes, and needlework contests have bolstered regional and even national interest in the tradition that they practice and to which they are utterly committed.

PROGRESSIVE ERA COLLABORATIONS IN BEHALF OF WOMEN'S ART

It is ahistorical to assume that collaborative efforts among philanthropic women are a modern development, but few are aware that a large network of women's amateur arts societies began to form and flourish at the turn of the twentieth century. Members of these organizations were involved in many of the same patterns of philanthropy we have just observed in the 1980s. In hundreds of American cities and towns, a dozen or more art-loving neighbors met monthly or even weekly (except in summertime) to study art history for their own edification, acquaint themselves with the work of contemporary artists, and foster cultural development by creating cultural opportunities in their communities. These groups were not composed of the richest women—those traditionally associated with philanthropy in America. Rather, they were made up of middle-class wives of successful business and professional men in America's big cities and small towns. The women were generally Protestant, white, and economically comfortable, with the time, taste, and background to pursue the arts. They built and exhibited art collections, created arts centers, and became the earliest supporters of municipal art commissions—the forerunners of today's network of government arts supports, from the National Endowment for the Arts to state, county, and city arts councils. In each community, their achievements were small rather than extraordinary, but as a whole, their efforts nationwide to deliver knowledge of and access to women's art were sizeable.[7]

Members of amateur arts associations felt entitled, even obliged, to act as taste-makers in their communities. Their above-average levels of education and their husbands' stature and influence contributed to this attitude. So did their gender, for nineteenth-century "ladies" were thought to be especially sensitive to beauty. In fact, women preferred to cultivate the arts in the company of other women, and they routinely declined opportunities to join coed arts societies. In mixed societies they did not hold executive offices and did not have the clout they enjoyed in women-only arts groups. In addition, middle-class American women justified their role as arts advocates by citing a long tradition of service through voluntary effort. Members' mothers and grandmothers had joined women's societies and auxiliaries for a wide range of purposes, including guilds that supported benevolent institutions, church sewing circles, and ladies' aid societies for war relief.[8]

Most women's arts groups formed initially for the purpose of studying art history. This was true of the Hartford Art Club in Connecticut, the Mankato Art History Club in Minnesota, the Decatur Art Club in Illinois, and the Auburn Art Club in Maine. Sometimes a handful of women met to exchange reviews of exhibitions they had attended or to offer papers they had researched. Sometimes the art enthusiasts were actually a department of a larger women's club that also had sub-groups devoted to the study of literature, music, languages, current events, or social problems. The New England Woman's Club in Boston, for example, created an Arts and Crafts Division in 1899, but the club had also formed groups devoted to botany and political economy.[9] Whether they formed independent clubs or divisions of larger associations of women, women arts advocates tended to concur with the general reverence for the Western canon of Old Masters. However, they invariably widened their curriculum to include the study of local artists—especially women—and crafts, notably the art of pottery, in which women were excelling. When the Hartford Art Club embarked on a study of American art, they devoted separate meetings to the study of women illustrators, women sculptors, women portrait painters, and women miniaturists. They also included women in their examination of Connecticut artists.[10] Probably this catholicism arose for a variety of reasons, including the members' lack of access to the Old Masters, their local pride, a sense of sisterhood, limited finances for collecting artworks, and taste in home decoration.

It was not long before members of these groups observed the dearth of opportunities for women in the arts and defined it as a problem they should solve. This is hardly surprising, given the reform impulse that had gripped many middle-class women of the day, who routinely addressed social problems by creating parks, playgrounds, and free health clinics and by lobbying for clean milk, mothers' pensions, and child labor laws.[11] We can document club efforts to provide—as a group, rather than individually—a wide range of support for women artists. To women enrolled in art schools, clubs offered scholarships and urban residences, such as the Three Arts Clubs in New York and Cincinnati; to professional women artists, they offered jobs as instructors at club meetings and increased exposure through exhibitions, commissions, and donations of their art to their communities. Through these efforts, women in arts clubs furthered the careers of women artists of their day. Club members did the work that well-heeled philanthropists have done, but they accomplished their goals as a group and learned how multitudinous were the results that their collaborations could yield.

Women in turn-of-the-century clubs built a strong tradition of publicizing the work of women artists by holding exhibitions, even if limited budgets tempered their ambitions. The General Federation of

Women's Clubs (GFWC), claiming a membership of four million in 1926, displayed fifty sculptures by twenty American women at its biennial convention, including the work of Brenda Putnam, Edith Baretto Parsons, Bessie Potter Vonnoh, Grace Mott Johnson, Laura Gardin Fraser, Anna Vaughn Hyatt-Huntington, Harriet Payne Bingham, and Harriet Frishmuth.[12] They also circulated an exhibition of art pottery from studios in which women were noteworthy, including Rookwood, Overbeck, Newcomb, and Grueby potteries.[13] Such activities were logical services for member clubs, who had long supported the arts with impressive zeal. In 1912, for example, two thousand clubs in the GFWC reported that they had offered lectures on art that year, and three hundred clubs had held their own exhibitions.

Many other networks of women art lovers also championed the accomplishments of women. When the Friends of the Arts in Pittsburgh acquired 134 works of art to hang in public school classrooms, forty-seven of those works were by women.[14] The Woman's Art Club of Cincinnati bought a painting by Mary Spencer in 1912, a gift for the Cincinnati Art Museum. In Richmond, Indiana, the woman-run Art Association purchased Indiana art for the high school art gallery, including sculpture by Janet Scudder and pottery by the Overbeck sisters, which appeared alongside the work of male artists like William Merrit Chase.[15]

Women supporters of women's arts persuaded other clubwomen to support the cause. Some women's organizations that existed for other purposes nevertheless became patrons of the arts in order to accomplish their work. Patriotic societies of women needed designers for tablets, historical plaques, memorials, markers, and statues of heroes. The Women's Roosevelt Society, for example, wanted to issue a bronze medal with the image of Theodore Roosevelt in 1919, and they commissioned Anna Hyatt to design it. She would also create a bronze statue of Sybil Luddington, a Revolutionary War heroine, for the Daughters of the American Revolution (DAR).[16]

Much of the work that women's clubs commissioned for the decoration of their clubrooms was created by women artists. The Daughters of the American Revolution purchased work by L. Pearl Sanders for Continental Hall in Washington, D.C., and statuary by Gertrude Vanderbilt Whitney, which in 1929 was placed in the courtyard at DAR headquarters. Violet Oakley, renowned for her mural paintings at the Pennsylvania State Capitol at Harrisburg, was revered by the Philadelphia Republican Women's Club. The club bought the home of Charlton Yarnall to save Oakley's mural decorations inside it. A bronze fountain by Janet Scudder was commissioned as a memorial shrine to Mrs. E. J. Robinson, president and founder of the Woman's Department Club in Indianapolis, and was placed at the entrance to the main hall of the clubhouse. The Junior Lounge of the American Women's Association building in Manhattan contained a series of murals by Lucile Howard and M. Elizabeth Price. The Wednesday Club in San Diego hired Anna Valentien to produce all of the door plates, hardware, and copper and glass lanterns for its clubhouse. The Daughters of the Republic of Texas commissioned Elisabet Ney to create statues of Stephen Austin and Sam Houston; these never adorned their clubrooms, but went instead to the United States Capitol.[17]

Club members honed the skills to press women's arts before general audiences. The GFWC's art director, Rose Berry, urged all clubwomen to study the work of American women painters Mary Cassatt, Elizabeth Bourse, Cecilia Beaux, Helen Maria Turner, Lilian Westcott Hale, Jean McLane, Gertrude Fiske, Lillian Genth, Anna Fisher, Felicia W. Howell, M. DeNeale Morgan, Helen Dunlop, Marie Danforth Page, Alice Kent Stoddard, Ellen Emmet Rand, Lydia Field Emmet, Violet Oakley, Dorothy Ochtman, Evelyn Withrow, Pauline Palmer, Mary Foote, Jane Peterson, Johanna K. Hailman, and Marie Oberteufer, as well as American sculptors Harriet Frishmuth, Anna Vaughn Hyatt-Huntington, Malvina Hoffman, Edith Barretto Parsons, Bessie Potter Vonnoh, Laura Gardin Fraser, Brenda Putnam, Evelyn Beatrice Longman, Beatrice Fenton, Gertrude Vanderbilt Whitney, Grace Talbot, Margaret French Cresson, Abastenia Eberle, and Lucy Perkins Ripley.[18] The Federation used its 1911 edition of *Handbook of Art in Our Own Country* to recognize numerous examples of women's art in public spaces, including a statue called "Southern Womanhood" by Belle Kinsey (Atlanta); statues of Lady Macbeth, General Albert Sidney Johnston, Sam Houston, and Stephen Austin by Elisabet Ney (Austin); "Leif Ericson" by Anne Whitney (Boston); the "Inspiration" statue at the front of the Buffalo Historical Building by Gertrude (Mrs. Harry Payne) Whitney; the "Mother Bickerdyke" statue in Galesburg, Illinois, by Mrs. Theodore Ruggles Kitson; the "Daniel Boone" statue in Louisville by Enid Yandell; "Soldiers' Monument" in Newburyport, Massachusetts, by Sally James Farnsham; the Carrie Brown Bagnotti Memorial Fountain in Providence, Rhode Island, by Enid Yandell; a statue of Admiral Esek Hopkins by Mrs.

Theodore R. Kitson (Providence); "Beatrice Cenci" by Harriet Hosmer (St. Louis); "Awakening of Spring" by Clara Pfeiffer Garrett (St. Louis); the Carnegie Library designed by Julia Morgan in Seminary Park, California; the Hamilton S. White Memorial by Gail Sherman Corbett in Syracuse; "Admiral David Farragut" by Mrs. V. R. Hoxie in Washington, D.C.; a bust of Alice Freeman Palmer in Wellesley, Massachusetts, by Anne Whitney; a bas relief portrait in the Woodstock, Vermont, courthouse by Mar Stickney; and the women's clubhouse designed by architect Josephine Wright Chapman in Worcester, Massachusetts.[19]

Members of women's groups ostentatiously furthered public familiarity with women's art still more when they began, after World War I, to build spacious and luxurious clubhouses with money from government bonds they had acquired to support the war effort. Some commissioned women architects. Julia Morgan shaped many California clubhouses; the Berkeley Woman's City Club is probably the most admired. Mrs. Minerva P. Nichols designed the New Century Clubhouses in Wilmington and Philadelphia. In both Worcester and Lynn, Massachusetts, Josephine Wright Chapman designed the women's clubhouses. Hazel Wood Waterman designed the Wednesday Club's hall in San Diego, and Gertrude Sawyer designed the Junior League Building in Washington, D.C. While these buildings provided space for a variety of club functions, including meeting rooms for business, kitchen and dining areas for luncheons, and auditoriums for speeches and concerts, the new halls additionally offered high-ceilinged, elaborately furnished gallery spaces for women's art, as well as reception areas for gala gallery openings. The Des Moines Women's Clubhouse, for example, included a separate gallery. Sometimes the exhibits were open only to club members, but frequently the club opened its shows to the general public; club members thus educated their neighbors about the strength, beauty, and value of women's art. These new galleries and reception halls, often elegant and splendid, lent a luster to the art of women similar to that created by Wilhelmina Holladay in her modern-day women's art showplace.

The advantages of collectively supporting women's art went beyond the increased financial base available to a project supported by hundreds of women. For instance, members shared a responsibility for supporting the arts projects. (In one Pennsylvania town, no committee was established to locate an appropriate clubhouse to meet the club's architectural needs and desires. Instead, everyone belonging to the organization was expected to tour the spaces available![20]) A sizeable club also ensured wide publicity for an arts program and thus increased an artist's visibility. Furthermore, the work of funding, assembling, hanging, and advertising art shows gave women in the sponsoring club valuable lessons in arts administration, training not very available to them elsewhere.

The disadvantages, however, were also apparent. A great number of donors inevitably brought conflicting opinions to each issue and practicality was sometimes lost in the ambitions of dreamers. In New York City, the National Association of Women Painters and Sculptors gave up their showplace after five years, undone by the expense of and debate over the details of clubhouse management.[21] There were as many project planners who were finally daunted by limits on time, space, collections, and security as who succeeded.

One of the clubwomen's strategies for supporting local artists was unsurprising, given their willingness to democratize the canon, broaden public access to the arts, and widen patterns of giving, all goals destined to increase women's role in the arts. They became early champions of government aid to the arts, in the form of municipal arts commissions. Women were not major players in the first city arts committee in America—the privately funded New York City Municipal Arts Commission, chartered by the City of New York in 1897— but they soon became major exponents of the idea. For example, the Minnesota Commission, antecedent of the modern state arts council, was formed in 1903, thanks in large part to pressure from Minnesota's State Federation of Women's Clubs. Members of St. Cloud's Art and History Club, while studying the subject of France, embraced the French government's notion of support for the arts. Determined to replicate this arrangement, the group's officers introduced the concept at their district convention in 1898 and won the support of the president of Minnesota's State Federation of Women's Clubs, Mrs. Margaret J. Evans. With the entire federation behind the proposal, Governor Van Sant and the 1903 legislature agreed to establish a state arts commission (also known as the State Art Society). The government appropriated two thousand dollars per year for the endeavor. The commission's objects were ambitious: "to advance the interest of the fine arts, to develop the influence of art in education and foster the introduction of art in manufactures"—goals that incorporated the contributions of women artists.[22]

The modest budget of the Minnesota art commission, even supplemented by memberships and donations, would not have permitted appreciable activity had not women's volunteer power fueled the agency. Clubwomen on the State Art Society's board delivered the unpaid labor that established its lecture service, a traveling exhibition program, the loan of photographs of Western art masterpieces, and the beginnings of an original art collection. Through the cooperation of the St. Cloud Reading Room Society, the organization initiated an annual exhibition. In 1911, with an increased appropriation of $7,500, the society hired Maurice Irwin Flagg as part-time director to expand its services.[23] This advance did not mean that clubwomen dropped out, however. They lent funds for special projects, and when funding for the Society collapsed, clubwomen soon revived it in 1921. It foundered in 1927 and was again revived in the mid-1940s. Women's collective efforts to broaden American access to the arts in the early twentieth century were tenacious, creative, and ambitious. Clubwomen's insistence on informing themselves about women artists of the past and present, commissioning work by women artists, and pressing government to enhance public access to art (including that by women) was bold and invaluable. Furthermore, their interests and influence awakened the general public to the existence and importance of women's creativity.

On the face of it, the contexts of the two eras under discussion here are sufficiently dissimilar as to make their stories incomparable. By the final decades of the twentieth century, the United States had changed considerably from what it had been in the first decades of that century. American economic, political, and social influence had grown and woman's piece of the pie had grown with it. Yet gender inequity persisted in arts and in women's access to resources that could correct the imbalance. However, women's determination to create a more just society in both periods launched a collaborative effort to push women's art before the public for appreciation and recognition. In both eras, women philanthropists supporting women artists successfully worked together to assemble the resources necessary to establish venues for showcasing women's art. However indifferent or even hostile to women's creative voice their world might be, they collectively forged paths to reach a broad public that might otherwise have remained ignorant of women's artistic capabilities.

NOTES

An earlier version of this chapter appeared in Wanda Corn, ed., *Cultural Leadership in America: Art Matronage and Patronage* (Boston: Isabella Stewart Gardner Museum, 1998).

1. NMWA Papers, National Museum of Women in the Arts Library, Washington, D.C.; Anne Higonnet, "Woman's Place," *Art in America* 76 (July 1988), 127–49; Wilhelmina Cole Holladay, interview by author, 6 and 7 August 1991, Washington, D.C.; *National Museum of Women in the Arts* (New York: Harry N. Abrams, 1987); and Eleanor Tufts, *American Women Artists, 1830–1930* (Washington, D.C.: International Exhibitions Foundation for the National Museum of Women in the Arts, 1987).

2. In 1987, Kansas and Colorado sponsored the first state exhibitions; in 1994, shows were produced by committees in northern and southern California. Texas sent its first show in 1988, Washington State and North Carolina in 1989, upstate New York in 1990, Arkansas in 1992, and Utah and Tennessee in 1993.

3. Twelve artists came from the Seattle area and three were from the eastern part of the state. They were Sonja Blomdahl, Rachel Feferman, Lorna Pauley Jordan, Francesca Lacagnina, Solveig Landa, Marilyn Lysohir, Janice Maher, Inge Norgaard, Connie J. Ritchie, Jennifer Stabler-Holland, Sarah Jane Teofanov, Barbara E. Thomas, Liza vonRosenstiel, Linda E. A. Wachtmeister, and Patti Warashina.

4. Ruth Gerberding, Beverly Criley Graham, Corinne Kramer, Nancy Lewis, and Irish Nichols, interviews with author, January 1995, Seattle, Washington.

5. The show was exhibited in Pullman, Ellensburg, two sites in Seattle, Yakima, Richland, Ilwaco, Pasco, Everett, and Walla Walla.

6. Carter Houck, "Museum Quilts," *Quilter's Newsletter Magazine* (April 1994), 22–23; *Compass*, the newsletter of the New England Quilter's Guild, 1981–91; Marie Geary, telephone conversation with author, February 1994; Janet Elwin, telephone conversation with author, March 1994; Marjorie Dannis, telephone conversation with author, December 1993; Susan Raban, interview by author, July 1992, Lowell, Mass.; Gail Binney-Stiles and Una Baker, telephone conversation with author, July 1992; and Papers of the New England Quilt Museum, New England Quilt Museum Library, Lowell, Massachusetts.

7. See especially chapter 4 of Karen J. Blair, *The Torchbearers: Women and Their Amateur Arts Associations in America, 1890–1930* (Bloomington: Indiana University Press, 1994).

8. Barbara J. Berg, *The Remembered Gate: Origins of American Feminism: The Woman and the City, 1800–1860* (New York: Oxford University Press, 1978); and Paula Baker, "Domestication in Politics: Women and American Political Society, 1780–1920," *American Historical Review* 89 (June 1984), 620–47.

9. Massachusetts State Federation of Women's Clubs, *Progress and Achievement: A History of the Massachusetts State Federation of Women's Clubs, 1893–1962* (Lexington: Massachusetts State Federation of Women's Clubs, 1962); and Jane Cunningham Croly, *The History of the Woman's Club Movement in America* (New York: Henry G. Allen, 1898).

10. Yearbooks, 1921–23, Hartford Art Club, Stowe-Day Foundation, Hartford, Conn.

11. Karen J. Blair, *The Clubwoman as Feminist: True Womanhood Redefined, 1868–1914* (New York: Holmes and Meier, 1980), especially chapter 6.

12. Rose V. S. Berry, "The Spirit of Art," *Eighteenth Biennial Proceedings, General Federation of Women's Clubs* (1926): 270–73.

13. "Art Department," *General Federation Magazine* 12 (April 1914), 9–10.

14. Catherine Kaiser, "Those One Hundred Friends," *Carnegie Magazine* (September/October 1984), 22–24. In McPherson, Kans., the community featured Anna Keener's painting "Mountain Ranch" ("An Exhibition in a Kansas High School," *American Magazine of Art* 9 [January 1918]: 111–13).

15. Ellis Bond Johnson Papers, Richmond Art Museum, Richmond, Ind.

16. Beatrice G. Proske, *Brookgreen Gardens Sculpture* (Brookgreen, S.C.: Trustees, 1943).

17. *American Art Annual* 26 (1929): 18; *American Art Annual* 24 (1927): 17; *American Art Annual* 25 (1928): 18; *American Art Annual* 28 (1931): 18; Vernon Loggins, "Ney, Elisabet," in *Notable American Women,* vol. 2, ed. Edward T. James, Janet Wilson James, and Paul S. Boyer (Cambridge, Mass.: Belknap Press of Harvard University Press, 1971), 623–25; and Bride Neill Taylor, *Elisabet Ney, Sculptor* (Austin, Tex.: Thomas F. Taylor, 1938), 75–78.

18. *Scribner's,* June 1928, 792 g, h, and 76.

19. Mrs. Everett W. Pattison, *Handbook of Art in Our Own Country,* 2nd ed. (St. Louis, Mo.: General Federation of Women's Clubs, 1911).

20. "Club Financing by the Extravagant Sex," *Woman Citizen* 7 (26 August 1922): 8.

21. Ronald Pisano, *One Hundred Years: The National Association of Women Artists* (New York: National Association of Women Artists, 1989), 15.

22. Mrs. E. W. Pattison, "Art and the Women's Clubs," *Federation Bulletin* 7 (May 1909), 38–40; General Federation of Women's Clubs, *Eighth Biennial Proceedings* (1906): 106; Minnesota State Art Society, *Brief History of the Minnesota State Art Society* (St. Paul: Minnesota State Art Society, ca. 1949); and Minnesota State Art Society, *Report of the Minnesota State Art Society, 1903–4* (St. Paul: Minnesota State Art Society, 1904).

23. Mrs. Phelps Wyman, "State Art Society of Minnesota," *American City* 7 (August 1912), 142–43.

PART III.
        THE POLITICS OF PHILANTHROPY
        IN WOMEN'S EDUCATION:
        RACE, CLASS, AND GENDER

11. "Nothing More for Men's Colleges": The Educational Philanthropy of Mrs. Russell Sage

Ruth Crocker

> I am sorry not to help you, but Mrs. Sage . . . has told me repeatedly that she was going to do nothing more for men's colleges.
>
> —THEODORE C. JANEWAY to Rutgers president
> William H. Demarest, 1916[1]

Late in life, Margaret Olivia Slocum—a Syracuse-born schoolteacher and the wife of New York financier Russell Sage (business partner to robber baron Jay Gould)—reinvented herself as "Mrs. Russell Sage," a philanthropist, moral authority, and advocate for women.[2] The Sages had no children, and it was rumored that she intended to give away the entire fortune amassed over a lifetime by her husband (equivalent to about one and one half billion dollars today).[3] So long as her miserly husband was alive, she had been unable to spend freely, and so for years her philanthropy was confined to moral pronouncements and good works.[4] What causes would the philanthropic Mrs. Sage now support? One sympathetic observer believed he had the answer: "Women and education—there is the key."[5]

Expectant college fundraisers had not long to wait. Russell Sage died in July 1906, a few weeks short of his ninetieth birthday, leaving everything to his widow. Olivia had encouraged her correspondents to believe that her interests lay in women's education above all. But as she considered which schools and colleges to support she faced a bewildering array of choices. Should she found a single, great institution, a Sage University for Women in the East, as the University of Chicago was Mr. Rockefeller's university in the West? Should she support the coeducational universities like Syracuse and Cornell, limit her gifts to women's colleges like Vassar, or support coordinate colleges like Barnard? And what about all the trade and professional schools for women that were begging for her money? When the financial officer from

Syracuse University called at her New York home in May 1906, he found her anxiously pondering these questions. He reported to the university president, "She inquired very minutely about the working of coeducation with us."[6]

CREATIVE AND COERCIVE SPENDING

Historian Margaret Rossiter has described how late-nineteenth-century advocates of women's advancement made their donations to universities conditional on the admission of women or in other ways attempted to leverage new opportunities for women in education. Some examples of such "creative and coercive spending" will be familiar to readers.[7] Female philanthropists funded the era's most famous reform institution, Hull House.[8] Wealthy female donors also funded fellowships to help younger women pursue careers in new fields—as juvenile court officers, visiting nurses, and social workers.[9] The Association of Collegiate Alumnae (ACA) supplies another example of women's creative philanthropy; it supported women scientists studying for their Ph.D.s in Germany at a time when no American graduate school would admit them.[10] A striking example of how women's philanthropy could serve as an "entering wedge" into higher education occurred in Baltimore. Here a group of wealthy women gave $119,000 toward a medical school where "women should be admitted upon the same terms which may be prescribed for men." Mary Elizabeth Garrett gave the Johns Hopkins Medical School an additional $306,977 in 1893.[11]

Olivia was aware of these attempts to use monetary donations to force universities to admit women. Her ally, physician Mary Putnam Jacobi, had recently tried unsuccessfully to leverage women's entry to Harvard Medical School.[12] And her friend Elizabeth Cady Stanton, better known as a strong advocate of coeducation, also urged women to financially support their own institutions. At the sixtieth anniversary of the Troy Female Seminary in 1892, Stanton appealed passionately for endowed college scholarships for girls. "This is the best work women of wealth can do," she declared, "and I hope in the future they will endow scholarships for their own sex instead of giving millions of dollars to institutions for boys."[13] At a parlor suffrage meeting in New York City, Stanton sounded the same theme. If there were any rich women present who were soon to make their wills, let them leave their money for the advancement of their own sex, she declared. Yale and Harvard "had received millions from women but very, very little had been done for the education of deserving girls."[14] When Stanton later learned that the president of Cornell was trying to interest Russell Sage in endowing a civil engineering chair, she urged him to "help the girls and not the boys."[15]

But Stanton would die in 1902 and Jacobi a few years later. Sage embarked on her educational philanthropy without the support of these feminist friends and with the influence of her patrician lawyer and advisor Robert de Forest (1848–1931) in the ascendant.[16] Just how ascendant is revealed in a memo from de Forest dated February 1907, in which he advises her how to proceed with her philanthropy to institutions. De Forest brushed aside the claims of most of the four thousand institutions that had already applied to her, confidently asserting that the institutions to which she would want to donate were those that had *not* applied.[17]

FIRST GIFTS

Within months of her husband's death, Olivia made her first, great donations to education. All of these were gifts that expressed sentiment, memorialized family ties, and rewarded long associations. Her initial large gift was for a teachers' college at Syracuse University; then, in December 1906, she gave one million dollars to the Emma Willard School (as the Troy Female Seminary was renamed), enabling it to build an entirely new campus.[18] Finally, in January 1907, she donated half a million to Troy Polytechnic (now Rensselaer Polytechnic Institute, or RPI) as a memorial to her husband, subsequently doubling the amount.[19]

NEW YORK UNIVERSITY

At the same time, Sage was planning to endow a coordinate college for women at New York University (NYU). Her interest in NYU had developed in partnership with Helen Gould (1870–1938), for whom she served as a kind of philanthropic mentor. Helen's donations to NYU expressed a passionately felt sense of stewardship, and they were unconditional.[20] In contrast, Olivia intended her donation to open the doors to women. New York University would provide a test case of coercive spending.

In New York University, Sage believed she had found a worthy recipient of her money: a progressive New York institution that was friendly to women. Henry MacCracken, NYU's chancellor since 1891, was an imaginative and ruthless fundraiser. Though he pursued a masculinist vision of undergraduate education, he was mindful of the need to cultivate the goodwill of wealthy men and women who were potential donors. In 1890 he admitted women as students to professional programs in law and pedagogy at the university's Washington Square campus.[21] A women's law class was started, and a group of wealthy women paid the salaries of instructors, notably Emily Kempin, a doctor of law from the University of Zurich. As one of the attendees explained, the class did not "aim to prepare students for the practice of law, but to give to women who are likely to have responsibility for the care of property or who . . . desire to have fuller knowledge of the laws . . . the opportunity to study the fundamental of Modern American law."[22]

MacCracken also appointed Olivia to a new Women's Advisory Committee, charged with preparing "plans and recommendations for the advancement of the University's work for women." (She served from 1896 to 1906.[23]) Coeducation was no part of MacCracken's plan for educational excellence, however. His new "up-town campus" at University Heights was for male undergraduates only.

"NO BETTER PLACE EXISTS IN THE WORLD FOR A NEW WOMAN'S COLLEGE"

MacCracken had been trying for a decade to interest Russell Sage in giving to NYU, but the Sages were not among fifty large donors who contributed to the purchase of the University Heights property for NYU between May 1891 and February 1898.[24] Meanwhile, in 1897 a bold proposal landed on the desks of the University Council. This was a petition from a Mrs. Vanderpoel "for leave to submit a plan for the formation of a Woman's College to be carried on at University Heights in connection with the university."[25] MacCracken saw the plan as worth pursuing, if only a donor could be found to underwrite the new college. He again turned to Russell Sage in December 1898. "I remind you of your general promise to me, since 1892 to do somewhat for New York University," he wrote, adding, "No better place exists in the world for a new woman's college than University Heights. If we use our plant and professors somewhat as Radcliffe College uses Harvard or Barnard College uses Columbia you could tell Mrs. Sage to organize here the best woman's college in the world."[26] For Olivia, the proposal was irresistible.

The chancellor continued to lay careful siege to Olivia. He agreed to include a bust of Emma Willard in NYU's grandiose new Hall of Fame, at her request. And in 1904, he persuaded the University Council to grant Olivia an honorary master of letters degree. Her letter of acceptance shows surprise and genuine delight. "With great diffidence I take my pen in hand to reply to your letter of April 30th. . . . But my loyalty to my own Alma Mater and to its Founder Mrs. Emma Hart Willard, induces me to write my acceptance and to thank the Corporation of New York University for the great honor they have done me."[27]

Just weeks after her husband's death, Olivia agreed to give NYU $294,250 on condition that "some part of the property at least will be used by New York University as a center for women's working and living, for a women's building, or for other University activities in connection with women."[28] But this poorly drafted clause was vague and unenforceable. The board of trustees insisted that the needs of the engineering school came first, and when MacCracken retired in 1910 the terms of Olivia's gift were still unfulfilled.[29] His successor, Elmer E. Brown, later admitted to Olivia's brother Joseph Jermain Slocum ("Jermain") that he had heard about "the unfortunate situation which had arisen, in which Mrs. Sage had expected a woman's college to be erected on the Schwab property and had been disappointed in this expectation." Although he had "the utmost sympathy with everything which has to do with the higher education of women"—indeed, he noted that the university had "not given up hope of having eventually a college for women on the magnificent property which Mrs. Sage has made available"—nevertheless, he informed Slocum, the university had decided to erect an engineering building on the land purchased with her gift.[30]

The donor is generally seen as powerful in the philanthropic relationship. Historian Kathryn Kish Sklar has written, "Women reformers of the Progressive era did indeed inhabit a separate political culture—one that gave generously of its own resources in the process of remaking the larger political society."[31] But the story of Olivia Sage's gift to NYU suggests it was not easy for women to retain control over their gifts. Olivia's gift to NYU was her most ambitious and its failure was the most disappointing.[32]

The shadow of the NYU fiasco hangs over the rest of Olivia Sage's philanthropy to education. Disappointed with the university's broken promises, Sage became suspicious of university fundraisers in general. Even at Syracuse University, her favorite institution, she now customarily inquired whether her conditions were being met—clearly a sign of her increasing unease. In September 1912, she wrote to Chancellor Day to inquire whether the scholarships she had endowed there five years earlier were still open to women as she had specified. The chancellor reassured her: "We intend to keep the doors open to both men and women and to give scholarship assistance to any woman who wishes to pursue agricultural instruction as they do at the State Universities like Wisconsin, Purdue, etc."[33]

SOMETHING FOR WOMEN'S WORK

Olivia Sage's philanthropy for women at Syracuse University, where she had already donated land and a building for a teachers' college in 1905, was more successful than her gifts to NYU.[34] In 1909, Henry de Forest, brother of and law partner to Robert de Forest, wrote informing Chancellor Day that Olivia wanted to give the university $50,000 on her birthday. He added, "Mrs. Sage's interest, as you know, particularly attaches to woman's work and she asks me to write you to inquire in connection with what special line of woman's work such gift would be the more acceptable."[35] Chancellor Day responded, inquiring whether Mrs. Sage would "be interested in a proposition of segregation here at the University." He suggested a women's coordinate college, "the College to be the Margaret Olivia Slocum College for Women or Woman's College." He offered her the opportunity to found a college that would be "more prominent and equally useful with Radcliffe, Barnard, Wellesley, and Vassar."[36]

The idea does not seem to have been taken up. Instead, President Day sent Olivia encouraging updates on the progress of the teachers' college, even as he continued to ask her for more funds. Another Syracuse official, writing in June 1912, informed her that "[t]here are over 400 students in the Teacher's College, nearly all of whom are women." Syracuse was training three times as many teachers for the public schools as any other institution in the state, he pointed out. Its Teacher's College "should be made one of the great factors in giving an opportunity to women, and training them for service as educators."[37]

"A FEW STRATEGIC EDUCATIONAL INSTITUTIONS OF NATIONAL SCOPE"

Gender was not the only factor motivating women donors. Helen Gould and fellow Emma Willard alumna Nettie McCormick, Olivia's closest friends, were both spectacular philanthropists. Gould gave generously to all kinds of civic, religious, educational, and benevolent institutions. McCormick was a leading benefactor of the Presbyterian Church and a major donor to dozens of colleges and universities, with gifts to educational and religious institutions estimated at $8 million. Neither of the women specified that their gifts should support women's causes or institutions.[38]

Philanthropists often prefer to give to the most prestigious, not the most needy, entities.[39] In the same year that Sage donated $150,000 to Syracuse University Teachers' College, she gave Yale over half a million. Why did she consistently give more to men's institutions than to women's?

Robert de Forest continued to play a vital role. He kept most petitioners away while nudging her philanthropy toward institutions that he favored. He suggested, reminded, cautioned, but never dictated: he was the soul of tact. Olivia respected his opinion, sometimes using it as an excuse for inaction. For example, in July 1910 her secretary answered an appeal from Cornell, "She will have to postpone the consideration of it . . . as Mr. de Forest is not here now, and she would like to talk with him about the matter."[40] Occasionally, de Forest suggested a dollar amount. In response to an appeal for a "Colored Chatauqua" near Nashville "where they are gathering the different ignorant negro clergymen from different parts of the South for some elementary and I imagine very useful instruction," he advised Olivia, "I would not give more than $5,000. I would not give less than $1,000. I think $2,500 would be deemed a very liberal contribution."[41]

De Forest's role in guiding Sage philanthropy is well illustrated in the maneuvering that produced the Sage donation to Yale. A Yale alumnus, de Forest was strategically placed to direct a large chunk of the Sage fortune toward his alma mater. The correspondence between de Forest and Yale president Anson Phelps Stokes, Jr., reveals how the latter played on Olivia's pride in her family's descent from Rev. Abraham Pierson, Yale's first rector. The elderly widow's vulnerability seems quite palpable as fundraisers conspired with her closest advisor.

Even before Russell Sage's estate was settled, Stokes was writing to Olivia about Yale's needs, enclosing a photograph of a statue of her eminent ancestor. Intrigued, she wrote back, requesting a sample signature of Reverend Pierson. De Forest confided to Stokes, "I think you have planted good seed, but . . . the harvest is not yet. She has been giving very liberally of late, . . . and I know she does not wish to give to Yale at the moment."[42] Stokes continued to correspond with Olivia. He wanted her to purchase the thirty-acre Hillhouse Estate for university expansion and to build new dormitories. In language that captured well the conflicting purposes of the American university in transition between older moral verities and the new social sciences, he wrote, "The great need of our country today is the strengthening of a few strategic educational institutions of national scope which stand for scholarship and high Christian ideals."[43] De Forest urged him on. "Why not write a line to the lady yourself at once, addressing her at Sag Harbor, where she is and where she will be likely to read any mail that comes to her?" he wrote. The timing was just right. In December 1909, Olivia Sage agreed to give the university the huge sum of $650,000, and the end of December found Stokes thanking her for the "wonderful offer" which had "put a new spirit in us all and a renewed determination to make the university stand truer than ever to its ideals of democracy, public service, and Christian faith."[44]

"START IN BY GIVING TO THOSE THAT ARE DISTINCTLY WOMEN'S COLLEGES"

By July 1910, the pressure on Olivia to start giving to women's colleges prompted Robert de Forest to remind her, "If you have in mind to do something for women's colleges, as you have several times suggested, I think in your place I would start in by giving to those that are distinctly women's colleges, such as Wellesley, for instance. . . . $100,000, $50,000, or even $25,000 apiece . . . would undoubtedly be a great boon." He named amounts significantly lower than she had been giving to men's colleges.[45]

Olivia made her first large donation to a women's college in 1911. (Her early donations to Vassar and Radcliffe had been modest and, in some cases, anonymous.) In this year, she gave $150,000 to Vassar for the Olivia Josselyn Hall—a dormitory named for her grandmother—adding another $50,000 the following year.[46] President James M. Taylor's letter of thanks was carefully crafted: "I have recently reviewed Emma Willard's 'Address,'" he confided, "and more than ever I am admiring her work, her ideals, and her progress beyond her age."[47]

"WELLESLEY IN TROUBLE IS LIKE A FRIEND IN DISTRESS"

Meanwhile, the administrators of the other women's colleges, like Wellesley, were on a roller-coaster of anticipation and disappointment. In February 1908, Wellesley president Caroline Hazard had optimistically hailed Mrs. Sage's new wealth. "By the providence of God you are placed in a position in which you can grant great things."[48] After Wellesley lost its main building in a disastrous fire in 1913 Sage received a request from the college for half a million dollars. She sent only $25,000, and college official Anna Palen chided her for sending so little, calling Wellesley "a friend in distress."[49] De Forest gently reminded her again in 1914, "Has it possibly occurred to you to anticipate your future intentions toward Wellesley by giving them something now when their main building has burned down?"[50] She was even receiving letters of complaint about the situation at Wellesley, some of which have survived. "Shall we have our girl students unhoused, scattered, and with imperfect supervision, or shall we be able to place them in such a Hall as now rejoices the boys of Harvard?" asked William Lawrence, bishop of Massachusetts, an officer of Harvard as well as a trustee of Wellesley. Referring to Standish Hall, the dormitory recently completed with Sage money at Harvard, he asked for "a girls' Standish from you." Wellesley mathematics instructor Euphemia Worthington declared, "Now [after the fire] there is an opportunity for someone to give where there is really urgent need, in fact almost to refound the college." Finally, in 1914, Olivia gave Wellesley $250,000.[51]

Why was Sage so slow to help Wellesley? Probably she was uneasy about the direction the women's colleges were taking. Wellesley abandoned compulsory chapel attendance in 1900 and by 1914 had become a "secular liberal-arts college for women," in the words of one scholar.[52] A letter from Helen Gould to Mary Wooley of Mount Holyoke in 1903 expressed displeasure that an instructor in the Chair of Biblical Study—which she, Gould, had endowed—was using critical analysis, "being destructive in her criticism and sweeping away faith without putting anything in its place."[53] Vassar, too, was changing. Helen Gould was so dissatisfied that the college had become "too liberal" that Vassar returned the money she had donated for four scholarships. A $40,000 endowed chair at Mount Holyoke (set up in 1902) was later transferred to the ˙Department of Romance Languages, and a $50,000 endowment of the Wellesley Biblical Department was withdrawn and reassigned to the Department of Mathematics![54] Ten years before, Sage had seen Vassar, as a women's college in New York State, as her dreamed-of "Willard University," upholding Christian ideals as it prepared women to become teachers. Now she wasn't so sure.

An additional explanation comes to light in a February 1914 letter from Olivia's secretary, E. Lilian Todd, to Barnard College president Virginia Gildersleeve. In informing Barnard's president why Mrs. Sage refused to consider a gift to the college, Todd explained, "She feels that her gift to the Emma Willard School is her contribution to women's education, and the few buildings given elsewhere were merely special cases."[55]

SCHOLARSHIPS FOR WOMEN

Disappointed by the NYU debacle and distracted by numerous appeals, Olivia nevertheless continued to fund scholarships and fellowships for girls. Her years as a struggling teacher and governess before her marriage had convinced her that the best education for a young woman was a practical course of training that led to paid work. Dozens of examples of such donations are scattered throughout her correspondence, from a gift in November 1909 of $10,000 to the New York State Federation of Women's Clubs girls' college scholarship fund, to a $125,000 donation to the New York School of Applied Design for Women in 1916.[56] In acknowledging a $2,500 donation to the Pennsylvania School of Horticulture for Women, its director assured Sage, "Your name is so connected throughout the country with projects for helping women to help themselves."[57] Sage also gave to industrial high schools. She endowed the Margaret Sage Industrial School at Lawrence, Long Island, with $150,000 in August 1907. The Idaho Industrial School, a self-described "absolutely non-sectarian but thoroughly Christian" school, received massive support after its principal, E. A. Paddock, wore Sage down with solicitations and personal visits over a period of several years. His school received $25,000 in 1910, $20,000 in 1916, and $200,000 in 1918.[58]

A lifelong interest in Protestant missions and admiration for evangelist Dwight L. Moody prompted Olivia's donations to Northfield Training School. This Presbyterian missionary training center received one of her first major gifts ($150,000) in 1907. She subsequently endowed five scholarships for women at Northfield in 1912 at a cost of $25,000.[59]

TUSKEGEE AND HAMPTON

When it came to donating to educational institutions for African Americans, Sage selected Hampton and Tuskegee, both of which represented themselves as institutions for industrial education. Personal connections came into play here also. A well-placed word from her friend Andrew Dickson White served to bring Booker T. Washington's Tuskegee Institute to Sage's attention, another word brought Washington to a conference with Robert de Forest in New York City, and Tuskegee received its first gift from Sage in May 1908. On her death it received $800,000 more.[60] Another friend, Robert Ogden, managed to interest Sage in the cause of Hampton Institute. Ogden, a nationally known spokesman for southern educational reform and one of the original trustees of the Russell Sage Foundation, strongly promoted the requests of President H. B. Frissell in his correspondence with Sage, and she responded, giving $25,000 in February 1908.[61] After Ogden's death, Olivia's secretary refused to send Frissell's letters on to Sage, even though his proposal for a training school for nurses at Hampton would probably have appealed to her. "Mr. Carnegie has promised $300,000," Frissell wrote, but his blunt appeals went nowhere. "*I'm* not going to give this to Mrs. Sage," Lilian wrote to Jermain. Fortunately for Hampton, the school already stood to benefit from a change in her will. The new codicil of February 1908 assigned the college one part of her legacy, or approximately $800,000.[62]

Another friend who influenced Sage's philanthropy was Nettie McCormick. In 1908, McCormick urged Olivia to join with McCormick and three other friends in a donation to Wooster University. Make some inquiries about the institution first, "and if the investigation is satisfactory, . . . take an interest with us in this cause," she wrote.[63] The women's friendship continued into old age, sustained by visits, letters, and gifts. Philanthropy and affectionate tokens were intertwined. In 1913, Lilian wrote to McCormick on Olivia's behalf, sending thanks for "two beautiful shawls, and the slippers," and conveying a promise from Olivia to send "the check for the fifteen hundred dollars additional that is required for the scholarship [at Fowler Theological Seminary] over the one thousand she gave you a few days ago."[64]

"EXERCISING A DIRECT AND MOST HAPPY INFLUENCE UPON THEM"

The theme of many carefully crafted appeals was the need to protect the morals and improve the living standards of undergraduates in these days of dancing, smoking, and other "new-woman" behaviors. Colleges that invested in new dormitories, dining halls, and chapels supported a paternalistic vision of supervising student morals as well as improving their living conditions. For example, in appealing to Sage for funds to build a dormitory at Cornell for female students, Andrew Dickson White argued that the dormitory would allow them to benefit from the care of "an excellent and accomplished Lady Dean exercising a direct and most happy influence upon them." White also successfully invoked Emma Willard's vision of civic womanhood. Writing to Olivia in January 1911, he described Cornell as "a great educational center, . . . sending out through the whole country young women unaccustomed to luxury, but brought up in respectable families, under good influences, instructed here under the advantages of a thoroughly equipped University."[65] Two weeks after receiving this letter Olivia gave Cornell the enormous sum of $300,000 for a women's residence hall.[66]

At a time when a backlash at Chicago and other universities threatened to remove female students from the classroom, White was defending the integrated classroom on the grounds that the presence of women students was good for male undergraduates. Female students helped to civilize their male counterparts; thus the admission of women to Cornell had been "good—good for them, good for the young men, good for the community at large," he informed Olivia. "[The] lecture rooms, laboratories, libraries, and public rooms of every sort, are far more quiet and orderly and civilized than they would be if only men were admitted." She was pleased that the civilizing presence of women was at work, she replied, adding that their influence would be even more effective once they had the vote.[67]

FRIENDS AND FAMILY: CORNELL AND AFTER

Olivia's interest in Cornell points to the fact that her philanthropy continued to be highly personal and idiosyncratic. Cornell president Andrew Dickson White was, like her, a native of Syracuse and their families had been close. White, who at seventy-seven was younger than Olivia, appealed to her pointedly: "I can think of nothing which would be a greater satisfaction to me on leaving all earthly scenes than the knowledge that these young women and those succeeding for hundreds of years are to be suitably housed." Naming decisions were difficult for Olivia; for us they are revealing. She named Cornell's new dormitory Prudence Risley Hall for her late husband's mother, commemorating the women of her husband's family as she had commemorated those of her own at Vassar. At Syracuse she chose the name Caroline Longstreet College for Women Teachers over the objection of Dean Jacob Street, who asked her to remove the word "women" since 25 percent of the students training there were men![68]

Other donations attempted to salvage her late husband's reputation. What better way to rescue the name Russell Sage from public opprobrium than to link it with some prestigious college or university? And if her husband's millions had been amassed by dubious means, if he had been born in obscurity and received only a meager schooling, at least his name would be linked after death with the nation's finest universities.

"MY ANCESTORS COULD WELL HOLD UP THEIR HEADS"

Other gifts confirm that Olivia wished to draw attention to her descent from Mayflower ancestors. For example, in donating to Vassar and naming the building she funded "Olivia Josselyn Hall," she advertised her descent on her mother's side through Josselyn from her colonial ancestor Miles Standish.[69] Correspondence in the papers of Harvard president A. Lawrence Lowell reveals how fundraisers persuaded Sage to donate to prestigious universities, all of which excluded women. Princeton fundraiser John Cadwalader went to Sage "not knowing her, and asked her if she would put up a building for the students of Princeton."[70] To his surprise, she agreed to donate $250,000 for a building that was then (after additional gifts totaling over $165,000) named Holder Hall after Christopher Holder, a seventeenth-century ancestor.[71] Securing an additional amount was remarkably easy, Cadwalader boasted to a friend. He "returned to her and showed her what part of the building she had built, being one side of a quadrangle. She asked: 'Why not the whole?', and he said, 'Because the whole cost more money than you furnished,' whereupon, after consideration, she gave the rest." She had no prior connection to Princeton.[72]

"MY FEMININE NAME DID NOT SEEM SUITABLE"

President Lowell of Harvard commented, "It is encouraging to hear that Mrs. Sage has given money to a dormitory at Princeton, for she may be willing to do the same for us." He secured an interview with Sage in March 1911.[73] Then, in July, Henry de Forest informed him that Mrs. Sage was "inclined, . . . if you so desire, to make donation of *say $225,000*," or half the cost of a dormitory.[74] To J. P. Morgan, Jr., a trustee and go-between, the Harvard president wrote, "I suppose there is no use in trying to persuade Mrs. Sage further, and *as we have no claim upon her*, I feel that her giving this amount is very generous, and I am exceedingly grateful for it."[75]

A year later, Henry de Forest informed Lowell that she had agreed to give a further $125,000. He went on, "She suggests that it be called the 'Russell Dormitory,' that being the first name of her late husband and the middle name of Mr. James Russell Lowell." The question of the name gave Lowell an excuse to correspond with Olivia. Lonely and isolated, the elderly philanthropist encouraged his visit: "My Secretary is off on her vacation," she wrote to the Harvard president. "Mr. de Forest, too, is on vacation trip and in the south of France."[76] The subsequent correspondence allows us to follow a curious discussion of a name for the new building. Since Harvard already had a "Russell Hall," she should name the new building after herself, he suggested.[77] Olivia recorded what came next. "I then told Mr. de Forest I would give the new dormitory the name of 'Standish Hall' if there was no other building with that name, for my feminine name did not seem suitable for a boys' building, the boys might resent being 'womanized' to coin a word in these 'new woman' days." In choosing the alternative "Standish," she was naming the building "for my great Grandmother 'Olivia Standish.' "[78] This revealing letter shows Sage confused over purpose and identity. Giving to a university that excluded women, she refused even a female name for the building, while substituting another name that appeared unmarked, but in fact commemorated a female ancestor!

Standish Hall gave Olivia much satisfaction. She wrote to the Harvard president, "I am sure Captain Myles would say 'Well done.' Ancestral names attract me, and with 'Standish Hall' in Cambridge, and Holder Hall at Princeton, my ancestors could well hold up their heads and be proud as I am of their works." She signed the letter, "Margaret (Olivia Standish) Sage."[79]

Other donations carried multiple meanings as this one did. Sage's gifts to RPI helped establish schools of electrical and mechanical engineering, with postgraduate programs that were among the earliest in the nation. Some of the monies were designated for a Russell Sage Laboratory commemorating Russell Sage's nephew and adopted heir, Russell Sage, Jr., who had studied at the Institute from 1856 to 1859 and had died in 1892. A further donation to RPI of $100,000 for a dining hall in 1915 was also a memorial to this nephew, as were two fellowships at $15,000 each.[80]

Affection for the memory of her father Joseph Slocum (1800–1863) prompted many gifts to Syracuse. Olivia donated over $250,000 for the Joseph Slocum College of Agriculture, commemorating the clever inventor and promoter of agricultural improvement whose business failures had made her childhood so uncertain.[81] And each year she gave another $25,000 or $50,000 to Syracuse University on her birthday. In September 1912, she gave $83,000, to correspond to her age, leaving its spending to the discretion of the university.[82]

Wealthy women clearly gave to educational institutions in order to remake the culture, but they also did so for many other reasons. The theme of "women's work" is woven through all of Olivia's correspondence, but her other concerns sometimes took priority. Her will, drawn up in October 1906, rewarded twenty-two schools, colleges, and universities with legacies amounting to $13 million. The list comprised coeducational Syracuse and Cornell, women's colleges (Vassar, Wellesley, Bryn Mawr, Barnard, Smith), and also male-only research universities and colleges.

These women's gifts were not able, however, to remake the culture. It was certainly ironic that at the very moment when Sage and women like her were poised to spend the fortunes reaped by their husbands and fathers in the great free-for-all of late-nineteenth-century capitalism, the universities were being redesigned to keep women out or to relegate them to special programs or units. University administrators, even at Chicago, where there was an initial commitment to coeducation, were beginning to draw back and to talk about professionalism in ways that conflated rising academic standards with male-only student bodies, constructing as "scientific" those disciplinary discourses from which women's voices were absent.[83]

The new colleges of engineering were the most obvious sign of this transformation. University presidents like RPI's Palmer Ricketts measured progress by the distance their universities put between themselves and the classically oriented universities of the nineteenth century. By giving to RPI and to NYU, Sage was in effect sustaining institutions that would exclude her sex until the mid-twentieth century or even later.[84]

RUTGERS: "NOTHING MORE FOR MEN'S COLLEGES"

By 1912, Olivia was funding scholarships for girls while refusing those for boys. When the principal of Pierson High School in Sag Harbor, Long Island, wrote to inquire about scholarships, Jermain Slocum responded, "Mrs. Sage directs me to say that *boys* have no scholarship in the 'Pierson High School."[85] And when a fundraiser from Rutgers (a male-only college connected with her own beloved Reformed denomination) approached her in 1916, he was told by her physician, "I am sorry not to help you, but Mrs. Sage takes very little interest now in helping the education of men, and has told me repeatedly that she was going to do nothing more for men's colleges."[86]

In the same year that she refused funds to Rutgers, Olivia founded the Russell Sage College of Practical Arts, a women's vocational college in Troy, New York. I have described elsewhere how the new college came into existence through the concerted lobbying of two extraordinary women, Eliza Kellas, principal of the Emma Willard School, and E. Lilian Todd, a remarkable engineer and inventor, who by 1911 had become Sage's private secretary. In 1916, Sage gave $250,000 to start the college, subsequently increasing her gift to $500,000, and the combined institution became the "Emma Willard School and Russell Sage College."[87] Olivia Sage was now nearing ninety. Founding a brand-new women's college in Troy was a belated affirmation of her belief in women's advancement.

Educational philanthropy can shore up elite institutions or fund alternatives. It can effect transformations of curriculum, engineer a more diverse faculty body, or support more varied student populations.[88] Olivia Sage remained a believer in women's advancement, but she pursued this goal inconsistently. She found it hard to resist appeals from colleges and universities when the connection seemed to flatter her own family or offer national recognition, and many of these institutions were for men only. Her educational philanthropy has an air of improvisation. In the end it was a scattershot affair that divided her splendid inheritance into many small donations. It reflected not so much any one philanthropic vision as it did the competing pressures of a number of determined fundraisers on an elderly donor made vulnerable by age and isolation.

APPENDIX: UNIVERSITIES, COLLEGES, AND SCHOOLS NAMED IN MARGARET OLIVIA SAGE'S WILL,
25 OCTOBER 1906[89]

Each of the following was to receive one share, or approximately $800,000, unless noted:

Schools: The Emma Willard School; Idaho Industrial Institute; the Northfield Schools.

Colleges and universities: The Troy Polytechnic Institute (now RPI); Union College, Schenectady, New York; Syracuse University; Hamilton College, New York; New York University; Yale University; Amherst College; Williams College; Dartmouth College; Middlebury College; Princeton University; Rutgers College; Bates College; Barnard College; Bryn Mawr College; Vassar College; Smith College; Wellesley College; Tuskegee Normal and Industrial Institute.

An unusual clause in the will caused dismay among legatees when it was known. It directed that payments made during her lifetime were to be considered advances, and that the legacies would be adjusted accordingly.

First Codicil, 17 February 1908. Revoked legacies to Middlebury College, Bates College, Rutgers College, and the Northfield Schools and gave one additional share ($800,000) to Syracuse University, as well as one to Hampton Institute.

Second Codicil, 19 July 1911. Added $5 million for Sage's brother, Joseph Jermain Slocum.

NOTES

This essay is adapted from my full-length work *Mrs. Russell Sage: A Life,* forthcoming from Indiana University Press. I would like to thank the other participants at the "Women, Philanthropy, and Education" workshop at the School of Education, Indiana University, Bloomington, Ind., 7 December 2001, and especially editor Andrea Walton and fellow participant Linda Eisenmann for suggestions and encouragement.

1. Theodore C. Janeway, M.D., to Rev. William H. S. Demarest, president, Rutgers College, 8 March 1916, Rutgers University Archives, New Brunswick, N.J.

2. Irvin Wyllie, "Sage, Margaret Olivia Slocum," in *Notable American Women, 1607–1950,* vol. 3, ed. Edward T. James, Janet Wilson James, and Paul S. Boyer (Cambridge, Mass.: Belknap Press of Harvard University Press, 1971), 222–23; Ruth Crocker, "From Widow's Mite to Widow's Might: The Philanthropy of Margaret Olivia Sage," *Journal of Presbyterian History* 74 (winter 1996): 253–64; idem, " 'I Only Ask You Kindly to Divide Some of Your Fortune with Me': Begging Letters and the Transformation of Charity in Late Nineteenth-Century America," *Social Politics* 6 (summer 1999): 131–60; idem, "Margaret Olivia Slocum, 'Mrs. Russell Sage': Private

Griefs and Public Duties," in *Ordinary Women, Extraordinary Lives: Women in American History,* ed. Kriste Lindenmeyer (Wilmington, Del.: Scholarly Resources, 2000), 147–59; and idem, "The History of Philanthropy as Life-History: A Biographer's View of Mrs. Russell Sage," in *Philanthropic Foundations: New Scholarship, New Possibilities,* ed. Ellen Condliffe Lagemann (Bloomington: Indiana University Press, 1999), 318–28.

3. Russell Sage left a fortune of over $75 million. For conversion of early-twentieth-century currency, see John J. McCusker, *How Much Is That in Real Money? A Historical Commodity Price Index for Use as a Deflator of Money Values in the Economy of the United States,* 2nd ed. (Worcester, Mass.: American Antiquarian Society, 2001).

4. On Russell Sage's stinginess, see "Mrs. Russell Sage on Marriage," *Syracuse Sunday Herald,* 21 June 1903, 29; "Russell Sage—A Man of Dollars: The Story of a Life Devoted Solely to the Chill Satisfaction of Making Money for Its Own Sake," *World's Work* 10 (May–October 1905), 6299; and "A Bashful Millionaire," *Brooklyn Eagle,* 17 January 1897, 6.

5. Arthur Huntington Gleason, "Mrs. Russell Sage and Her Interests," *World's Work* 13 (November 1906), 8183.

6. James D. Phelps to Chancellor James Day, 11 May 1906, box 2, Day Correspondence, Syracuse University Archives, Syracuse, N.Y. (hereafter cited as SUA); Thomas Woody, *A History of Women's Education in the United States,* 2 vols. (New York: Science, 1929); Barbara Miller Solomon, *In the Company of Educated Women: A History of Women and Higher Education in America* (New Haven, Conn.: Yale University Press, 1985); and Lynn D. Gordon, *Gender and Higher Education in the Progressive Era* (New Haven, Conn.: Yale University Press, 1990).

7. Margaret W. Rossiter, *Women Scientists in America: Struggles and Strategies to 1940* (Baltimore, Md.: Johns Hopkins University Press, 1982), 46–47.

8. Kathryn Kish Sklar, "Who Funded Hull House?" in *Lady Bountiful Revisited: Women, Philanthropy, and Power,* ed. Kathleen D. McCarthy (New Brunswick, N.J.: Rutgers University Press, 1990), 94–115. See also "Bowen, Louise de Koven (1859–1953)," in *Notable American Women: The Modern Period,* ed. Barbara Sicherman and Carol Hurd Green with Ilene Kantrov and Harriette Walker (Cambridge, Mass.: Belknap Press of Harvard University Press, 1980), 99–101. In addition, a "fellowship system" linked wealthy friends to the settlement house through regular monthly donations.

9. Robyn Muncy, *Creating a Female Dominion in American Reform, 1890–1935* (New York: Oxford University Press, 1991), 17–18; Ellen Fitzpatrick, *Endless Crusade: Women Social Scientists and Progressive Reform* (New York: Oxford University Press, 1990); Regina G. Kunzel, *Fallen Women, Problem Girls: Unmarried Mothers and the Professionalization of Social Work, 1890–1945* (New Haven, Conn.: Yale University Press, 1993); and Penina Migdal Glazer and Miriam Slater, *Unequal Colleagues: The Entrance of Women into the Professions, 1890–1940* (New Brunswick, N.J.: Rutgers University Press, 1987).

10. Rossiter, *Women Scientists in America: Struggles and Strategies,* 42; and John D. Rousmaniere, "Cultural Hybrid in the Slums: The College Woman and the Settlement House, 1889–1894," *American Quarterly* 22 (spring 1970), 45–66. The ACA was the precursor to the American Association of University Women.

11. Sarah Knowles Bolton, *Famous Givers and Their Gifts* (New York: Thomas Y. Crowell, 1896), 326–27; and Paul S. Boyer, "Garrett, Mary Elizabeth (1854–1915)," *Notable American Women*, ed. James, James, and Boyer, vol. 2, 21–22.

12. Mary Roth Walsh, *"Doctors Wanted, No Women Need Apply": Sexual Barriers in the Medical Profession, 1835–1975* (New Haven, Conn.: Yale University Press, 1977), 173–77.

13. Theodore Stanton and Harriot Stanton Blatch, eds., *Elizabeth Cady Stanton As Revealed in Her Letters, Diary, and Reminiscences*, vol. 1 (New York: Harper, 1922), 340–45. Stanton, like Sage, was a Troy alumna.

14. "Woman's Debt to Woman," *New York World*, 29 April 1894, in *The Papers of Elizabeth Cady Stanton and Susan B. Anthony*, ed. Patricia G. Holland and Ann D. Gordon (Wilmington, Del.: Scholarly Resources, 1991), microfilm, 700–701, reel 32, CMS 8: 137.

15. Stanton and Blatch, eds., *Elizabeth Cady Stanton*, vol. 2, 295 n. 1.

16. "Feminist" is my term; the label was not coined until the early twentieth century. See Nancy Cott, *The Grounding of Modern Feminism* (New Haven, Conn.: Yale University Press, 1987). For Robert Weeks de Forest, see James A. Hijiya, "Four Ways of Looking at a Philanthropist: A Study of Robert Weeks de Forest," *Proceedings of the American Philosophical Society* 124 (December 1980), 404–18.

17. Robert W. de Forest (RW de F) to Margaret Olivia Sage (MOS), 7 February 1907; Gertrude Rice to RW de F, 27 April 1907; both in folder 11, box 2, Russell Sage Foundation Papers, Rockefeller Archive Center, Sleepy Hollow, N.Y. (hereafter cited as RSFP). For the begging letters from individuals, see Crocker, "I Only Ask You."

18. [William Gurley], press release, January 1907, 3; Robert W. de Forest, "Estimate of Cost—Emma Willard School, Troy, New York," 18 December 1906; William Gurley to RW de F, 10 December 1906; RW de F to Gurley, 3 January 1907; all four in Gurley Papers, Archives of the Emma Willard School, Troy, N.Y. (hereafter cited as Gurley Papers).

19. Palmer Ricketts to MOS, 1 January 1907, 5 March 1908, 15 February 1909, and 19 June 1909, all four in folder 896, box 92, RSFP. See also Paul Sarnoff, *Russell Sage, the Money King* (New York: Ivan Obolensky, 1965), 279–80.

20. Theodore Francis Jones, *New York University, 1832–1932* (New York: New York University Press, 1933), 169–70, 323. Helen lost both her parents in the 1890s, and Olivia fancied herself "like a mother" to the younger woman.

21. Phyllis Eckhaus, "Restless Women: The Pioneering Alumnae of New York University," *New York University Law Review* 66 (December 1991), 1996–2013; and Elizabeth Cady Stanton, Susan B. Anthony, and Matilda Joslyn Gage, eds., *History of Woman Suffrage*, vol. 4 (1881; reprint, New York: Arno, 1969), 871.

22. Martha Buell Plum (Mrs. John P.) Munn, "The Law and Liberal Culture," speech to Woman's Law Class, New York University, n.d., Munn Papers, folder 7, box 1, series 1/C, New York University Archives, New York, N.Y. (hereafter cited as NYUA); and "Records of the Women's Law Class and Women's Legal Education Society of New York University," 1983, record group 22.1, NYUA. *New York University, Law Lectures to Women* (1 May 1897) lists the curriculum of four courses on law, describes the Woman's Legal Education Society and the Alumnae Association, and lists the graduates of the 1897 class (folder 5, series 1/C, MC2, Munn Papers,

NYUA). See also Virginia Drachman, *Sisters in Law: Women Lawyers in Modern American History* (Cambridge, Mass.: Harvard University Press, 1998).

23. "Records of the Woman's Law Class and Woman's Legal Education Society," *Finding Aid,* record group 22.1, NYUA; Henry M. MacCracken to MOS, n.d., folder 851, box 88, RSFP; and Henry M. MacCracken, "University Heights South," 31 October 1907, marked "Private and Confidential," 1, folder 4, box 18, series III, record group 3.0.3, Administrative Papers of Henry Mitchell MacCracken, University Heights South, NYUA.

24. MacCracken to Russell Sage, 3 March 1893, folder 850, box 88, RSFP.

25. Minutes of the executive committee of the Council of New York University, 25 November 1895, quoted in Teresa R. Taylor, "No Extra Expense: The Education of Women from New York University, 1870–1918," NYU graduate seminar paper, January 1988, 12–13.

26. MacCracken to Russell Sage, 19 December 1898, NYUA.

27. "Pick First Women for Fame's Hall," unidentified newspaper clipping, folder 850, box 88, RSFP; and MOS to MacCracken, 31 May 1904, Honorary Degrees file, NYUA.

28. MacCracken, "University Heights South," 1–3; RW de F to MacCracken, 15 October 1906; both in folder 850, box 88, RSFP.

29. MacCracken, "University Heights South," 4; and Nancy M. Cricco, NYU archivist, to the author, 12 December 1994.

30. Dr. Elmer E. Brown to J. J. Slocum, 20 November 1917, box 62, folder 1, Dr. Elmer E. Brown Papers, NYUA.

31. Sklar, "Who Funded Hull House?" 111; and Susan A. Ostrander and Paul G. Schervish, "Giving and Getting: Philanthropy as a Social Relation," in John Van Til et al., *Critical Issues in American Philanthropy: Strengthening Theory and Practice* (San Francisco: Jossey-Bass, 1990), 67–98.

32. Margaret Rossiter lists other failed attempts. The University of Michigan accepted Dr. Elizabeth Bates's large gift, but never carried out the terms of the gift. And Joseph Bennett's gift of $400,000 for an undergraduate College for Women at the University of Pennsylvania met a similar fate. See Rossiter, *Women Scientists in America: Struggles and Strategies,* 47, 88.

33. Day to Slocum, 18 September 1912, folder 940, box 94, RSFP. But the college yearbooks show that at Syracuse, as elsewhere, female students were moving into departments of home economics, leaving agriculture and most of the sciences to their male peers.

34. Phelps to MOS, 29 July 1907, acknowledging "your great gift to Syracuse University"; Dean Jacob Street to Slocum, 22 September 1908; both in folder 939, box 94, RSFP.

35. Henry de Forest to Day, 3 September 1909, box 3, Day Correspondence, SUA.

36. Day to Henry de Forest, 4 December 1909; Street to Slocum, 22 September 1908; RW de F to Day, 5 February 1910; all three in box 3, Day Correspondence, SUA; Street to MOS, 10 October 1909, thanking Olivia for permission to use her name, folder 939, box 96, RSFP.

37. Unsigned letter to MOS, 14 June 1912, box 4, Day Correspondence, SUA. In *The Goose-Step: A Study of American Education,* Upton Sinclair viciously spoofs Day's

narrow-minded evangelicalism, calling Syracuse "The University of Heaven" (Pasadena, Calif.: published by the author, 1922), 277–81.

38. "Nettie Fowler McCormick," in *Emma Willard and Her Pupils, Or Fifty Years of Troy Female Seminary, 1822–1872,* comp. Mrs. A. W. Fairbanks (New York: published by Mrs. Russell Sage, 1898), 814; and Charles O. Burgess, "McCormick, Nettie Fowler (1835–1923)," *Notable American Women,* ed. James, James, and Boyer, vol. 2, 454–55.

39. On motivations for giving, see Paul G. Schervish, Platon E. Coutsoukis, and Ethan Lewis, *Gospels of Wealth: How the Rich Portray Their Lives* (Westport, Conn.: Praeger, 1994).

40. Catharine Hunter, secretary, to Hon. Andrew D. White, 14 July 1910, Cornell University Archives, Cornell University, Ithaca, N.Y. (hereafter cited as CUA).

41. RW de F to MOS, 1 February 1911, folder 894, box 92, RSFP.

42. RW de F to Anson Phelps Stokes, Jr., 4 May 1907, Robert de Forest file, office of the secretary, YRG 4-A, series 11, Yale University Archives, Sterling Memorial Library, New Haven, Conn. (hereafter cited as YUA). The letter was marked "Personal." See also Stokes to RW de F, 13 June 1907; RW de F to Stokes, 14 June 1907; Stokes to RW de F, 19 December 1907; all three in Robert de Forest file, YUA. The request for the Pierson signature is MOS to Stokes, 30 July 1907, folder 1001, box 98, RSFP.

43. Stokes to MOS, 7 April 1908, folder 1001, box 99, RSFP. See also David A. Hollinger, "Inquiry and Uplift: Late Nineteenth-Century American Academics and the Moral Efficacy of Scientific Practice," in *The Authority of Experts: Studies in History and Theory,* ed. Thomas L. Haskell (Bloomington: Indiana University Press, 1984), 142–56; George M. Marsden, "The Soul of the American University: An Historical Overview," in *The Secularization of the Academy,* ed. George M. Marsden and Bradley J. Longfield (New York: Oxford University Press, 1992), 9–45; and Edwin E. Slosson, *Great American Universities* (1910; reprint, New York: Arno, 1977).

44. RW de F to Stokes, 20 November 1909, YUA; Stokes to MOS, 31 December 1909, folder 1001, box 99, RSFP; and *Yale Alumni Weekly,* 7 January 1910.

45. RW de F to MOS, 18 July 1910, folder 690, box 75, RSFP.

46. Mrs. A. L. Hadley to MOS, 30 April 1904; President James M. Taylor to MOS, 20 June 1904; Helen Hadley to MOS, 30 April 1910; Taylor to MOS, October 1910, 31 July 1911, and 24 August 1911; all six in folder 965, box 96, RSFP. See also Henry Whittemore, *History of the Sage and Slocum Families of England and America* (New York, 1908); and Gordon, *Gender and Higher Education,* 121–64.

47. Taylor to MOS, 24 August 1911, folder 965, box 96, RSFP.

48. President Caroline Hazard to MOS, 24 February 1908, folder 970, box 96, RSFP.

49. Anna Palen to MOS, 3 April 1914, folder 970, box 96, RSFP.

50. RW de F to MOS, 5 April 1911, folder 738, box 79, RSFP. In RW de F to MOS, 25 March 1914, folder 970, box 96, RSFP, de Forest advised Mrs. Sage to consider "balancing Harvard's needs and resources as against the needs and resources of other universities, notably women's colleges, gifts to which you have been considering in the past."

51. The decision is noted in her hand on the back of an envelope dated 10 April 1914, in folder 970, box 96, RSFP.

52. Helen Lefkowitz Horowitz, *Alma Mater: Design and Experience in the Women's Colleges from Their Nineteenth-Century Beginnings to the 1930s* (New York: Knopf, 1984), 205, 213–14; and Patricia Ann Palmieri, *In Adamless Eden: The Community of Women Faculty at Wellesley* (New Haven, Conn.: Yale University Press, 1995), 53–54, 74–76.

53. Helen Miller Gould to Mary Wooley, 16 May 1903, quoted in Glazer and Slater, *Unequal Colleagues*, 39, 255 n. 21.

54. Hunter, secretary, to White, 14 July 1910, CUA; and Alice Northrop Snow with Henry Nicholas Snow, *The Story of Helen Gould, Daughter of Jay Gould, Great American* (New York: Fleming H. Revell, 1943), 279–80.

55. E. Lilian Todd to G. A. Plimpton, 25 February 1914. I am grateful to Dr. Nancy Slack, Russell Sage College, for this reference.

56. Memorandum, "Margaret Olivia Sage: Trustee 1907 to November 1918," typescript, folder 1, box 1, RSFP; and Frances Hamilton to MOS, 6 December 1915; Daisy Allen Story, New York Federation of Women's Clubs, to MOS, 8 November 1909; both in folder 3, box 1, RSFP.

57. Mary Rutherford Joy to MOS, 14 January 1914; Gertrude Ely, secretary, Pennsylvania School of Horticulture for Women, to MOS, 15 February 1916; both in folder 869, box 90, RSFP.

58. Five Towns Community House Collection, folder 1; Margaret Olivia Sage, "To the Trustees of the Margaret Sage Industrial School, Lawrence, Long Island," 16 June 1910, Social Welfare History Archives, University of Minnesota; and E. A. Paddock, president, Idaho Industrial Institute, to Hunter, 5 March 1908; Paddock to MOS, 5 May 1910; Mrs. S. B. Dudley to MOS, 30 March 1916; all three in folder 755, box 80, RSFP.

59. MOS to W. R. Moody, March 1907, folder 857, box 89, RSFP. See also Patricia R. Hill, *The World Their Household: The American Woman's Foreign Mission Movement and Cultural Transformation, 1870–1920* (Ann Arbor: University of Michigan Press, 1985), 127, 146–47; and James F. Findlay, *Dwight L. Moody, American Evangelist, 1837–1899* (Chicago: University of Chicago Press, 1969). Northfield Training School consisted of the Mount Hebron School for Boys and the Northfield School for Girls.

60. Andrew Dickson White to unspecified recipient [letter of introduction for Booker T. Washington], 13 November 1906; Booker T. Washington to MOS, 2 May 1908, acknowledging a donation of $20,000 for Tuskegee Institute; both in folder 952, box 95, RSFP.

61. Eric Anderson and Alfred A. Moss, Jr., argue that scholars have been too harsh on "Ogdenism," which they characterize as an amalgam of belief in "the Baptist faith, white supremacy, and industrial training for Negroes" (*Dangerous Donations: Northern Philanthropy and Southern Black Education, 1902–1930* [Columbia: University of Missouri Press, 1999], 57). See also Ralph E. Luker, *The Social Gospel in Black and White: American Racial Reform, 1885–1912* (Chapel Hill: University of North Carolina Press, 1991); and James D. Anderson, *The Education of Blacks in the South, 1860–1935* (Chapel Hill: University of North Carolina Press, 1988).

62. H. B. Frissell to MOS, 1 May 1913; Frissell to MOS, 5 March 1914, with attached response from Lilian Todd and J. J. Slocum; both in folder 737, box 79, RSFP.

63. Nettie McCormick to MOS, 7 February 1908, January–March 1908 file, box 12, McC MSS 1B, Papers of Nettie Fowler McCormick (Mrs. Cyrus McCormick, Sr.), State Historical Society of Wisconsin (hereafter cited as McCormick MSS.)

64. Todd to McCormick, [1913], "Todd, E. Lilian" file, box 133, McC MSS 2B, McCormick MSS; James G. K. McClure to MOS, 22 February 1916, 15 March 1916, both in folder 795, box 83, RSFP. In 1915, McCormick thanks Sage for "the 'wireless apparatus,'" a birthday gift, along with another check for $1,000 "for Missions" (McCormick to "My dearest friend" [MOS], [1915], Foreign Missions file, box 15, McC MSS 1B, McCormick MSS).

65. White to Slocum, 21 January 1911, CUA.

66. Slocum to White, 2 February 1911, CUA; and White to MOS, 15 April 1910; "Mrs. Sage Guest at Dedication of Risley Hall," newspaper clipping, n.d.; White to Slocum, 4 February 1911; White to MOS, 4 February 1911; all four in folder 690, box 75, RSFP.

67. Hunter, secretary, to White, 14 July 1910; White to MOS, 12 October 1910; Slocum to White, 18 January 1911; White to Slocum, 21 January 1911; Slocum to White, 2 February 1911; all five in CUA. On the resegregation of classes at the University of Chicago, see Gordon, *Gender and Higher Education*, 112–17; and Rosalind Rosenberg, *Beyond Separate Spheres: Intellectual Roots of Modern Feminism* (New Haven, Conn.: Yale University Press, 1982), 51–53.

68. White to MOS, 8 July 1910, CUA; see also Henry de Forest to MOS, 25 October 1909, folder 939, box 94, RSFP. Olivia had lived at Yates Castle (now incorporated into the Teachers' College) in the 1860s, when it belonged to the Longstreet family.

69. Taylor to MOS, October 1910, 21 November 1910, 31 July 1911, and 24 August 1911, all four in folder 965, box 96, RSFP. Kathleen McCarthy labels this motive "tribalism."

70. Henry Lee Higginson to President A. Lawrence Lowell, 16 December 1910, Harvard University Archives, Nathan Marsh Pusey Library, Harvard University, Cambridge, Mass. (hereafter cited as HUA).

71. MOS to trustees of Princeton University, 7 April 1908, 19 June 1911; W. Wilson to MOS, 2 November 1908; MOS to John L. Cadwalader, 3 June 1910; RW de F to MOS, 2 January 1912; all five in folder 1001, box 99, RSFP. Mrs. Sage requested a copy of her ancestor's signature.

72. Higginson to Lowell, 16 December 1910, HUA; and Cadwalader to MOS, 3 June 1910, folder 892, box 91, RSFP.

73. Lowell to Higginson, 19 December 1910; Higginson to Lowell, 21 January 1911; both in HUA.

74. "She has decided not to donate the $450,000 which she understands will cover the cost of one dormitory." Henry de Forest to Lowell, 19 July 1911, my italics. See also Lowell to MOS, 28 March 1911; Lowell to Henry de Forest, 21 July 1911; MOS to Lowell, 13 September 1911; Henry de Forest to Lowell, 13 September 1911; all four in HUA.

75. Lowell to J. P. Morgan, Jr., 21 July 1911, HUA, my italics.

76. Henry de Forest to A. Lowell, 18 July 1912; MOS to Lowell, 26 August 1912; both in folder 379, box "Freshman Dormitories," HUA.

77. Henry de Forest to Lowell, 18 July 1912; and Lowell to Henry de Forest, 23 July 1912, HUA.

78. MOS to Lowell, 26 August 1912, HUA; and president and fellows of Harvard College to MOS, 24 April 1911; Lowell to MOS, 13 May 1911; RW de F to Lowell, July 1912; Lowell to MOS, 3 September 1912; all four in folder 739, box 79, RSFP.

79. MOS to Lowell, 17 September 1912, HUA.

80. Sage's gift to RPI is acknowledged in Ricketts to MOS, 1 January 1907, folder 896, box 92, RSFP; and Ricketts to MOS, 5 March 1908, folder 897, box 92, RSFP. See also RPI board of trustees minutes, 5 May 1915, vol. 4, 101; RPI board of trustees minutes, 24 September 1913, vol. 4, 73, 75; both in RPI Archives, Rensselaer Polytechnic University, Troy, N.Y.

81. Chancellor James Day, "Report of Chancellor Day to the Honorable Board of Trustees of Syracuse University, 13 June 1922," SUA, 300. "Mrs. Sage Will Build New College Building," newspaper clipping, Onondaga Historical Society, Syracuse, N.Y., estimated the cost of the Joseph Slocum College of Agriculture at between $250,000 and $300,000.

82. Slocum to Day, [September 1912], box 4, Day Correspondence, SUA; Slocum to Day, 6 September 1913, box 5, Day Correspondence, SUA.

83. Alexandra Oleson and John Voss, eds., *The Organization of Knowledge in Modern America, 1860–1920* (Baltimore, Md.: Johns Hopkins University Press, 1979). This prestigious anthology excludes women from its survey of "knowledge." Compare with Helene Silverberg, ed., *Gender and American Social Science: The Formative Years* (Princeton, N.J.: Princeton University Press, 1998).

84. David Noble describes RPI as the first modern engineering school. See David F. Noble, *America by Design: Science, Technology, and the Rise of Corporate Capitalism* (New York: Knopf, 1977), 20–26; and idem, *A World without Women: The Christian Clerical Culture of Western Science* (New York: Knopf, 1992).

85. Slocum to Grover C. Hart, 3 September 1912, box 4, Day Correspondence, SUA, emphasis in original.

86. Janeway to Demarest, 8 March 1916, Rutgers University Archives.

87. [Margaret Olivia Sage], addendum to "Release of Restrictions upon Use of Gifts," 17 September 1917, n.p. (typescript); Paul Cook, treasurer, to MOS, 12 January 1918; both in Gurley Papers.

88. For a striking modern example, see Rosa Proietto, "The Ford Foundation and Women's Studies in American Higher Education: Seeds of Change?" in *Philanthropic Foundations*, ed. Lagemann, 271–84.

89. "The Last Will and Testament of Margaret Olivia Sage," 25 October 1906, 8–12, in the papers of the late Mrs. Florence Slocum Wilson, Pasadena, Calif.

12. The Texture of Benevolence: Northern Philanthropy, Southern African American Women, and Higher Education, 1930–1950

Jayne R. Beilke

From 1930 to 1950, higher educational opportunity for southern African American women underwent dramatic changes. Motivated by the desire to render service to black colleges and universities and to contribute to racial advancement, an increasing number of black women obtained master's and doctoral degrees despite the constraints of the southern caste system. Confident of their ability to succeed in graduate school and convinced of their right to be there, they viewed education as a path to upward mobility, occupational fulfillment, and middle-class status. In pursuit of graduate and professional education, hundreds of talented southern African Americans applied for prestigious fellowship awards from northern educational philanthropic funds to defray the costs of attending northern institutions. But, as this chapter explores, black women who used philanthropic fellowships to surmount barriers to higher education were confronted by a more insidious set of constraints, namely, prejudicial attitudes toward their race and gender on the part of foundation officials and black college administrators.

The number of African American men and women who graduated from college each year increased steadily after 1920. From 1920 to 1933, the number of black graduates from northern colleges increased by 181 percent (to 439), while the number of graduates from black colleges and universities increased by 400 percent (to 2,486). At the graduate and professional level, eighty-five doctorates were granted to blacks between 1876 and 1933. Only ten of those, however, went to black women.[1] Studies of the occupational distribution of college graduates prior to 1933 confirm low numbers of black female professionals: for example, 2.5 percent (or 27) of 1,079 physicians and dentists were women, and only two of 186 lawyers were women. Although 63 percent of all black high school teachers and 71 percent of all black elementary school teachers were women, they were largely absent from educational leadership positions. Only one of every fifteen black high school principals was a woman, as was one of every five black elementary school principals. Among twenty-one black college presidents, there was only one woman as of 1936.[2] This exception was probably Mary E. Branch, who became president of Tillotson College (Austin, Texas) in 1930 and served until her death in 1944.[3] Tillotson had been founded by the American Missionary Association as a women's college and remained so until 1935, when it began to admit men.

By the mid-1940s, black women were attending colleges at a higher rate than either white women or black men. Many of these women were employed in traditional "women's professions": nursing, teaching, and social work. Others, however, were seeking degrees in nontraditional fields, such as mathematics, the natural and physical sciences, and school administration. By the early 1950s, black women were receiving 62.4 percent of all degrees from black colleges—this at a time when the percentage of women graduates was 33.4 percent across *all* colleges. The percentage of black women graduates was, in fact, just slightly less than that of male graduates in all schools (66.4 percent) and substantially higher than that of black men (35.6 percent).[4] More African American women were also earning degrees beyond the baccalaureate. A 1956 report by Jeanne L. Noble notes that 73 percent of black women college graduates had studied beyond the bachelor's degree and 48 percent had received a master's degree. The consequence of this was a rise in the number of black professional women (in areas such as teaching, medicine, law, and social work); by 1950 these women constituted 58 percent of all black professionals. Although more black women than black men now held master's degrees, few women had earned Ph.D. or medical (M.D.) degrees.[5]

Prior to the United States Supreme Court ruling in *Brown v. Board of Education* (1954), southern blacks who desired postbaccalaureate degrees had few options. Excluded from southern white institutions by de jure segregation, African Americans had to choose among only a few black colleges and universities in the South that offered course work beyond the baccalaureate (primarily Fisk University in Nashville,

Tennessee, and Howard University in Washington, D.C.). Faculty at black colleges labored under heavy teaching loads and service responsibilities that often prevented them from pursuing doctoral degrees. And although blacks could legally enroll in advanced courses of study at northern institutions, they encountered financial hardship, northern de facto segregation, and the isolation of living apart from family and friends. Black families, churches, social clubs, and other organizations did provide some financial support, and African Americans drew upon state scholarships and philanthropic fellowship programs. To offset the financial burden of attending northern institutions, the large majority of blacks who enrolled in northern graduate schools made do with out-of-state tuition scholarships.

These scholarships had been established in nearly all southern states in an effort to circumvent black demands for public support of advanced education. Southern school officials argued that the provision of state scholarships to northern schools meant that they did not have to appropriate funds to build local facilities for black education or face black demands to integrate white graduate and professional schools. Many of these out-of-state scholarship programs dated from the 1930s and were maintained in violation of the ruling in *State of Missouri ex rel. Gaines v. Canada et al.* (1938). In rendering its decision in the *Gaines* case, the U.S. Supreme Court essentially declared the practice of awarding out-of-state scholarships as illegal on the basis of the Fourteenth Amendment, ruling that "the payment of tuition fees in another state does not remove the discrimination." Generally administered by state departments of education or black colleges and universities located within individual southern states, the scholarships awarded only meager amounts in any case, and the application and distribution process was riddled with bureaucracy.[6]

A more lucrative and prestigious form of financial assistance was available through fellowship programs established by northern educational philanthropic foundations. However, the fellowship programs were highly competitive and fund officials often placed unrealistic demands on fellowship recipients. For example, Ph.D. candidates were frequently expected to finish all course work and dissertation requirements within one or two years. This accelerated pace was made still more difficult by the fact that many northern institutions would not accept credits earned at black colleges. Students were "conditionally" admitted to northern schools with the stipulation that they enroll in additional courses (often in the liberal arts) in preparation for graduate study. An added complication was fund officials' insistence that fellowship awards and out-of-state scholarships were to be mutually exclusive: blacks had to choose either a state scholarship or a philanthropic fellowship. In some cases, the General Education Board (GEB), a Rockefeller-founded organization intended to promote education, demanded reimbursement from GEB Fellows who had also received state tuition funds.[7]

The most comprehensive philanthropic fellowship programs were those of the General Education Board and the Julius Rosenwald Fund. Under these programs, southern blacks were awarded fellowships to study at prestigious northern institutions such as the University of Chicago, Teachers College at Columbia, Harvard University, and the University of Michigan. Fellowship grants generally covered tuition, fees, and living expenses incurred while studying for master's or doctoral degrees. From 1902 to 1954 (when the program was transferred to the Council of Southern Universities), the GEB fellowship program awarded nearly two thousand grants to black and white individuals.[8] The GEB initially allocated funds in the South only to white public school teachers who had been identified as possessing sufficient leadership potential to exert political influence on the public school system. In 1924, the GEB began to award fellowships to promising black instructors in southern colleges and universities. By 1938, candidates for fellowships were required to have earned a master's degree.[9] The amount of the stipend granted to black Fellows ranged from $1000 for an unmarried man to $1500 for a married man, to be used for expenses related to travel, living expenses, and other costs. Significantly, no such accommodation based on marital status was made for women.

The Julius Rosenwald Fellowship Program began with informal requests made by petitioners to Julius Rosenwald personally. Clearly reflecting Rosenwald's educational and political alignment with black leader Booker T. Washington, the fund's early instrumentalist emphasis meant that program monies were targeted to develop leadership for the areas in which the Fund had an interest (black schools, hospitals, and library programs). The Rosenwald Fellowship Program initially emphasized advanced training for black medical and nursing personnel, vocational and industrial teachers, and librarians. The relatively large number of fellowships given for work in social science is directly related to the influence of fellowship committee member Charles S. Johnson, who used the program to identify talented students for Fisk

University's Department of Social Sciences. After Rosenwald's death in 1932, the program was administratively formalized and awards were granted to "superior individuals" in the liberal arts, fine arts, and social sciences. The program's directive—"to identify a group of superior mentalities"—reflected the influence of Yale-educated Edwin Embree, who steered the course of the Rosenwald Fund from its date of incorporation (1928) to its close in 1948.[10]

The Rosenwald Fellowship Committee consisted of William C. Haygood, director; Edwin Rogers Embree, president; and a core group including Charles S. Johnson, Will W. Alexander, and Robert C. Weaver. As the fellowship program director, Haygood played a largely administrative role. As the president of the Rosenwald Fund and ex officio chairperson of the fellowship committee, Embree had a pre-eminent influence. The grandson of John G. Fee—white abolitionist and founder of Berea College—Embree was a self-described "philan-thropoid," or fund manager, and had served as director of the Division of Studies and vice president of the Rockefeller Foundation before joining the Rosenwald Fund in 1927.

Committee member and sociologist Charles S. Johnson was a co-founder of *Opportunity,* the official publication of the National Urban League, and director of the nationally respected Department of Social Sciences and Race Relations Institute at Fisk University. In 1947, he became Fisk University's first African American president. Will Alexander was a white southerner who had helped to establish the Commission on Interracial Cooperation in Atlanta in 1919 and was a driving force behind the founding of historically black Dillard University (New Orleans, La.). Robert Weaver, an African American and a Harvard-educated economist, had worked for the United States Department of the Interior (1933–1937) and the U.S. Housing Authority (1937–1940) prior to his affiliation with the fellowship committee.

A total of 586 African Americans received fellowships from the Rosenwald Fund. Of that number, 189 (or 32 percent) were women. An analysis of the distribution of fellowship awards granted to women between 1928 and 1948 reveals that most awards were meant to pre-pare scholars for work in traditionally female occupations (table 12.1).[11]

In addition to the preponderance of women in teaching, by the mid-1930s women accounted for 83 percent of the black librarians and 70 percent of the black social workers in the South.[12] While the Rosenwald Fund undoubtedly helped to professionalize those areas

Table 12.1. Rosenwald Fellowship Awards to Women, 1928–1948

Field	Number of awards
Domestic arts (home economics)	27
Social sciences	23
Library science	19
Public health/nursing/hospital administration	18
Liberal arts	18
Music performance	18
Rural education	18
Education	17
Fine arts	11
Music education	6
Other	14
Total	189

Source: Embree and Waxman, *Investment in People*, 238–52.

through the fellowship program, it also reinforced the pattern of placing black women in service occupations.

The cases of Rosenwald Fellows Florence Beatty Brown, Lillian Burwell Lewis, and Georgia C. Poole, as well as GEB Fellow Carrie Coleman Robinson, are representative of the constraints that accompanied philanthropic support of educational opportunity for black women. In 1943, Florence Beatty Brown applied for a fellowship from the Julius Rosenwald Fund for one year's study at the University of Illinois in order to develop study aids for rural social science programs. Born in Cairo, Illinois, in 1912, she had received a bachelor of arts degree from Fisk University in 1933 and a master of arts in history from the University of Illinois in 1936. In 1939, she had earned a master's degree in sociology from the University of Illinois. In addition, she studied at Teachers College (Columbia) during 1940–1941 and had also served as a regional field worker in the North Carolina rural school program. After finishing the proposed additional year of study at Illinois, Brown intended to return to her current position as a social science instructor at State Teachers College in Fayetteville, North Carolina. Her previous applications for a Rosenwald Fellowship (in 1938, 1940, 1941, and 1942) had been unsuccessful.[13]

One of Brown's letters of recommendation in her 1943 application came from Bruce Barton, whose father had been a circuit rider in

Tennessee. When he was a child, his family had taken in "a mulatto boy"—Webster Barton Beatty—who was "the son of a black woman who had been a slave and of a worthless drunken white man." Beatty remained with the Barton family and graduated from Berea College. Since that time, Barton had extended "some small help" to Webster Beatty's three children, including Florence Beatty Brown, the oldest daughter. Barton continued, "Florence worked her way through Fisk University and . . . earned an A.M. also. She married a Negro who, as I recall it, was working for his doctor's degree and subsequently became principal of a normal school in one of the southern states." Barton had "no reservations whatever about Florence Beatty-Brown. She has come up by her own character, hard work, and self-respect, and deserves to go further."[14]

While good character and a laudable work ethic were valuable assets, the fact that Brown was pregnant jeopardized her chances for a fellowship. Haygood suggested that she defer the fellowship until she could pursue her graduate studies full-time, without the distraction of caring for a new baby. Brown responded that "My subsequent plans for my career are to remain in the teaching field since I apparently have been 'called,' my [institutional] President says, a born teacher, and because I love to teach . . . especially misguided rural students who have neither a fair chance nor good conscientious teachers who teach for the love of it rather than for the money in it." During negotiations with the Rosenwald Fund, she changed the focus of her research. As the result of her work in the North Carolina rural school program, she had gained access to an extraordinarily complete set of records and diaries kept by a black family, and she now wished to write a generalized study of the middle-class black family. She intended to continue teaching in Fayetteville while she sifted through the materials that would be used in her thesis.[15] Charles S. Johnson expressed his concern to Director Haygood about Brown's ability to continue teaching or even residing at State Teachers College. Johnson believed that she needed "close institutional supervision" and worried that "she will not do justice to the fellowship and will set a rather questionable precedent." He suggested that a former Rosenwald Fellow, sociologist E. Franklin Frazier (then at Howard University), undertake this "close supervision."[16]

At this latter stage of the Fellowship program (1942–1948), applicants were not as plentiful as they had been between 1936 and 1941. The effects of World War II, in particular, had decreased the fellowship applicant pool. Some potential applicants were serving in the armed forces while others were taking advantage of employment opportunities offered by the United Service Organization (USO) and wartime industries. The decline in student enrollments at many colleges and universities had caused retrenchment and faculty layoffs, leading to bitter competition over a declining number of faculty positions, and thus limiting the placement opportunities for fellowship recipients.[17]

It is difficult to know whether it was the relatively small number of applicants that year, Barton's reference to Berea College in his letter of reference, or Brown's persistence that finally influenced Embree to cast the deciding vote in favor of Brown. Most likely, the decision turned on Brown's willingness to change her research topic. The fellowship committee was very interested in research on "Negro problems" and deliberately steered applicants in the direction of problems related to black history, sociology, literature, and culture. In any event, Brown was awarded a Rosenwald Fellowship for 1943–1944. The following year, Brown reported that she was an assistant professor of sociology at historically black Lincoln University (Pennsylvania). By 1946, she had become acting head of the Department of Sociology at Lincoln and reported that she was rewriting her thesis, "A Study of the Middle Class Negro Family from 1870–1945," for possible publication.[18]

Without doubt, state tuition grants and philanthropic fellowships helped southern African American women surmount barriers to higher education during this period. But the opportunity afforded by the fellowship award was muted by the responsibilities undertaken by (and expected of) black women, many of whom were the economic mainstays of their families. Accepting the fellowship meant, at the least, leaving those families while attending a northern university. And upon returning to the southern institutions where they were employed after completing graduate work, they often met with jealousy on the part of colleagues or the indifference of administrators who considered advanced training or graduate study superfluous, particularly for women. Not always commensurately rewarded or respected for their educational achievements, they returned to paternalistic institutions that rewarded women on the basis of service to the institution and loyalty to its president.

Lillian Burwell Lewis was teaching biology at Tillotson College when she applied for a Rosenwald Fund fellowship for doctoral studies in zoology at the University of Chicago. She had received her high school diploma from Tougaloo College in 1919 and the bachelor of science degree in 1925 from Howard University, where she studied with well-known biologist (and Rosenwald Fellow) Ernest E. Just. With the assistance of a GEB fellowship, she had earned a master of science degree from the University of Chicago in 1931 after three summers and one semester of study. The next year, the Rosenwald committee awarded her a fellowship of $1000 to study zoology at Chicago during the 1932–1933 academic year. But when notified of the award, Lewis responded that the grant would not cover all her expenses. Besides being in debt from the financial burden of earning the master's degree, she wrote,

> My mother was stricken with paralysis and is now an invalid. My father is too old to support her and take care of her needs properly. In rearing the thirteen children, my parents were unable to save very much for a time of need like this and I am the only one of the children without a family and able to contribute materially to their needs. If I should stop [teaching at Tillotson] they would be reduced to absolute want and so I must continue to make my monthly contributions.[19]

Neither the Rosenwald Fund nor the University of Chicago was willing to supplement the grant, and Lewis's award was canceled.

She continued to teach at Tillotson and attend summer sessions at the University of Chicago. It was not until 1946, however, that she earned the doctor of philosophy degree. The next year, she and her husband (a native of Winston-Salem, N.C.) left Tillotson when Lewis accepted a position as head of the science department and professor of biology at Winston-Salem Teachers College. The following letter from Lewis to Francis L. Atkins, president of the college, suggests that her hard-earned doctoral degree from Chicago was not entirely appreciated:

> A look at the salary scale for the Winston-Salem Teachers College since the 1959 legislature provided 3.5 million dollars for faculty salary increases, as "has been worked out by institutions and the State Department of administration," will show that the raise you agreed to give me previous to this appropriation puts me in the rank of an assistant.

In view of the appropriation and the fact that you are trying to qualify Teachers College for the Southern Association rating with additional PhDs, I believe you will agree that it is fair that I receive at least the salary of an associate, $7500, if not more.

As I stated to you previously, if I were just beginning to teach I would have time to capitalize upon my advanced degree, but with me it is now or never.

Because of the effort to pay teachers more, it is going to be increasingly difficult to obtain a person with a doctorate for under $7000. A. and T. [North Carolina Agricultural and Technical] still has that vacancy in Biology for a PhD. Along with a need of several others with a doctorate to qualify for the Southern Association rating.[20]

Interestingly, Atkins himself had received a GEB fellowship for 1923–1925 and was therefore thoroughly familiar with the limited opportunities African American women had for graduate education. The fact that Lewis's husband was also employed as a faculty member at Winston-Salem undoubtedly provided Atkins with leverage. It appears that the two arrived at a somewhat satisfactory solution, because Lewis remained at Winston-Salem until her retirement in 1970.[21]

By the 1930s, new accreditation requirements for colleges and universities required faculty to earn advanced degrees in order to retain their positions. But administrators of black colleges, coping with the reality of scarce resources and increased institutional competition for students, were often reluctant to institute a hierarchical reward system of salary increases, faculty rank, or promotion to administrative positions. This is exemplified by Georgia Poole's experience upon finishing her Rosenwald fellowship year and returning to Georgia State Industrial College.

Georgia Cowen Poole had received an A.B. from Talladega College. She taught at Georgia State Industrial College (Savannah) for four years prior to receiving a Rosenwald Fellowship in 1936. Poole pursued a master's degree in children's literature, and she planned to develop age- and grade-appropriate materials for rural children while studying at the University of Chicago. Upon completion of her studies, she requested an increase in salary. President Benjamin F. Hubert responded,

I realize that you have done your work well and have been loyal to the institution, but I think you must agree that the institution has provided for you an opportunity to show what you can do. It is also through the institution that you were able to receive a scholarship. Other employees have asked for recommendations in order that they might have scholarship awards permitting them to study. We feel that when we excuse a person to study that we have favored them as well as the institution which they have agreed to service.[22]

Disappointed with Hubert's response, Poole discussed the situation with L. M. Lester, associate director of the Division of Negro Education of the Rosenwald Fund. Lester spoke with President Hubert and found him to be "not inclined to offer [Poole] an increase in salary next year. He feels that the opportunity for study meant more to you than to the college."[23] Convinced that the situation was unlikely to improve, in 1937 Poole accepted an offer to teach at Spelman, a historically black women's college in Atlanta, Georgia.

It is likely that Hubert's reaction was intensified by his own professional frustrations. Through the efforts of Will Alexander, Hubert had received a scholarship to Harvard University to work on a Ph.D. in agricultural economics. In 1929, he received a scholarship from the Laura Spelman Rockefeller Memorial Scholarship Program for Negro Social Science and Social Work. Illness and the responsibilities of the presidency of Georgia State College forced him to apply for extensions from the LSRM through 1937. Although he was able to finish the course work, he never completed his dissertation.[24]

Race and gender discrimination not only played a prominent role in the fellowship selection process, they also affected fellowship recipients during their terms of study at northern universities. Carrie Coleman Robinson was one of six children born to a Mississippi schoolteacher and a farmer. She earned a bachelor of arts degree at Tougaloo College in 1931 and spent a year at Hampton Institute, earning a bachelor's degree in library science in 1932. She was employed as the librarian at Western Kentucky Industrial College from 1932 to 1934. From 1934 to 1940 she was employed by the American Missionary Society and worked for several AMA-affiliated institutions (Barber Scotia College, Tillotson College, and Avery Institute). After her marriage to Thomas Robinson in 1940, she enrolled at Teachers College, Columbia University. Like many others, Robinson was admitted on a conditional basis and required to take additional courses as she worked toward a master's degree. She explained, "Tougaloo was not an A-rated school when I graduated from it. So I took courses in humanities [at Columbia]. I spent one year there, then I enrolled in the masters program."[25] She remembered that "the racial animosity I encountered on the part of one professor in English literature at Columbia was liberally offset by the delight I derived from Willard Heaps' course in school library science administration and from courses taught by other professors, especially in religion, philosophy and political science."[26] She left Teachers College in 1941 without a degree. In 1946, she was recruited by H. Councill Trenholm—president of Alabama State College and former Rosenwald Fellow—to build a library training program at Alabama State.

Still without an advanced degree, Robinson was awarded a GEB Fellowship to study at the Graduate Library School of the University of Illinois in 1948, as preparation for teaching graduate courses in library education at Alabama State Teachers College.[27] To her, the GEB scholarship "made a tremendous difference. When I came home from Illinois I had a master's degree in library science from one of the Big Ten universities. The university to which I was denied entrance [the University of Alabama] was offering only a minor in library science. And all of those white librarians thought they had a master's! But the master's was in education with a minor in library science. So I had a degree that was accepted throughout this country."[28]

In pursuit of her dream of earning a doctorate in school librarianship, she returned to the University of Illinois for the 1953–1954 academic year. While studying at Illinois, Robinson moved her family to Chicago in order to care for them. After Robinson finished the course work, however, her mother sustained a hip fracture in a fall. Beyond these family responsibilities, a further complication for Robinson was her academic advisor's insistence that her dissertation focus on a school program in Indianapolis, Indiana. Historically, like other states on the North-South border, Indiana has exhibited an uneven pattern of de facto segregation. Local school officials prevented Robinson from pursuing the topic "because I was black. I [was not allowed to] work for that school system." Moreover, Robinson was convinced that her academic advisor at Illinois had been fully cognizant of this barrier from the very beginning. Burdened by the pressures of caring for her family and discouraged by manifestations of northern racism, she resumed her position at Alabama State. Years later, the failure to obtain the doctorate in school librarianship remained a bitter disappointment.[29]

In her study of black women who earned baccalaureate degrees from the Seven Sister colleges between 1880 and 1960, Linda Perkins concluded that the experience "gave them the freedom, exposure and opportunity to prove themselves intellectually on the same basis as Whites, and opened to them opportunities for a wider range of careers." But while the degrees did function as windows of opportunity, they also brought with them a new set of constraints that prevented black women from capitalizing on their improved occupational and professional status. Like the subjects of Perkins's study, southern black women who obtained graduate degrees at northern institutions through philanthropic fellowships "had little choice but to go South to teach in segregated . . . schools."[30]

In fact, the original application forms of both the Rosenwald and GEB fellowship programs contained the query, "Do you intend to return to the South?" The question was an important one for foundation officers who had been charged with building the competence of selected black institutions. Since the foundation officers relied heavily upon the recommendations of institutional presidents in their search for top candidates, the inclusion of that query may also have been intended to reassure black college administrators that the fellowships would not decimate their faculty ranks. Without doubt, it also served to remind blacks of "their place" within the economic and political landscape. In regard to black women, who were valuable economic contributors to the black community, there was certainly concern that the opportunity for graduate study in the North might educate them out of their sphere. Whatever their reasons, more black women graduates of northern schools than men returned to the South.[31] This would remain the case as long as teaching was the largest field of opportunity for black women.

Beyond race, gender stereotypes figured heavily into the valuation of black women's educational potential. A middle-class emphasis on good character and work habits often overshadowed a recognition of women's intellectual abilities and potential. The dissertation study of Marion Vera Cuthbert, a Rosenwald Fellow, focused on black women college graduates. Cuthbert herself was nearly the victim of age discrimination, but she met the standard for character. In a report to the Rosenwald Trustees on the fellowship awards for 1941, the Rosenwald Fellowship Committee noted that Cuthbert was "older than we usually consider [but a] remarkably fine person with a brilliant record and definite and timely topic."[32]

When undertaken by women, the Ph.D. degree in particular was often viewed as superfluous and self-indulgent. Like their white counterparts, highly educated black women were accused of contributing to race suicide by marrying later in life (after completing their education) and bearing fewer children. Cuthbert's study confirms that educated women made different choices concerning marriage and childbearing than did women with less formal education. In "Education and Marginality: A Study of the Negro Woman College Graduate" (1942), she pointed out the escalating tensions between black men and black college women that were beginning to manifest themselves. For example, educated middle-class black women tended to marry later (3–4 years after graduation) and to give birth to fewer than four children.[33] This is corroborated by Noble's 1956 study, in which 38 percent of the women college graduates she studied had one child, 15 percent had two children, and 6 percent had between three and six children. Significantly, 41 percent were childless.[34]

Black women were never exempt from rendering service to the black college or university or to the larger community. In some cases, highly qualified—and educated—women filled such positions as secretary to black institutional presidents. While those positions carried with them a certain amount of prestige (the "halo" effect of working for an important man), the women who held them generally abdicated any serious academic leadership role. While their male counterparts often became institutional presidents, respected scholars, and researchers at black colleges and universities, African American women generally rose no higher than department chairs. Those who became department heads often had their careers attenuated by virtue of the length of time necessary to finish the degree, leaving little time, as Burwell Lewis observed, "to capitalize upon my advanced degree."

Graduate and professional degrees were valued for more than economic reasons. The degrees offered some measure of autonomy (if only for their portability) as well as verifying intellectual competence and self-worth. Graduate degrees also afforded black women options. For example, obtaining a doctoral degree enabled Lillian Burwell Lewis to negotiate more effectively with President Atkins by threatening to leave Winston-Salem to "take the position at [North Carolina] A. and T." Beyond that, the graduate degrees earned by southern black women between 1930 and 1950 ultimately contributed to the development of a cadre of leadership that culminated during the Civil Rights era. In 1960, Lewis became the first black woman to be elected to the county school board in Forsyth County, North Carolina.[35]

Carrie Coleman Robinson provides another example. In 1969, the Alabama State Department was reorganized and a white woman, a recent graduate from Louisiana State University, was hired to supervise the secondary school libraries. Although she was a secondary education specialist, Robinson was relegated to the elementary education division. A life member of the National Education Association, Robinson and the NEA filed suit against the state of Alabama. In 1971, the case was settled out of court in her favor. Robinson's educational history would come full circle in 1972 when William Hug, the director of the library media program at traditionally white Auburn University, asked Robinson to teach in his program. She went to Auburn as an associate professor and retired three years later.[36]

In the end, however, the relationship between northern philanthropy and southern African American women during this period was hegemonic. While philanthropic fellowships expanded higher educational access and occupational opportunity, the gendered expectations of male fund officials and institutional presidents prevented women from fully realizing their academic potential. Torn between family obligations and institutional loyalty on the one hand and the desire for educational attainment on the other, educated black women nevertheless remained convinced that, in the words used to describe Florence Beatty Brown, they "deserved to go further." Although their choice to pursue higher education was often compromised, it laid the foundation for educational leadership in the crucial decades preceding the decision in *Brown v. Board of Education* and the Civil Rights era.

NOTES

An earlier version of this chapter was presented at the 1999 American Educational Research Association Annual Meeting, Montreal, Canada; my research was partially supported by a Rockefeller Archive Center grant-in-aid.

1. Charles S. Johnson, *The Negro College Graduate* (Chapel Hill: University of North Carolina Press, 1938), 9–11, 92–130.
2. Ibid., 92–130. See also Fred McCuistion, *Graduate Instruction for Negroes in the United States* (Nashville, Tenn.: George Peabody College for Teachers, 1939).
3. Elizabeth L. Ihle, ed., *Black Women in Higher Education: An Anthology of Essays, Studies, and Documents* (New York: Garland, 1992), 177.
4. Jeanne L. Noble, *The Negro Woman's College Education* (New York: Columbia University Bureau of Publications, 1956), 29.
5. Ibid.
6. For a discussion of out-of-state (public) scholarships, see Mary B. Holmes Pierson, *Graduate Work in the South* (Chapel Hill: University of North Carolina Press,

1947); and Jayne R. Beilke, "The Politics of Opportunity: Philanthropic Fellowships, Out-of-State Aid, and Higher Education for Blacks in the South," *History of Higher Education Annual* 17 (1997): 53–71.

7. For a history of the GEB, see Raymond B. Fosdick, Henry F. Pringle, and Katharine D. Pringle, *Adventure in Giving: The Story of the General Education Board* (New York: Harper and Row, 1962).

8. Ibid., 311.

9. Ibid., 309–14.

10. The papers of Edwin R. Embree are stored at the Sterling Memorial Library, Yale University. The business diary he kept while at the Rockefeller Foundation is located at the Rockefeller Archive Center, Sleepy Hollow, N.Y. (hereafter cited as RAC).

11. The total number of awards made to African Americans by the Rosenwald Fund is often listed as 800. That number, however, includes renewal awards to Fellows. Awards were made to 586 individuals, and this chapter uses that number. See Embree and Waxman, *Investment in People*, 238–52; and Jayne R. Beilke, "To Render Better Service: The Role of the Julius Rosenwald Fund Fellowship Program in the Development of Graduate and Professional Educational Opportunities for African-Americans" (Ph.D. diss., Indiana University, 1994).

12. Darlene Clark Hine, Elsa Barkley Brown, and Rosalyn Terborg-Penn, eds., *Black Women in America: An Historical Encyclopedia*, vol. 1 (Bloomington: Indiana University Press, 1993), 385–86.

13. Application digest of Florence Beatty Brown, folder 2, box 397, Julius Rosenwald Fund Papers, Fisk University Library Special Collections, Nashville, Tenn. (hereafter cited as JRF Papers).

14. B. Barton to G. M. Reynolds, folder 2, box 397, JRF Papers.

15. Application digest of Florence Beatty Brown, folder 2, box 397, JRF Papers.

16. Ibid.

17. For a discussion of the evolution of the Rosenwald Fellowship Program, see Jayne R. Beilke, "The Changing Emphasis of the Rosenwald Fellowship Program, 1928–1948," *Journal of Negro Education* 66 (winter 1997): 3–15.

18. Application digest of Florence Beatty Brown, folder 2, box 397, JRF Papers.

19. Application digest of Lillian L. Burwell, 19 October 1932, folder 1, box 399, JRF Papers.

20. Lillian Burwell Lewis to Francis L. Atkins, 31 July 1959, C. G. O'Kelley Library, Winston-Salem State University Archives, Winston-Salem, N.C.

21. Carter B. Cue, archivist, C. G. O'Kelley Library, conversation with author, 18 August 1998, Winston-Salem, N.C.

22. Benjamin F. Hubert to Georgia Cowen Poole, 14 July 1937, folder 1, box 441, JRF Papers.

23. L. M. Lester to Poole, 15 July 1937, folder 1, box 441, JRF Papers.

24. John H. Stanfield, *Philanthropy and Jim Crow in American Social Science* (Westport, Conn.: Greenwood, 1985), 83.

25. Carrie Coleman Robinson, interview by author, 9 May 1995, Montgomery, Ala.

26. Carrie C. Robinson, "First by Circumstance," in *The Black Librarian in America*, ed. E. J. Josey (Metuchen, N.J.: Scarecrow, 1970), 277.

27. Application for Fellowship, folder 2354, box 233, General Education Board Papers, RAC.

28. Robinson, interview.

29. Ibid.

30. Linda M. Perkins, "The African American Female Elite: The Early History of African American Women in the Seven Sister Colleges, 1880–1960," *Harvard Educational Review* 67 (winter 1997), 718–56.

31. One study indicated that 31.9 percent of African American women and 28.1 percent of men returned to the South after attending northern schools (Johnson, *Negro College Graduate*, 129).

32. Report to the Trustees, 1940 Awards to Negroes, box 374, JRF papers. Awards were always made for the following year.

33. Marion V. Cuthbert, "Education and Marginality: A Study of the Negro Woman College Graduate" (Ph.D. diss., Teachers College, Columbia University, 1942), 28. See also Paula Giddings, *When and Where I Enter: The Impact of Black Women on Race and Sex in America* (1984; reprint, New York: Bantam, 1988), 244–48.

34. Noble, *Negro Woman's College Education*, 20.

35. "Lillian Lewis Made Headway for Blacks," *Winston-Salem Journal*, 10 March 1998, B2.

36. Robinson, interview.

13. "Contributing to the Most Promising Peaceful Revolution in Our Time": The American Women's Scholarship for Japanese Women, 1893–1941

Linda L. Johnson

What Katharine McBride, president emeritus of Bryn Mawr College, called a "peaceful revolution"[1] was the work of the American Women's Scholarship for Japanese Women (AWSJW), which provided financial aid for Japanese students to attend Bryn Mawr College, and the Committee for Miss Tsuda's School for Girls, which endowed Joshi Eigaku Juku, an elite school for educating women teachers. These two committees (largely composed of the same members) played a critical role in the development of Japanese women's higher education and the training of women teachers. The scholarship provided financial aid for eleven students to attend Bryn Mawr between 1893 and 1941. The first scholarship recipient, Tsuda Ume,[2] became Japan's leading expert on English-language instruction and women's education. The most outstanding graduates of her school became the later recipients of Bryn Mawr scholarships. In comparison to other scholarship programs and gifts to colleges analyzed in this volume, the endowments raised by the AWSJW and the Committee for Miss Tsuda's School for Girls were small; nevertheless, their impact on Japanese women's higher education was substantial. Tsuda's school and other women's schools established by Bryn Mawr scholarship recipients prepared Japan's leading female intellectuals and professionals, as well as large numbers of the teachers who staffed girls' primary and secondary schools before World War II.

This study examines the factors that enabled Tsuda Ume to develop American philanthropic support for Japanese women's higher education. The collaboration between Tsuda and her benefactors was made possible by shared beliefs about gender, class, education, and social change. They all believed that education was fundamental to emancipating women from their dependence on men, and that women had the same intellectual capacity as men and deserved the same rigorous educational opportunities. Their educational vision for women was limited, however, by their implicit assumption that the privilege of higher education was reserved for women of the middle and upper classes.[3] This study is divided into three parts: an examination of the elements of Tsuda Ume's education that enabled her to be the beneficiary of American philanthropy, an analysis of the administration of the scholarship program, and a study of the varied philanthropic efforts that made Joshi Eigaku Juku possible.

A RESPECT FOR TRUE CULTURE: THE AMERICAN EDUCATION OF TSUDA UME

Tsuda Ume's unique career in Japanese higher education was initially made possible by a Japanese government scholarship that financed her precollegiate education in the United States. At the end of the nineteenth century, the Japanese Ministry of Education sent students to the United States, Great Britain, France, and Germany to be trained as teachers for the public school system then being created. According to a government document, in Western countries students could "master the character, government, customs, and nature of the people. . . . This will help the Japanese people to advance and will aid in the development of a civilized Japan, so that the country can prosper."[4] The plan to include females in overseas study was authorized by the emperor, who acknowledged the lack of formal educational opportunities for women. "Due to the inadequate provisions for the education of women in our country, most of them are not able to understand the meaning of civilization," he said.[5]

In order to study the foundations of Western power, a Japanese delegation—led by Prince Iwakura Tomomi and including almost half of Japan's political leaders—was to set sail for the United States and Europe at the end of 1871. Both female and male students were to accompany the Iwakura Mission; they would study in the United States for a ten-year period, financially supported with free tuition, a travel allowance, room and board, and $800 spending money. In spite of the lucrative offer, two recruiting efforts failed to identify female applicants. Ultimately, however, five girls, ranging in age from six to fourteen, were found. Tsuda Ume, daughter of Tsuda Sen, an educator and Western enthusiast, was the youngest.[6] Tsuda Ume's strong sense of an obligation to serve came from the imperial commission with which the girls were sent to the United States. In a break with tradition, the five girls were granted a private audience with Empress Haruko and given a document sending them abroad "to study for the good of our countrywomen."[7]

Upon their arrival in the United States, the girls were placed with American families so that they might become "fully acquainted with the blessings of *home life* in the United States," learning "all those kinds of information which will make them true ladies" and developing a "respect for what is called true culture."[8] Tsuda Ume was placed with Charles Lanman, secretary to the Japanese legation, and his wife Adeline. Impressed by the young girl's intelligence, dedication to study, and refined manners (characteristics for which she was praised by her American benefactors throughout her career), the Lanmans became devoted to Tsuda, choosing to educate her in neighborhood academies so that she might continue to live with them. She graduated from Georgetown Collegiate Institute and the Archer Institute. Understanding their mandate in the broadest possible terms, the Lanmans sought to educate Tsuda Ume about as many aspects of the United States and American culture as possible.

While Tsuda Ume's formal schooling was on a par with the best precollegiate educations for women available in the United States, it was the informal education she received as a member of the Lanman family that ultimately enabled her to work effectively with American mentors and patrons. Her American biographer, Barbara Rose, has argued that Tsuda's American education instilled in her the values of domesticity then prevalent in American society, values that constrained the version of women's education that she developed upon her return to Japan.[9] I contend that the Lanmans sought not to prepare Tsuda Ume for marriage, but rather to empower her to be a national leader in Japan. The education directed by the Lanmans prepared Tsuda Umeko for the public world of service to Japanese women.

A significant aspect of Tsuda's informal education was the Lanman house itself. Tsuda read widely in the Lanmans' collection of three thousand books and she observed walls covered with Charles Lanman's landscape watercolors (he was a noted amateur) as well as the original works of British and American artists. A newspaper reporter described the Lanman home as "a veritable museum" and "a little picture gallery."[10] The school that Tsuda later established in the former house of a Japanese aristocrat can be seen as her effort to replicate the Lanman house—the residence of a Victorian couple of arts and letters. The Lanman residence may have been influential in another aspect of Tsuda's thinking as well. When Charles Lanman became secretary of the Japanese legation, he had begun adding Japanese books and objets d'art to the collections that he displayed at home. This eclecticism may have informed Tsuda Ume's thinking about the viability and desirability of combining things Japanese and American.

The decor of the Lanman home provided a backdrop for entertaining refined guests, enjoying elevated conversation, cultivating artistic talents, and learning social graces. In the company of the Lanmans, Tsuda Ume played piano, read for pleasure, painted watercolors, wrote essays, and composed poems. In a memoir she later wrote for *Joshi Sekai* (Women's World), Tsuda recalled that at the age of eleven or twelve she was reading Scott, Dickens, and the poems of Longfellow and Bryant, as well as enjoying the biographies of Caesar, Josephine, and Darwin.[11] The Lanmans' circle of friends included Washington Irving, John Whittier, and other American men of letters. When literary celebrities such as Dickens and Longfellow toured, they were entertained in the Lanman home. Tsuda Ume's talents were on display when the Lanmans entertained their distinguished guests, and it was during these social occasions, one might conclude, that she developed her sense of propriety and maturity of thought. It was also in the Lanman home that Tsuda Ume was introduced to Mary Morris, a Philadelphia Quaker and philanthropist and the wife of a Philadelphia railroad baron, who was to become her personal benefactor as well as the major patron of her school and scholarship fund.[12] Additionally, Tsuda Ume learned to value education and appreciate the value of domestic relations that were based on respect for the intellect. Beyond the formal education for which the Japanese government paid, the Lanmans provided Tsuda Ume with an invaluable informal education that prepared her to charm the upper classes in the drawing rooms of America, where she would later solicit the assistance of benefactors for her mission of educating Japanese women and elevating their status.

"A FREE GIFT FROM AMERICAN LADIES": THE AMERICAN WOMEN'S SCHOLARSHIP FOR JAPANESE WOMEN

After eleven years in the United States, Tsuda Ume returned to Japan, which had become more conservative and less supportive of women's education. In correspondence to Adeline Lanman, Tsuda Ume expressed her despair about the condition of women and their lack of desire for change. "Oh women have the hardest part of life to bear in more ways than one. Even in America I often wished I were a man. Oh how much more so in Japan! Poor, poor women, how I long to do something to better your position! Yet why should I, when they are so well satisfied, and do not seem to know any better?"[13] The Japanese government had legally confirmed women's traditional subordinate status. A wife was treated as a minor by law and could not enter into a contract without her husband's consent. Her property was placed at the disposal of her husband and family property was inherited by the eldest son. Not only were women denied the franchise, but the Peace Preservation law prohibited them from attending political meetings.[14] Japan's Ministry of Education had made little progress in establishing secondary schools for girls or educating women teachers. Foreign missionaries continued to educate girls, but anti-Western sentiment was frequently heard in Tokyo and educated women were derided in the popular press. Writing to Adeline Lanman, Tsuda expressed her need to be circumspect. "We must not make enemies, or offend their taste, but conform as much as possible, yet improve their customs, and methods of dressing, of society, etc. in our own little circles."[15] In spite of her frustrations, Tsuda asserted her desire to remain in her homeland, expressing, perhaps for the first time, the sense of alienation she had experienced in the United States: "You know I never want to be an American citizen. . . . Many times I have felt that I was of different race and blood, and there were none whose blood was kin to mine, who had the characteristics of our race."[16] Tsuda's sense of her Japanese identity appears to have been strengthened by her encounters with Westerners in Japan. Unlike the cosmopolitan guests in the Lanman household who were charmed by Japanese culture, Westerners such as American missionaries Tsuda met in Tokyo were less enamored of the Japanese. Tsuda criticized "their excessive narrow-mindedness, and their want of appreciation of anything whatever good in Japan or anywhere outside of America and American ways."[17] Tsuda Ume felt more keenly that, as an educated Japanese woman, she was uniquely qualified to improve the condition of Japanese women.

Initially, Tsuda Ume did not receive the government-sponsored teaching position that she anticipated upon her return. The government agency that sponsored her study in the United States had disbanded and its girls' school had closed after only four years. But in 1884, her English-language skills, knowledge of American culture, and social skills with foreign dignitaries finally brought her to the attention of Itō Hirobumi, who was to become Japan's first prime minister. She entered his private household as an English-language tutor and consultant on Western style and customs. On Itō's recommendation in 1885, Tsuda Ume was appointed a teacher of English in the Peeresses' School, newly established to teach the daughters of Japanese nobility. The empress was the school's patron and Shimoda Utako—Japan's most venerated female intellectual, a poet who had received a classical Japanese education—was its headmistress. The position was precisely what she had hoped for; it offered Tsuda financial security, professional standing, and the prestige of court rank. It appeared that Tsuda finally had the opportunity to fulfill her mission of elevating the status of Japanese women through education.

It was not long, however, before Tsuda became disillusioned with teaching at the Peeresses' School and fearful that her lack of a college education would jeopardize her professional future. From the outset, Tsuda was frustrated with the elementary level of English-language instruction offered at the school and the time wasted with formalities and court ritual.[18] In addition, Tsuda began to feel personal limitations, realizing that her unique experience in the United States would not guarantee her professional status in Japan. With the development of normal schools in Japan, a college degree would soon become the necessary professional credential.[19] In 1886, Tsuda wrote to Adeline Lanman, "I sometimes wonder if it would be feasible for me to think of, or hope for such a thing as trying to get to America for a little further study and for examining the school methods, and ways of teaching in the United States. I intend to be a teacher all my life, as it is, but I should like to fit myself to be a first-rate teacher, and though I may have enough education to carry me along through ordinary paths, I want more than that. . . . I want to be well-fitted for my work, and we need all our brains and ability in Japan."[20] Tsuda Ume's wish came to the attention of Mary Morris, who had met Tsuda earlier in the Lanman home. Morris sought assistance for Tsuda through her family connections at Bryn Mawr, the newly established women's liberal arts college. Bryn Mawr agreed to admit Tsuda as a special student and waive the tuition; Morris offered to pay her personal expenses. In 1891, Tsuda was granted a two-year leave of absence from the Peeresses' School in order to study instructional methods.

At Bryn Mawr, Tsuda Ume was introduced to the educational vision of its academic dean, M. Carey Thomas. Tsuda later emulated aspects of this vision in her own school. Thomas carefully shaped Bryn Mawr as a female-centered learning community, offering undergraduate women the highest standard of university training in the United States: the equivalent of the finest men's universities.[21] As a language teacher herself, Tsuda was drawn to Thomas's view that language study would "cultivate the taste [and] judgment" of the "girls and women of the upper classes."[22] Tsuda flourished at Bryn Mawr, studying with students, many of them former teachers like herself, who shared her abiding sense of a duty to work for the advancement of women.[23] She studied English literature, philosophy, German, and biology. She excelled in laboratory science; her paper entitled "Orientation of the Frog's Eggs" was published in the British *Quarterly Journal of Microscopial Science* in 1894. Mindful of her obligation to study instructional methods, however, in January 1891 Tsuda began a term at Oswego Teacher's College in New York, where she studied the language instruction methods of Johannes Pestalozzi, which had a following among Japanese male educators who had studied in the United States. When she finished her studies at Bryn Mawr, President James Rhoads issued a certificate describing Tsuda's course of study and testifying that "Miss Tsuda has shown at this college all the virtues that grace and adorn the womanly character, and bears with her the honour, esteem, and kindly regard of all the officers and students of the college."[24] Anna Hartshorne, a Bryn Mawr classmate who later taught with Tsuda in Japan, concluded that the "best qualities of Bryn Mawr, broadmindedness, thoroughness, exact standards of scholarship, became rooted in her and were an integral part of her educational ideal."[25] Ultimately more valuable than the formal education that Tsuda received at Bryn Mawr, however, were the "honour, esteem, and kindly regard" afforded her by a valuable network of women educators and advocates for the higher education of women.

While studying at Bryn Mawr, Tsuda received frequent invitations to speak about the lives of Japanese women. Hartshorne recalled that Tsuda "made a wonderful impression"; American audiences thought that she was "like a princess."[26] Tsuda's experience in the Lanman home enabled her to move comfortably in the homes of faculty and friends of the college. Her "parlor talks" (as Hartshorne called them) were of interest to a growing segment of a social elite, who, like Mary Morris, were curious about Japanese culture and eager to offer hospitality to Japanese visitors.[27] During summers and school breaks, Tsuda spoke throughout the eastern United States, retracing earlier journeys she had made with Charles and Adeline Lanman as she talked to audiences sympathetic to the cause of women's higher education.

Tsuda's parlor talks were expanded into a book, *Japanese Girls and Women*, which she co-wrote with Alice Mabel Bacon in the summer of 1891.[28] Bacon had grown up with Yamakawa Sutematsu, one of the girls who accompanied Tsuda on her first trip to the United States; further, she was a faculty member at Hampton Institute in Virginia and founder of the Dixie Hospital. In *Japanese Girls and Women*, Tsuda and Bacon described the life cycle of Japanese females and analyzed their daily lives in terms of the productive labor carried out by women of the nobility, the middle class, the peasantry, and the urban artisan class. They cautioned readers to take account of cultural differences when making value judgments, particularly with respect to matters of Japanese women's morality. Tsuda and Bacon identified arranged marriages, limited opportunities for productive work, the misogynist ideas of Buddhism and Confucianism, and the absence of formal educational opportunities as the chief obstacles Japanese women had to overcome. They argued that educational opportunities (which would enable women to become financially independent) and the spread of Christian values would be the most effective means for elevating the status of Japanese women. Middle-class women, they concluded, offered the best hope for providing the leadership that would benefit all Japanese women.

Recognizing a growing audience interested in the cause, Tsuda initiated a project to raise money for Japanese women's higher education. With the assistance of her personal patron, Mary Morris, Tsuda launched "The Scholarship for Japanese Women," an effort to build an endowment of $8,000 that would allow Japanese women to attend college in the United States. In support of the scholarship program, Tsuda began giving more formal lectures (written with the assistance of M. Carey Thomas) to larger audiences in more public settings, but she continued to proclaim, as she had in her parlor talks and book, that education was the key to Japanese women's emancipation. Tsuda expressed her admiration for women's position in the United States, which she attributed to the power of education. "While I have been in this country, the one thing which has struck me particularly, and filled me with admiration, is the position which American women hold, the great influence that they exercise for good, the power given them by education and training, the congenial intercourse between men and women, and the sympathy existing in the homes, between brothers and sisters, husbands and wives." Tsuda was confident that the same advances were possible in Japan, and she reassured potential donors that "there has seemed to me no reason why this should not be so in my own country, for in Japan there has never been any great prejudice against women such as we find in so many countries of the East." She acknowledged, however, that due to the influence of what she termed "foreign" religions—Buddhism from India and Confucianism from China—Japanese women were subjugated by men. But, she proclaimed, "happily, the influence of Buddha and Confucius is growing, year by year, less powerful in Japan, and we are hoping that Christianity will fill the void." Tsuda boasted of the speed with which Japan had moved from feudalism to a constitutional monarchy with a popularly elected parliament, but she lamented that "with all these advances for the nation, and much progress for men, no corresponding advantages have been given to the women."[29]

From her perspective of having lived in an American home, Tsuda explained that what struck her most when she returned to Japan was "the great difference between men and women, and the absolute power which men held." Tsuda's central concern was Japanese women's lack of autonomy. "The women were entirely dependent, having no means of self-support, since no employment or occupation was open to them. . . . A woman could hold no property in her own name and her identity was merged in that of her father, husband, or some male relative. Hence, there was an utter lack of independent spirit."[30] Drawing on her own convictions, and in a calculated appeal to the audiences she addressed, Tsuda spoke to "the need of education for women of the upper classes. We should expect them to have the greatest influence." She allied herself with "the advocates of the new education," who "believe that one has a more serious part to play in the world than to be a mere ornament for the house, or plaything for the men."[31] In Japan, she said, "Christian men and those who had been abroad wished to marry cultivated women and desired that their daughters as well as their sons should be well educated."[32] Tsuda envisioned a society in which relations between men and women, husbands and wives, would be more harmonious and satisfying if women were the educated, intellectual equals of men.

Having identified the reasons for optimism, Tsuda finally arrived at the critical question: "Where are the teachers who are to train and help the eager students?"[33] She asserted that there were Japanese women who were anxious to undertake the responsibility: "They are willing to devote their lives to it, if only they were suitably prepared, but few of them have opportunities of study such as men have, for none of the higher institutions are open to women, still less have they the means to come abroad for study." While explaining the limitations of foreign missionaries, Tsuda coyly described her own advantages, asserting that "a well educated, cultivated, native woman, even though she is herself not of high rank, can as a teacher find her way to the homes of this exclusive class, and through education, the lesson of Christianity could be taught."[34] Tsuda described the goal of the scholarship program as being to educate women like herself to undertake the mission to which she, herself, was committed. Tsuda's experience in the Lanman household, her Bryn Mawr education, and her collaborations with Mary Morris, Alice Bacon, and M. Carey Thomas enabled her to craft a message to potential donors that appealed to their deeply held reform commitments and beliefs that education and Christianity were the means by which the status of women would be elevated.[35]

Tsuda and Mary Morris envisioned a permanent scholarship fund, making it possible for Japanese women to study for four years at an American institution of higher learning. The idea was to institutionalize the gift that Bryn Mawr College and Morris had bestowed upon Tsuda and make the opportunity available to women throughout Japan. "It would be open to all Japanese women, as an incentive to them, a free gift from American ladies, to show the interest which has been taken in them, and the high value attached by American ladies to education."[36] Competitive examinations, apparently modeled on Bryn Mawr's rigorous admission exams, would be used to select a student who excelled not only in English-language study, but also in Japanese language and literature. The selection of the candidate was to be made by a committee of both men and women in Japan "anxious for the spread of Christianity, and the elevation of women." In a direct appeal to members of her audience who were most clearly motivated by a desire to support foreign mission work, Tsuda concluded, "I feel that such a scholarship offered in this way, directly to the Japanese would have a very great influence, and would help to do away with the feeling now so prevalent in Japan that higher education is antagonistic to Christianity." Through the AWSJW, Tsuda sought to multiply the number of women in Japan who shared her expertise and her commitment to elevating the status of Japanese women. "The great need," she saw, was "for teachers of the higher education, for Japanese women fitted to enter, at once, into the government and private schools, to educate the Japanese girls according to American methods, to teach them by example and precept the benefits of a Christian civilization."[37]

While a shared commitment to women's higher education motivated the members of both the Japanese and American committees that administered the scholarship, disagreements over the administration of the program reflected cultural differences and the interests of individuals. The early years of the program were characterized by explicit disagreement about authority and responsibilities and implicit disagreement about the extent to which the scholarship was intended to promote Christianity. Misunderstandings between the American and Japanese committees were exacerbated by a dependence on written communication, with infrequent face-to-face meetings between the principals.[38]

The composition of the original American committee, which solicited money and supervised the education of scholarship recipients, was mandated by a constitution. Mary Morris was the chair from the establishment of the program in 1893 to her death in 1925, and M. Carey Thomas served as the committee's academic consultant. Members were drawn from the social and economic elite of three Protestant denominations in Philadelphia that were active in mission work in Japan—Episcopal, Presbyterian, and Quaker. There were no set terms: members served for the entirety of their lives, and their female descendants or women who had teaching experience in Japan replaced them. Noriko Araki and Louise Ward Demakis, who have studied the backgrounds of the committee members, characterize them as active in their churches and missionary societies. They were the wives and daughters of railroad and industrial executives, many of whom served on the board of Haverford College (a Quaker college for men). They were Republicans, although not active politically; they were not involved in women's suffrage organizations. Finally, the original members, most of whom were married and began their families in the 1870s, had never attended college. They endeavored to bestow, then, a privilege on Japanese women that they themselves had never received.[39]

With the exception of M. Carey Thomas, members of the American committee were motivated by the desire to spread Christianity, but scholarship recipients were not required to be Christian. Araki and Demakis have speculated that the conscious omission of such a requirement suggests that members of the American committee were more concerned about educating than proselytizing. Pious themselves, committee members began their meetings with a Bible reading, followed by a prayer.[40] Although AWSJW committee members chose not to require a Christian commitment, they sought to provide the students with the experience of a Christian home life. Bryn Mawr College did not offer formal religious instruction, but the AWSJW constitution stated that the committee members should offer scholarship recipients "the hospitality of their own Christian homes."[41] Committee members invited scholarship recipients to their homes, included them in family vacations, and interceded on their behalf when they experienced personal problems.

The awarding of scholarships to Japanese women was groundbreaking. Tsuda Ume established the Japanese committee, charged with the selection of the scholarship recipients, after her return to Japan in 1892. She became its chair and appointed four men and three women; in Japan at the time, a committee including both men and women was virtually unprecedented. While Mary Morris had appointed members of the American committee on the basis of personal acquaintance and social connections, Tsuda sought to establish the prestige of the scholarship program in Japan by engaging the assistance of national leaders in women's higher education. The male members of the committee were administrators of women's schools, while the female members had been educated in the United States. To ensure that the committee members in Japan shared the American women's values, all Japanese members had to be approved by two Christian ministers and were to "be such as are anxious for the spread of Christianity and the elevation of women in Japan."[42] Tsuda demonstrated that she was politically astute by appointing committee members from both public and private educational institutions, but, in keeping with her reservation about missionaries, none of the committee members was associated with a foreign mission school. The establishment of the scholarship program and the committee to administer it enabled Tsuda to move into a position of leadership in women's higher education in Japan.

The most significant conflict between the Japanese and American committees was the selection of scholarship recipients. The American committee set the criteria for selection, but the Japanese committee was responsible for advertising the scholarship, conducting competitive examinations, and selecting the final candidate. An early conflict was evident in the writing of the Japanese committee's constitution, when the American women required the deletion of the statement that the scholarship was intended to train teachers.[43] In general, the Americans wanted the criteria for selection to be as general as possible, and the recipient to have as wide a choice of studies as possible. Scholarship recipients had the option to study at Bryn Mawr, a liberal arts college, and they were also permitted to study at the Women's Medical College of Pennsylvania or Drexel Institute, a technical school. The Japanese committee, on the other hand, sought to restrict the pool of potential candidates and select only those applicants who would return to teach in Japan.

While the wording of the scholarship advertisement sparked open disagreement, in other instances the Japanese committee was able to thwart the intentions of the Americans simply because the latter understood so little about the circumstances in which the selection process was implemented. For example, while the Americans chose not to limit the selection solely to Christians, the requirement that the recipient be fluent in English meant that in all likelihood the most successful candidate would have been educated in mission schools and accustomed to conversing with native English speakers, most likely missionaries. The competitive examination, lasting five days and modeled on Bryn Mawr's rigorous entrance examination, was designed to establish an objective basis for selection, but personal tutoring, particularly by Tsuda herself, increased the likelihood that the successful candidate would be a person known to members of the Japanese committee. Ultimately, the examination requirement was contested and there were times when circumstances forced the American committee to waive it.[44] The Japanese committee was adamant that the scholarship recipient literally come from Japan; one highly qualified candidate, already in the United States, was disqualified because she could not be present in Tokyo for the selection process. It was consistent with Japanese values to create a selection system that enabled the committee members to exercise their judgment and select an individual whose personal character they could guarantee.

Financial considerations also restricted the pool of eligible students. While the scholarship funded tuition and living expenses in the United States, the recipient's family was required to pay transportation costs from Tokyo to Philadelphia, as well as the costs of a Western wardrobe. As a result, all but upper-middle-class women were eliminated from the competition. For more than a year, Tsuda had devoted time to soliciting funds for the scholarship, but they fell short of the $8,000 endowment necessary to create sufficient annual interest income. Moreover, even before the first scholarship recipient arrived in Philadelphia, the American committee recognized the need to fund one or two years of preparatory work, which was completed at Ivy House, a school in Germantown, Pennsylvania. Over the years, the American committee faced financial challenges, particularly following recession in the national economy or special expenses associated with unanticipated travel opportunities or emergency medical expenses for students. To meet these needs, American committee members charged themselves annual membership dues and the committee was expanded to include contributors who did not participate in the program's administration.

In addition to its financial challenges, the American committee faced unanticipated difficulties in providing personal assistance to and supervision of the scholarship recipients. Members' correspondence, particularly in the early years of the scholarship program, reveals that they had unrealistically high expectations of the scholarship recipients' English skills and familiarity with American culture. Their expectations had been based on the standard of Tsuda Ume, who had been raised in an American family and educated in the United States.

Over the years, committee members were advised by American women who had taught in Japan, and some traveled to Japan themselves; however, particularly in the early years, members of the American committee were ill-prepared to understand how difficult it was to bring the necessities of daily life from Japan or how unsuitable the students' personal possessions were for life in the United States. Matsuda Michi, the first of the scholarship recipients, carried the greatest burden resulting from cultural misunderstanding. When her $12 monthly personal allowance proved insufficient for the purchase of Western clothing and its repair, the American committee became particularly concerned about her "extravagance." Matsuda's most critical failing in the eyes of the American committee women was her inability to mend her own clothing. The American women were unaware that Japanese girls were taught to weave rather than sew because a kimono is a garment that is wrapped—not seamed, hemmed, or held together by buttons. During her first summer in the United States, the American committee enrolled Matsuda in a domestic course. They were concerned, not because she was in their estimation ill-prepared for marriage, but because she would not be able to take care of herself. They valued the independence afforded by a skill that they considered fundamental.[45]

While the early problems encountered by the American committee reflected the cultural insularity of its members, later experience reflected increased sensitivity and a continuing commitment to hospitality. For example, a scholarship recipient experiencing medical problems was brought to New York by a committee member so that she could be treated by a Japanese doctor, and her medical expenses, first covered by an emergency loan, were ultimately paid by the committee. The administration of the AWSJW was characterized by intensely close personal relationships between the scholarship recipients and members of the committee—relationships that paralleled the family-like ties between Tsuda Ume and the Lanmans, providing students with a broader view of American culture.

From the scholarship's establishment in 1893 to the beginning of World War II, eleven Japanese women were AWSJW recipients. International politics between the world wars created complications for the scholarship recipients, who experienced increasing anti-Japanese sentiment in the United States and charges of disloyalty when they returned to Japan. During World War II, two scholarships were awarded to Japanese-American students. Between 1949 and 1976, twelve scholarships were awarded to students for graduate work, a change that reflected the increased opportunities for women to attend college in Japan following World War II. The scholarship committee disbanded in 1976 and donated the remaining $20,000 to a Bryn Mawr College scholarship fund for Japanese students.[46]

JOSHI EIGAKU JUKU AND THE COMMITTEE FOR MISS TSUDA'S SCHOOL FOR GIRLS

The network of personal friends, professional contacts, and financial supporters Tsuda had developed in the United States made it possible for her to establish her own school, Joshi Eigaku Juku, in 1900. The demands of administering her own school both increased her dependence on members of the AWSJW American committee and made their collaboration on the scholarship more problematic. However, it was with the establishment of her own school that Tsuda ultimately felt herself to have fulfilled the imperial commission with which she had originally been sent to the United States: to educate Japanese women and increase their opportunities.

Tsuda had long dreamed of establishing her own school, and had prepared to do so by studying in the United States, developing a patronage network, and undertaking a fact-finding tour in which she visited the newly developing women's academies in England.[47] At Bryn Mawr, Tsuda had imbibed an elitist approach to women's higher education that focused on serving upper-class women, maintaining rigorous entrance requirements, and demanding the same level of academic performance that was expected in the most prestigious men's schools. M. Carey Thomas, a pioneer administrator in women's higher education, communicated to Tsuda the value of developing rituals (opening ceremonies, theatricals, commencement exercises) to define the identity of the college, building a strong alumnae base to support the college, and soliciting funds not only from individuals, but also from foundations that favored projects in higher education.[48] In the classrooms and laboratories of Bryn Mawr, Tsuda had learned to appreciate personal mentoring by faculty who expected their students to think independently and express their opinions. Tsuda's experience at Oswego's Teacher's College gave her knowledge of cutting-edge English-language instruction methods that, along with her fluency in English, enabled her to become recognized as the leading authority on English-language instruction in Japan. Her tour of women's schools in Britain reinforced Tsuda's belief in the education of women in women-only schools, as opposed to the men's institutions that marginalized women in related but unequal "annex schools." Perhaps most importantly, the progress that some women's schools had made in a short period of time filled Tsuda with hope that her dream was a real possibility.[49]

Tsuda timed the opening of her school to take advantage of both her own professional preparation and national legislation. The Act of Girls' High Schools (1899) required every prefecture (state) to have at least one public high school for girls. By 1900, fifty-two schools enrolled twelve thousand girls, but no institution existed to offer them broader educational opportunities after graduation. Moreover, no educational institutions certified women to teach English at the girls' schools. Tsuda developed Joshi Eigaku Juku to fill these needs. The early national reputation of the school was secured by Tsuda's association with the AWSJW and by the texts and magazines she published about teaching English. With the 1903 Act of Vocational Colleges, Joshi Eigaku Juku became the only government-approved women's college in Japan. Graduates of the school had a reputation for being able to converse easily in English, and in 1905, Joshi Eigaku Juku became the first and only women's institution whose graduates were exempted from taking government examinations for teaching certification. Thereafter, the two most prestigious men's schools, the Tokyo Higher Normal School and the Tokyo Foreign Language School, sent their students to observe language instruction at Tsuda's school.[50] Remarkably, this achievement was made possible in great part because of the philanthropic efforts of American women benefactors.

Joshi Eigaku Juku was established with an endowment raised by Tsuda's longtime colleagues and benefactors. In March 1900, Alice Mabel Bacon—co-author of *Japanese Girls and Women*—went to Philadelphia to talk about plans for the school with a group of Tsuda's old friends. Bryn Mawr classmate Anna Hartshorne spoke of the practical issues that she had discussed with Tsuda in Tokyo. M. Carey Thomas presided over the meeting, speaking of the values that Tsuda and the assembled women shared. Mary Morris, Tsuda's benefactor, was named chair of the Committee for Miss Tsuda's School in Japan. She contributed half of the two thousand dollars collected that summer to provide the initial capital for the school.[51]

While the memberships of the American committee of the AWSJW and the Committee for Miss Tsuda's School for Girls overlapped significantly, the establishment of Tsuda's own school complicated the administration of the AWSJW. Contrary to the wishes of the American committee, Tsuda wanted to use the scholarship, which she had campaigned so hard to develop, exclusively for the benefit of her school and its graduates. Seeking a well-qualified faculty for her school, Tsuda also aimed to decrease the scholarship recipients' period of study in order to permit more women to receive funding. The American committee was determined, however, that the scholarship would remain open to all qualified applicants and that all recipients would earn college degrees. At times there was a direct conflict of interest; for example, in 1902 Tsuda offered to prepare scholarship recipients at her school for an annual payment of $500. Miss Stevens, a member of the AWSJW committee and principal of the academy in Philadelphia that prepared the first scholarship recipients, insisted that a two-year period of preparation take place in the United States. In 1904, a member of the Japanese committee traveled to Philadelphia to present Tsuda's request that the AWSJW be awarded exclusively to graduates of her own school. The American committee's rejection of the request offended Tsuda, and during a 1907 visit with the American committee she requested release from her responsibilities as chair of the Japanese committee, citing the hard feelings and criticism that appeared when a scholarship recipient came from her own school. The request was approved, but Tsuda remained on the Japanese committee, serving in the capacity of secretary, and she continued to control the committee's decisions.[52] While conflicts resulted from Tsuda's efforts to promote the interests of her school and the efforts of the American committee to retain their original intent, the AWSJW was critical to the success of Joshi Eigaku Juku. Scholarship recipients represented their alma mater when they studied at Bryn Mawr and, like Tsuda before them, they did extensive fundraising for the school. Upon returning to Japan, they provided Joshi Eigaku Juku with a well-qualified, loyal cadre of faculty.

In addition to the financial support of the AWSJW committee and the Committee for Miss Tsuda's School for Girls, Joshi Eigaku Juku benefited from a variety of forms of philanthropic service. Foremost was the willingness of women to teach as volunteers. Alice Mabel Bacon took a two-year leave from her teaching position at Hampton Institute to assist Tsuda when she opened the school. She accepted no salary (Tsuda herself accepted only a half-salary) and even taught part-time in other schools in Tokyo to contribute toward the operating expenses of Joshi Eigaku Juku. Following Bacon's departure in 1902, Anna Hartshorne traveled to Japan and devoted her life to teaching at the school, assisting Tsuda and also fundraising in the United States. During the early decades of Joshi Eigaku Juku, Bryn Mawr alumnae and daughters of members of the AWSJW American Committee also supplemented the Japanese faculty. Like Tsuda herself, these American women were uniquely qualified to provide the educational opportunities that became the hallmark of the school. They developed students' capacities to speak English fluently, understand American and British values through the study of literature, and think independently. These women shared a sense of Christian calling to the mission field, and their presence enhanced the Christian influence in the school's curriculum and residential program. Like Tsuda, they believed that educational opportunities and the spread of Christian values would elevate the status of women.[53]

The dependence of Joshi Eigaku Juku on American philanthropy took Tsuda out of the classroom, making her a full-time fundraiser. Tsuda noted, ruefully, that the Japanese government supported the best men's universities, but higher educational opportunities for women were dependent on donations. Tsuda made frequent trips to the United States to maintain personal relationships with the Committee for Miss Tsuda's School and the AWSJW American committee. She lectured and met with individual donors on American tours organized largely by the affluent and socially well placed Bryn Mawr alumnae and their husbands. When she was in Japan, her days were frequently devoted to hosting American donors. Tsuda was constantly engaged in correspondence as well, mostly with Bryn Mawr alumnae; she asked for donations to capital projects and specific gifts of used items, such as books for the library and a phonograph player for the music room.[54]

Perhaps because of the extent to which Joshi Eigaku Juku was dependent on gifts of money and the work of volunteer teachers, and because she often articulated her own project in terms of moral obligation to the empress and the nation, Tsuda consistently reminded students and alumnae about the importance of service. While enrolled, students participated in raising funds for the school, often by presenting theatricals much like those Tsuda had seen at Bryn Mawr. Graduates were asked to volunteer at least once a week, using their skills and talents to enrich the curriculum and program of residential students. Ultimately, Tsuda asked her students to devote their lives to service, to raise the status of Japanese women through their individual actions. In 1915, she urged students, "Humbly strive to be worthy of respect so that all must acknowledge the value of your training, and bear in mind always that where much has been received, much must be given to others. If you can succeed in these things even in part, you will pave the way for privileges and the honor of Japanese women."[55]

NOTES

1. Katherine E. McBride, quoted in "Japanese Alumnae, 1973," *Bryn Mawr Alumna Bulletin* (1973), 8.

2. Tsuda is her family name and Ume is her given name. In adulthood, she added the suffix "ko" to her given name, becoming Tsuda Umeko.

3. The values shared by these women have been identified as representative of "Victorian liberal feminism"; see Joyce Senders Pedersen, "Education, Gender and Social Change in Victorian Liberal Feminist Theory," *History of European Ideas* 8 (1987): 503–19.

4. Quoted in James T. Conte, "Overseas Study in the Meiji Period: Japanese Students in America, 1867–1902" (Ph.D. diss., Princeton University, 1977), 45.

5. Translated by and quoted in Michio Nagai, "Westernization and Japanization," in *Tradition and Modernization in Japanese Culture,* ed. Donald H. Shively (Princeton: Princeton University Press, 1971), 47.

6. The girls were Yoshimasu Ryoko (age fourteen), Ueda Teiko (fourteen), Yamakawa Sutematsu (eleven), Nagai Shigeko (seven), and Tsuda Ume (six).

7. Tsuda Umeko, "Japanese Women Emancipated," reprinted in *Tsuda Umeko monjo* (The writings of Tsuda Umeko), ed. Furuki Yoshiko (Kodaira, Japan: Tsuda Juku Daigaku, 1984), 78–79.

8. Charles Lanman, *The Japanese in America* (New York: University Publishing Company, 1872), 48.

9. Barbara Rose, *Tsuda Umeko and Women's Education in Japan* (New Haven, Conn.: Yale University Press, 1992), 6–7. Rose does not cite specific sources in which Tsuda articulated the values of domesticity. Rather, she assumes that popular figures such as Catharine Beecher would have shaped Tsuda's thinking (31–32).

10. Quoted in Yoshiko Furuki, *The White Plum: A Biography of Ume Tsuda, Pioneer in the Higher Education of Japanese Women* (New York: Weatherhill, 1991), 20.

11. Tsuda Umeko, "Waga Knonode Yomishi Shomotsu" (Books I enjoyed reading), in *Tsuda Umeko monjo,* 65–68.

12. Louise Ward Demakis, "No Madam Butterflies," *Journal of American and Canadian Studies* 4 (1989): 5.

13. Yoshiko Furuki, ed., *The Attic Letters: Ume Tsuda's Correspondence to Her American Mother* (New York: Weatherhill, 1991), 23.

14. Sadako Ōgata, "Women's Participation in the Modernization of Japan," *Studia Diplomatica* 30 (1977): 205.

15. Furuki, *Attic Letters,* 3.

16. Ibid., 82.

17. Ibid., 51.

18. Ibid., 223.

19. Rose, *Tsuda Umeko,* 79.

20. Furuki, *Attic Letters,* 250.

21. Helen Lefkowitz Horowitz, *Alma Mater: Design and Experience in the Women's Colleges from Their Nineteenth-Century Beginnings to the 1930s,* 2nd ed. (Amherst: University of Massachusetts Press, 1993), 115–16.

22. Ibid., 119.

23. Rose, *Tsuda Umeko,* 83.

24. Quoted in Furuki, *The White Plum,* 86. See also "The Years of Preparation: A Memory of Miss Tsuda," *Alumnae Report* (Bryn Mawr College), no. 35 (1930).

25. Hartshorne quoted in Furuki, *The White Plum,* 86.

26. Hartshorne quoted in Rose, *Tsuda Umeko,* 84.

27. T. J. Jackson Lears, *No Place of Grace: Antimodernism and the Transformation of American Culture, 1880–1920* (New York: Pantheon, 1981), 148–49.

28. Alice Mabel Bacon, *Japanese Girls and Women* (Boston: Houghton Mifflin, 1891). Although the book was co-authored by Tsuda, it was published under Bacon's name in order to protect Tsuda from criticism in Japan.

29. Tsuda Umeko, "The Education of Japanese Women," in *Tsuda Umeko monjo*, 19, 20, 21. Tsuda was a baptized Christian. Akiko Tokuza has observed, "As a social philosophy, Confucianism emphasized a hierarchical order, upheld by loyalty and the submission of inferiors to superiors. Women were seen as fundamentally inferior, this subordination thus having philosophical justification. Moreover, Japanese Buddhism tended to teach that '[women] by nature are covetous and sinful,' and thus at a grave disadvantage in seeking enlightenment. This criticism of women's intelligence, autonomy, and moral worth was essential to the total subordination of women that society demanded" (Akiko Tokuza, *The Rise of the Feminist Movement in Japan* [Tokyo: Keio University Press, 1999], 40–41).

30. Tsuda, "The Education of Japanese Women," 23.

31. Ibid., 22.

32. Ibid., 24.

33. Ibid., 25.

34. Ibid., 26.

35. Describing the women's foreign mission movement, Patricia R. Hill has observed, "Gradually, education of women in foreign lands became not so much a strategy for evangelization as an instrument for social change. The ablest students were selected for further education . . . not for marriage and maternity, but for positions of leadership in their own societies" (Patricia R. Hill, *The World Their Household: The American Women's Foreign Mission Movement and Cultural Transformation, 1870–1920* [Ann Arbor: University of Michigan Press, 1985], 134).

36. Tsuda, "The Education of Japanese Women," 26.

37. Ibid., 27.

38. Noriko Araki and Louise Ward Demakis, "The Scholarship for Japanese Women," *Japan Christian Quarterly* 53 (1987): 30.

39. Ibid., 18.

40. Ibid., 18, 16.

41. AWSJW Constitution, Tsuda College Archive, in the library of Tsuda Juku Daigaku, Kodaira, Tokyo (hereafter cited as TCA).

42. Japan Scholarship Committee Constitution, 3–4, TCA.

43. Minutes of the Japan Scholarship Committee Meeting, 9 April 1892, MSS, TCA.

44. Minutes of the Japan Scholarship Committee Meeting, 29 January 1906, MSS, TCA.

45. Mary E. Stevens to Juliana Wood and Mrs. Robert Haines, 15 May 1895, MSS, TCA.

46. Araki and Demakis, "The Scholarship for Japanese Women," 31.

47. Tsuda made the tour at the suggestion of her mentor, M. Carey Thomas, who had made a similar tour of American women's colleges before she began her appointment as dean of Bryn Mawr College (Helen Lefkowitz Horowitz, *The Power and Passion of M. Carey Thomas* [New York: Knopf, 1994]).

48. Both Bryn Mawr College and Tsuda's Joshi Eigaku Juku received lucrative grants from the Rockefeller Foundation to fund capital projects. Following the Great Earthquake of 1923, which destroyed the Joshi Eigaku Juku campus, the Laura Spelman Rockefeller Memorial pledged one hundred thousand dollars in matching funds. See Furuki, *The White Plum*, 132.

49. Ibid., 96.

50. Ibid., 103, 108, 110–11, 121.

51. Ibid., 103.

52. Araki and Demakis, "The Scholarship for Japanese Women," 24.

53. See Maude Whitmore Madden, *Women of the Meiji Era* (New York: Fleming N. Revell, 1919), 28–45 for profiles of women who taught at Tsuda's school.

54. Rose, *Tsuda Umeko*, 136–37.

55. "Miss Tsuda's Address to the Graduates," Alumnae Report of the Joshi Eigaku Juku, July 1915, in *Tsuda Umeko monjo*, 151.

14. Supporting Females in a Male Field: Philanthropy for Women's Engineering Education

Amy Sue Bix

Through most of the twentieth century in the United States, science was commonly assumed to belong to men's intellectual sphere and workplace. Narrow assumptions about proper gender roles discouraged many women from pursuing scientific studies, while many science programs discouraged women's applications or flatly denied women access. For those women who chose to persist, moving ahead in the scientific profession required fighting persistent employment discrimination and institutional obstacles within academia, government, and business. In the face of such structural barriers, the force of "creative philanthropy" helped generate a few meaningful opportunities, as Margaret Rossiter has detailed. Endowments specifically established for hiring female scholars brought women into new slots on the faculties of both Harvard and the University of Michigan during the post–World War II period, Rossiter explains. Radcliffe dean Bernice Brown Cronkhite took one step toward remedying universities' usually miserable treatment of female graduate students by raising funds to open a dormitory and living center for those women in Cambridge in 1957. Meanwhile, ever since the late 1800s, the American Association of University Women had awarded fellowships to female students. By the late 1960s, generous donations from members enabled the AAUW to increase both the number and the size of its fellowships; in cases where departments proved reluctant to support female graduate students, AAUW assistance was especially valuable.[1]

Just as the organizers of such efforts strove to help women scientists overcome some of the difficulties facing them in graduate school

and in the professions, the same power of "female creative philanthropy" also played a role in shaping conditions facing women in
American engineering. Even more than in science, American engineering has a gendered history, one which for decades prevented
women in any significant numbers from finding a comfortable place
in the predominantly male technical world. In the United States during the 1950s, women studying or working in engineering defied traditional gender norms and were popularly perceived as oddities at best
and outcasts at worst. Overall, women made up less than 2 percent of
students in college and university engineering programs during those
years. Yet by century's end, women's presence in American engineering
had become accepted, even encouraged (at least officially). In 1996,
women made up roughly 18 percent of students earning bachelor's
degrees in engineering. Such a substantial gain was no coincidence.
This dramatic change in the gender dimensions of this field reflects
in part a strategic use of philanthropy to counter barriers rooted in
the institutional culture of higher education and in the social culture
of engineering.

In the narrower sense of the word "philanthropy"—that is, in the
realm of financial donations—women supported other women by endowing scholarships for female engineering students or by funding the
construction of women's dormitories. But the true historical force of
philanthropy becomes clear when the more expansive sense of the
word is considered. Philanthropy as benevolence—doing good—was
crucial to expanding opportunities for women in engineering. Women
volunteered countless hours to assist other women and young girls in
pursuing the dream of an engineering education. In individual efforts,
female engineers mentored others, taught special classes, and offered
informal advice on both career and personal questions. At a group
level, female engineering students at dozens of colleges banded together to organize support networks and numerous activities. At an
institutional level, the Society of Women Engineers (SWE) established many different support mechanisms that expanded over the
years.

This tradition of help extended across generations. Well into her
eighties, Lillian Gilbreth (whose family life was famously portrayed in
Cheaper by the Dozen) traveled around the country to meet with female
engineering undergraduates. In turn, these college students hosted
outreach programs for girls in high school, junior high, and elementary
school. The net effect contributed significantly toward making the

intellectual, social, and personal atmosphere for women in engineering far more welcoming during the 1950s, 1960s, 1970s, and 1980s. Philanthropy, of course, had its limitations; voluntary efforts could not satisfy all needs, could not always overcome ingrained institutional lethargy or individual resistance, and did not instantly turn the field of engineering into a female paradise. Much work still remains to be done to draw more women into engineering and enable them to advance in the profession. Across the United States today, many individuals and groups continue to develop outreach and support programs for women in engineering. This article offers the background history of such ongoing work, female creative philanthropy aimed at addressing the traditional gender limitations of engineering and at broadening women's opportunities in this avenue of education.

MIT, A PHILANTHROPY CASE STUDY: MONEY AND MUTUAL SUPPORT

For decades, Americans treated the professional study of technology as men's territory. Well into the twentieth century, preeminent engineering schools remained largely closed to women. Rensselaer Polytechnic Institute only opened its doors to female students as a World War II emergency measure. Other universities took even longer to acknowledge women: Caltech, Georgia Tech, and Princeton did not admit female undergraduates until the 1950s and 1960s, and then only after extensive agonizing and argument. In each case, shifting composition of the student body forced universities to rethink their physical, social, and academic environments. Faculty, administrators, and students faced the challenge of creating space for women in an intellectual world and a campus climate assumed to be for men.[2]

The Massachusetts Institute of Technology had actually been co-educational since 1871. Its first female graduate, Ellen Swallow Richards, had created the Women's Laboratory, a special program that she hoped would keep MIT involved in training other women in chemistry. But school trustees resisted admitting "coeds" (as female students were called, and as I will therefore refer to them here) to regular courses, citing the lack of suitable accommodations. In 1882, alumnae raised $8,000 to build women's bathrooms, aiming to ensure that MIT could no longer excuse its neglect by citing inadequate facilities. The first women's lounge was "a tiny cubbyhole with one rocking chair and little else in the way of comfort"; the next contained "a sink, locker, some old sofas, and . . . numberless cockroaches." A renovated Margaret Cheney Suite opened in 1939; coeds called it "a feminine retreat in the midst of a male environment," a "refuge" where they could study, relax, and eat lunch.[3]

Between the 1920s and the 1940s, MIT averaged fifty female students on campus each year, amidst about five thousand men. In one sense, coeds represented a curiosity. The student newspaper introduced a 1940 class member as a New York "glamor girl" who wanted to work on cancer research and won a hundred-dollar bet from fellow debutantes by gaining admission.[4] But officially, women students remained invisible. President Karl Compton told incoming students, "In choosing MIT, you've taken on a man-size job," and campus traditions represented masculinity itself. As an official welcome, the institution held a "smoker" for freshmen and their fathers; initiation took place at MIT camp and featured water fights with the sophomores, baseball games with faculty, and plenty of male bonding. Even curricular activities seem to have presented problems for inclusion of coeds. For instance, civil engineering students learned surveying and other field techniques at a rough camp whose accommodations were judged unsuitable for females. Mechanical engineering class required round-the-clock observations of engine performance; generations of male students turned the "twenty-four-hour boiler tests" into beer parties. The prospect of women hanging out with men overnight in the lab seemed inappropriate.[5]

World War II brought massive upheavals to campus routine, and Compton seized the occasion to rethink policy. Contemplating the postwar place of women at MIT, he wrote, "For reasons, some logical and some traditional, technology has been predominantly of interest to the male of the species. [Nevertheless] the female continues to display both interest and effectiveness in technological pursuits, . . . slowly but definitely increasing." Compton noted that MIT had never helped coeds find housing in Cambridge, a "serious" problem that made parents nervous about letting their daughters attend. One mother, "afraid that her daughter will develop into a queer sort of person interested only in her work," had wanted supervised housing "as a good influence and balance wheel." Compton recommended that MIT rent or buy an old house to fix up as a women's dorm, an idea seconded by Florence Stiles, advisor to women students. Stiles noted regretfully that while coeds entered MIT with records at least equal to their male counterparts, only one in twenty completed degrees. She hoped a centralized residence could create "esprit de corps" among female students and prevent so many from dropping out.[6]

In 1945, as "a small scale experiment," MIT opened a women's house at 120 Bay State Road in Boston. The location—a half-hour distant from campus by subway and trolley—proved inconvenient. More unfortunately, since the Bay State house held only fourteen first-year women, MIT capped female enrollment at that number (plus a few married and commuter students). Admissions officers discouraged many high school girls from applying and ultimately evaluated women more selectively than men. Typically, MIT rejected four qualified women each year due to lack of dorm space alone. Throughout the foreseeable future, officials admitted, coeds would "continue to be grossly outnumbered by men in classroom and lab."[7]

This attitude summarized the postwar stance of the school: as long as MIT could fit in a few women without much trouble, it would, while generally ignoring the existence of this anomalous population. In 1947, the dean of students defined MIT as an institution intended "to prepare men for . . . engineering, . . . [and] educate . . . men for responsible citizenship."[8] As women's advisor, Stiles explained, the sense was that "women in general do not make acceptable engineers."[9] One observer later wrote, "Before 1960, women entered MIT at their own risk. If they succeeded, fine; if they failed—well, no one had expected them to succeed."[10] The few coeds enrolled hesitated to rock the boat. "I was very conscious of having to represent women in each class. If I did anything wrong, . . . said anything stupid, it would be ammunition for all the men who didn't want us there in the first place," recalled engineering graduate Christina Jansen. "Discriminatory events were so common that it didn't occur to us to object." Besides, "other engineering schools weren't accepting women, . . . so even though MIT was only accepting twenty a year . . . I felt MIT was doing us an enormous favor to have us there at all."[11]

Skeptics doubted it would ever prove "possible to provide a small group of women . . . with a sound environment for study in an institution primarily designed for men."[12] The 1950s brought further makeshift housing arrangements. MIT tried putting coeds in Boston University dorms, but noise made studying impossible. Bexley Hall at MIT, which housed the few women students who survived their first year, had no dining hall or social areas to foster any sense of community. In addition, coed life offered few amenities: MIT's gym barred women and granted swimming pool access only at rare, inconvenient hours. In terms of facilities, administrators conceded, "Women are the 'forgotten men' at MIT."[13]

The dean of students concluded that MIT faced a fundamental choice: either "eliminate women students . . . ; or, decide we really want women, plan an adequate set-up, and then deliberately go out and get more good girls."[14] Many argued for eliminating coeducation, noting that six of twenty-three new women had run into first-semester academic trouble. Margaret Alvort, women's-house supervisor, wrote that her "doubt as to whether [coeds] belong . . . has grown into certainty that they do not." If MIT wanted to serve the nation by turning out as many excellent scientists and engineers as possible, then "there is little in the records of the girls . . . to justify their continuance."[15] MIT's medical director agreed: "[W]hen there is such a shortage of engineers, one wonders if we are justified in taking positions away from male students for female." Coeds brought "pleasure and ornamentation" to campus, but could rarely hold their own against "high-grade intellects." Further, to try to do so would be self-detrimental: while MIT men displayed healthy competitiveness, aggression in women signified emotional "conflicts" and rejection of femininity. In short, he declared, "except for the rare individual woman, [MIT] is an unsuitable place."[16]

Significantly, MIT president James Killian believed some women could succeed and therefore deserved access. He wrote, "I do not see how the Institute, having admitted women for so long, can now change"—nor should it, considering that Cold War competition against the Soviets demanded that the U.S. develop *all* professional talent. Striving to "think more boldly . . . about recognizing [women's] presence," Killian broached the idea of setting up a women's college inside MIT, similar to Oxford's system or the Harvard-Radcliffe arrangement. Women would attend classes with men but have a separate dormitory with self-contained eating and recreation facilities. Plans for a women's college could attract support from private donors, Killian predicted, and for the first time "really justify . . . admitting women students."[17]

In 1960, Katharine Dexter McCormick pledged $1.5 million to build MIT's first on-campus women's dorm. At the turn of the century, McCormick had attended MIT as a "special student" for three years to prepare for qualifying exams, then earned a degree in biology after four additional years. In her will, she wrote, "Since my graduation in 1904, I have wished to express my gratitude to the Institute for its advanced policy of scientific education for women . . . , which has been of inestimable value to me throughout my life." McCormick knew that in her day, MIT had enrolled forty-four women, a figure that had risen only slightly five decades later. When announcing McCormick's donation, MIT president Julius Stratton observed that the gift "affords us an unprecedented opportunity to improve [women students'] residential and social environment, advance the[ir] development . . . in the scientific professions. . . . Indeed, woman's potential for achievement in these fields represents one of the great latent resources of the country."[18]

The new building was conveniently located just one block away from MIT's main instructional complex. The architect took pains to plan feminine amenities, such as bathroom space for hand laundry and places downstairs for residents to receive male visitors. Dedication of McCormick Hall in 1963 attracted national publicity. "Hardly anyone imagines girls attending mighty MIT," *Time* reported. "Yet last week Tech . . . dedicated its first women's dormitory to go with its first women's dean, an attractive blonde lured from nearby Radcliffe."[19] *Seventeen* touted MIT's "luxurious new women's dorm overlooking the Charles River."[20]

MIT used McCormick Hall's opening to draw attention to its female students. Noting that "opportunities for women in science [and] engineering . . . are clearly increasing," the 1963 catalog mentioned up front that MIT was coed. In 1964, women's applications jumped fifty percent. McCormick wrote to Stratton that she was "happy to hear of the increase. . . . I have been so grateful for all I received from the Institute that I realize how much Tech will mean to them, and I am happy to think that perhaps the women's dormitory has been a factor in this increase."[21] Backers of coeducation hailed McCormick Hall as a "vote of confidence," "testimony . . . that women are to remain a permanent part of MIT."[22] Now that the university had finally created physical place on campus for female students, women's dean Jacquelyn Mattfeld called on MIT to integrate coeds intellectually and socially. A "conservative . . . Wall Street attitude toward women still runs through MIT's veins," she declared; many male professors and students regarded female undergrads as "incompetent, unnatural, and intruders."[23]

McCormick initially provided beds for 120 coeds, more than ever before. Yet with increased applications, deans forecast that MIT would soon run short of women's housing again. Furthermore, Mattfeld considered the first phase of construction insufficient to improve women's living environment. McCormick residents had difficulties establishing a healthy sense of community and creating a workable student government association. Coeds bemoaned "the drawn out struggles of living with two girls known to be suicidal, the feeling of being trapped in an elegant hotel with no place to get away to when one's own room felt oppressive, the sense that . . . 'no faculty member really cares if you ever get to be a scientist.' "[24]

To raise morale, Mattfeld looked to McCormick's funding for the second stage of construction, which could double women's housing. Admissions staff confirmed they could find another fifty good female candidates each year, doubling the number per class.[25] There was no reason for "fear that MIT will suddenly be over-run by the Fair Sex," Mattfeld reassured doubters; raising female enrollment to four hundred would only lift women from 3 to 8 percent of the total student body. Moreover, she argued, improving "educational opportunities for one portion of the population cannot help but be beneficial to the whole." Mattfeld wanted MIT to become a model academic community recognizing women's scientific and engineering potential. She emphasized that McCormick's second tower should include not just more beds, but also recreational facilities such as swimming pools and music studios. Coeds would perform better, Mattfeld insisted, once they felt at home.[26]

Even as Mattfeld pored over blueprints for expanded undergraduate housing, McCormick instead suggested that the second tower house female graduate students, whose greater professional commitment seemed to make them better "investments." MIT worked to persuade her that female undergraduate enrollment had not yet reached optimum size. Women would only continue on to graduate study in science if they had a supportive undergraduate climate, officials stressed. Moreover, graduate women, especially married ones, did not want dormitory life.

Administrators convinced McCormick that undergraduate women's housing remained essential, and indeed, her donation of dormitory funds proved vital. In days when many factors discouraged girls from pursuing professional interests, MIT presented positive pictures of female science and engineering majors. Descriptions of McCormick life suggested that coeds were not unwomanly freaks obsessed with mathematics; one article observed that the "condition of floor kitchenettes and . . . sewing machine[s] suggests that [coeds] cook and sew as well as run computers." Administrators made dorm activity part of strategies encouraging women to succeed in male-dominated fields. MIT brought female visiting professors, such as neurobiologist Rita Levi-Montalcini, to spend weeks in residence at McCormick, talking to coeds about their research and their experiences as female professionals.[27]

Even as they met with renowned women scholars, this new McCormick generation of MIT coeds gained national visibility themselves as they began to confront frustrations more openly and band together to consider remedies. After receiving degrees, numerous MIT graduates encountered employment discrimination: companies questioned how long a woman engineer would remain on the job. To address such issues, the newly invigorated Association of Women Students (AWS) helped organize a "Symposium on American Women in Science and Engineering" at MIT in 1964. Planners hoped to attract widespread media coverage, teaching industry professionals and the public that women could be good scientists and engineers. Organizers also wanted to encourage young women to consider those careers, aiming to describe "the mythical and actual difficulties they may . . . encounter, to convey that these are not insurmountable, and to assure that the satisfaction and rewards are high." The symposium attracted college faculty and administrators, high school students and guidance counselors, and more than 250 delegates from Smith, Radcliffe, Wellesley, the University of California, Georgia Tech, Northwestern, Purdue, and other institutions. The novel coming together of such a large group served an important purpose in itself; one mechanical engineering major from Michigan State University said she found it "reassuring to see so many other women in the same situation." Speakers such as Radcliffe president Mary Bunting called on employers to provide day care and flexible schedules to help women balance motherhood and work. University of Chicago professor Alice Rossi urged society to cultivate girls' independence, curiosity, and reasoning. Psychologist Erik Erikson encouraged women to stop depending on men for approval, to envision a future beyond being a husband's domestic helpmate.[28]

In the early 1970s, MIT instituted an ad hoc committee "to review the environment . . . for women students." Co-chaired by engineering professor Mildred Dresselhaus and engineering major Paula Stone, the committee reflected fundamental feminist principles. It declared, "A discriminatory attitude against women is so institutionalized in American universities as to be out of the awareness of many of those contributing to it." Institute coeds faced both open hostility and more subtle prejudice, the committee wrote.

> If many people (professors, staff, male students) . . . persist in feeling that women jeopardize the quality of MIT's education, that women do not belong in traditionally male engineering and management fields, that women cannot be expected to make serious commitments to scientific pursuits, that women lack academic motivation, that women can only serve as distractions in a classroom, . . . then MIT will never . . . be a coed institution with equal opportunities for all.[29]

The committee's report represented a self-directed rallying cry, telling MIT women that gender discrimination would change only when female students, faculty, and staff organized to demand improvement.

The early 1970s brought a burst of activism, as MIT women drew strength from the national feminist movement to assert their presence physically, intellectually, socially, and politically. Listing all the awards coeds received, advocates documented that women could lead and succeed in difficult studies. AWS produced pamphlets encouraging high school girls to apply, emphasizing that "there is an enormous pride in being a 'tech coed,' . . . great satisfaction in having done something difficult and worthwhile."[30]

To help MIT women establish a positive sense of identity within a male-dominated atmosphere, campus women's groups initiated monthly colloquia addressing wide-ranging feminist subjects such as the nature of androgyny, sexism in popular culture, and the strengths and difficulties of two-career marriages. Dresselhaus and Professor Emily Wick created a new organization, the Women's Forum, which brought together undergraduates, graduate students, faculty, staff, and wives of all of these to develop "consciousness-raising skits," express concerns about women's health, athletic opportunities, day care, and career planning, and otherwise raise gender awareness.[31]

MIT women continued worrying, especially about the question of numbers. In the early 1970s the admissions office revised photographs and text in the Institute's catalog to highlight coeds and sent special recruiting material to all female national merit and national achievement scholarship semifinalists. AWS feared that such measures would not suffice to overcome social forces pushing girls away from science and engineering. It would take "high-powered" efforts to increase female enrollment, "to de-mythify incorrect assumptions about women at MIT."[32] Women's advocates worried that MIT's "educational counselors," members of the male alumni network who spoke to potential applicants, would not encourage high school girls to enter nontraditional fields or address their concerns about coming to MIT. AWS urged coeds to contact hometown seniors over Thanksgiving and Christmas vacation. "The women in particular may just need an encouraging word from you before taking the plunge."[33] AWS members also volunteered to sit in the admissions office during the peak interview period, ready to chat with interested young women.

Mattfeld and her successor, Professor Wick, served as administrative advocates for female students throughout the sixties. Wick wrote, "As the number of women students increases (and it cannot fail to do so if admissions criteria are the same for all applicants) it is essential that MIT be sensitive to their needs . . . , prepared to assist women students as they make their way through this very male institution."[34] Precisely because of their small numbers, "women are treated differently from men in MIT classes."[35] Mattfeld and Wick stepped in to mediate when coeds encountered trouble dealing with advisors, professors, or teaching assistants. Similarly, most of MIT's few women faculty considered it their responsibility, as successful professionals, to lobby on behalf of other women on campus. Professor Sheila Widnall complained, "Engineers may have a view of engineering which is twenty years out-of-date, and they communicate that to other people. Engineers have an image of engineering that is very masculine . . . [and] takes a long time to change." In 1976, she described women's activism as a "very exciting" force that could open wonderful opportunities for new generations of girls. "There's obviously a direct connection between militant feminism in the junior highs and the ultimate enrollment of women in engineering. . . . Everybody, mothers in particular . . . are much more aware of the importance of encouraging their daughters to take life seriously."[36]

Widnall and other female professors worked behind the scenes to convince deans to back women's education. In 1975, MIT's Center for Advanced Engineering Study produced a film entitled *Engineering: Women's Work*. It was one of the first movies aimed at combating the field's macho image. The film followed "real-life" female students and professionals through their daily routines to show high school students, parents, guidance counselors, and the public that affirmative action had opened up interesting and lucrative opportunities. The film's release drew national attention, and administrators considered it a major contribution to promoting the cause of women in engineering.[37]

Earlier, in 1973, MIT had convened another workshop on women in science and engineering, featuring panels on women's professional status and workshops on career planning. Organizers hoped to convert parents, schools, and the national media into agents of change, helping to break down outdated sex-role stereotypes that steered women into low-paid, shrinking occupations such as teaching. "Enlarging opportunities for women must include not only opening all doors, but also helping women to have the motivation and the courage as well as the educational preparation for walking through them." Embracing feminist language, MIT president Jerome Wiesner spoke about a need "to encourage women's participation in every aspect of our technological society. This is another front in the almost universal battle for equality of opportunity." Workshop leaders called for revising lower-school curricula in order to attract girls toward nontraditional fields, sensitize parents to girls' ambitions, and teach boys to "understand the importance of eliminating sex barriers."[38]

Women's advocates considered 1973 a year for celebration. In June, the Association of MIT Alumnae (AMITA) commemorated the one hundredth anniversary of MIT's women graduates. AMITA hailed the fact that female enrollment had tripled in just ten years, reaching 816 (roughly 13 percent of the total student body). In the freshman class, the number of enrolled women went from 48 out of 958 students in 1965 (5 percent) to 211 out of 1036 in 1974 (20 percent). The evidence seemed to validate supporters' belief that women's academic performance would improve with more favorable living conditions now available in McCormick Hall. The proportion of coeds completing degrees on time rose from 33 to 64 percent (equivalent to male students' performance) during the early 1970s; women graduated with higher GPAs than men, and a larger proportion moved on to graduate studies.[39]

A number of activities sponsored by faculty and alumnae also aimed to continue improving the lot of women engineers. By 1974, female faculty and staff were getting together for monthly lunches, hoping to multiply their impact on Institute policy. Pursuing an activist stance inside the engineering school, Professors Dresselhaus and Widnall inaugurated a freshman seminar entitled "What Is Engineering?" Though not restricted to coeds, the course was geared primarily toward them, starting from an assumption that women often avoided technical subjects simply because they sounded unfamiliar. Researchers in various engineering fields visited the class to explain their work. In order to make women comfortable with manual skills, the syllabus also included lab projects in electronics, welding, drafting, and building Heath Kits (a popular brand of do-it-yourself electronics sets). Dresselhaus further helped organize meetings entitled "Let's Talk about Your Career"; at these gatherings, female students consulted faculty, staff, and guest lecturers for advice about graduate school, employment, and the eternal question of combining marriage with work. Arguing that male students' familiarity with the business world gave them a competitive advantage, AMITA started an annual seminar, "Getting the Job You Want in Industry: A Woman's Guerrilla Guide to the Pin-Striped World." By advising coeds on resume writing and interview techniques, alumnae hoped to level the playing field.

Advocates drew heavily on their teamed strength as potential difficulties loomed. By 1976, budget cuts had prompted the admissions office to limit targeted mailings and start skimping on other "extras" needed to draw female applications. While MIT once led efforts to recruit high school girls talented in math and science, other colleges, such as Cornell, Caltech, and Purdue, had since launched campaigns competing for that small pool. AWS undergraduates, faculty, and staff redoubled efforts to welcome potential coeds. During a spring vacation telethon in 1978, volunteers called 172 high school women who had been accepted; two-thirds of those contacted ultimately chose to attend the Institute. The sense that this personal touch made a difference in raising the "yield" convinced a few undergraduates to undertake a more intensive project. Noticing that women made up just seven out of forty-one students accepted from their home state of Michigan, these coeds sent out hundreds of newsletters seeking to combat the stubborn "perception among most . . . girls that science and technology are not appropriate or desirable fields of study or work for them." At symposia in Southfield and Kalamazoo, Michigan, MIT professors and recent graduates encouraged high school women to keep their educational and career prospects open by staying in math and science classes.[40]

By the late 1970s, female students made up 17 percent of MIT undergraduates, 16 percent of the graduate body, and 12 percent of engineering majors. The sheer increase in population mattered; as women became more of a presence on campus, activists gained a critical mass for organization. Female graduate students formed their own society, as did women in architecture, in chemistry, and at Lincoln Laboratory—a federally funded research center which was part of MIT. Such groups kept women's issues on the front burner, providing a sense of visibility, an identity, and a cause for many individuals. These societies proved especially valuable to female faculty and graduate students based in departments with few other women.

Advocates had successfully established the principle that women's success in the classroom depended on providing both a literal and a psychological home for them in the midst of a male-oriented, often hostile landscape. For decades, MIT had used lack of housing as an excuse to ignore coeds. Only with money from a powerful alumna did the university finally decide that "girls" really "belonged." Only with the construction of McCormick Hall did MIT offer women viable, visible space in the campus community.

THE SOCIETY OF WOMEN ENGINEERS: THE POWER OF PHILANTHROPIC SUPPORT

In their battle to secure expansion and improvement of women's position at MIT, advocates volunteered their money, time, and effort. Both their philosophical dedication and the particular strategies they embraced were echoed at dozens of schools across the nation during the 1960s, 1970s, and 1980s. Such commitments owed much to the Society of Women Engineers, which initiated, coordinated, and supported literally hundreds of undertakings—both small and large, local and national—to help women pursue an engineering education and career.

In 1946, about twenty female engineering students at Iowa State University had organized a local group called the "Society of Women Engineers" to assist "in orienting new women students in the division." That same year, female students at Syracuse and Cornell vented their frustration at being either excluded from several major engineering honor societies or else restricted to a "woman's badge" instead of full membership. Pi Omicron, the new honorary society they created, soon had chapters at schools around the country. Members held orientations for new female engineering majors and hosted speakers such as Lillian Gilbreth. Its mission was "to encourage and reward scholarship and accomplishment . . . among the women students of engineering . . .

[and] to promote the advancement and spread of education in . . . engineering among women."[41]

In 1950, female engineers in New York, Boston, Philadelphia, and Washington, D.C., began meeting with each other; in 1952 they officially incorporated as the Society of Women Engineers (SWE), a professional, nonprofit educational service organization. According to an early statement, SWE was organized around the following objectives:

> To inform the public of the availability of qualified women for engineering positions; to foster a favorable attitude in industry toward women engineers; and to contribute to their professional advancement. To encourage young women with suitable aptitudes and interest to enter the engineering profession, and to guide them in their educational programs.

In an effort to reach these young women (along with their parents, teachers, and counselors), one of SWE's first acts was to set up a Professional Guidance and Education Committee, which would supply information on college programs and engineering in general.[42]

Volunteer efforts at disseminating information reflected one of SWE's primary beliefs: that girls often shied away from entering technical studies simply because they did not realize that women could and did pursue engineering, or because they lacked a basic understanding of engineering itself. Irene Carswell Peden, associate professor of electrical engineering at the University of Washington in the 1960s (its sole female engineering faculty member), wrote,

> It is important to think of women engineers as real people doing real jobs which the student could do, too. . . . A girl is not likely to choose a career field disapproved by her parents, teachers, classmates, and friends. All of these people . . . seem to be responding in part to an erroneous but popular image of the woman engineer as a cold, . . . aggressive female who trudges through life in her flat-heeled shoes without a man in sight (away from the job). . . . Many women engineers are very attractive; most represent a perfectly normal cross section of femininity. The only way that this image can be brought into line with reality, of course, is by way of personal contact. Few women engineers would refuse an opportunity to talk with interested girls and their parents and teachers. Society of Women Engineers . . . members are their own best public relations experts.[43]

In 1954 and 1955, members of the Cleveland section of SWE appeared on local television programs to personally illustrate women's presence in the engineering profession. At a time when many Americans perceived female engineers as odd, manlike creatures, SWE members took pains to offer a presentable feminine image, emphasizing how many of them were married and had children. In 1958, the Boston SWE put out a pamphlet "for young women who might like to enter the field of engineering, and for teachers who are helping them to decide." It contained biographical sketches of a few "typical" women engineers and gave readers information about qualifications for studying engineering and about potential career directions. SWE's authors concluded, "If this pamphlet shall have inspired one young woman to consider an engineering career . . . and one parent to 'encourage' the daughter's desire to enter the technical field, this pamphlet will then have been a worthwhile venture."[44]

Advocates believed that women engineers could gain greater acceptance in society simply by making themselves more visible, and thus SWE soon expanded outreach efforts. In the mid-1950s, college campuses began holding "Junior Engineer and Scientist Summer Institute" (JESSI) programs, thirteen-day courses to let high school students explore pure and applied science and also receive educational and career guidance. Each year, SWE members volunteered to assist with JESSI programs and to discuss women's job opportunities in engineering. For example, at Colorado State University's JESSI program in 1961, fifty-three girls listened to a five-woman panel discuss why they chose an engineering career, supply information on engineering colleges, and answer audience questions. On other occasions, women engineers led JESSI students on visits to industry and gave the girls (and boys) tours of their laboratories.[45]

In the heady rush of creating a new organization with a crusading vision, SWE's leaders dedicated enormous effort to the cause. They poured personal attention into reaching potential converts; members of SWE's professional guidance and education committee wrote to dozens of high school girls, sending pamphlets and replying to questions. In 1954, four SWE members had lunch with one William and Mary first-year woman looking at engineering as a way of using her talent for math. Elsie Eaves wrote, "Roslyn Gitlin, Althea Thornton and myself . . . and Betty Mills . . . gave her a pretty well rounded picture of civil, chemical and mechanical engineering and suggestions of how she could check with Columbia for planning her liberal arts work so that she could transfer to engineering if she wishes."[46]

By 1957, female engineering students at Drexel, Purdue, the University of Colorado, CCNY, the University of Missouri, and several schools in Boston had founded student sections of SWE, and the parent organization enthusiastically welcomed its new junior counterparts. Many established SWE women vividly recalled their sense of initial isolation; as Carnegie Mellon associate engineering dean Helen O'Bannon later wrote, "being one of a small group following a path that appears to violate society's norms is lonely." SWE members spoke passionately about the anxieties and pressure facing a coed who found herself the sole woman in class. Many wrestled with a lack of self-confidence and a low self-image, factors worsened by teasing or hostility. Coeds needed a chance "to see by example that women can 'make it' in engineering," wrote Mildred Dresselhaus in 1975; they needed to receive advice and reassurance from older mentors. "Visibility of successful role models often provides the necessary encouragement to 'keep going when the going gets rough' or when she begins to ask, 'Is it worth it?' It is important for women students to see in some tangible way that there are career opportunities ahead of them, and to find out what it is like to be a professional woman engineer."[47]

Older professionals especially sympathized with young women at schools such as Georgia Tech, where many male classmates, faculty, and alumni bluntly expressed their disapproval of the fact that the institution had chosen to admit women at all. In 1958, the Atlanta section of SWE sent members to participate in Georgia Tech's start-of-the-year camp for first-year women.

> Usually these coeds are completely unaware of future tasks in industry, and we feel that the revealing of our experiences and the impressing on them that they have a great responsibility as women engineers is a basic necessity. They are also encouraged to consult with members of SWE should they encounter any difficulties, even tutoring. One must realize that there are this year approximately 1300 freshmen at Georgia Tech and only 19 freshman coeds. There will be numerous problems and SWE Atlanta Section is proud to play an integral part in the quite difficult assimilation of female engineering students in an almost all male school.[48]

Through the 1960s, the number of SWE student chapters multiplied, reaching colleges and universities across the country. Established members offered support; for instance, the Los Angeles section of SWE provided speakers and counselors to student sections at USC, UCLA, Loyola Marymount, Harvey Mudd, Cal State Long Beach, Pomona, Fullerton, and Cal Poly San Luis Obispo. Overall, campus

SWE groups offered vital intellectual, social, and psychological support for female engineering majors. Advocates stressed the value of
"critical mass," having enough coeds for mutual encouragement and a
commitment to "stick together." Karen Lafferty Instedt, a student at
Ohio State University in 1968–1971, later wrote that SWE gave her
"an opportunity to meet the other female engineers who, like me, were
isolated in their respective fields and classrooms. The SWE section
functioned as a refuge of sorts—where one could find an understanding ear from a peer or a kindhearted, encouraging professor or dean."[49]
By the end of the 1970s, student sections had been chartered in over
170 colleges, universities, and technical institutes. SWE held an annual national student conference featuring technical sessions and exhibits, professional workshops, industrial tours, and even sessions on
career planning, power dynamics, management, personal assertiveness
training, and how to "dress for success."

By the late 1970s, SWE's overall membership totaled over ten
thousand women and men. As SWE grew, its leaders not only were
able to draw on its own expanding membership resources, but also
mobilized the political clout necessary for drumming up outside support. In the most obvious manifestation of this kind of philanthropy,
SWE members donated and collected money to help young women
finance their higher education. Starting in 1958, SWE had instituted
the Lillian Moller Gilbreth scholarship for a woman in her junior or
senior year of engineering school. Local chapters in the Southwest, in
Kentucky, and elsewhere soon created their own scholarship funds.
The Pittsburgh section offered awards to women engineering students
who had finished freshman year in a Pennsylvania university or were
Pennsylvania residents. By the end of the 1970s, SWE administered
nineteen annual scholarship competitions worth more than $27,000 in
all. The RCA Company supported SWE scholarships for third- and
fourth-year women enrolled in electrical engineering, while the West-
inghouse Educational Foundation funded Bertha Lamme–Westing-
house Scholarships (named in honor of that company's pioneering
woman engineer) for first-year women.[50]

SWE activities at the college, regional, and national levels exploded
during the 1970s, driven by members' enthusiasm and dedication, by
the feminist movement, by government equal opportunity laws, and
by university public relations needs. One of the most energetic programs was at Purdue University's engineering school, which had created a special staff position in 1968 to increase its female enrollment

and promote retention. That intensive campaign paid off: Purdue's number of women engineering students rose from 46 in 1968 to 280 in 1974, and to more than one thousand in 1979, when the university boasted the nation's largest female engineering enrollment. The campus had one of the country's most active student SWE chapters. Among other activities, engineering coeds published their own newsletter, ran a "big sister" program pairing entering women with upperclass mentors, offered help in locating summer jobs, and produced an annual members' "resume book" for sale to potential employers. Each weekday, SWE "hostesses" volunteered to talk to prospective engineering students, take them to lunch, or offer a tour of residence halls.[51]

The 1970s witnessed the organization of dozens of conferences, open houses, and other public events in many states to celebrate and assist women pursuing engineering. Some meetings were organized by and for women already out in the work world, to give each other encouragement and suggestions for promotion. For example, a 1974 "Women in Engineering" conference jointly sponsored by SWE, the Engineering Foundation, and the Engineers' Council for Professional Development focused on advising women on how to update their skills (especially after temporary child-rearing leave) and advance into other areas, including management. Other conferences were designed for women still in college. These meetings sought to bring collegiate women together with each other and with older mentors who might help undergraduates succeed in their studies and prepare to enter the professional world. For instance, the University of Washington (with 230 women engineering students in 1975, and 445 in 1977) hosted an annual conference where those coeds met with working professionals such as Bonnie Dunbar, a Rockwell ceramics engineer. The SWE section at the University of North Dakota sponsored a 1979 conference entitled "Transitions: College to Careers," which brought in corporate representatives (many of them alumni) to talk about how to project a professional image, how to have a successful interview, how to handle postcollege finances, how to set career goals, and how to balance work and marriage. Speakers offered practical advice; for example, they suggested that women make an effort to communicate with their bosses, making a point to describe their career goals and suggest a schedule for accomplishing them.[52]

Other conferences were organized by women engineering students themselves as a way of encouraging the potential interest of younger girls. SWE assumed that, in general, girls and boys possessed a similar ability to excel in math and science, and that girls could be as interested as boys in technology. Activists blamed girls' relative lack of interest in engineering on socialization patterns that provided girls with dolls and boys with toy tools, that directed girls to home economics classes and boys to "shop." SWE further attributed girls' underrepresentation in engineering to failures of the school system, and especially to guidance counselors who didn't take girls' career ambitions seriously and who let them drop math and science classes. To counter such problems, the University of Iowa hosted a 1974 meeting entitled "Women in Engineering: Why Not You?" A brochure distributed to high schoolers read,

> Right now you're probably going through the list of things you do and don't want to do with your life. College, teaching, the Peace Corps, marriage, or just getting a job are a few of the things you may have considered. Well, if you're looking into a career, we'd like you to think of one more possibility—engineering. While engineering has always been thought of as a man's profession, it is no more masculine than cooking is feminine. All you need to be a good engineer is an interest in math and science, and the desire to plan and solve problems. In fact, most engineering students are a lot like you.

At the Iowa conference, current and former coeds spoke about "student life: trials and tribulations, joys and expectations," while industry representatives and educators discussed course options and career opportunities.[53]

Similar events occurred across the country, with the aims of familiarizing young women with engineering, talking up employment opportunities, showing the most exciting sides of technical work, and allowing girls to meet role models. In 1976, the New Jersey Institute of Technology hosted an all-day program for three hundred young women; organizers had received more than six hundred attendance requests, far beyond their capacity. Faculty member Marion Spector said, "Typically women just let things happen, they float along with the current, not making any effort to set career goals. What we are trying to do is to give them an introduction to personal direction and to introduce alternatives while they are young enough to make strong changes."[54] A 1973 University of Illinois conference, "Women in Engineering: It's Your Turn Now," gave high school junior and senior girls a chance to participate in "rap sessions"—informal conversations with college SWE members and older women engineers. A 1974 symposium sponsored by SWE sections at the Universities of Florida and South Florida featured a tour of the Kennedy Space Center, plus discussions of student financial aid, co-op programs, career problems and openings, and men's reactions to women engineers. The promotional material declared,

> As an engineering student you'll gain something most women don't get in college, a professional skill which can be used immediately upon graduation . . . , [with] the highest starting salary bracket of the major professional job categories for women holding a bachelor's degree. . . . You owe it to yourself to look into the possibilities and opportunities offered by engineering.[55]

Other SWE chapters went directly into the high schools as self-described "missionaries" seeking to spread the gospel of technical study. Starting in 1976, Berkeley's SWE section sent teams of three or four students and engineers to visit local junior high classes; in 1980, members gave presentations to about one thousand students in ten Bay Area schools. Presenters described how they became interested in engineering and sought "to dispel myths about women in engineering . . . and give special encouragement to girls who are interested in math and science." One mechanical engineering major prepared posters showing how an engineer might design a pair of skis, another team brought slides showing construction of a hydropower plant. An organizer commented,

> We discovered that women engineering students can be excellent role-models for girls in grades 7–12. A practicing engineer or scientist may be inspiring, but her achievement may seem unattainable to students who have not even started college. Junior high students, in particular, are more willing to take advice from those closer to their own age. "I was happy to find out that there are women engineers!" said one enthusiastic student. . . . "It showed me another kind of work I might be interested in."[56]

Berkeley section noted that running this community outreach program benefited SWE members themselves: it gave them experience in public speaking, led to useful professional contacts, and provided favorable publicity. Berkeley members even compiled a handbook for other SWE chapters that contained advice on how to start a similar outreach program. Taking outreach even further in the 1980s, SWE's San Francisco section hosted a program entitled "Tinker . . . Toys . . . Technology," in which seventy-one teenage Girl Scouts spent two weeks learning computer programming, running physics experiments, touring Silicon Valley companies, and talking with women engineers and astronauts.[57]

Other SWE members hoped to influence even younger girls, those still in elementary school. In the 1970s, the Boston section sought to "infuse a seven- or eight-year-old" with enthusiasm and curiosity about how things worked. It wrote and published a coloring book entitled *Terry's Trip*, the story of a girl visiting her aunt, a mechanical engineer who worked in a toy factory. The heroine, Terry, talked to industrial engineers supervising the production line, chemical engineers mixing polystyrene, electrical engineers with fancy calculators, and then announced, "Maybe some day I'll be an engineer like Aunt Jennifer and her friends at the factory."[58] The North Carolina section of SWE prepared a 1983 booklet called *Betsy and Robbie,* which told of a girl who visited her cousin at a university engineering fair and became fascinated with Robbie, a computer-controlled robot designed by a female student.[59] Such material emphasized that women were fully qualified for engineering, a discipline that required creativity and logic more than physical strength. Illustrations and photos documented the daily activities of women who worked in safety engineering for General Motors, as government environmental engineers, or as university professors. By making such role models visible and attractive, SWE strove to win young women's interest and public confidence.

Some SWE experts admitted that in the end it was virtually impossible to find a direct causal correlation between advocacy efforts and changing patterns of women's engineering education. Taken in isolation, a child's coloring book, a conference for high school girls, or even a new dormitory seemed to do little to affect such momentous decisions as where to attend college, what major to choose, or which career to follow. Yet as a whole, the multidimensional actions undertaken after 1950 by the national Society of Women Engineers, local chapters, student sections, and individual women add up to a substantial force. It was Katherine McCormick's funding that made it physically possible for MIT to expand female enrollment, paving the way for advocates who pushed for broader changes in campus intellectual and social culture. Donations by other women established scholarships and awards for female technical students, giving them vital financial assistance and recognition. Philanthropy in a broader sense—contributions of time and service—played an equally crucial role. Pioneering female engineers poured immense effort into nurturing their successors, offering advice and encouragement. SWE set up a social and professional bridge between generations that was rich with meaning both for those giving and for those receiving support. College women benefited from the guidance of older members even as they themselves volunteered as outreach ambassadors to younger girls. Such philanthropy helped transform educational trends: by 1980, the number of female engineering students had skyrocketed. Today, high school girls take for granted that they have a right to study engineering if their interests lie in that direction. Philanthropists of the postwar decades have achieved their vision, creating a space for women in the traditionally masculine world of engineering education.

NOTES

1. For a discussion of women's use of "creative" and "coercive philanthropy" to pressure institutions to accept women graduate students and appoint women faculty, see Margaret W. Rossiter, *Women Scientists in America: Struggles and Strategies to 1940* (Baltimore, Md.: Johns Hopkins University Press, 1982), 39; and Mary Ann Dzuback's chapter in this volume. For information on the AAUW, see Marion Talbot and Lois Kimball Mathews Rosenberry, *The History of the American Association of University Women, 1881–1931* (Boston: Houghton Mifflin, 1931).

2. For background, see Margaret W. Rossiter, *Women Scientists in America: Before Affirmative Action, 1940–1972* (Baltimore, Md.: Johns Hopkins University Press, 1995); idem, *Women Scientists in America: Struggles and Strategies;* Marilyn Bailey Ogilvie, *Women in Science: Antiquity through the Nineteenth Century: A Biographical Dictionary with Annotated Bibliography* (Cambridge, Mass.: MIT Press, 1986); and Amy Bix, "'Engineeresses' Invade Campus: Four Decades of Debate over Technical Coeducation," *IEEE Technology and Society Magazine* 19 (spring 2000): 20–26.

3. Mrs. Frederick T. Lord to Karl Compton, 11 January 1938; Louise P. Horwood to Mrs. Lord, 5 January 1938; both in file 12, box 240, AC 4, Massachusetts Institute of Technology Archives, Cambridge, Mass. (hereafter cited as MITA). For background, see Amy Bix, "Feminism Where Men Predominate: The History of Women's Science and Engineering Education at MIT," *Women's Studies Quarterly* 28 (spring/summer 2000): 24–45.

4. "Glamor Girl MIT," *The Tech*, 8 October 1940, 1.

5. *Massachusetts Institute of Technology Handbook, 1941,* MIT.

6. *Report of the President*, MIT, 1944; Florence Ward Stiles to Compton, 3 February 1945; memo from Stiles, 22 February 1945; all three in file 18, box 210, AC4, MITA.

7. Memo from L. F. Hamilton to Julius A. Stratton, 24 October 1956; memo from Stratton, "A Statement of Policy on Women Students," 24 January 1957; Roland

B. Greeley to Devrie Shapiro, 4 October 1961; all three in "Women Students," box 116, AC134, MITA.

8. Memo from Everett Baker, 26 January 1947, file 12, box 26, AC4, MITA.

9. Stiles to Carroll Webber, Jr., 28 March 1946, file 2, box 2, AC220, MITA.

10. Emily L. Wick, "Proposal for a New Policy for Admission of Women Undergraduate Students at MIT," 9 March 1970, box 9, MC86, MITA.

11. Christina Jansen, interview by Shirlee Shirkow, 1977, box 9, MC86, MITA.

12. Stratton, "A Statement of Policy on Women Students," 24 January 1957, "Women Students," box 116, AC134, MITA.

13. Greeley to Shapiro, 4 October 1961, "Women Students," box 116, AC134, MITA.

14. Hamilton to Stratton, 14 November 1956, box 2, AC220, MITA.

15. Margaret Alvort to Hamilton, 21 June 1956, box 2, AC220, MITA.

16. Herbert I. Harris to Hamilton, 31 July 1956, quoted in Evelyn Fox Keller, "New Faces in Science and Technology: A Study of Women Students at MIT," August 1981, file "MIT-women," box 17, AC220, MITA.

17. Memo from J. R. Killian, Jr., to Stratton, 22 October 1956, file 7, box 1, AC4, MITA.

18. Press release, 12 April 1960, MITA; see also press release, "Residence for Women Students at the Massachusetts Institute of Technology," n.d. (ca. 1963); and "A Tribute to Katharine Dexter McCormick," 1 March 1908; all three in file "women students," box 116, AC134, MITA.

19. "Where the Brains Are," *Time,* 18 October 1963, 51.

20. Joan Hawkes, "Looking Ahead to College and Careers," *Seventeen,* October 1964, 44, 46.

21. Katharine McCormick to Stratton, 15 January 1965, file 2, box 4, AC220, MITA.

22. *This Is MIT,* 1963–64, file 2, box 4, AC220, MITA.

23. Memo from Jacquelyn A. Mattfeld to Malcolm G. Kispert et al., 21 January 1964, file 2, box 4, AC220, MITA.

24. Memo from Mattfeld, "Information on Women's Program, MIT, 1964–65," 1 July 1965, file 2, box 4, AC220, MITA.

25. Academic council, minutes of 2 March 1965, box 1, AC134, MITA.

26. Notes of Mattfeld, in "Academic Council 6/64–6/65," box 1, AC134, MITA.

27. Association of Women Students, *This Is MIT for Women,* 1963–64, file 16, box 85, AC118, MITA.

28. "Female Scientist Image Blasted," *Michigan State News,* 4 November 1964; Marilyn S. Swartz to Joann Miller et al., 8 August 1972; both in file 1, box 57, AC12, MITA. See also Rossiter, *Women Scientists in America: Before Affirmative Action,* 366–68.

29. Ad Hoc Committee on the Role of Women at MIT, report, n.d. (ca. 1972), box 13, MC485, MITA.

30. Association of Women Students, *This Is MIT for Women,* 1969–70, file 16, box 85, AC118, MITA.

31. Mildred Dresselhaus, interview by Shirlee Shirkow, 1976, box 8, MC86, MITA.

32. Ad Hoc Committee on the Role of Women at MIT, report, n.d. (ca. 1972), box 13, MC485, MITA.

33. Association of Women Students, flyer, November 1974, file 14, box 1, AC220, MITA.

34. Emily Wick to Paul Gray, 16 November 1971, "MIT," box 13, MC485, MITA.

35. Ad Hoc Committee on the Role of Women at MIT to J. Daniel Nyhart, 28 February 1972, "MIT," box 13, MC485, MITA.

36. Sheila Widnall, interview by Shirlee Shirkow, 1976, box 8, MC86, MITA.

37. Walter McKay to Greeley, 4 May 1972; "Women in Engineering," film draft proposal, 27 June 1974; both in "Films—Women in Engineering," box 57, AC12, MITA.

38. Swartz to Miller et al., 8 August 1972; *Women in Science and Technology: A Report on the Workshop on Women in Science and Technology*, 2–4, file "1973 workshop"; both in box 57, AC112, MITA.

39. Association of MIT Alumnae, report, n.d. (ca. 1973), file 12, box 1, AC220, MITA.

40. Holliday Heine to James Mar, 14 November 1979, "Ad Hoc Committee on Women's Admission," box 13, MC485, MITA.

41. "New Society Organizes," *Iowa Engineer*, May 1946, 222.

42. Pamphlet, "Facts about the Society of Women Engineers," n.d. (ca. 1980), "Student Affairs," box 86, Society of Women Engineers Collection, Wayne State University Archives, Walter P. Reuther Library, Detroit, Michigan (hereafter cited as SWEC).

43. Irene Carswell Peden, "Women in Engineering Careers," 1965 SWE booklet, in "Women in Engineering," box "SWE bio/subj.," SWEC; and "Career Opportunities for Women in Engineering: Engineering Can Be Your Future," in "Career Guidance 1958," box 118, SWEC. See also Joy Miller, "Women Engineers: They're Feminine and So Bright," *Perth Amboy (N.J.) News*, 30 July 1964, unpaginated clipping, MITA.

44. Pamphlet, 1958, in "Women in Engineering," box "SWE bio/subj.," SWEC.

45. Alta Rutherford, "Women Engineers in Redlands Spotlight," *Detroit News*, 19 April 1954; "JESSI Panels Hailed a Success," *SWE Newsletter*, November 1961, 2; and "JESSI Program," *SWE Newsletter*, November 1965, 5.

46. Elsie Eaves to Rose Mankofsky, 22 April 1954, "Misc. Corr. Eaves, 1942, 1946, 1951–57," box 187, SWEC.

47. Helen O'Bannon, "The Social Scene: Isolation and Frustration"; Mildred S. Dresselhaus, "A Constructive Approach to the Education of Women Engineers"; both in "Women in Engineering—Beyond Recruitment Conference Proceedings, June 22–25, 1975," box 128, SWEC. See also Mildred S. Dresselhaus, "Some Personal Views on Engineering Education for Women," *IEEE Transactions on Education* 18 (February 1975), 30–34.

48. "Orientation Program for Georgia Tech Coeds Initiated by Atlanta Section," *SWE Newsletter*, March 1962, 4.

49. Karen Lafferty Instedt, "How Should SWE Serve Undergraduates?" *SWE Newsletter*, June/July 1978.

50. Starting in the 1960s, SWE also presented financial prizes and certificates of

merit to high school girls who had demonstrated excellence in math or science or who had presented outstanding technical exhibits at local or national science fairs. As a separate example of women's engineering philanthropy, it is worth noting that Zonta International, a service organization of executive and professional women, in 1938 began awarding annual Amelia Earhart Fellowships to women for graduate study in aeronautical engineering or aerospace science (*SWE Newsletter*, March 1978).

51. Purdue flyer, n.d. (ca. 1970s), "Student Activities 1974–75," box 70, SWEC; and "Progress Report: Women in Engineering at Purdue Univ.," n.d. (ca. 1978), "Women Engineering Students," box "SWE bio/subj.," SWEC. Many other universities established programs with similar elements; for example, SWE chapters at Ohio State and Lehigh ran "big and little sisters" programs during the 1970s.

52. Press release, 29 May 1974, "Henniker IV," box 129, SWEC; and booklet "Women in Engineering: Role Models from Henniker 3," "Role Models," box 119, SWEC.

53. "Women in Engineering: Why Not You?" n.d. (ca. 1974), "Iowa, Univ. of," box 139, SWEC.

54. New Jersey Institute of Technology press release, n.d. (ca. April 1976), "Newark College of Engineering," box 140, SWEC.

55. "A Symposium on the Opportunities for Today's Woman," n.d. (ca. 1974), "Florida," box 138, SWEC.

56. SWE student section, University of California at Berkeley, *Junior High School Outreach: A Practical Guide*, 1980, "Junior High School Outreach 1980," box 118, SWEC.

57. "Tinker . . . Toys . . . Technology," brochure, n.d. (ca. fall 1982), "A-V material," box 133, SWEC. See also Deborah S. Franzblau, "Have You Considered Outreach?" *U.S. Woman Engineer*, December 1980, 15. To note two similar examples among many, the SWE section of the Lawrence Institute of Technology made presentations to Detroit girls, while the University of Michigan's SWE worked with the Ann Arbor school system's career planning office to give talks at elementary schools and at junior and senior high schools.

58. *Terry's Trip*, n.d. (ca. 1979), "Terry's Trip," box 131, SWEC. See also Sarah Sloan, "Terry's Trip," *SWE Newsletter*, November/December 1979.

59. *Betsy and Robbie*, n.d. (ca. 1983), "Betsy and Robbie," box 119, SWEC.

CONTRIBUTORS

Jayne R. Beilke is Associate Professor of Educational Studies at Ball State University. Her publications have focused on philanthropy and black education and include articles in the *History of Higher Education Annual* and the *Journal of Negro Education.*

Amy Sue Bix is Associate Professor of History at Iowa State University and author of *Inventing Ourselves out of Jobs? America's Debate over Technological Unemployment, 1929–1981.*

Karen J. Blair is Professor and Chair of History at Central Washington University. She is author of *The Torchbearers: Women and Their Amateur Arts Associations in America, 1890–1930* and *The Clubwoman as Feminist: True Womanhood Redefined, 1868–1914,* as well as a reference book and several articles on women in the Pacific Northwest.

Ruth Crocker is Professor of History at Auburn University and author of *Social Work and Social Order: The Settlement Movement in Two Industrial Cities, 1889–1930* and *Mrs. Russell Sage: A Life* (forthcoming).

Mary Ann Dzuback is Associate Professor of Education and History at Washington University in St. Louis and a past president of the History of Education Society. She is author of *Robert M. Hutchins: Portrait of an Educator* as well as articles on women scholars in social sciences.

Linda Eisenmann is Associate Professor of Education at the University of Massachusetts and currently Vice President of Division F (History and Historiography) of the American Educational Research Association and Vice-President of the History of Education Society. She will become Dean of the College of Arts and Sciences at John Carroll University in 2005. She is editor of *A Historical Dictionary of Women's Education in the United States.*

Marybeth Gasman is Assistant Professor of Higher Education at the University of Pennsylvania and co-author (with Patrick Gilpin) of *Charles S. Johnson: Leadership beyond the Veil in the Era of Jim Crow*.

Frances Huehls is Assistant Librarian of the Joseph and Matthew Payton Philanthropic Studies Library at Indiana University–Purdue University Indianapolis.

Linda L. Johnson is Professor and Chair of History at Concordia College, Moorhead, Minnesota. Her research on cross-cultural women's history includes articles in *Women's Studies Quarterly* and *Women's Studies International Forum*.

Sarah Henry Lederman teaches history at the Dalton School in New York City.

Eleanore Lenington is a doctoral candidate at Florida State University and co-author (with Victoria-María MacDonald) of a public history project, *A History of Kate Sullivan Elementary School, 1948–1998: Access and Achievement in the Last Half of the Twentieth Century*.

Victoria-María MacDonald is Associate Professor of History and Philosophy of Education at Florida State University. Most recently, she has edited *Latino Education in U.S. History, 1513–2000*.

Amy E. Wells is Assistant Professor of Higher Education at the University of New Orleans. Her work has appeared in the *History of Higher Education Annual*.

Roberta Wollons is Professor of History at Indiana University–Northwest and editor of *Children at Risk in America: History, Concepts, and Public Policy* and *Kindergartens and Cultures: The Global Diffusion of an Idea*.

Christine Woyshner is Assistant Professor of Education at Temple University and co-editor (with Holly S. Gelfond) of *Minding Women: Reshaping the Educational Realm*. Her work has appeared in *Teachers College Record* and *History of Education Quarterly*.

Andrea Walton is Assistant Professor of Education at Indiana University, Bloomington, where she teaches in the Higher Education and Foundations of Education programs and is also a member of the Philanthropic Studies faculty. She has published articles on women's philanthropy, women's higher education, and the history of universities and voluntary associations in such venues as *History of Education, Historical Studies in Education,* and *History of Education Quarterly.* She is currently completing a book on the history of women at Columbia University from the founding of Barnard College in 1889 to the admission of women to Columbia College in 1983.

INDEX

academies, 15, 39, 45, 81. *See also* schools; seminaries

Addams, Jane, 3, 8, 11, 71, 74

African American education: black colleges and their graduates, 194–236, 281–297; foundation support of, 13, 281–297; ideal of race uplift, 196, 229; ideal of service, 19, 194–236; in the South, 81; women's involvement in, 194–214, 215–236

African American women: and civil rights activism, 195; club movement, 215–236; and gender discrimination, 194, 293, 294; parent-teacher associations, 215–236; as philanthropists, 194–214; in the professions, 194, 285; scholarship on, 292; sororities, 194–214

African Americans: and desegregation, 19, 206; fellowships for, 281–297; networks, 228; as philanthropists, 225; in the professions, 201, 205; racial discrimination, 194, 291; as recipients of philanthropy, 201, 281–297; and self-help, 194–211

agricultural education, 86

Alpha Kappa Alpha, 197–205

American Association of University Women (AAUW), 106, 109–111, 151, 320

American Board of Commissioners for Foreign Missions (ABCFM), 169–193

American Council on Education (ACE), Commission on the Education of Women, 151

American exceptionalism, 181

American Missionary Association, 81, 282

American Philanthropy, 7, 12. *See also* Bremner, Robert

American Women's Scholarship for Japanese Women, 21, 298–319

Anderson, Florence, 19, 155, 159

Anglo-Saxon ethos, 91, 92, 95–96

Association of Collegiate Alumnae (ACA), 106, 109, 151, 161, 258, 320. *See also* American Association of University Women (AAUW)

Bailyn, Bernard, 15, 16

Baltimore Charity Organization Society, 66, 67, 68

Beard, Mary Ritter, 126, 219, 222

Beecher, Catharine, 6, 39–59; conceptualization of ties between philanthropy and education, 54; definition of benevolence, 49; view of charity, 51; view of teaching as philanthropic activity, 50

benevolence: and charity, 2, 41; definition of, 34, 40, 49; in nineteenth-century America, 6, 7, 41; and Protestant theology, 41, 172, 180, 182, 188; and social control, 13; and teaching, 50; and voluntary societies and associations, 6, 40, 41

bequests, 142

Berkeley, University of California, 110, 111–115

Berry, Martha McChesney, 17, 81–104

Berry College, 85, 99

Berry schools, 64, 84–86; connections to regional pride, 86

biography, as a lens, 128

Bremner, Robert, 9, 12. See also *American Philanthropy*

Brown *v.* Board, 23, 203, 282, 295